POLITICAL INSTITUTIONS AND FINANCIAL

DEVELOPMENT

POLITICAL INSTITUTIONS AND FINANCIAL DEVELOPMENT

Edited by

STEPHEN HABER, DOUGLASS C. NORTH,

AND BARRY R. WEINGAST

STANFORD UNIVERSITY PRESS

Stanford, California 2008

Stanford University Press
Stanford, California

Printed in the United States of America on acid-free,
archival-quality paper

Library of Congress Cataloging-in-Publication Data

Political institutions and financial development / edited by
Stephen Haber, Douglass C. North, and Barry R. Weingast.
    p. cm. — (Social science history)
  Includes index.
   ISBN 978-0-8047-5692-1 (cloth : alk. paper) —
ISBN 978-0-8047-5693-8 (pbk. : alk. paper)
   1. Finance—Political aspects. 2. Finance—Government
policy. 3. Monetary policy. I. Haber, Stephen H., 1957–
II. North, Douglass Cecil. III. Weingast, Barry R.

HG173.P655 2008
332—dc22

                                        2007029138

Typeset by Newgen in 10.5/13 Bembo AR

CONTENTS

CONTRIBUTORS

James R. Barth is the Lowder Eminent Scholar in Finance at Auburn University and a Senior Finance Fellow at the Milken Institute.

Gerard Caprio is Professor of Economics at Williams College and is currently Chair of the Center for Development Economics there.

Peter Gourevitch is Professor of Political Science and founding Dean of the Graduate School of International Relations and Pacific Studies at the University of California, San Diego. He is also a former editor of *International Organization.*

Stephen Haber is A. A. and Jeanne Welch Milligan Professor in the School of Humanities and Sciences and Peter and Helen Bing Senior Fellow of the Hoover Institution at Stanford University.

Philip Keefer is a Lead Research Economist in the Development Research Group of the World Bank.

Ross Levine is the Harrison S. Kravis University Professor and Professor of Economics at Brown University. He is also the Paul Dupee Faculty Fellow at the Watson Institute for International Studies and a Research Associate at the National Bureau of Economic Research. He is an Editor of the *Journal of Financial Intermediation* and an Associate Editor of the *Journal of Economic Growth.*

Aldo Musacchio is Assistant Professor at Harvard Business School in the Business, Government, and International Economy Unit.

Douglass C. North is the 1993 Nobel Laureate in Economic Science. He is Professor of Economics at Washington University and a Senior Fellow of the Hoover Institution at Stanford University.

James Shinn is Visiting Professor at Georgetown University's School of Foreign Service, where he teaches courses on technology and foreign policy. Previously he worked in the U.S. State Department's East Asia Bureau and was later a general manager, entrepreneur, and outside director in the high-tech sector.

Mary M. Shirley is President of the Ronald Coase Institute, a nonprofit organization working to improve lives by building capacity to understand

and address economic problems. She is a founder and past president of the
International Society for New Institutional Economics.

William R. Summerhill is Professor of History at the University of California,
Los Angeles.

Richard Sylla is Henry Kaufman Professor of the History of Financial
Institutions and Markets and Professor of Economics at the Stern School of
Business, New York University. He is also a Research Associate of the National
Bureau of Economic Research and a former editor of the *Journal of Economic
History*.

John Joseph Wallis is Professor of Economics and Director of Undergraduate
Studies in the Department of Economics at the University of Maryland. He is
also a Research Associate at the National Bureau of Economic Research.

Barry R. Weingast is Ward C. Krebs Family Professor in the Department of
Political Science and a Senior Fellow of the Hoover Institution at Stanford.
He is also a member of the American Academy of Arts and Sciences.

ACKNOWLEDGMENTS

This volume was the product of a series of conferences that occurred over a three-year period. We wish to express our gratitude to the institutions that provided generous support for these conferences as well as for the preparation of this volume: the Liberty Fund, the Mercatus Institute of George Mason University, the William and Flora Hewlett Foundation, the Freeman Spogli Institute for International Studies at Stanford University (through its Bechtel Global Studies Initiative), and the Stanford Center for International Development.

Logistical support for the conference series and the preparation of this volume came from the Mercatus Institute and Stanford's Social Science History Institute (SSHI). We wish to thank Paul Edwards, then of Mercatus, who helped initiate the first program. We also wish to thank two individuals in particular, Scott Wilson and Marie Toney (SSHI's Associate Director and Administrator, respectively), without whom this volume would not have happened. Finally, we wish to thank John Raisian, Director of Stanford's Hoover Institution, not only for supporting our research in multiple ways but for creating an intellectual environment that encourages the free exchange of ideas among scholars from a broad range of disciplines.

POLITICAL INSTITUTIONS AND FINANCIAL

DEVELOPMENT

Chapter 1

Political Institutions and Financial Development

STEPHEN HABER, DOUGLASS C. NORTH,

AND BARRY R. WEINGAST

A broad consensus exists among economists that there is a strong positive association between the extent of a country's financial development and the material well-being of its population. There is also consensus that causality runs from financial development to economic growth: countries do not have large banking systems and securities markets because they are wealthy; they are wealthy *because* they have large banking systems and securities markets (King and Levine 1993a, 1993b; Levine 1997, 1998; Levine and Zervos 1998; Rajan and Zingales 1998; Levine, Loayza, and Beck 2000).

Considerably less consensus exists, however, when trying to understand why there is a high degree of variance in financial development across countries. If it is common knowledge that a key input to economic growth is a large financial system, then why don't poor countries simply create the conditions necessary for financial development?

Broadly speaking, scholars provide two answers to this question—which as shorthand we shall call the legal origins view and the political institutions view. The legal origins view argues that contemporary levels of financial development are largely determined by a country's colonial history: countries that were colonized by Great Britain, and that therefore adopted the legal institutions of British common law, provide better protection to minority shareholders and hence have larger financial systems than countries that adopted the French Civil Code. Politics and political institutions, according to this view, either do not matter (La Porta et al. 1998) or they

1

matter but are less important than legal origin (Beck, Demirgüç-Kunt, and Levine 2003; Levine 2005).

The political institutions view suggests that legal origin has little effect on financial development (Rajan and Zingales 2003; Acemoglu, Johnson, and Robinson 2004; Lamoreaux and Rosenthal 2005; Acemoglu and Johnson, forthcoming; see also North 1981, 1990). Rather, financial development is an outcome of specific laws and regulations, which are the product of politics and political institutions. At its core, the political institutions view is concerned with the government's inherent conflict of interest: the growth of banks and securities markets is not possible without a government that can enforce financial contracts; but the government relies on those same banks and markets to provide it with a source of finance. Unless there are self-enforcing political institutions that limit the government's authority and discretion, it will have strong incentives to govern the financial system so as to facilitate its own political survival, at the expense of the development of the securities markets and banking systems that can finance the private economy.

The resolution of the debate about the causes of financial development and underdevelopment is not purely an academic matter: the legal origins view and the political institutions view imply very different policy prescriptions. If the legal origins view is right, then financial system development can be accomplished by reforms to legal codes—in particular, by strengthening the rights of financial claimholders generally, including those of minority shareholders and creditors. If the political institutions view is right, then what is needed are far-reaching institutional reforms designed to limit the authority and discretion of public officials. In the absence of political reform, tinkering with legal codes might actually make countries worse off: the process of reform may allow vested interests to shape the new laws to their advantage, or newly empowered regulators might use their authority to behave opportunistically vis-à-vis private economic agents.

The essays in this book—the result of three years of research and discussion among the chapter authors and editors—come down on the side of the political institutions view. They do more, however, than take sides in a debate. Indeed, it is has become commonplace in the social sciences to observe that "institutions matter." The challenge taken up by the authors in this book is to explore *which* political institutions matter and *how* those institutions matter.

As the chapter by Richard Sylla makes clear, financial systems are composed of private banks, securities markets, a money supply, a central bank, and a system of public finance. Some of these entities, most particularly the banks and the securities markets, tend to be predominantly under the control of private economic agents. The other entities—the money supply, the central bank, and the system of public finance—tend to be predominantly under the control of the government. None of these entities, however, operates in isolation from the others. For example, the government's system of public finance uses private securities markets to place its bonds. Similarly, the central bank often controls the number of corporate charters granted to private banks, as well as sets their reserve requirements and regulates their lending practices. Private banks, to cite another example, play a crucial role in the development of stock and bond markets: banks often serve as underwriters for corporate bond issues, and banks are often among the first corporations whose shares are traded on organized stock exchanges.

The implication is that the government can decisively influence the development of private banks and securities markets. For example, the government can force the banks to lend it their deposit base by establishing reserve requirements (and then increasing reserve requirements); grant corporate charters only to politically favored constituents; refuse to enforce financial contracts when the debtors are from politically crucial groups; or expropriate the holders of government securities by defaulting on the public debt.

Private investors, of course, are not potted plants. They know that their wealth is subject to expropriation if the authority and discretion of government are not limited by political institutions. In the presence of this risk, investors therefore behave accordingly: most will refrain from investing their wealth in banks, in public corporations, or in government debt, whereas a small portion may deploy their wealth but require compensation, in the form of high rates of return, for the risk of doing so. In short, the actions of private investors have implications for the amount of credit available to the government.

Governments and private investors interact to generate a broad range of institutions that affect the size and structure of the financial system. To cite an obvious example, when the authority and discretion of government are not limited by political institutions, bankers seek compensation for expropriation risk by demanding that the government constrain the number of bank charters it will grant. The government, needing a financial sector from which it can borrow, accedes to the demands of the bankers for regulated entry but, in turn, requires that the banks provide credit to the government. The result is a concentrated banking sector that earns monopoly rents—some of which are then shared with public officials as individuals (in the form of bribes) and with the government in general (in the form of lines of credit at below market interest rates or in the form of bank shares granted to the government gratis) (see Haber, Razo, and Maurer 2003, chap. 4).

Limits on government discretion that are weak or not binding also have consequences for the enforcement of contract rights, and weak contract rights, in turn, have negative consequences for the development of banks and securities markets. The very same institutions that make property rights transparent and enforceable, and that allow private parties to enforce financial contracts—for example, up-to-date and accurate property registers, efficient police and courts—also facilitate the government's ability to expropriate property. In societies in which the authority and discretion of the government are not limited, individuals and firms not only have weak incentives to lobby for the creation of institutions that make their property rights transparent and enforceable but they also have strong incentives to frustrate the development of those institutions. The effect of weak property rights, of course, is that financial development is stunted: banks limit the types of contracts that they write and limit the range of individuals with whom they will write contracts; individuals tend not to purchase shares in corporations that are outside their direct control; and individuals and firms are reluctant to purchase corporate debt.

Precisely because political institutions are the key to the development of the banking systems and securities markets that finance the private economy, the essays in this volume focus on those political institutions and how they connect to the development of banks and markets. The following five chapters—by Haber, Sylla, Wallis, Keefer, and Barth, Caprio, and Levine—focus on how the political institutions that limit government affect the development of banking systems. The next three chapters—by Gourevitch and Shinn, Summerhill, and Musacchio—focus on how the political institutions that limit government affect corporate governance and the development of private stock and bond markets.

We begin with three chapters that use historical case studies to explore how political institutions and banking systems jointly evolved over time. The first of these, "Political Institutions and Financial Development: Evidence from the Political Economy of Bank Regulation in Mexico and the United States," by Stephen Haber, traces the process by which the banking systems of the United States and Mexico developed from independence to 1913. Haber's analysis indicates that the major reforms in banking law in both countries were motivated by governments seeking sources of public finance, and that one feature of those government initiatives was constraints on competition.

The difference in long-run outcomes was not caused by differences in the motivations of the U.S. and Mexican governments but by the institutions that limited those governments. Attempts to constrain competition in U.S. banking failed because they were inconsistent with the competitive nature of the political system. Attempts to constrain competition in Mexico succeeded because the Mexican political system lacked the broad range of *mutually reinforcing institutions*—federalism, separation of powers, electoral suffrage, and party competition—necessary to constrain public officials. As a result, the Mexican government was able to structure the regulations governing banking so as to maximize short-run government revenues and permit rent seeking by public officials. In contrast, American officials faced a range of these institutional constraints that led to different outcomes. Whereas the centralized political control in Mexico allowed Mexican officials to create a system of segmented monopolies, the decentralized system in the United States created competition among jurisdictions and levels of government. Officials in the United States seeking to maximize revenue from the banking system were therefore led to create a competitive system.

The next two chapters, by Richard Sylla and John Wallis, focus on the U.S. case in detail. Both make a strong case for the pivotal role played by political institutions in the process of American financial development. Sylla's chapter, "The Political Economy of Early U.S. Financial Development," demonstrates that the political structure of the United States, as well as the leadership exerted by particular individuals, led the United States to a modern financial system beginning in the 1790s. He also demonstrates that changes in leadership resulted in financial reversals in the 1810s and 1830, even though the underlying legal institutions of British common law did not change.

Wallis's chapter, "Answering Mary Shirley's Question, or: What Can the World Bank Learn from American History?" continues this line of analysis, looking at U.S. financial development through the nineteenth century. He exploits the considerable variance across states to demonstrate that British legal origin did not inevitably lead American states to adopt policies that were positive for financial development. Indeed, American states experimented with many different ways of creating and regulating banks and developed new institutions that did not draw on their British inheritance. Initially, the American banking system was much like that of Mexico: a cartelized industry providing rents both to banks (as favored governmental constituents) and to the state. Competition among states, as noted, led over several decades to a more competitive banking system.

Do the results from these in-depth case studies travel beyond the U.S. and Mexican cases? Philip Keefer's chapter, "Beyond Legal Origin and

Checks and Balances: Political Credibility, Citizen Information, and Financial Sector Development," employs large-n techniques to look at political
institutions and financial development in cross section—and his results are
broadly consistent with those that emerge from the country case studies.
Keefer demonstrates that legal origin primarily proxies for political phenomena. His analysis also shows that variables that proxy political institutions come up as statistically significant even when controls for legal origin are introduced. Finally, he demonstrates that the influence of political
institutions on financial development works, at least in part, through the
security of property rights.

Governments that are not limited by institutions can behave opportunistically vis-à-vis private banks. From this it follows that much of the
advice given by multilateral institutions to developing countries—they
should strengthen the hand of bank regulators so as to promote financial
development—might actually be counterproductive. In the context of
weak limits on the authority and discretion of public officials, strengthening the hand of bank regulators might allow them to use their increased
supervisory power to extract rents from banks or encourage banks to lend
to politically favored groups. James Barth, Gerard Caprio, and Ross Levine
test this implication econometrically in their chapter, "The Microeconomic Effects of Different Approaches to Bank Supervision." They show
that the traditional public interest view of regulation, in which regulators
are presumed to be motivated by promoting social welfare, does not square
with the evidence: rather, regulators are apt to be privately interested. In
the context of weak limits on political officials, these authors conclude that
regulatory systems that focus on information disclosure are more likely to
promote financial development than regulatory systems that focus on strong
supervision by government regulators.

The impact of political institutions extends beyond banking systems:
they also affect the development of securities markets. We begin our discussion of the political economy of securities market development with a
large-n analysis by Peter Gourevitch and James Shinn, "Political Drivers
of Diverging Corporate Governance Patterns." They question the dominant view, that the strength of minority shareholder rights is determined
by legal origin, and demonstrate that legal family does not fully capture the
political processes at work in the creation of the laws covering corporate
governance. Their analysis indicates not only that a wide variety of institutions matter for a country's approach to corporate governance but that
these institutions change within countries over time.

If political institutions, rather than legal origin, determine the development of financial markets, then it follows that we should observe the growth of securities markets in French Civil Code countries. We therefore turn to two case studies of Brazil. The first study, by William R. Summerhill, "Credible Commitment and Sovereign Default Risk: Two Bond Markets and Imperial Brazil," demonstrates that between 1824 and 1889 Brazil had a government whose authority and discretion were limited by formal political institutions. The Constitution of 1824 placed multiple veto points on the sovereign's ability to tax, spend, borrow, or default. In addition, beginning in the 1850s monetary policy was delegated to a quasi-private entity, the Banco do Brasil. The result was that the Brazilian government was able to borrow progressively larger sums at progressively lower interest rates.

The second study, "Legal Origin vs. the Politics of Creditor Rights: Bond Markets in Brazil, 1850–2002," by Aldo Musacchio, demonstrates that Brazil also developed an extremely active market for corporate bonds after 1890, when the rights of creditors were made even stronger than they had been during the 1824–89 period studied by Summerhill. Thus, regardless of the existence of a civil law system, turn-of-the-century Brazil had a larger corporate bond market than many contemporary European countries. It also had a larger market for corporate bonds than Brazil does today.

The chapters by Summerhill and Musacchio both explore why Brazil's bond market ultimately fell apart. Summerhill argues that the erosion of limits on government after the military coup of 1889 meant that the government could borrow and spend without check. Ultimately, this lack of checks damaged the quality of Brazilian sovereign debt issues. Musacchio further points out that creditor rights were diminished after 1930, when Getulio Vargas came to power via another military coup. Bondholders no longer had primacy in the case of corporate bankruptcy: they came behind workers and government tax liens. The net result was that private markets for debt dried up.

The final chapter, "Conclusion: Economics, Political Institutions, and Financial Markets," by Douglass C. North and Mary M. Shirley, ties together many of the themes that run through the eight preceding chapters. They point in particular to three issues. First, politics and political institutions, rather than legal origin, appear to be determinative of financial development. Second, countries undergo both financial revolutions and financial reversals, as the Brazilian case illustrates. Third, there tends to be congruence between the openness and competitiveness of political systems and the openness and competitiveness of their financial systems.

The implications of the themes highlighted by North and Shirley are far reaching and have obvious implications for developing countries. They suggest, for example, that China's combination of competitive markets and repressive style of government is inherently unstable and that one or the other will change. They also suggest, however, that the creation of a competitive political system is not a phenomenon that is well understood by social scientists. In short, they suggest that the essays in this volume should not be taken as the last word on the political economy of financial development but should be taken as a call for a turn toward more microlevel analysis of the politics and economics of economic change.

References

Acemoglu, Daron, and Simon Johnson (Forthcoming). "Unbundling Institutions." *Journal of Political Economy.*

Acemoglu, Daron, Simon Johnson, and James Robinson (2004). "Institutions as a Fundamental Cause of Long Run Growth." In Philippe Aghion and Steve Durlauf, eds., *Handbook of Economic Growth.* Amsterdam: North-Holland.

Beck, Thorsten, Asli Demirgüç-Kunt, and Ross Levine (2003). "Law and Finance: Why Does Legal Origin Matter?" *Journal of Comparative Economics* 31: 653–75.

Haber, Stephen, Armando Razo, and Noel Maurer (2003). *The Politics of Property Rights: Political Instability, Credible Commitments, and Economic Growth in Mexico, 1876–1929.* Cambridge, UK: Cambridge University Press.

King, Robert G., and Ross Levine (1993a). "Finance and Growth: Schumpeter Might Be Right." *Quarterly Journal of Economics* 108: 717–38.

——— (1993b). "Finance, Entrepreneurship, and Growth: Theory and Evidence." *Journal of Monetary Economics* 32: 513–42.

Lamoreaux, Naomi, and Jean-Laurent Rosenthal (2005). "Legal Regime and Contractual Flexibility: A Comparison of France and the United States during the Era of Industrialization." *American Law and Economic Review* 7: 28–61.

La Porta, Rafael, Florencio López-de-Silanes, Andrei Shleifer, and Robert W. Vishny (1998). "Law and Finance." *Journal of Political Economy* 106: 1113–55.

Levine, Ross (2005). "Law, Endowments, and Property Rights." *Journal of Economic Perspectives* 19: 61–88.

——— (1998). "The Legal Environment, Banks, and Long Run Economic Growth." *Journal of Money, Credit, and Banking* 30: 596–620.

——— (1997). "Financial Development and Economic Growth: Views and Agenda." *Journal of Economic Literature* 35: 688–726.

Levine, Ross, Norma Loayza, and Thorsten Beck (2000). "Financial Intermediation and Growth: Causality and Causes." *Journal of Monetary Economics* 46: 31–77.

Levine, Ross, and Sara Zervos (1998). "Stock Markets, Banks, and Economic Growth." *American Economic Review* 88: 537–58.

North, Douglass C. (1990). *Institutions, Institutional Change, and Economic Performance.* Cambridge, UK: Cambridge University Press.

——— (1981). *Structure and Change in Economic History.* New York: W. W. Norton.

Rajan, Raghuram G., and Luigi Zingales (2003). "The Great Reversals: The Politics of Financial Development in the 20th Century." *Journal of Financial Economics* 69: 5–50.

——— (1998). "Financial Dependence and Growth." *American Economic Review* 88: 559–86.

Chapter 2

Political Institutions and Financial Development
*Evidence from the Political Economy of Bank Regulation
in Mexico and the United States*

STEPHEN HABER

Over the past decade, social scientists have created a broad literature on the role of institutions in economic development. That literature demonstrates that there is a relationship between democratic governance, secure private property rights, and high levels of material welfare (Barro 1991, 1997; Levine and Renelt 1992; Brunetti 1997; Przeworski et al. 2000).

Social scientists do not yet, however, fully understand the mechanisms that underlie this relationship. Which way does causality run? Do democratic institutions promote economic growth? Does economic growth promote democratic institutions? Or are democracy and growth jointly caused by a third, unspecified, set of institutions (Acemoglu et al. 2005)? Social scientists are similarly unsure about how and why particular political institutions affect the security of property rights (Keefer 2004). Finally, social scientists are unsure about where institutions come from and how they evolve. Some broad theories have been proposed (Engerman and Sokoloff 1997; Bates 2001; Acemoglu, Johnson, and Robinson 2001, 2002, 2004), but there is, as yet, no consensus view.

This chapter offers a contribution to the literature on institutions and growth by exploring the origins and dynamics of a particular set of institutions—those that govern the development of banking systems. I focus on banking because there is a broad consensus among economists that banks are a crucial part of the financial system and that an efficient

10

financial system is a necessary requisite for economic growth.[1] World history provides no case of a society with a high per capita income without a well-developed financial system and no case of a well-developed financial system without a banking system.[2]

The argument I advance runs in the following terms. The size and structure of banking systems are influenced by both the demand for and the supply of financial services. The demand for banks is an endogenous outcome of the size and structure of the real economy. When wealth is highly concentrated and when the overall level of development is low, the demand for banks is modest. As economies grow and as wealth becomes more broadly distributed, the demand for banks increases.

The supply of banks does not, however, respond automatically to increases in demand for their services. This can be the case for any of four reasons: bankers fear expropriation by the government; the government purposely limits the number of banks; bankers cannot enforce financial contracts with debtors; and investors (depositors and outside shareholders) fear that bankers will behave imprudently and therefore do not deploy their wealth in the banking system.

In order to overcome these problems, bankers, outside shareholders, depositors, debtors, and the government must create institutions that align their incentives. Societies have experimented with a number of different institutional solutions, but what they all tend to have in common is an active role for the government. To cite just a few examples, the government can compensate bankers for expropriation risk by raising bank rates of return through regulations that limit competition or by granting lucrative privileges to some banks. Similarly, the government can be charged with enforcing financial contracts through its system of laws, courts, and police. Or the government can mitigate the risk to outside investors by granting limited liability to shareholders and insurance to depositors. It might also create rules of prudent behavior by bankers and enforce these through various mechanisms, including supervisory agencies and deposit reserve requirements.

The active role of government creates a thorny problem: at the same time that the government plays a role in the creation of the institutions that make the banking system possible, it looks to the banking system as a source of finance for its own operations. The government therefore has an inherent conflict of interest. It may structure the institutions that govern banking so as to meet the demand that comes from the private economy, or it can structure the institutions that govern banking so as to facilitate its own political survival. It might create bank monopolies that share rents with the government. It may allocate charters only to politically favored constituents. Government officials may demand bribes in order to grant a bank charter. Or the government may refuse to enforce financial contracts when the debtors are from politically crucial groups.

Precisely because government has this conflict of interest, the political institutions that limit the authority and discretion of government play a crucial role in the development of the banking system. These political institutions vary across societies. There does not appear to be any single algorithm for their optimal organization. Nevertheless, these institutions operate according to a single unifying principle: they create institutionalized forms of competition within the political system that allow the ambitions of individuals or groups to be counteracted by the ambitions of other individuals or groups.[3]

The presence of institutionalized competition—through such institutions as electoral suffrage, political parties, separation of powers, and federalism—increases the probability that there will be ex ante vetoes over policies that allow the government's own short-term needs to take precedence over those of economic development. Similarly, the presence of institutionalized competition increases the probability that there will be ex post sanctions for public officials or government entities that exceed their authority or who engage in rent seeking at the expense of economic development.

The lack of institutionalized political competition does not necessarily mean that there will be no banking system at all. It does imply, however, that the institutional solutions to expropriation risk, default risk, and imprudent behavior are likely to be inefficient. As we shall see in the following discussion, the interaction of these inefficient institutions strongly works against the development of the banking system. Indeed, it gives rise to systems in which there may be few banks, and in which banks severely limit the range of services they provide to individuals and firms.

I develop the logic and evidence of these claims in the pages that follow. I first provide a theoretical framework. Next, I discuss the methods and approaches to evidence of the chapter. Finally, I explore how the development of banking systems was conditioned by the existence of institutionalized political competition in two widely divergent cases: the United States and Mexico.

Theoretical Framework

THE PROBLEM OF EXPROPRIATION

In order for individuals to invest their wealth in a bank, they must believe that the returns to them outweigh the risk that the government will expropriate the bank. Expropriation, it should be pointed out, does not have to take the form of the government seizing bank assets—although history offers us numerous cases of this phenomenon. Expropriation can also take more subtle forms: the government can renege on loans made to it by banks; it can force banks to lend to it at below-market interest rates; it can raise taxes to the point that profits are below the opportunity cost of capital; it can require banks to hold reserves against deposits in the form of government bonds that pay negative real rates of interest; or it can expand the money supply, setting off an inflation that amounts to a tax on the holders of cash.

The problem of expropriation means that for bankers to deploy their wealth, there must be institutions that align the incentives of the government and the bankers. One solution is the creation of political institutions that limit the authority and discretion of government. In cases where the government's authority and discretion are not limited, however, the incentives of bankers and government are aligned by the creation of institutions that raise the rate of return to banking high enough to compensate bankers for the risk of expropriation. These institutions typically allocate a set of lucrative privileges to one or more banks and/or limit the number of banks allowed in any market. That is, the government takes a direct role in structuring the market because it is in the interest of both the government and the bankers to do so.

THE PROBLEM OF CONTRACT ENFORCEMENT

Bankers will not write financial contracts if they cannot enforce those contracts. They therefore need to align the incentives of debtors with their own by credibly threatening to take possession of the physical assets represented by debt contracts. There is a broad range of institutions necessary to make this threat credible. Bankers must be able to draw upon institutions that allow them to determine who owns a particular asset (a property register, for example) and that allows them to repossess that asset in the case of default (a system of laws regarding bankruptcy and foreclosure, an efficient system of courts, and a police force with the power of coercion).

These institutions, it must be emphasized, emerge only in part because of demand by bankers. More fundamentally, they emerge because governments have a vested interest in creating mechanisms that allow them to monitor and enforce taxation, and because individuals and firms have an interest in protecting their property rights against encroachment by other individuals and firms. Indeed, firms and individuals have strong incentives to clearly demarcate (make transparent, in the parlance of property rights theory) and enforce property rights: transparent and enforceable property rights are easier to transfer—and hence are more valuable.

The need of governments, individuals, and firms to create institutions that make property rights transparent and enforceable creates a fundamental dilemma. *The same institutions that make property rights more transparent and enforceable make them more subject to expropriation by the government.* In societies in which the authority and discretion of government are limited by political institutions, the threat of expropriation does not loom large. In societies in which the authority and discretion of the government are not limited, however, individuals and firms have weak incentives to lobby for the creation of institutions that make their property rights transparent and enforceable. That is, if the government has unlimited discretion and authority, it is not in the interest of individuals and firms to have an efficient system of laws, courts, and police. Indeed, a government with unconstrained discretion that possesses efficient police and courts is likely to be a tyranny.

It logically follows that when the government has unlimited authority and discretion, the institutions that make property rights transparent and enforceable tend to be weak. The population does not necessarily frustrate the development of efficient property laws, property registers, courts, and police—although it may do so; rather, the population does not lobby for reforms in these institutions that would make them more efficient. Over time, the effect is the same: disorganized property registers, arcane laws, poorly paid and inefficient police, and a court system that is cumbersome and subject to bribery.

These inefficient institutions are reinforced by the government's inability to collect taxes. Precisely because property rights tend not to be transparent when government is not limited, the government cannot easily tax wealth or transactions involving wealth. Hence, even if the government wanted to make the institutions that specify and enforce property rights more efficient, it would not have the fiscal resources to do so. The result is a paradox: unconstrained governments tend to be poor and weak, whereas governments whose authority and discretion are limited tend to be wealthy and powerful (North and Weingast 1989).

When property rights are not transparent and enforceable at low cost, bankers respond by limiting the types of contracts that they write. Alternatively, they may limit the range of individuals and firms with whom they write contracts. As we shall see, one strategy they may pursue is to lend primarily to members of their own families, to other bank directors, and to themselves because they can monitor and enforce those contracts without recourse to the society's inefficient legal institutions.

THE PROBLEM OF IMPRUDENT BANKERS

For banks to grow beyond the wealth of their initial shareholders, they must attract the wealth of outside individuals and firms. These outsiders (most typically depositors and minority shareholders) will not, however, deploy their wealth if they perceive that the bankers will behave imprudently—that is, write credit contracts that have a high probability of default and/or a low probability of enforcement. At the extreme, bankers may loan the funds provided by outside investors to themselves and then default on the loans—in effect looting their own banks. Thus, institutions must be created that align the incentives of the depositors, the outside shareholders, and bank directors. Alternatively, institutions can be created that minimize the extent to which the wealth of depositors and shareholders is at risk, even if the bankers are imprudent.

Different societies have experimented with a range of institutions to align the incentives of bank directors, shareholders, and depositors. Some of these institutions, such as outside directors, are created out of the interaction of the bank directors and outside shareholders. Other institutions, however, are created by the government. These include laws that require banks to hold minimum levels of capital or that require banks to create reserve accounts that provision for risk. Governments may also create institutions that align the incentives of outsiders with those of directors by reducing the risk that those outsiders face. One common example is limited liability for shareholders. Another common example is deposit insurance.

THE CENTRALITY OF POLITICAL INSTITUTIONS

All of these institutions have a common thread: they directly involve the government. The government structures the banking system—allocating privileges, regulating entry by controlling bank charters, and limiting the types of contracts that may be written by banks. The government also enforces financial contracts through its system of laws, property registers, courts, and police. Finally, the government plays a key role in aligning the incentives of depositors and outside shareholders with those of bank directors and managers: it creates laws governing limited liability, reserves against risk, and the rights and responsibilities of bank directors; it creates and funds the agencies that supervise and regulate banks; and it creates (and often funds) the system of deposit insurance.

The problem is that the government is not a disinterested party in this process. At the same time that the government specifies and enforces the rules that govern banking, it also looks to the banking system as a source of finance. These sources include revenues from taxes on bank capital or bank profits, dividend income from the ownership of bank stock, credit lines from banks, and the mandatory purchase of government bonds as a chartering or reserve requirement.

Precisely because government has a conflict of interest, the political institutions that limit the authority and discretion of government play a crucial role in the development of the banking system. As we shall explore in detail, the political institutions that limit the authority and discretion of government by promoting political competition interact, reinforcing one another. Indeed, the evidence that we present suggests that political institutions that constrain government co-evolve. A somewhat parallel process occurs when governments are unconstrained by institutions that promote political competition. In these cases, bankers and governments create institutions that mitigate the problems of expropriation, contract default, and imprudent behavior. These institutions also interact, but they do so in ways that constrain the number of banks and the services that they will offer.

Case Selection

Operationalizing this argument requires that we proceed in three steps. First, we need to understand the origins and evolution of the political institutions of particular societies. Second, we need to understand how those political institutions structured the economic institutions that governed banking systems. Third, we need to understand how those economic institutions affected the supply of banks.

Connecting the causal links in this chain requires that we depart from the kinds of cross-country regression techniques that are standard in much of the financial economics literature and instead draw on the historical records of particular countries. In an ideal world, we would focus on a large number of case studies. Understanding the evolution of political institutions, the economic institutions that govern banking, and the subsequent structure and performance of banking systems is not, however, an enterprise characterized by increasing returns. Inevitably, the more cases one includes, the less one is bound to know about each case.

I therefore focus on two extreme cases—the United States and Mexico during the period 1781–1932.[4] I focus on the United States because it was characterized by institutionalized political competition on four dimensions: electoral suffrage, organized political parties, separation of powers within the central government, and federalism. As the ensuing pages shall show, these different forms of competition worked to reinforce one another in ways that were not, in fact, fully foreseen at the time that the Constitution was written.

The net effect of these institutions was an equilibrium: political actors articulated their demands and adjudicated their differences by staying within the governance structure, rather than going outside it by making demands through the use of violence. There was, as Hofstadter (1969) put it, a "legitimate opposition"—one that used formal institutions to oppose the policies of the government, rather than oppose the government itself. This equilibrium broke down over only a single issue—slavery—requiring that differences in interests on this issue be adjudicated not through institutional channels but through armed force.

I focus on Mexico because it was characterized by an almost complete absence of institutionalized political competition of any type. This is not to say that there were not formal rules governing political action. In fact, Mexico had various constitutions—some federal and republican, others centralist and decidedly anti-republican. The problem was that the sets of political institutions created by these constitutions were not mutually reinforcing. Instead, Mexico had alternating periods of federal republics and centralized dictatorships, punctuated by coups d'état, civil wars, and foreign interventions. Thus, during the first 55 years after Mexico's independence from Spain (1822–76), most political competition in Mexico took place outside the channels prescribed by the country's formal institutions—that is, at gunpoint. Indeed, those first 55 years saw 75 presidents, with one military leader serving as president on 11 different occasions.

In the last decades of the nineteenth century Mexico finally obtained political stability, under the dictatorship of Porfirio Díaz (1876–1911). Díaz drew upon a preexisting constitution to craft a governance structure that was nominally federal and republican, but that was in fact ruled by a network of political and economic elites who used the government's regulatory powers to create and share rents with one another. In short, neither during the period when the political system was unstable (1821–76) nor when it was stable (1876–1911) was there institutionalized political competition in Mexico.

These differences in political institutions had a powerful effect on long-run economic outcomes. In the United States, attempts by governments to limit the supply of banks in the face of increasing demand for banking services tended to be sustainable only for short periods of time. The nature of U.S. political institutions allowed the population to quickly undermine whatever restrictive arrangements had been made. In 1800, the U.S. banking system was characterized by segmented monopolies erected by state legislatures and a private commercial bank with special privileges that served as the financial agent of the federal government. Within a few decades this organization of banking markets was completely transformed: there were thousands of banks, the overwhelming majority of banks had no branches, and the federal government had no bank at all. Not until 1913 would the federal government once again have access to an institution that could serve as a central bank (when the Federal Reserve was founded), but by that time there were more than 25,000 banks in operation in the United States.

In Mexico, on the other hand, the absence of institutionalized political competition meant that the banking system always remained small—even in the face of increasing demand for banking services. During the decades before 1876, bankers faced expropriation risk because of the types of political institutions in Mexico. Bankers also could not count on the government to enforce their contract rights. As a consequence, there was virtually no chartered banking system at all. In the decades after 1876, the economy grew rapidly. Nevertheless, even as demand for financial services increased, the supply of banks was constrained. In exchange for limiting the number of charters granted, bankers shared some of their rents directly with the federal treasury and with government officials as individuals. The result was a market structure virtually the opposite of that in the United States: two banks with national branch networks controlled 60 percent of total assets; virtually no market had more than three banks in it. Moreover, unlike U.S. bankers, Mexican bankers faced an environment in which it was not possible to enforce their property rights. They therefore lent most of the funds in the banking system to themselves. The combination of a small number of banks and insider lending meant that there was differential access to capital in Mexico: a small group of entrepreneurs were awash in funds, while everyone else was starved for credit.

Case Studies

THE UNITED STATES

During the early republican period, banking in the United States was characterized by segmented monopolies. In exchange for regulations that protected banks from competition, bankers shared their monopoly rents with state treasuries—and with state legislators as individuals. The central government had a commercial bank as well, the Bank of the United States—modeled on the Bank of England, which had a series of special privileges, including the sole right to operate branches across state lines.

These arrangements constraining the supply of banks, however, were inconsistent with the fact that U.S. political institutions fostered political competition. Moreover, that competition did not arise only because the United States had democratic elections—though the existence of electoral suffrage figures as part of our story. In addition to electoral suffrage, four other institutions were crucial to the erosion of limits on the supply of banks: the development of political parties that could articulate coherent policy options; the existence of horizontal competition among states for capital and labor; the existence of vertical competition between states and the central government; and the existence of separation of powers within the central government, which gave states the ability to use their congressional and Senate delegations to undermine federal initiatives.[5]

Political Institutions, Public Finance, and Bank Chartering

The political institutions of the United States began to take shape even before independence was achieved in 1781. During the colonial period, each colony had essentially governed itself through a system of elected colonial assemblies and an appointed British governor. When independence came, the British governors and their supporters were thrown out, electoral suffrage was broadened somewhat, and the colonial assemblies became state legislatures. There was never any doubt that the United States would have democratic elections and a federal system of government. What was up for debate, however, was how strong the central government would be.

The first experiment produced an extremely weak central government, under the Articles of Confederation. The new government did what almost all new governments do: it founded a commercial bank—the Bank of North America (BNA)—whose purpose was to serve as the government's fiscal agent. The problem was that the Articles of Confederation was ambiguous as to whether the central government had the authority to charter a bank. The BNA was therefore rechartered by the state of Pennsylvania—and then almost immediately came into conflict with the Pennsylvania state legislature. The BNA had been founded with the understanding that it would hold a monopoly on the issue of paper currency. It therefore took a strong position on the states' issuing bills of credit, which was paper money by another name. In retaliation, the Pennsylvania state legislature revoked the BNA's charter in 1785. After a two-year battle, the BNA got its charter restored, but only after accepting a series of restrictions on its activities (Bodenhorn 2003, p. 128).

The extreme federalism of the Articles soon proved unworkable because the central government lacked any independent taxation authority. In 1789, the Articles of Confederation was replaced with the Constitution, which conferred on the central government a great deal more policy and taxation authority—in exchange for which it assumed the (quite considerable) debts that the states had accumulated. Nevertheless, the American political system was still strongly federal: all policy-making authority not explicitly delegated to the federal government by the Constitution was vested in the states.

The delegation of power to the states meant that they had the right, and the incentive, to charter and regulate banks. Under the Constitution, the states lost both the right to tax imports and exports and the right to issue paper money—both of these powers were vested with the federal government. These constitutional provisions created two problems for state finances: tax revenues were dependent on cumbersome poll and property taxes, and states could no longer finance their expenditures in excess of taxes by issuing paper money. The response of the states was to sidestep the Constitution: the states might no longer be able to issue paper money, but the Constitution said nothing about states chartering banks of issue, whose banknotes would circulate as currency (Sylla, Legler, and Wallis 1987).

The ability to charter banks allowed states to find a ready source of finance. A bank charter was not just a license to do business; it conferred two very valuable concessions on its holders—the right to issue banknotes (and thereby profit from seignorage) and the right to limited liability. Potential bankers were thus willing to pay handsomely for a charter, especially if they believed that they were receiving the only one. States, for their part, had every incentive to sell charters so that they could fill their treasuries. Thus, bankers offered (and states demanded) the payment of charter "bonuses." These bonuses came in various forms—one-time cash payments, the promise to lend to the state government at preferential rates, or the cession of blocks of bank shares to the state (which generated a stream of dividend income) (Sylla, Legler, and Wallis 1987; Wallis, Sylla, and Legler 1994; Bodenhorn 2003, p. 15).

State governments therefore owned sizable amounts of bank stock. In Virginia, for example, the state owned one-fifth of the stock in the Bank of Virginia (chartered in 1804)—a purchase that it financed by borrowing the funds from that very same bank. The state government later simplified matters by demanding that new banks provide the state with shares gratis. In Massachusetts, the state government was a major investor in the Union Bank (chartered in 1793) and the Bank of Boston (chartered in 1803), giving it control of one-eighth of all banking capital until 1812. In Pennsylvania, the state owned more than $1 million in bank shares, most of it in the Bank of Pennsylvania, whose concession made it the state's fiscal agent.

New states, as they entered the Union, copied the chartering model of the original 13 states: all of them were major owners of bank stock. Kentucky, Tennessee, Illinois, Arkansas, and Alabama went even further: their first banks were 100 percent state owned. Indeed, the basic pattern of state governments being major bank stockholders held just about everywhere— with the exception of New York, where (as we will discuss later) bankers did not just share rents with the state treasury but shared them directly with legislators as individuals.[6]

The chartering of banks helped solve the problem of state government finance. Sylla, Legler, and Wallis have calculated that circa 1810, bank dividends and bank taxes accounted for 6 percent of total state revenues in New York, 9 percent in Connecticut and South Carolina, 12 percent in Delaware and Virginia, 29 percent in Maryland, and 38 percent in Pennsylvania. These 1810 estimates do not include a number of states that we know (from subsequent observations) relied heavily on bank dividends or taxes. Thus, their first observation for North Carolina is in 1820 (when banks accounted for 31 percent of state revenues), and their first observation for Massachusetts is in 1830 (when bank taxes accounted for an amazing 61 percent of state revenues). Moreover, none of these figures include one-time cash payments by banks to state treasuries, the market value of bank stock distributed gratis (or discounted) to states, or the transfers created by bank financing of public works projects or credit lines provided to states at favorable rates (Wallis, Sylla, and Legler 1994, p. 126).

The financing of state expenditures via chartering bonuses created a problem of moral hazard: it created incentives for incumbent banks to offer bonuses to state legislatures to deny the charter applications of potential competitors; and it created incentives for state legislatures to accept those bonus payments—unless the newcomer was willing to offer a substantial share of its future stream of rent.[7] It was, therefore, in the interest of state governments to restrict entry into banking to maximize the amount of rent earned by incumbent banks, and then share in those rents via the dividend stream created by the state's ownership of bank stock. States thus had to make sure that there was not a competitive fringe of private banks that operated without charters. They therefore nearly all passed laws that required private banks to obtain a corporate charter from the state government—and then turned down many of those charter applications (Bodenhorn 2003, pp. 17, 244).

In some states, problems of moral hazard extended beyond the incentives of the state treasury and affected the behavior of legislators as individuals. The most notorious such case was New York. From the 1810s to the late 1830s, bank chartering in New York was controlled by the so-called Albany Regency—a political machine controlled by Martin Van Buren. Bank charters were only granted to friends of the Regency. The incentives of legislators were aligned with those of the bankers by allowing the former to subscribe to initial public offerings of bank stock at par, even though the stock traded for a substantial premium because the banks earned monopoly rents. In addition, banks also made direct bribes to legislators. Not surprisingly, in 1818 the Regency expanded the state laws (initially passed in 1804) that restricted unchartered institutions from providing banking services. It later amended the state constitution (in 1821) so that new bank charters required a two-thirds vote of the legislature, instead of the simple majority that had been required up to that time (Gatell 1966, p. 26; Bodenhorn 2003, pp. 134, 186–88, 2004; Moss and Brennan 2004, p. 7).

Banking in the early republican United States, therefore, tended to be characterized by segmented monopolies. In fact, the four largest cities in the United States in 1800—Boston, Philadelphia, New York, and Baltimore—had only two state-chartered banks apiece. Smaller markets typically had only one bank, if they had a bank at all. These banks, it should be pointed out, did not lend to all comers. Indeed, they discriminated on the basis of profession, social standing, and political party affiliation (Wallis, Sylla, and Legler 1994, pp. 135–39; Bodenhorn 2003, p. 142; Majewski 2004a).

The federal government pursued a similar strategy to that of the states and chartered its own commercial bank, the Bank of the United States (BUS), in 1791. Unlike the state incentives, the incentive of the federal government was not to produce a source of dividend income (dividends from the BUS were on the order of 1 percent of total federal revenues). Rather, it was to provide the federal government with a financial agent that could issue banknotes against customs duties and that could hold federal balances.

Nonetheless, the BUS was founded and operated in much the same way as the segmented monopolies created by the states: it was a commercial bank fully capable of making loans to private individuals, and 20 percent of its stock was owned by the federal government. The federal government did not actually pay for its $2 million stake in the bank: rather, the bank lent the government the money for the shares, which the government then paid for out of the flow of dividends. In addition, 75 percent of the private capital in the bank could be paid for with federal government bonds at par, providing a mechanism to soak up federal debt. In other words, the BUS allocated a 20 percent ownership stake in the bank to the federal government in exchange for a series of valuable concessions: the right to hold federal government specie balances; the right to charge the federal government interest on loans from the bank (notes issued by the bank to cover federal expenses); and the sole right to open branches throughout the country. This gave it a tremendous competitive advantage over state-chartered banks, which were not allowed to branch across state lines and which did not have the advantage of having the federal government as their biggest depositor. Needless to say, the existence of the BUS generated considerable resentment from bankers who held state charters, and therefore from state legislatures. Some states even tried (unsuccessfully) to tax the banknotes of the BUS to constrain it from competing against their own banks (Wettereau 1942; Lane 1997; Sylla 2000).

Political Competition and the Breakdown of Segmented Monopolies
The strategies of the state and federal governments made sense from their points of view. In addition, the Bank of the United States made sense from the point of view of a sound system of public finance. That sound system of public finance was, in turn, an important ingredient in the creation of a government that honored property rights: investors did not fear that the government would have to fund itself via inflation or the seizure of assets (Sylla 2000; Majewski 2004a).

Nevertheless, the system of segmented state monopolies and a single national bank was not an equilibrium that was stable given the political institutions of the United States. As the U.S. economy grew, so too did the demand from the public for banking services. That demand was channeled via the country's political institutions—parties, elections, separation of powers, and federalism—and it quickly undermined the initial organization of the banking system at both the national and state levels.

The first source of competition, and the one that has received the most attention from historians, was that between states and the federal government. Bankers with state charters, and hence state legislatures, had opposed the BUS from the time of its initial chartering in 1791. The reason for their opposition was straightforward: branches of the BUS undermined local banking monopolies (Rockoff 2000). These state bankers formed alliances with the Jeffersonians, who were ideologically opposed to chartered corporations and "aristocratic" bankers. Indeed, though the Founders were all opposed to the concept of political parties, two parties (the Federalists and the Democratic Republicans) quickly formed around the broad set of debates initiated by Hamilton and Jefferson regarding banking and public finance (Hofstadter 1969). Thus, when the BUS charter expired in 1811, it was not renewed by Congress. The War of 1812 demonstrated, however, the importance of a bank that could serve as the financial agent of the federal government, and thus a new charter (for a Second Bank of the United States) was granted in 1816.

The Second Bank of the United States was founded on the same principles as the first bank and met the same fate. The Second Bank was a private enterprise, but the federal government owned 20 percent of its $35 million in stock—which it paid for with a $7 million loan from the bank to the government. In addition, the bank paid a charter bonus to the government of $1.5 million. Much as happened with its predecessor, the holders of state banking charters, as well as state governments, resented the fact that the Second Bank held tremendous government balances—balances that state bankers believed should be part of their reserve base. They also resented the fact that the Second Bank could compete in their markets by opening branches at will. The history of the closure of the Second Bank would take us beyond the space limitations of this chapter. Suffice it to say, however, that in the end the state bankers prevailed by forming an alliance with Jacksonian populists. When the bank's charter came up for renewal in Congress, it passed by only a single vote and was therefore successfully vetoed by Jackson. It was forced to close in 1836 when its charter expired. The United States would therefore be without a central bank until the Federal Reserve System was created in 1913 (Hammond 1947; Temin 1968; Engerman 1970; Rockoff 2000).

A second, and less obvious, source of competition was that between states for business enterprise and population. The fact that the United States had a federal system meant that population and business enterprises could easily relocate to other states. The fact that it also had an expanding frontier meant that the pressures on state legislatures to hold their populations and businesses from emigrating were especially severe.

Competition between states undermined the incentives of legislators to maintain the monopoly banks they had earlier established. State legislatures were under considerable pressure to provide public works projects, particularly canals, because powerful constituents (urban merchants and large-scale farmers) stood to gain from the increase in commerce they would generate. The pressure to carry out these projects was made particularly intense by the fact that the failure to do so would result in commerce (and hence labor and capital) moving to those states that had made these improvements. Indeed, state legislatures tended to be highly aware of canal and port improvement projects in neighboring states, and of the consequences of those projects for the flow of commercial traffic within their own borders (Goodrich 1961; Majewski 2004a).

State legislatures tended not, however, to have the ability to fund public works projects out of their meager tax revenues. One response by states was to issue bonds, thereby funding public works out of future tax revenues. This strategy had a limit, because states could issue debt only to the point that investors believed that the state would have sufficient future revenues to repay it (Grinath, Wallis, and Sylla 1997; Sylla 2000; Wallis and Weingast 2004).

Many states therefore found supplementary funding for public works projects from "bonuses" levied on new bank charters. Such charter bonuses created, however, an incentive for state legislatures to renege on their arrangements with incumbent banks. As a consequence, quite a few banks were granted charters that undermined the monopolies of preexisting banks, in exchange for which they provided financing for canals, ports, and (somewhat later) streetlights and railroads. These schemes were employed across the country, even including Southern states that tended to be highly resistant to undermining their initial monopoly banks (Bodenhorn 2003, pp. 86, 148, 152, 228–34).

One might wonder why incumbent banks did not simply outbid potential entrants by agreeing to finance state infrastructure projects themselves. Incumbent banks at times tried this strategy. In order to successfully outbid all potential entrants, however, they would have had to devote nearly all of their rents to public goods provision. They were better off forcing new entrants to shoulder the costs of infrastructure projects (costs that could sometimes be ruinous for those new banks). The rents earned by incumbent banks were thus dissipated by competition, but that process took place over time. Incumbent banks therefore avoided the "Krueger paradox," but they did so at the cost of their long-run monopoly positions.

Competition over capital and labor also drove states to expand the suffrage, and an expanded suffrage undermined the political coalitions that had supported restrictions on the number of bank charters. All of the original 13 states restricted the right to vote based on a person's economic standing: some had minimum property qualifications; others had a qualification based on a minimum tax payment. With the exception of Louisiana, all of the states that subsequently joined the Union, however, either eliminated these qualifications entirely or reduced them to the point that they were not binding. The logic of these voting rules was transparent: new states were eager to attract population. As a consequence, the original 13 states were forced to respond by ratcheting their voting restrictions downward. By the mid-1820s, property qualifications had been dropped or dramatically reduced in virtually all of the original states (Engerman and Sokoloff 2001). As we shall see, the extension of the suffrage allowed citizens to bring pressure to bear on legislatures, voting in legislators who were willing to remove constraints on the chartering of banks.

De Facto "Free Banking"

Political competition within and among states undermined the incentives of state legislatures to constrain the number of charters they granted. Massachusetts began to increase the number of charters it granted as early as 1812. This required that the state abandon its strategy of holding bank stock as a source of state finance (the value of those shares and their dividend streams would decline as the original banks faced increased competition) and instead levy taxes on bank capital. Pennsylvania followed Massachusetts's lead with the Omnibus Banking Act of 1814. The act, passed over the objections of the state's governor (he had vetoed an earlier bill), ended the cozy Philadelphia-based oligopoly that, until then, had dominated the state's banking industry. The act divided the state into 27 banking districts and allocated at least one bank to each district. In all, it chartered 42 new banks. Rhode Island also followed Massachusetts's lead: in 1826 it sold its bank shares, increased the number of charters it granted, and began to tax bank capital as a replacement for the income it had earned from dividends. It soon became, on a per capita basis, America's most heavily banked state.

A necessary condition for this change in the institutions governing banking was that there be pent-up demand within states for bank credit. That is, there had to be constituencies that demanded access to credit but had been unable to obtain it under the earlier set of institutions. The existence of this demand can be clearly seen by four features of Pennsylvania's 1814 Omnibus Act. The first was that merchants, manufacturers, and farmers had long complained that the lack of capital and specie had constrained their enterprises. The second was a peculiar requirement of the new law: banks had to lend at least 20 percent of their capital to those same three groups. The third was that the law spread the new banks throughout the state, with particularly prosperous counties getting multiple banks. The fourth was that the stockholders of these new banks viewed them as being extremely lucrative: demand for shares at the initial subscription prices far outstripped the supply. In fact, a Pennsylvania bank chartered prior to the 1814 Omnibus Act (the Mechanic's Bank in 1809) was viewed by potential shareholders as being so lucrative that they rioted in the streets of Philadelphia when they found that there were not enough shares to go around (Bodenhorn 2003, pp. 142–43; Majewski 2004a, 2004b).

Southern states tended to be a good deal slower than Northern states to make the shift toward more liberal chartering. They did not uniformly refuse to grant any new charters beyond those issued to their original, partially state-owned, banks but tended to grant additional charters quite sparingly by the standards of Northern states. Historians have not yet systematically pursued the reasons for this difference in the treatment of bank chartering. One explanation often advanced is that the demand for capital was lower in the South. Although this is almost certainly true, it is difficult to reconcile with the fact that some Southern states later embraced free banking—and chartered large numbers of banks as a consequence. A second explanation is that, as Gavin Wright (1986) has pointed out, slavery reduced the demand for public goods. The lower political pressure for public works projects in the South would, in turn, have reduced the need for states to charter progressively larger numbers of banks to fund those projects via charter bonuses. As a consequence, the dividend streams generated by the state ownership of bank stock would not have been diminished by competition, and states would have had little incentive to shift away from the ownership of bank shares and toward more liberal bank chartering.

Even with the relative slowness of Southern states to undo their monopolies and oligopolies, the U.S. banking system grew remarkably quickly. In 1818, there were 338 banks in operation, with a total capital of $160 million—roughly 3 times as many banks and 3 times as much bank capital as in 1810 (Fenstermaker 1965, pp. 401–4). By 1835, there were 584 banks. Larger cities may have had a dozen or more banks, whereas small towns may have had 2 or 3 (Bodenhorn 2003, p. 12). To put the size of this banking system into perspective, consider the case of England, which is usually thought of as the world's financial leader in the nineteenth century. In 1825, the United States had roughly 2.4 times the banking capital of England, even though the United States had a smaller population (Rousseau and Sylla 1999).[8]

De Jure Free Banking

By the late 1830s the de facto policies of many states in the Northeast to grant virtually all requests for bank charters became institutionalized as a series of laws known as free banking. Under free banking, bank charters no longer had to be approved by state legislatures. Rather, individuals could open banks provided that they registered with the state comptroller and deposited state or federal bonds with the comptroller as a guarantee of their note issues. Some states also had minimum capital requirements and speci-fied a minimum number of directors. Many required that bank stockhold-ers be doubly liable. These features of free banking laws were meant to encourage prudent behavior by the bankers: they prevented bankers from overissuing notes and gave shareholders strong incentives to monitor the bank directors.[9]

The first state to make the switch (New York in 1838) to de jure free banking was not one that had previously carried out a de facto reform.[10] Indeed, free banking in New York was unambiguously a consequence of political competition undermining the coalition of upstate interests that had supported restrictions on bank charters. New York was among the last of the original 13 states to broaden its electoral laws: not until 1826 did it finally shift to universal manhood suffrage. Once that happened, Whig can-didates began to outpoll Democratic Republicans in elections for the state legislature. By 1837, the Whigs had gained a majority, ending the reign of the Albany Regency. In the wake of the panic of 1837, which highlighted the fragility of unsecured banknotes, the Whig-dominated legislature was able to push through the free banking law. The new law made the establish-ment of a bank an administrative, rather than a legislative, procedure. Pru-dent behavior was enforced by requiring all banknotes to be 100 percent backed by high-grade securities. By 1841, New Yorkers had established 43 free banks, with a total capital of $10.7 million. By 1849, the number of free banks mushroomed to 111, (with $16.8 million in paid capital). By 1859, there were 274 free banks with paid-in capital of $100.6 million (Atack and Passell 1994, p. 105; Wallis, Sylla, and Legler 1994; Bodenhorn 2003, pp. 186–92; Moss and Brennan 2004).

Other states soon followed New York's lead: Georgia passed a free banking law in 1839; Alabama, in 1849; and then New Jersey, Illinois, Massachusetts, Ohio, Vermont, Connecticut, Indiana, Tennessee, Wisconsin,
Florida, Louisiana, Iowa, and Minnesota, during the 1850s. Some variant
of the New York law was ultimately adopted in 21 states.[11]

Readers may wonder how such a system of free entry could have been
compatible with the fiscal needs of state governments. The answer lies in
the fact that under free banking all banknotes had to be 100 percent backed
by high-grade securities that were deposited with the state comptroller of
the currency. The putative reason for this was protection of the noteholders
(if the bank failed, the comptroller of the currency could sell the bonds and
compensate the noteholders). States tended, however, to gradually restrict
the range of securities that they would accept as backing for banknotes.
Initially, they accepted federal government bonds, bonds issued by other
states, and even bonds that secured mortgages on real property. Increasingly, however, they required that notes be backed only by federal bonds
or by bonds of the state in which the bank operated (Bodenhorn 2003,
chap. 8). As Moss and Brennan (2004) have shown, free banks were forced,
in essence, to grant a loan to the state government in exchange for the
right to operate. Inasmuch as bankers could have earned higher returns
than those available from investing in state bonds, this feature of the free
banking laws constituted a form of financial repression.

Bankers realized that this feature of free banking laws prevented them
from being able to serve as credit intermediaries. They responded with an
institutional innovation of their own: they began to pursue deposit banking,
opening demand deposit (checking) accounts and then lending the funds in
those accounts without restriction. This step meant that banks were now
subject to runs on their deposits, even if their notes were fully protected.
The growth in deposit banking explains, in fact, why state governments
found it necessary to introduce double liability into subsequent free banking laws: they wanted to give shareholders strong incentives to monitor
bank directors (Moss and Brennan 2004).

The problem of runs was exacerbated by the fact that banks were single-
unit enterprises. Individual small banks tended to be susceptible to failure
because of changes in local business conditions. This problem would have
been mitigated had there been branch banking, which would have allowed
banks to transfer funds from one branch to another in the event of a run on
any single branch. It also would have been mitigated had there been a central bank, which could have acted as a lender of last resort, by buying and

holding the notes of banks that were in trouble. Unfortunately, the U.S. banking system after the closure of the Second Bank of the United States had neither. To a remarkable degree, this problem was largely mitigated by the specie standard and the Suffolk System during the antebellum period. As research by Rockoff has shown, bank failure rates were surprisingly low.[12]

A reader prone to skepticism might be tempted to argue that the passage of these laws demonstrates that there were no politically determined supply constraints in banking—as demand for banking services increased, states changed their laws. Such a view would be extremely difficult to reconcile, however, with one of the curious features of free banking laws: they almost uniformly precluded the chartering of branch banks. Virtually all banks in the nineteenth-century United States, except those in some Southern states, were unit (single branch) banks. This unusual organization of the banking system was the outcome of an unlikely political coalition: populists who feared bank monopolies at the state level allied to bankers who wanted to create local monopolies.

This system of free entry and unit banks did confer several advantages. One obvious advantage was that the number of banks and bank capital mushroomed. Circa 1860, the United States had 1,579 banks, with a total capital of $422.5 million (Lamoreaux 1991, p. 540). A second, less obvious advantage was that large numbers of small banks (the average capitalization was only $268,000) made it easier for bankers to overcome information asymmetries. The only reliable information that bankers had about borrowers was what bankers could obtain via repeated business dealings with them, via information obtained from local (and informal) networks of businesspeople and farmers, or via their kinship ties. Bankers tended, therefore, to lend primarily to people that they knew personally. Under these circumstances, a system made up of large numbers of small banks embedded in individual communities was a rational way to organize the banking industry.[13]

As Naomi Lamoreaux has shown, this fairly unusual organization of the banking industry allowed New England banks in particular (one-third of all U.S. banks were in New England) to operate as investment pools—the nineteenth-century equivalent of modern mutual funds. New England's banks were not the independent credit intermediaries of economic theory. Rather, they were the financial arms of kinship groups whose investments spread across a wide number of economic sectors and enterprises. Basically, kinship groups tapped the local supply of investable funds by founding a bank and selling its equity to both individual and institutional investors. The founding groups then lent those funds to the various enterprises under their own control. Investors in the banks knew full well that the banks lent only to insiders. They bought bank stock precisely in order to invest in the broad range of business enterprises controlled by the founding group of entrepreneurs (Lamoreaux 1994).

Had legal restrictions been placed on the founding of banks, these insider arrangements would have concentrated capital in the hands of a small number of kinship/business groups. The fact that entry into banking was essentially free, however, meant that large numbers of entrepreneurs could tap the capital of nongroup investors by using banks as investment pools. The crucial point is that the rules of the game were not constructed to allow some entrepreneurs to play while excluding others.

Political Institutions, War Finance, and the National Banking System
From the point of view of the federal government, unit banking had another major drawback: a system of small, state-chartered banks did not provide the government with a source of finance. This had not been a major problem during the 1840s and 1850s (after the closure of the Second Bank of the United States in 1836), because the federal government had a low demand for debt. To the degree that it ran deficits, it was able to cover these by selling treasury bonds to the public and to European investors. The Civil War, however, dramatically increased the financial needs of the federal government. The response of the government was to do what most governments do when they need to finance a war: they turn to the banking system. It therefore passed laws in 1863, 1864, and 1865 designed to eliminate the state-chartered banks and replace them with a system of federally chartered banks that would finance the government's war effort.

The laws creating national banks were designed to centralize bank chartering in the hands of the federal government. The laws did not abrogate the rights of states to charter banks—that would have violated the Constitution. They also did not abrogate the right of state-chartered banks to issue banknotes, as that too would have been unconstitutional. A follow-up act to the National Banking Act (in 1865) did, however, impose a 10 percent tax on banknotes and then exempted federally chartered banks from the tax. This created a strong incentive for state banks to obtain new, federal charters. In fact, the expectation of the federal government was that state banks would disappear.

TABLE 2.1
Number of U.S. commercial banks, 1860–1932

Year	STATE-CHARTERED BANKS		NATIONAL BANKS		TOTAL BANKS		NATIONAL BANKS AS % OF TOTAL	
	Number	Assets (millions U.S. $)	Number	Assets (millions U.S. $)	Number	Assets (millions U.S. $)	Number	Assets (millions U.S. $)
1860	1,579	423			1,579	423		
1865	349	231	1,294	1,127	1,643	1,358	79	83
1870	325	215	1,612	1,566	1,937	1,781	83	88
1875	1,260	1,291	2,076	1,913	3,336	3,204	62	60
1880	1,279	1,364	2,076	2,036	3,355	3,400	62	60
1885	1,661	2,005	2,689	2,422	4,350	4,427	62	55
1890	4,717	3,296	3,484	3,062	8,201	6,358	42	48
1895	6,103	4,139	3,715	3,471	9,818	7,610	38	46
1900	9,322	6,444	3,731	4,944	13,053	11,388	29	43
1905	13,103	10,186	5,664	7,325	18,767	17,511	30	42
1910	18,013	13,030	7,138	9,892	25,151	22,922	28	43
1914	20,346	15,872	7,518	11,477	27,864	27,349	27	42
1919	20,079		7,780		27,859		28	
1924	20,292		8,080		28,372		28	
1929	16,974		7,530		24,504		31	

SOURCES: Lamoreaux (1991, p. 540); Davis and Gallman (2001, p. 268); Calomiris and White (1994, p. 151); and U.S. Federal Reserve (1943, p. 24).

The incentive of the federal government for doing this is not obvious until you consider a principal feature of the new law: federally chartered banks had to invest one-third of their capital in federal government bonds (which were then held as reserves against note issues by the comptroller of the currency). Consistent with the goal of maximizing credit to the federal government, the National Banking Act made the granting of a charter an administrative procedure—as long as minimum capital and reserve requirements were met, the charter was granted. It was free banking on a national scale (Sylla 1975).

In the short run, the response of private banks was as the federal government expected: the number of state-chartered banks declined from 1,579 in 1860 to 349 by 1865 (see Table 2.1). Federal banks grew dramatically: from zero in 1860 to 1,294 in 1865. They then continued growing, reaching 7,518 by 1914, controlling $11.5 billion in assets in that year.

In the long run, however, the political institutions of the United States frustrated the federal government's goal of a single, federally chartered banking system. They also undermined the barriers to entry in banking that had been created by the National Banking System. The federal government had effectively nationalized the right to issue banknotes by creating a 10 percent tax on the notes of state-chartered banks in 1865. The 1865 law did not, however, say anything about checks drawn on accounts in state-chartered banks. State banks therefore aggressively pursued deposit banking, and checks drawn on those accounts became a common means of exchange in business transactions.[14] Moreover, the states rewrote their banking laws, reducing even further the requirements to obtain a charter. Most states did away with the requirement of "double liability" that had been part of most state free banking laws. State charters also tended to require lower minimum capital requirements than for national banks and had less onerous reserve restrictions. Finally, national banks were not allowed to lend on real estate. State banks faced no such restrictions (Sylla 1975, pp. 62–73; Davis and Gallman 2001, p. 272).

The result was that state-chartered banks actually outgrew federally chartered banks during the period 1865–1914. In 1865, state banks accounted for only 21 percent of all banks and 13 percent of total bank assets. By 1890, state banks outnumbered national banks and controlled the majority of assets. Circa 1914, of all banks, 73 percent were state banks, which controlled 58 percent of assets (see Table 2.1).

The end result of this competition between states and the federal government was a banking system unlike that of any other country: (1) circa 1930 there were 21,309 banks in the United States; and (2) virtually all of these banks were unit banks: many states had laws that prevented branch banking, even by nationally chartered banks; most other states did not explicitly forbid branching, but their laws provided no provision for branch banking (Davis and Gallman 2001, p. 272). As Calomiris and White (1994) have shown, of the 21,309 banks in operation, only 723 had branches. The average number of branches operated by these banks was less than five. Large numbers of small unit banks created problems of volatility, which were only partially compensated by the fact that the national banks had correspondent relationships. It also made it difficult for banks to capture scale economies (Bordo, Rockoff, and Redish 1994).

Unit banking did, however, confer two advantages. First, unit banking meant that all markets were contestable. Second, embedding banks into communities meant that bankers could overcome information asymmetries by tapping into local (and informal) networks for information about potential borrowers. Indeed, one feature that is particularly striking about this system was how many banks there were per person in the United States and how geographically dispersed banks were (see Table 2.2).

TABLE 2.2

U.S. commercial bank lending resources per capita,
by region in 1909

Region	Number of banks	Population (millions)	Persons per bank
New England	657	6.3	9,527
Eastern	2,477	20.1	8,121
Southern	4,961	25.4	5,130
Midwest	7,059	26.0	3,681
Western	4,276	6.7	1,573
Pacific	1,326	3.7	2,828
United States	20,756	88.3	4,253

SOURCE: Davis and Gallman (2001, p. 270).
NOTE: "Eastern" region consists of the Mid-Atlantic states from New York to Washington, D.C.

In sum, constraints on the supply of banks in the United States tended to be short-lived, not because there were not attempts to constrain supply but because barriers to entry tended to be dissipated by the effects of competition—competition not among firms but among (and within) the different political entities that could charter and regulate firms.

MEXICO

The colonial political institutions of Mexico were starkly different from those of the colonial United States. Rather than having elected colonial assemblies, Mexico had a viceroy who ruled through provincial-level colonial officials. Until the late eighteenth century, these colonial officials typically married into, and became part of, the local economic elite. Even after a series of reforms changed the policies governing the recruitment and compensation of royal officials, the basic point remained: colonial political institutions were hierarchical and nondemocratic. Their purpose was to maintain a society that was composed of Native Americans and mestizos but that was run by, and for the benefit of, a numerically small Spanish (and Mexican-born, but culturally and ethnically Spanish) elite.

As a consequence, the process of Mexican independence was the polar opposite of the process in the United States. Mexican elites pushed for independence not because they resented royal authority but because they were royalists. They had earlier sided with the viceroy against an independence movement whose goal was to challenge the colonial system of privilege and hierarchy (the Hidalgo revolt of 1810)—and had put down that insurgency with extreme brutality. They finally declared independence (in 1821) precisely because the king of Spain had been forced to accept a liberal constitution by his own army.

Mexico's post-independence elite were not, however, all of one mind regarding the institutions that should govern the new country. Some sought to create a constitutional monarchy and to maintain all of the other political and economic institutions of the colony, including the centralization of political power and exemptions from trial in civil courts for the army and clergy. Others wanted a federal republic—though one in which suffrage would be restricted on the basis of literacy, in a society where very few were literate. The one factor that unified both groups was their aristocratic inclinations: neither had any real intention of sharing power with the country's vast indigenous and mestizo populations.

These two groups, one conservative and centralist, the other liberal and federalist, were unable to craft a set of political institutions through which political conflict could be channeled. Instead, they engaged in a series of coups, countercoups, and civil wars—often mobilizing the indigenous and mestizo populations in the process. When one or the other emerged victorious, they would scuttle earlier constitutions and redraft a new one.

The result was quite unlike what had occurred after independence in the United States. There, the Republicans and Federalists had each come to believe that they would be better off if they competed with one another through the country's formal political institutions (for example, elections, Congress, state legislatures) rather than go outside them. In order to do so, they each built an additional institution—political parties with coherent ideologies. In contrast, the conservatives and liberals in Mexico each saw one another as illegitimate. The purpose of political competition was not just to take power but to eliminate the other side.

Political Institutions, Public Finance, and Banking, 1821–76

The first government after independence was a monarchy, whose leader (Agustín Iturbide) soon dissolved Congress and declared himself emperor. The dissolution of Congress left him with few supporters, and he was successfully overthrown by the liberals, who then instituted a federal republic. It lasted less than a decade and was replaced by a conservative government headed by a military strongman (Antonio López de Santa Anna), who threw out the constitution and eliminated the federal system. (It was this move against the states' autonomy that prompted the Texans to secede from Mexico.) A series of weak governments followed, most of them lasting only a few months. Their disorganization invited the United States to invade Mexico in 1846 and take half of Mexico's territory in the peace settlement.

In the early 1850s the conservatives made another effort to build a centralized state. They reinstalled Santa Anna (he served as president on 11 separate occasions between 1832 and 1853), who soon decreed that his rule should last indefinitely. This provided a lightning rod for the liberals to build a coalition to depose him, which resulted in yet another liberal government and yet another federal constitution in 1857. This liberal government was then challenged by the conservatives in a three-year civil war. The liberals emerged triumphant, but exiled conservatives encouraged France to invade and occupy Mexico in 1862 (the nominal reason was to enforce payment of Mexico's external debt). When France withdrew its support in 1867 from the puppet regime of Archduke Maximilian, the liberals retook power. Nevertheless, even this restored liberal regime was torn by internal conflict and was overthrown in 1876 by Porfirio Díaz, a popular army officer who led a revolt against the government because the president (Sebastian Lerdo de Tejada) was attempting to centralize power and arrange his own reelection, in contravention of the constitution of 1857.

We will return to Díaz at length, but for now, let us consider the impact that this long period of political instability had on the development of the banking system.

All sides in Mexico's nineteenth-century coups, rebellions, and civil wars preyed on the property rights of their vanquished opponents. Indeed, the logic of the situation virtually required that they do so: they had to reward their allies; and the most readily available resource at hand to do so was the wealth of their enemies (Haber, Razo, and Maurer 2003, chap. 8).

Every government that came to power also inherited a depleted treasury and no ready source of income that could be used to create a durable government. Desperate governments with short time horizons tend to raise taxes to the point that producers can recover only their variable costs. Mexico's nineteenth-century governments were no exception to this general rule. The most productive part of the colonial economy had been silver mining. Indeed, in the eighteenth century Mexico had been the world's leading producer of silver, and the colonial government had steadily dropped the tax rate in order to keep the mines profitable. In the decades after independence, Mexico's various governments (state as well as central) pushed tax rates through the roof (they were on the order of 25 percent of *revenues* in the 1860s) in order to fill their empty coffers. In so doing, they removed the incentives of mining companies to invest in new exploration and to resurrect colonial mines (Haber, Razo, and Maurer 2003, chap. 7).

Mexico's governments also could have instituted a land tax. The reason why they did not do so, however, follows another general rule of political economy: when a small group of wealthy men control the state, they prefer not to tax themselves to fund its operation. A broadly based land tax in nineteenth-century Mexico would have been expensive to administer; it would have required cadastral surveys and the creation of a public registry of land titles (and clear demarcation of parcel boundaries). It would also have required a collection mechanism. Under these circumstances, the easiest land to tax would have been the land held in large commercial farms. This land, however, tended to be owned by the same small elite that ran the government. Indeed, when governments changed hands in the nineteenth century, they tended to allocate these estates to their military allies as compensation for their service. Taxing these estates was therefore politically difficult.

The government therefore had to rely on taxes on imports and exports. The problem was that Mexico actually exported and imported very little. Moreover, the fact that Mexico's nineteenth-century governments faced the very real threat of being overthrown meant that they needed large infusions of cash in the short run, not the modest stream of revenues that would trickle in from customs duties.

Mexico's nineteenth-century governments therefore borrowed from the country's private bankers (the *agiotistas*). The problem was that when governments changed, or when governments faced sufficient threat, they reneged on these debts. Private bankers therefore demanded interest rates that would compensate them for this risk. They also realized that they needed to collateralize the loans, so the government mortgaged the customs revenues. The problem was, however, that new governments could (and did) abrogate these agreements, which only lowered the mortgage value of the customs in the next round of loans (Tennenbaum 1986; Walker 1986).

In this environment—in which property rights were insecure and the government did not have a sound system of public finance—the incentives of private bankers to obtain charters were extremely low. Charters confer two advantages on bankers: they allow them to issue banknotes (and profit from seignorage), and they allow them limited liability (which allows them to sell equity to outsider investors). The disadvantage is that a charter makes the property rights of the banker transparent. In a situation in which bankers are subject to expropriation, they do not want their property rights to be more transparent—they want them to be *less* transparent, because transparency makes property rights easier to expropriate.

As a consequence, Mexico had no chartered banks at all until 1863— and that bank charter was the product of very special circumstances. The specifics of this charter, in fact, give us an indication of why there had not been others previously: the charter was granted to a foreign bank (the British Bank of London, Mexico, and South America) by the puppet government of a foreign power (Emperor Maximilian, who had been installed by the French). The British stockholders of this bank (known in Mexico as the Banco de Londres y México—BLM) believed that the French government would not expropriate them.

One might be tempted to argue that Mexico had no chartered banks prior to 1863 (and then only one from 1863 to the late 1870s) because there was insufficient demand. Such an argument would not, however, square with two pieces of evidence. The first is that Mexico's fledgling industrialists were clamoring for more credit than could be provided by the private bankers. For that reason, they convinced the government to create a national industrial development bank, the Banco de Avío, in 1830. That bank was scuttled in 1842, when the central government, desperate for revenue, ransacked its vaults. That is, the government expropriated its own development bank (Potash 1983).

The second is that the Mexican government was itself clamoring for more credit at lower interest rates than could be provided by the private bankers. Clearly, it was in the government's interest to create a semiofficial commercial bank (such as the Bank of England or the Bank of the United States) that would provide it with credit in exchange for a set of special privileges. The problem was that Mexican governments in the nineteenth century did not have a way to make a credible commitment to the bankers that the governments would not expropriate the banks as soon as they deployed their capital. The only threat that bankers could make was the threat implicit in all sovereign debt contracts: there would be no future loans if past loans were not repaid. When governments have long-time horizons, this threat carries great force. But when time horizons are short, threats of this nature have little impact.

Regulated Entry and Insider Lending in Porfirian Mexico, 1876–1911
The unstable nature of Mexican politics, and the underdeveloped state of Mexico's banking system, changed dramatically during the 35-year dictatorship of Porfirio Díaz (1876–1911). Díaz's solutions to Mexico's weak institutions, however, only mitigated some of the problems facing the banking system. The banking institutions that developed alleviated the problem of expropriation and imprudent behavior, but they did not overcome the problem of contract enforcement. As we shall see, the institutional solution to expropriation risk interacted with weak contract enforcement to

produce a banking system that was stable and served as a source of public finance but provided little credit to anyone who was not a bank director or a family member of a bank director.

Díaz confronted the same problem as all of the governments before him. He lacked sufficient tax revenues to finance a government capable of unifying the country and putting an end to internecine warfare. Borrowing his way out of this situation was difficult, because Mexico had a long history of defaulting on its debts to its international and domestic creditors. In fact, Díaz himself had reneged on debts to some of the banks that had been founded in Mexico City during the early years of his rule (Marichal 2002; Maurer and Gomberg 2005).

Díaz did, however, have an advantage over earlier Mexican presidents. By the end of the nineteenth century the expansion of the U.S. railroad network and technological advances in transoceanic shipping had driven down international transport costs. Mexico could be integrated with the world economy in ways that were previously unimaginable. Díaz therefore had a tremendous source of rents to tap—from foreign direct investment in mining, petroleum, and export agriculture—that could be used to buy off opponents or build a state strong enough to intimidate them. The problem for Díaz was how to start the virtuous cycle of political stability, state capacity, foreign direct investment, and economic growth.

The solution that Díaz hit upon to jump-start this process was one that had been used by European governments since the eighteenth century: create a semiofficial superbank that received a set of lucrative privileges in exchange for providing a source of finance to the government. This solution mitigated the problem of expropriation risk (because the bank was compensated for risk with privileges that allowed it to earn supernormal returns) (Maurer and Gomberg 2005). Later banks were rewarded with protected markets, via a system of taxes on new entrants. The fact that this bank (and the ones that followed it) had to hold high levels of reserves against note issues mitigated the problem of imprudent bankers (Maurer and Haber 2004). Díaz's solution did not, however, alleviate the problem of contract enforcement. Thus, Mexico's bankers employed an informal institution—they lent primarily to themselves and their family members. The problem with this strategy, however, was that the lucrative privileges that Díaz bestowed on banks included restrictions on the number of banks in any market. Credit was thus restricted to those few entrepreneurs in any state who happened to have family members who had obtained one of only a few bank charters (Haber 1991, 1997; Maurer 2002; Maurer and Haber 2004).

The Transformation of Mexico's Political Institutions

Porfirio Díaz, having just overthrown Sebastian Lerdo de Tejada in 1876, and having installed himself as president, inherited an economy that had scarcely grown over the previous six decades. He also inherited a constitution, a Congress and Senate, and a federal system of government—all of which had been created in 1857 but little of which had actually had much of an opportunity to function. Díaz's goal—though he did not make this clear at the time—was to find a way to undermine whatever real bite these institutions had and, in so doing, perpetuate himself in power.

In the early years of his regime, Díaz was conscious of the fact that his grip on power was weak and that the country's formal political institutions could serve as a lightning rod for opposition to any attempt to succeed himself in office. He therefore handpicked a successor for the 1880–84 term (General Manuel Gónzalez) and arranged for his election. Díaz's allies in Congress then amended the constitution, removing term limits and lengthening presidential terms from four to six years. This step allowed Díaz to legally return to office in 1884 and then "win" every presidential election until he was overthrown in 1911.

By the late 1880s Díaz had effectively undermined the independence of Congress. As Armando Razo (2003) has shown, during the early years of Díaz's administration there was opposition to many of his public policy initiatives. After 1888, however, virtually all roll-call votes in the Mexican Senate were unanimous. The decline in dissension in Congress and the Senate was coterminous with a decrease in the rate at which seats in those bodies turned over. During the period when Díaz was still gaining control of the legislature (1876–90), a senator or federal deputy had about a one-in-three chance of being reelected. From 1890 to 1910, however, the probability of reelection doubled—to two in three. This change in legislative tenure was accomplished by the following simple mechanism: prior to elections, Díaz would send the state officials who ran the election a list of his "preferred" candidates. The officials' job was to make sure that those candidates were then "elected" (Razo 2003).

In order to pull this off, Díaz had to undermine Mexico's powerful state governors, who commanded state militias that outnumbered the federal army. Díaz gradually appointed men loyal to him to state-level posts—for example, chief of the federal police garrison—and then slowly promoted them into the governorship when the moment seemed propitious. These handpicked appointees—who were often from outside the state and had few local ties—remained in power for decades, and owed that power to Díaz. By the end of Díaz's rule in 1911, over 70 percent of the state governors were presidential favorites "imported" from outside (Knight 1986).

In those states where Díaz could not eliminate or undermine potentially recalcitrant governors, he co-opted them. For example, Governor Enrique Creel of Chihuahua (of the Terrazas-Creel clan, which had controlled the governorship of the state on and off since the 1870s) was named Díaz's foreign minister. Another example is Governor Olegario Molina, who ran the Yucatán as a private business enterprise, being named minister of development (Knight 1986, p. 16).

The undermining of the governors meant that rights formerly conferred on the states were all centralized in the federal government. Given the fact that Congress was a rubber stamp, this meant that policy-making authority was centralized in the hands of Díaz and his long-term minister of the treasury, José Yves Limantour (1892–1911). As of 1884 the granting of mining titles and the establishment of mining taxes were made federal, not state, functions. (Díaz got the governors to go along by allowing them to levy a 25 percent surtax on whatever federal taxes were charged. He later lowered the federal tax rates.) The same act gave the federal government, and not the states, the authority to grant concessions and to tax the rights to groundwater and petroleum deposits. By 1896, Díaz was strong enough to force states to remove taxes on interstate commerce. Finally, in a series of laws enacted between 1884 and 1897 Díaz centralized control of bank chartering in the hands of the federal government.

The glue that held this governance system together was the distribution of rents from private economic activities directly to politically crucial governors, senators, and federal deputies. Recent research by Razo (2003) and Musacchio and Read (2003) on the networks of political and economic elites in Porfirian Mexico demonstrates that the boards of directors of the country's largest publicly traded companies—particularly those that needed federal largesse and protection—were populated by a small group of powerful public officials. They went along with Díaz, in short, because they got rich in the process.

Regulated Entry, Public Finance, and the Supply of Banks in Porfirian Mexico
Once Mexico began to become stable and to grow in the early 1880s, states—particularly mining states on the U.S. border—began to charter banks. In addition, foreign-born merchants in Mexico City obtained charters from the national government to operate banks in Mexico City. By 1883, Mexico therefore had eight chartered banks.

The fact that the Díaz government was still, at this point, fragile gave it a strong incentive to monopolize bank chartering as a means to provide itself with a ready source of credit. Díaz therefore made two moves. First, in 1884, he engineered the merger of Mexico City's two largest banks, creating the Banco Nacional de México (Banamex). The intention of the government was to model Banamex on the Bank of England, granting it a monopoly over the issuance of paper money in return for providing a credit line to the federal government and acting as the treasury's financial agent. In addition, the federal government granted Banamex the rights to tax farm customs receipts and to run the mint (Maurer and Gomberg 2005). Second, the government simultaneously federalized the chartering of banks. As of 1884, states could no longer grant charters (Haber 1991).

What was crucial, from the point of view of Díaz and Banamex, was that the 1884 Commercial Code erected high barriers to entry. Not only had the federal government monopolized the granting of charters but it also required that new banks obtain the permission of Congress and the secretary of the treasury to obtain a charter. They also had to pay a 5 percent tax on the issuance of banknotes. Banamex was exempted from the tax. Finally, Banamex was permitted to issue banknotes up to three times the amount of its reserves. Other banks were not afforded this privilege. In short, the federal government was attempting to exchange a set of special privileges for access to credit (Haber 1991; Maurer 2002).

Mexico's extant banks, particularly the Banco de Londres y México, realized that the commercial code and Banamex's special privileges put them at a serious disadvantage. They therefore sued in federal court and managed to obtain an injunction against the 1884 Commercial Code on the basis that the 1857 constitution had an antimonopoly clause. The ensuing legal and political battle ground on for 13 years, until a compromise was finally hammered out by Secretary of Finance José Yves Limantour in 1897 (Maurer 2002, chap. 2).

Four groups pressured the federal government in the crafting of the 1897 General Credit Institutions and Banking Act: the stockholders of Banamex; the stockholders in the Banco de Londres y México; the stockholders in other, smaller, state-level banks; and the state governors (who wished to award cronies with bank charters). The resulting law could easily be predicted from knowledge of the players in the negotiations: Banamex shared many (although not all) of its special privileges with the Banco de Londres y México; the state banks were given local monopolies; and the state governors were able to choose which business group in the state would receive a bank charter from the federal government. Holding the arrangement to-

gether was the fact that the federal government monopolized bank chartering. Legal barriers to entry into banking could not be eroded by competition between states, or between states and the federal government, because
states did not have the right to charter banks.[15]

The resulting competitive structure had the following features. Banamex
and the Banco de Londres y México were granted a duopoly in the Mexico City market. In addition, only Banamex and the Banco de Londres y
México had the right to branch across state lines. Banamex was also granted
the exclusive privilege of providing financial services to the government:
collecting tax receipts, making payments, holding federal deposits, and underwriting all foreign and domestic federal debt issues. In short, the compromise was that Banamex would retain the special privileges granted to it
in 1884, and some of these privileges would also be extended to the Banco
de Londres y México (Maurer 2002, chap. 3).

State-level banks and their patrons—the state governors—were also
protected from competition. The law was written in such a way that, as
a practical matter, only one bank could be established in each state, although existing banks were grandfathered in. The law specified that bank
charters (and additions to capital) had to be approved by the secretary of
the treasury *and* the federal Congress. In order to make this policy credible beyond the tenure of José Limantour as treasury secretary, the law also
created three other barriers to entry. First, the law created very high minimum capital requirements, initially U.S. $125,000, which was later raised
to U.S. $250,000—more than twice the amount for national banks in the
United States. Second, the law established a 2 percent annual tax on paid-in
capital. The first bank granted a charter in each state, however, was granted
an exemption from the tax. Third, state banks were not allowed to branch
outside their concession territories. This prevented banks chartered in one
state from challenging the monopoly of a bank in an adjoining state. In
short, the only threat to the monopoly of a state bank could come from a
branch of Banamex or the Banco de Londres y México.[16]

The existence of these segmented monopolies was made incentive compatible with the interests of Mexico's most important public officials, who
received seats on the boards of the major banks (and thus were entitled to
directors' fees and stock distributions). Indeed, the Díaz government appears not to have chosen the groups that received a bank charter based on
their entrepreneurial talents but on their political connections. The board
of directors of Banamex, for example, was populated by members of Díaz's
coterie, including the president of Congress, the undersecretary of the treasury, the senator for the Federal District, the president's chief of staff, and

the brother of the secretary of the treasury. The chairman of the board of the Banco de Londres y México was none other than the secretary of war. Joining him on the board was a federal senator from the state of Sonora. The Banco International e Hipotecario (a mortgage bank) was similarly populated with political notables, including the president's son, the ambassador to Belgium and the Netherlands (who was also a federal senator), and the brother of the secretary of the treasury. The Banco Mexicano de Comercio e Industria was also a who's who of insiders. Its board chairman was the president of Congress. Joining him on the board was the governor of the Federal District.

Banks with limited territorial concessions were also chosen based on their political connections. The only difference was that state governors, rather than cabinet ministers, sat on their boards and received directors' fees, stock distributions, dividends, and in some cases loans made with no expectation of repayment. In some cases, the governor himself received the bank concession. In fact, the system was deliberately conceived to distribute benefits to the state governors and give them a stake in the maintenance of Porfirio Díaz's rule (Haber, Razo, and Maurer 2003, pp. 88–90; Razo 2003, chaps. 8, 9).

The resulting banking system had one major advantage and one major disadvantage. The advantage was that the construction of Banamex created, for the first time in Mexican history, a stable system of public finance. Credit from Banamex meant that the Díaz government did not have to prey upon property rights to maintain its fragile hold on power. Instead, it gave Díaz the financial breathing room he needed to slowly recraft the tax codes governing mining, petroleum, and interstate commerce, gradually increasing government tax revenues to the point that he ran balanced budgets (Carmagnani 1994; Haber, Razo, and Maurer 2003, chaps. 3, 6, 7). It also allowed Díaz, with the help of Banamex's directors, to renegotiate Mexico's foreign debt—which had been in default for several decades (Marichal 2002; Maurer and Gomberg 2005). Finally, the creation of Banamex allowed Díaz to subsidize the creation of a national railroad system—which had a huge positive impact on the country's overall growth (Coatsworth 1981; Kuntz Ficker 1995).

The disadvantage was that Mexico had a very concentrated banking system. In 1911, there were only 42 formally incorporated banks in the entire country. The United States, for comparison purposes, had more than 25,000 banks and trust companies in that year. The capital available to the Mexican banking system was also small: assets in 1911 totaled approximately U.S. $385 million (Mexico, Secretaria de Hacienda 1912, p. 255)

TABLE 2.3
The Mexican banking industry, 1896–1912

Year	Number of reporting banks	Total bank assets (millions U.S. $)	Banamex market share (%)	BLM market share (%)	Herfindahl Index
1896	6	50	58	28	0.42
1897	10	54	na	na	na
1899	13	78	51	26	0.34
1900	17	113	39	25	0.22
1901	20	107	38	22	0.20
1902	23	107	35	19	0.17
1903	25	130	37	17	0.18
1904	26	184	41	15	0.20
1905	26	205	39	18	0.20
1906	28	264	40	16	0.21
1907	28	301	44	14	0.23
1908	34	339	40	12	0.19
1909	35	283	37	12	0.17
1910	35	302	39	12	0.18
1911	35	385	39	12	0.18
1912	34	342	36	11	0.16

SOURCE: Maurer and Haber (2004).
NOTE: "Herfindahl Index," a measure of concentration, is the sum of the squares of the market shares of all firms in the industry.

(see Table 2.3). For comparison purposes, total assets of the U.S. banking system were $22.9 billion (United States, Department of Commerce 1975, series 10, pp. 580–87). Finally, not only were Mexico's banks few in number and of small size but the level of concentration was extremely high: Banamex and Banco de Londres y México accounted for more than 60 percent of all assets (Mexico, Secretaria de Hacienda 1912, pp. 236, 255). The vast majority of markets had, at most, three banks: a branch of Banamex, a branch of the Banco de Londres y México (BLM), and a branch of the bank that held that state's territorial concession. It was not uncommon for there to be only one or two banks in some states (see Table 2.3).[17]

The Economic Effects of Concentrated Banking

A skeptical reader might argue that a concentrated banking system with branch networks might have been an efficient solution in a country with a low gross domestic product (GDP). This hypothesis can be subjected to two kinds of tests against evidence, neither of which supports it.

The first test is an analysis of excess liquidity in the leading banks. Noel Maurer has demonstrated that the two largest banks in the system (Banamex and the Banco de Londres y México, which jointly controlled 60 percent of assets) acted like inefficient monopolists: they held excess liquidity in order to ration credit and drive up their rates of return. As a result, their stockholders earned substantial rents while they incurred very little risk: the yield on common stock (the value of dividends divided by the market value of common shares) of these two banks was about equal to that of Mexican government bonds (Maurer 2002, chap. 5).

The second test involves an analysis of the organization of Mexico's banking markets on downstream industries. Mexico's bankers and government had found a way to mitigate expropriation risk by limiting competition in banking markets—by constraining the number of banks. They had not, however, been able to build the broad range of institutions necessary to allow property rights to be enforced at low cost. The institutional solution that Mexican bankers hit upon was that they primarily lent to themselves. The evidence suggests that they hit upon this solution by trial and error, initially making arm's-length loans that went into default. The collateral for these loans then proved to be either fictitious or unrecoverable (Maurer and Haber 2004).

In the context of a banking system in which bankers primarily lent to themselves and their family members, constraints on the number of banks in any market acted as a barrier to entry in downstream industries. It is not possible, of course, to observe the universe of potential entrepreneurs who did not found firms for lack of credit. It is possible, however, to determine whether industries that are usually characterized by near-perfect competition were structured that way in Mexico. If we observe that industries with modest-scale economies had competitively structured markets, the implication would be that entrepreneurs did not face financial barriers to entry. If we observe, however, that industries with modest-scale economies had market structures similar to those of industries characterized by increasing returns to scale, then the implication would be that entrepreneurs faced financial barriers to entry.

A series of papers by Haber (1991, 1997, 2003) and Maurer and Haber (2004), which focus on the industrial structure of the Mexican cotton textile industry, addresses this question.[18] These papers specify three counterfactuals. The first compares Mexico to itself over time. Cotton textile manufacturing was an industry characterized by constant returns to scale technologies and the absence of entry barriers. We should expect that as the industry grew, concentration should have fallen. The second compares Mexico to three other countries (the United States, Brazil, and India) that had large textile industries but did not have Mexico's banking system. The third, following Sutton (1998), compares the Mexican textile industry's ac-

TABLE 2.4

Industrial concentration in cotton textiles:
Mexico, Brazil, India, and the United States

| | FOUR-FIRM RATIO | | | | | HERFINDAHL INDEX | | |
| | Mexico | | | | | | | |
Year	Mexico (%)	Expected (%)	Brazil (%)	India (%)	U.S. (%)	Mexico	Brazil	India
1888	18	19	37		8	0.022	0.058	
1893	29	15				0.038		
1895	33	17	35			0.042	0.059	
1896	30	16				0.041		
1900	30	14		19	7	0.038	0.028	0.018
1904	33	15	21			0.042		
1909	38	15				0.045		
1912	30	14		19	8	0.039		0.018
1913	31	14	14			0.041	0.014	

SOURCE: Maurer and Haber (2004).

tual market structure to a hypothetical, fully competitive industry, in which
the market structure was a function solely of industry size and a stochastic
growth process.

The results of these experiments are presented in Table 2.4. Concentration is measured in two ways: the four-firm ratio (the percentage of the
market controlled by the four largest firms); and the Herfindahl Index (the
sum of the squares of the market shares of all firms in the industry). Regardless of the measure employed, the data indicate that the Mexican cotton
textile industry was "too concentrated." First, concentration in Mexico
actually increased over time, even though the industry was growing rapidly.
(In the United States, Brazil, and India, unlike Mexico, concentration fell
or remained stable as the textile industry grew.) Second, the Mexican cotton textile industry was much more concentrated than the American, Brazilian, or Indian cotton textile industry. Third, the Mexican cotton textile
industry showed much higher four-firm ratios compared to the ratio that
would be expected in a perfectly competitive market. The implication is
that some entrepreneurs were awash in funds, while others were starved for
capital. In short, the evidence supports the view that the organization of
Mexico's banking industry came at a cost to the real economy.

A detailed discussion of Mexico's banking system after the fall of the Díaz
dictatorship would take us well beyond the space constraints of this paper.
Suffice it to say that the Mexican Revolution (1911–20) and the ensuing
political instability of the 1920s did little to create institutionalized political
competition. During the period 1911–29, political competition in Mexico

took place entirely outside formal institutions, which is to say at gunpoint. The property rights of bankers were once again expropriated. The banking system, as a result, contracted until postrevolutionary governments forged a new set of institutions in 1924 that would govern the industry.

These governments, much like Díaz's before them, were not constrained by institutionalized political competition. Indeed, until the late 1990s, none of their successors were either. Not surprisingly, they created economic institutions—and a resulting banking system—that were not dissimilar to those that had existed under Díaz (Maurer 2002; Del Angel-Mobarak 2002; Haber, Razo, and Maurer 2003; Haber 2005).

Conclusions and Implications

In the past two decades social scientists have embraced the notion that a wide variety of economic outcomes can be explained by institutions. A number of questions, however, remain: where do institutions come from; which way does causality run; and which institutions are crucial (and which are merely incidental) to the process of growth?

This chapter has offered a contribution to this literature by examining the causes and consequences of the economic institutions that govern banking. Obviously, sustaining the argument that institutions that encourage political competition translate into economic institutions that encourage competition in banking will require more empirical testing than I have provided here. Additional case studies, which focus on cases intermediate to those of the United States and Mexico, are required.

Nevertheless, the analysis presented here makes a strong case for the argument that competitive markets do not happen all by themselves. All markets are embedded in political systems, and some of these markets are highly sensitive to regulation by governments. When governments are unconstrained by institutionalized competition, they (and the public officials within them) will structure economic institutions so as to maximize short-run government revenues and/or permit rent seeking by public officials. The unintended result is smaller and less efficient markets, which, in turn, constrain economic growth.

One might be tempted to argue that one or another of the political institutions that encourage institutionalized competition are crucial and the others are merely incidental. Although I do not discount the possibility that research into cases beyond those analyzed here might support that view, the cases analyzed here suggest that political institutions mutually reinforce one another—they do not operate in isolation.

Alternatively, one might argue that electoral suffrage was the crucial institution, because it allowed voters in the United States to remove rent-seeking legislatures that maintained oligopolies. Although it is true that voters did remove such legislatures, it is also true that they could not have done so had state legislatures themselves not voted to broaden the suffrage. The reason they did so had everything to do with federalism—states competed with one another for business and population. In addition, federalism worked directly to undermine oligopolized banking systems, because states had strong incentives to increase the number of charters they granted: first, in order to fund public works projects necessary to keep business and population in the state; and second, in order to keep business and population from migrating to other states where it would be easier to obtain credit.

One might therefore be inclined to argue that federalism was the crucial institution. This view, too, holds some water. Federalism explains why the United States had a banking system composed of tens of thousands of unit banks, instead of a banking system composed of a few large banks that could branch wherever they pleased. At the same time, however, federalism alone cannot explain why the United States had no central bank for most of the nineteenth century. Clearly, federalism played a role, because the congressmen who voted against the renewal of the Bank of the United States did so because they were representing the interests of bankers in their states. But congressmen could do this only because of another institution: separation of powers in the national government.

An analysis of the Mexican case produces similar conclusions. When Porfirio Díaz came to power, he inherited a constitution, a federal system, and a bicameral legislature. What he did not inherit, however, were two other institutions that could have given federalism and separation of powers real bite: effective electoral suffrage and political parties. Díaz was therefore able to undermine the Senate, the Chamber of Deputies, and the governors. The resulting rent-seeking network could not be challenged—at least not within the existing set of institutions. The eventual challenge, in 1911, was by violent, not institutional, means.

The analysis presented here has an additional, practical implication. Much of the research in financial economics about bank regulation in less developed countries suggests that a major problem for financial development is inadequate regulation and supervision. The prescription is to give regulators more power and authority. This view assumes that regulators and supervisors are immune to politics—that their goal, and that of the government, is to maximize social welfare. Levine (2004) has recently suggested

that such a view might not only be naïve but be counterproductive, because politically motivated regulators and supervisors with more authority
might be tempted to use their power to structure institutions in ways that
provide sources of short-run revenues for the government (and for themselves), at the expense of economic development. The evidence presented
in this chapter is consistent with the Levine view: all of the major reforms
in banking law, in both the United States and Mexico, were motivated in
good part by governments seeking sources of public finance. The difference
in long-run outcomes was not caused by the motivation of government but
by the political institutions that limited the government.

Notes

Support for this research was provided by National Science Foundation Grant
SBR-9515222, the William and Flora Hewlett Foundation's Program in U.S.–
Latin American Relations, and the Bechtel Initiative of the Institute of International Studies at Stanford University. Earlier versions of this chapter were
presented at the 2002 meeting of the American Economics Association, at
Stanford's Center for Research on Economic Development and Policy Reform,
and at the 2004 Stanford Conference on the History of Congress. Richard
Bensel, Jeff Frieden, Ross Levine, Noel Maurer, James Robinson, Paul Snider-
man, Gabriel Sod Hoffs, Kenneth Sokoloff, Richard Sylla, Barry Weingast,
and Scott Wilson made helpful comments on earlier drafts.

1. King and Levine (1993a, 1993b); Levine and Zervos (1998); Beck,
Levine, and Loayza (2000); Rajan and Zingales (1998); Beck et al. (2001);
Levine (1997); Neusser and Kugler (1998); Rousseau and Wachtel (1998); and
La Porta et al. (2000).

2. In addition to a system of private banks, financial systems also include
securities markets, a central bank, a system of money, and a system of public
finance.

3. This chapter therefore builds upon the literature on "limited government." The central idea of that literature—political institutions must be structured so that ambition may be able to counteract ambition—goes back at least
as far as James Madison's writings in the *Federalist Papers*. In recent years these
ideas have generated a sizable social science literature, exemplified by North
(1981, pp. 154–57); Levi (1988); North and Weingast (1989); North (1990);
Weingast (1995, 1997a, 1997b); North, Summerhill, and Weingast (2000); and
Bates (2001).

4. I break off my analysis in 1932 because the creation of the Federal Deposit Insurance Corporation in the following year gradually weakened the
ability of states to charter and regulate banks independently of the federal
government.

5. Relevant literature on these institutions includes McCubbins and Schwartz (1984); Weingast (1995); Tsebelis (1995); and Haggard and McCubbins (2001).

6. See Sylla, Legler, and Wallis (1987); Wallis, Sylla, and Legler (1994); and Bodenhorn (2003, pp. 15, 84, 234–35, 2004).

7. The phenomenon of competing for bank charters by offering shares of the future rents appears to be an example of that modeled by Krueger (1974), in which rent seekers expend rents up the point that they earn the normal rate of return. Most of the rent is captured by the government and by public officials.

8. The relatively slower development of the British banking system can be tied to politically determined constraints on the supply of banks. The Bank of England was chartered as a monopoly. Until 1825, other banks were not allowed limited liability. Instead, they were restricted to unlimited liability partnerships of six or fewer people (Rousseau and Sylla 1999).

9. If a bank breached the requirement that its notes be redeemable on demand for specie, the comptroller closed the bank, sold the bonds held as collateral, and redeemed the bank's circulating notes from the proceeds. Some states also allowed banks to use mortgages on unencumbered property to back their note issues. Many states, for obvious fiscal reasons, later amended their laws, requiring that all reserves be held in bonds issued by that state (Bodenhorn 2003, chap. 8).

10. Michigan was actually the first state to pass a free banking law, in 1837, but revoked the law in 1839. It reinstituted free banking in 1857.

11. There has been considerable debate in the literature regarding the impact of free banking laws. The traditional view, associated with Rockoff (1974, 1985), was that free banking reduced barriers to entry, increased competitiveness, and reduced profits. This view was challenged by Ng (1988), who argued that free banking acts, with the exception of that of New York State, did not reduce barriers to entry because the competitive pressures that existed among states prior to the free banking acts had already eroded barriers to entry. Ng's argument was subsequently challenged by Economopoulos and O'Neill (1995), who demonstrated that free banking states were able to respond more elastically to changes in demand for banking services than chartering (non–free banking) states. A series of articles by Bodenhorn (1990, 1993) has also cast considerable doubt on Ng's view. Bodenhorn has demonstrated that one of the effects of free banking was to put competitive pressure on non–free banking states to grant more charters than they would have otherwise. In short, the weight of the evidence supports Rockoff's original interpretation: free banking increased entry and contributed to the rapid growth of the number of banks operating in most markets.

12. Rockoff (1974, 1985); also see Gorton (1996). Bank failures became more widespread in the 1920s, resulting in the creation of the FDIC in 1933 (Calomiris and White 1994).

13. Informal networks appear to have played an important role in commercial lending until the information revolution of the last decade (see Petersen and Rajan 2002).

14. Demand deposits were already becoming an important component of bank liabilities before the National Banking Act, as a consequence of the note security requirements of free banking acts (Moss and Brennan 2004). With the complete demise of state banknote issues after 1864, however, state banks had even stronger incentives to pursue deposit banking.

15. Had states had the right to charter banks, they would have been tempted to ratchet downward the minimum requirements for a bank charter as they competed against one another for bank business.

16. The law also allowed for the establishment of mortgage banks and *bancos refaccionarios*, which were allowed to make long-term loans. These banks were not granted, however, the right to issue banknotes and were subject to a variety of restrictions on the types of investments they could make. Without the right to issue notes, and with few ways to actually foreclose on a mortgage, these banks could not compete. Few charters for mortgage banks were ever taken out. See Riguzzi (2002).

17. Three states on the U.S. border, Nuevo León, Chihuahua, and Sonora, had more than three banks (four, five, and six, respectively) because of peculiarities of their banking histories.

18. This research focuses on cotton textiles because it was an industry characterized by the lack of barriers to entry created by advertising, branding, or technology. It was also characterized by a small minimum efficient scale of production and capital divisibilities. At the same time, the existence of financial barriers to entry in this industry would be expected to indicate similar barriers in other industries.

References

Acemoglu, Daron, Simon Johnson, and James Robinson (2004). "Institutions as a Fundamental Cause of Long Run Growth." In Philippe Aghion and Steve Durlauf, eds., *Handbook of Economic Growth*. Amsterdam: North-Holland.

——— (2002). "Reversal of Fortune: Geography and Institutions in the Making of the Modern World Income Distribution." *Quarterly Journal of Economics* 117: 1231–94.

——— (2001). "The Colonial Origins of Comparative Development: An Empirical Investigation." *American Economic Review* 91: 1369–1401.

Acemoglu, Daron, Simon Johnson, James Robinson, and Pierre Yared (2005). "Income and Democracy." CEPR Discussion Paper 5273.

Atack, Jeremy, and Peter Passell (1994). *A New Economic View of American History from Colonial Times to 1940*. 2d ed. New York: Norton.

Barro, Robert J. (1997). *Determinants of Economic Growth: A Cross-Country Empirical Study*. Cambridge, MA: MIT Press.

———— (1991). "Economic Growth in a Cross Section of Countries." *Quarterly Journal of Economics* 106: 407–43.

Bates, Robert H. (2001). *Prosperity and Violence: The Political Economy of Development*. New York: Norton.

Beck, Thorsten, Asli Demirgüç-Kunt, Ross Levine, and Vojislav Maksimovic (2001). "Financial Structure and Economic Development: Firm, Industry, and Country Evidence." In Asli Demirgüç-Kunt and Ross Levine, eds., *Financial Structure and Economic Growth: A Cross-Country Comparison of Banks, Markets, and Development*. Cambridge, MA: MIT Press.

Beck, Thorsten, Ross Levine, and Norman Loayza (2000). "Finance and the Sources of Growth." *Journal of Financial Economics* 58: 261–300.

Bodenhorn, Howard (2004). "Bank Chartering and Political Corruption in Antebellum New York: Free Banking as Reform." NBER Working Paper 1047.

———— (2003). *State Banking in Early America: A New Economic History*. New York: Oxford University Press.

———— (1993). "The Business Cycle and Entry into Early American Banking." *Review of Economics and Statistics* 75: 531–35.

———— (1990). "Entry, Rivalry, and Free Banking in Antebellum America." *Review of Economics and Statistics* 72: 682–86.

Bordo, Michael D., Hugh Rockoff, and Angela Redish (1994). "The U.S. Banking System from a Northern Exposure: Stability Versus Efficiency." *Journal of Economic History* 54: 325–41.

Brunetti, Aymo (1997). *Politics and Economic Growth: A Cross Country Data Perspective*. Paris: OECD.

Calomiris, Charles W., and Eugene N. White (1994). "The Origins of Federal Deposit Insurance." In Claudia Goldin and Gary D. Libecap, eds., *The Regulated Economy: A Historical Approach to Political Economy*. Chicago: University of Chicago Press.

Carmagnani, Marcello (1994). *Estado y mercado: la economía pública del liberalismo mexicano, 1850–1911*. Mexico City: El Colegio de México and Fondo de Cultura Económica.

Coatsworth, John H. (1981). *Growth Against Development: The Economic Impact of Railroads in Porfirian Mexico*. Dekalb: Northern Illinois University Press.

Davis, Lance E., and Robert E. Gallman (2001). *Evolving Financial Markets and International Capital Flows: Britain, the Americas, and Australia, 1865–1914*. Cambridge, UK: Cambridge University Press.

Del Angel-Mobarak, Gustavo A. (2002). "Paradoxes of Financial Development: The Construction of the Mexican Banking System, 1941–1982." Ph.D. diss., Stanford University.

Economopoulos, Andrew, and Heather O'Neill (1995). "Bank Entry During the Antebellum Period." *Journal of Money, Credit, and Banking* 27: 1071–85.

Engerman, Stanley L. (1970). "A Note on the Economic Consequences of the Second Bank of the United States." *Journal of Political Economy* 78: 725–28.

Engerman, Stanley L., and Kenneth L. Sokoloff (2001). "The Evolution of Suffrage Institutions in the New World." NBER Working Paper 8512.

———— (1997). "Factor Endowments, Institutions, and Differential Paths of Growth Among New World Economies: A View from Economic Historians of the United States. In Stephen Haber, ed., *How Latin America Fell Behind: Essays on the Economic Histories of Brazil and Mexico, 1800–1914*. Stanford, CA: Stanford University Press.

Fenstermaker, J. Van (1965). "The Statistics of American Commercial Banking, 1782–1818." *Journal of Economic History* 25: 400–413.

Gatell, Frank Otto (1966). "Sober Second Thoughts on Van Buren, the Albany Regency, and the Wall Street Conspiracy." *Journal of American History* 53: 19–40.

Goodrich, Carter (1961). *Canals and American Economic Development*. New York: Columbia University Press.

Gorton, Gary (1996). "Reputation Formation in Early Bank Note Markets." *Journal of Political Economy* 104: 346–97.

Grinath, Arthur III, John Joseph Wallis, and Richard E. Sylla (1997). "Debt, Default, and Revenue Structure: The American State Debt Crisis in the Early 1840's." NBER Historical Paper 97.

Haber, Stephen (2005). "Mexico's Experiments with Bank Privatization and Liberalization, 1991–2003." *Journal of Banking and Finance* 29: 2325–53.

———— (2003). "Banks, Financial Markets, and Industrial Development: Lessons from the Economic Histories of Brazil and Mexico." In José Antonio González, Vittorio Corbo, Anne O. Krueger, and Aaron Tornell, eds., *Latin American Macroeconomic Reforms: The Second Stage*. Chicago: University of Chicago Press.

———— (1997). "Financial Markets and Industrial Development: A Comparative Study of Governmental Regulation, Financial Innovation, and Industrial Structure in Brazil and Mexico, 1840–1930." In Stephen Haber, ed., *How Latin America Fell Behind: Essays on the Economic Histories of Brazil and Mexico, 1800–1930*. Stanford, CA: Stanford University Press.

———— (1991). "Industrial Concentration and the Capital Markets: A Comparative Study of Brazil, Mexico, and the United States, 1830–1930." *Journal of Economic History* 51: 559–80.

Haber, Stephen, Armando Razo, and Noel Maurer (2003). *The Politics of Property Rights: Political Instability, Credible Commitments, and Economic*

Growth in Mexico, 1876–1929. Cambridge, UK: Cambridge University Press.

Haggard, Stephan, and Mathew D. McCubbins, eds. (2001). *Presidents, Parliaments, and Policy*. Cambridge, UK: Cambridge University Press.

Hammond, Bray (1947). "Jackson, Biddle, and the Bank of the United States." *Journal of Economic History* 7: 1–23.

Hofstadter, Richard (1969). *The Idea of a Party System: The Rise of Legitimate Opposition in the United States, 1780–1840*. Berkeley: University of California Press.

Keefer, Philip (2004). "What Does Political Economy Tell Us About Economic Development—and Vice Versa?" In Nelson Polsby, ed., *Annual Review of Political Science*. Palo Alto, CA: Annual Review.

King, Robert G., and Ross Levine (1993a). "Finance and Growth: Schumpeter Might Be Right." *Quarterly Journal of Economics* 108: 717–38.

——— (1993b). "Finance, Entrepreneurship, and Growth: Theory and Evidence." *Journal of Monetary Economics* 32: 513–42.

Knight, Alan (1986). *The Mexican Revolution: Porfirians, Liberals, and Peasants*. Cambridge, UK: Cambridge University Press.

Krueger, Anne (1974). "The Political Economy of the Rent-Seeking Society." *American Economic Review* 64: 291–303.

Kuntz Ficker, Sandra (1995). *Empresa extranjera y mercado interno: el Ferrocarril Central Mexicano, 1880–1907*. Mexico City: El Colegio de México.

Lamoreaux, Naomi (1994). *Insider Lending: Banks, Personal Connections, and Economic Development in Industrial New England*. Cambridge, UK: Cambridge University Press.

——— (1991). "Bank Mergers in Late Nineteenth Century New England: The Contingent Nature of Structural Change." *Journal of Economic History* 51: 537–57.

Lane, Carl (1997). "For a 'Positive Profit': The Federal Investment in the First Bank of the United States, 1792–1802." *William and Mary Quarterly* 54: 601–12.

La Porta, Rafael, Florencio López-de-Silanes, Andrei Shleifer, and Robert W. Vishny (2000). "Investor Protection and Corporate Governance." *Journal of Financial Economics* 58: 3–27.

——— (1998). "Law and Finance." *Journal of Political Economy* 106: 1113–55.

Levi, Margaret (1988). *Of Rule and Revenue*. Berkeley: University of California Press.

Levine, Ross (2004). "The Microeconomic Effects of Different Approaches to Bank Supervision." Mimeo, University of Minnesota.

——— (1999). "Law, Finance, and Economic Growth." *Journal of Financial Intermediation* 81: 36–67.

——— (1998). "The Legal Environment, Banks, and Long Run Economic Growth." *Journal of Money, Credit, and Banking* 30: 596–620.

————— (1997). "Financial Development and Economic Growth: Views and Agenda." *Journal of Economic Literature* 35: 688–726.

Levine, Ross, and David Renelt (1992). "A Sensitivity Analysis of Cross-Country Growth Regressions." *American Economic Review* 82: 942–63.

Levine, Ross, and Sara Zervos (1998). "Stock Markets, Banks, and Economic Growth." *American Economic Review* 88: 537–58.

Majewski, John (2004a). "Jeffersonian Political Economy and Pennsylvania's Financial Revolution from Below, 1800–1820." Mimeo, University of California, Santa Barbara.

————— (2004b). "Toward a Social History of the Corporation: Shareholding in Pennsylvania Banking and Transportation Corporations, 1800–1840." Paper presented at the Conference on the Past and Future of Early American Economic History: Needs and Opportunities, Library Company of Philadelphia.

Marichal, Carlos (2002). "The Construction of Credibility: Financial Market Reform and the Renegotiation of Mexico's External Debt in the 1880's." In Jeffrey L. Bortz and Stephen H. Haber, eds., *The Mexican Economy, 1870–1930: Essays on the Economic History of Institutions, Revolution, and Growth*. Stanford, CA: Stanford University Press.

Maurer, Noel (2002). *The Power and the Money: The Mexican Financial System, 1876–1932*. Stanford, CA: Stanford University Press.

Maurer, Noel, and Andrei Gomberg (2005). "When the State Is Untrustworthy: Public Finance and Private Banking in Porfirian Mexico." *Journal of Economic History* 64: 1087–1107.

Maurer, Noel, and Stephen Haber (2004). "Related Lending and Economic Performance: Evidence from Mexico." Mimeo, Stanford University.

McCubbins, Mathew D., and Thomas Schwartz (1984). "Congressional Oversight Overlooked: Police Patrols Versus Fire Alarms." *American Journal of Political Science* 28: 165–79.

Mexico, Secretaria de Hacienda (1912). *Anuario de Estadística Fiscal, 1911–12*. Mexico City.

Moss, David, and Sarah Brennan (2004). "Regulation and Reaction: The Other Side of Free Banking in Antebellum New York." Harvard Business School Working Paper 04-038.

Musacchio, Aldo, and Ian Read (2003). "Bankers, Industrialists, and Their Cliques: Elite Networks in Turn of the Century Mexico and Brazil." Mimeo, Stanford University.

Neusser, Klaus, and Maurice Kugler (1998). "Manufacturing Growth and Financial Development: Evidence from OECD Countries." *Review of Economics and Statistics* 80: 636–46.

Ng, Kenneth (1988). "Free Banking Laws and Barriers to Entry in Banking, 1838–1860." *Journal of Economic History* 48: 877–99.

North, Douglass C. (1990). *Institutions, Institutional Change, and Economic Performance*. Cambridge, UK: Cambridge University Press.

——— (1981). *Structure and Change in Economic History*. New York: Norton.

——— (1961). *The Economic Growth of the United States, 1790–1860*. Englewood Cliffs, NJ: Prentice Hall.

North, Douglass C., William Summerhill, and Barry Weingast (2000). "Order, Disorder, and Economic Change: Latin America Versus North America." In Bruce Bueno de Mesquita and Hilton L. Root, eds., *Governing for Prosperity*. New Haven, CT: Yale University Press.

North, Douglass C., and Barry R. Weingast (1989). "Constitutions and Commitment: The Evolution of Institutions Governing Public Choice in Seventeenth-Century England." *Journal of Economic History* 49: 803–32.

Petersen, Mitchell, and Raghuram Rajan (2002). "Does Distance Still Matter? The Information Revolution in Small Business Lending." *Journal of Finance* 57: 2533–70.

Potash, Robert (1983). *The Mexican Government and Industrial Development in the Early Republic: The Banco de Avío*. Amherst: University of Massachusetts Press.

Przeworski, Adam, Michael Alvarez, José Antonio Cheibub, and Fernando Limongi (2000). *Democracy and Development: Political Institutions and Material Well-Being in the World, 1950–1990*. New York: Cambridge University Press.

——— (1998). "Financial Dependence and Growth." *American Economic Review* 88: 559–86.

Rajan, Raghuram G., and Luigi Zingales (1998). "Financial Dependence and Growth." *American Economic Review* 88: 559–86.

Razo, Armando (2003). "Social Networks and Credible Commitments in Dictatorships: Political Organization and Economic Growth in Porfirian Mexico, 1876–1991." Ph.D. diss., Stanford University.

Riguzzi, Paolo (2002). "The Legal System, Institutional Change, and Financial Regulation in Mexico, 1870–1910: Mortgage Contracts and Long Term Credit." In Jeffrey Bortz and Stephen Haber, eds., *The Mexican Economy, 1870–1930: Essays in the Economic History of Institutions, Revolution, and Growth*. Stanford, CA: Stanford University Press.

Rockoff, Hugh (2000). "Banking and Finance, 1789–1914." In Stanley Engerman and Robert Gallman, eds., *The Cambridge Economic History of the United States*, vol. 2. Cambridge, UK: Cambridge University Press.

——— (1985). "New Evidence on Free Banking in the United States." *American Economic Review* 75: 886–89.

——— (1974). "The Free Banking Era: A Reexamination." *Journal of Money, Credit, and Banking* 6: 141–67.

Rousseau, Peter, and Richard Sylla (1999). "Emerging Financial Markets and Early U.S. Growth." NBER Working Paper W7448.

Rousseau, Peter, and Paul Wachtel (1998). "Financial Intermediation and Economic Performance: Historical Evidence from Five Industrial Countries." *Journal of Money, Credit, and Banking* 30: 657–78.

Sinkin, Richard N. (1979). *Mexican Reform, 1855–1876: A Study in Liberal Nation-Building*. Austin: University of Texas Press.

Sutton, John (1998). *Technology and Market Structure*. Cambridge, MA: MIT Press.

Sylla, Richard (2000). "Experimental Federalism: The Economics of American Government, 1789–1914." In Stanley Engerman and Robert Gallman, eds., *The Cambridge Economic History of the United States*, vol. 2. Cambridge, UK: Cambridge University Press.

——— (1975). *The American Capital Market, 1846–1914: A Study of the Effects of Public Policy on Economic Development*. New York: Arno Press.

Sylla, Richard, John B. Legler, and John Wallis (1987). "Banks and State Public Finance in the New Republic: The United States, 1790–1860." *Journal of Economic History* 47: 391–403.

Temin, Peter (1968). "The Economic Consequences of the Bank War." *Journal of Political Economy* 76: 257–74.

Tennenbaum, Barbara (1986). *The Politics of Penury: Debt and Taxes in Mexico, 1821–1856*. Albuquerque: University of New Mexico Press.

Tsebelis, George (1995). "Decision Making in Political Systems: Veto Players in Presidentialism, Parliamentarism, Multicameralism, and Multipartyism." *British Journal of Political Science* 25: 289–326.

United States, Board of Governors of the Federal Reserve System (1943). *Banking and Monetary Statistics*. Washington, DC: U.S. Government Printing Office.

United States, Department of Commerce (1975). *Historical Statistics of the United States: Colonial Times to 1970*. Washington, DC: U.S. Government Printing Office.

Walker, David W. (1986). *Business, Kinship, and Politics: The Martinez del Rio Family in Mexico, 1824–1867*. Austin: University of Texas Press.

Wallis, John, Richard E. Sylla, and John B. Legler (1994). "The Interaction of Taxation and Regulation in Nineteenth Century U.S. Banking." In Claudia Goldin and Gary D. Libecap, eds., *The Regulated Economy: A Historical Approach to Political Economy*. Chicago: University of Chicago Press.

Wallis John, and Barry. R. Weingast (2004). "Equilibrium Impotence: Why the States and Not the American National Government Financed Infrastructure Investment in the Antebellum Era." Mimeo, Stanford University.

Weingast, Barry R. (1997a). "The Political Foundations of Democracy and the Rule of Law." *American Political Science Review* 91: 245–63.

———— (1997b). "The Political Foundations of Limited Government: Parliament and Sovereign Debt in 17th- and 18th-Century England." In John N. Drobak and John V. C. Nye, eds., *The Frontiers of the New Institutional Economics*. San Diego: Academic Press.

———— (1995). "The Economic Role of Political Institutions: Federalism, Markets, and Economic Development." *Journal of Law, Economics, and Organization* 11: 1–31.

Wettereau, James O. (1942). "The Branches of the First Bank of the United States." *Journal of Economic History* 2: 66–100.

Wright, Gavin (1986). *Old South, New South: Revolutions in the Southern Economy Since the Civil War*. New York: Basic Books.

Chapter 3

The Political Economy of Early U.S. Financial Development

RICHARD SYLLA

Introduction

Why do some nations grow faster economically and therefore become richer than others? That is a pressing question in a world that today features more economic inequality across nations and major geographical regions than at any other time in the past half millennium, and perhaps in all of history. Economic historians studying the long-term development of nations and economists analyzing more recent data from a much larger set of countries are converging on an answer: nations that have modern, more effective financial systems grow faster than those that do not.

As is often the case, the answer to one question leads to others. What is a modern financial system? Why do some countries have them and others do not? How did those countries having effective financial systems manage to get them? Nations are polities. Governments themselves require financing and therefore have an interest in financial systems. What are the relationships between political development, financial development, and economic growth?

The early history of the United States provides abundant material for answering such questions. This chapter examines how, in the first years of U.S. history, political and financial developments interacted, leading to improved political and financial systems. One immediate consequence was a higher rate of economic growth. The examination confirms that limited government achieved with horizontal (executive, legislative, judicial) and vertical (federal and state/provincial) separation of powers can facilitate achieving a more effective financial system and faster economic growth.[1]

The chapter also suggests, however, that limited government by itself is not sufficient. Other countries—neighboring Canada and Mexico, for example—had what appear to be limited governments but had nothing like the financial development of the United States in the nineteenth century.[2] Moreover, the horizontal and vertical separation of powers that facilitated financial development in the 1790s later, on more than one occasion (to be discussed later), led to difficulties in sustaining an effective financial system. Thus, in U.S. history there are examples of what some in other contexts have called "great reversals" in financial-system development.[3] And these reversals appear to have resulted from the very separation of powers that encouraged financial modernization. In the horizontal separation, if the executive is weak relative to the legislature, or vice versa, a financial system might be damaged. In the vertical separation of federalism, if state interests gain relative to the national interest, or vice versa, a financial system again might be weakened.

These possibilities, which became realities in U.S. history, suggest that favorable outcomes in financial development may depend as much on enlightened political and financial leadership as on such political structures as limited government, federalism, and separation of powers per se.

The U.S. Financial Revolution and Economic Growth

During the 1780s, the first decade of independence, the U.S. political system limited the discretion of government, which some analysts contend is necessary for effective financial systems and economic growth. But that limited government was, at the national level, an ineffective government tottering on the edge of, if not actually in, bankruptcy. At the state level, political stability and finances were only marginally better. And the U.S. financial system was primitive and premodern compared with those of the British and the Dutch at the time. Economic growth was also premodern, but in that respect the United States was like most of the world. Since the 1775 outbreak of revolution, which cut off Americans from external markets they had accessed under British rule, growth most likely was negative.

Then everything changed. The Constitution transformed the limited, ineffective national government of the 1780s confederation into the limited, effective federal government of the 1790s. By 1795, the United States had all the key institutional components of a modern financial system—strong public finances and debt management, a national dollar monetary unit based on precious metals, a central bank, a banking system, thriving securities markets, and a host of corporations. In 1788, when the new Constitution was ratified, it had none of these components. In short, between 1788 and 1795 the United States had what economic historians term "a financial revolution," the creation in a short period of time of a greatly improved and modern financial system.[4] Two centuries earlier, the Dutch Republic had a financial revolution. A century earlier, Great Britain also had one. John Law tried—and failed—to lead France to one between 1715 and 1720.[5] The U.S. financial revolution was based on these earlier positive and negative experiences. Its leader, Alexander Hamilton, was keenly aware of the historical precedents and drew heavily on them to create a modern financial system for the United States.

U.S. economic growth accelerated at the time of the 1790s financial revolution.[6] For the next century it likely was at the highest rate of any country's. Effective public finances combined with good luck and a few doses of imperialism to triple the territory of the country between 1803 and 1853. Effective private financial arrangements (banks, securities markets, corporations, and so on) compared with those of most other countries contributed greatly to U.S. economic expansion, although financial modernization also introduced occasional bank panics and failures, stock market crashes, and corporate malfeasance. Despite occasional setbacks, the benefits of modern financial arrangements in mobilizing and allocating capital resources far outweigh their costs. By the 1890s, U.S. population had grown so much that it exceeded that of any of the old European powers and overseas European offshoots. The country had become the world's largest national economy, the leader in manufacturing, and probably the equal of Britain, the "first industrial nation," in real income and output per person.

The "big bang" that gave the United States a modern financial system in the early 1790s cannot, of course, account for all of these developments. But it was a more important source of them than most of the history books indicate. When the industrial and transportation revolutions of early U.S. history took place, a modern financial system was there to finance them. The westward movement—territorial acquisitions, land purchases, settlement and property development—had to be financed, often externally from the formal financial system. In the nineteenth century nothing like the economic expansion that occurred in the United States happened in other large countries—in Canada, Latin America, Russia, China, India, Australia, and Africa—despite the availability of industrial and transportation technologies and a lot of land.

The big difference between the United States and these other nations and regions was in political and financial systems. Moreover, in the U.S. case, as in earlier cases of successful and unsuccessful financial revolutions, political and financial reforms were intimately bound up with one another. How did the intimate relationship between political and financial change unfold at the birth of the United States? Did getting the politics right allow the United States to get its finances right? Or did a need for better finance promote more effective politics? The U.S. case, we shall see, is consistent with an answer of "yes" to both questions. At the same time, perhaps inevitably, finance became highly politicized, and it has remained that way throughout U.S. history.

Political Origins of the U.S. Financial Revolution

The origins of political and financial change at the start of the United States as a nation can be found in the difficulties of financing the revolt against British rule. Those difficulties led to the financial messes of the late 1770s and early 1780s when the Confederation Congress saw its paper money become worthless and, having no taxing powers, had to struggle to find ways to pay its army and service its debts. Financial messes for governments and countries are common, however, whereas financial revolutions are few. The roots of the U.S. financial revolution were more specific.

Given what happened subsequently, we can trace the roots to three letters, which are really essays on political economy, written between late 1779 and early 1781 by Alexander Hamilton when he was an officer in the Continental Army. Since early 1777, after demonstrating military competence during the battles of New York, Trenton, and Princeton, Hamilton had served as a principal aide-de-camp to the U.S. military commander, General George Washington. In the early letter-essays, Hamilton, who was only in his mid-20s at the time, revealed an unusual grasp of financial history. The grasp included knowledge of the successful financial revolutions of the Dutch and the British, and the aborted one of John Law in France. Hamilton applied what he had learned from the European precedents to the U.S. situation. In the process, he began to outline plans for political and financial changes in which he would be a leading participant during the 1780s and 1790s.

The setting for Hamilton's three letter-essays was the dire situation of the American revolutionaries during 1779–81. The war had dragged on for five years. Continental paper money was well on its way to becoming worthless. State paper monies were not much better. Tax revenues were inadequate and mostly retained by states. Borrowing at home and abroad was difficult. From his central position in the army, Hamilton drew several conclusions from his direct military experience. First, Congress and the states were not providing the army with the resources of manpower and materiel it needed if it were to have any chance of success. Second, both Congress and the states complicated the war effort by greatly overissuing paper money, to the point where hardly anyone trusted it or would accept it. Third, as a consequence, the army had to resort to large-scale impressments, that is, confiscations and seizures, of resources to maintain itself as a viable force, and such involuntary seizures of resources from citizens were hardly a way to maintain for long the support and confidence of the people. Many historians take a rosy view of U.S. history and tend to ignore these less-than-glorious aspects of what it took to achieve independence.[7] To a soldier such as Hamilton, they were a frequent occurrence.

Because war in that era was a seasonal affair with long lulls between campaigns and battles, Hamilton used his free time to study whatever he could lay his hands on that might explain why the revolutionary cause was so ill-served by political and financial institutions that should have rendered more support but did not. He gave himself a crash course in economic, political, military, and especially financial history, the first prescient results of which appeared in the three letter-essays of 1779–81.

In the first letter (only an undated, unaddressed draft survives, and seems to have been written between December 1779 and March 1780), Hamilton says that the only solution to U.S. financial problems is a foreign loan. Part of that loan could be used to buy up and retire superfluous paper currency, but a better idea would be to use it to purchase and import military supplies from overseas. The more innovative part of Hamilton's plan was to have Congress charter what he called a "Bank of the United States" and use part of the foreign loan to capitalize the bank, with another part of the capital to come from stock subscriptions by private investors. Hamilton reasoned that the only way to create a good currency was to make it in the interest of those who routinely held and used currency—mainly the merchant class—to support it. That could be accomplished by having the bank's notes be made convertible into a specie base, thus anchoring paper currency in something intrinsically valuable. The new convertible currency would replace existing and rapidly depreciating national and state fiat paper monies.

The U.S. government in the plan Hamilton outlined would take a stake in the bank and share in its profits. And it would receive a large loan from the bank. Unlike the Bank of England, Hamilton's Bank of the United States was not to have exclusive banking privileges. This is interesting because in 1780 there were no banks at all in the United States, and yet Hamilton even then envisioned a competitive banking system. Hamilton further suggested that his proposed Bank of the United States could be tied to a market for public debt securities by having public securities become a part of the bank's capital, as was done in England.[8]

Hamilton's second letter-essay, dated September 3, 1780, was addressed to James Duane, a New York delegate to the Continental Congress. In it, Hamilton's political economy advanced to a higher plane. The fundamental defect of the United States was that the national government did not have sufficient vigor, and especially sufficient means, to provide for public exigencies. The lack of vigor resulted from weak administration by committees of Congress; Hamilton contended that responsible individuals, not committees, should lead administrative departments of government. The results of weak administration were that the army had difficulties recruiting and retaining troops and was poorly supplied.

Hence, Hamilton argued to Duane, the national governmental structure needed to be altered. The national government had to have the power of the purse, "for without certain revenues a government can have no power; that power, which holds the purse strings absolutely, must rule." There were two possible remedies. First, since a national government worthy of the name must have powers competent to meet public exigencies, Hamilton boldly asserted that Congress already had such powers. The problem was that Congress and its committees were too timid to use them. Realizing that not all would agree with this bold approach, Hamilton proposed as an alternative that Congress call immediately for a constitutional convention, the outcome of which would be to grant Congress competent powers. This, in September 1780, may be the first mention by any American leader of the need for the sort of constitutional restructuring of U.S. government that came seven years later.

Hamilton argued that in the interim, Congress should appoint single executive officers to administer its great departments. It should recruit troops for the duration of the war, or at least three or more years. Hamilton again called for a foreign loan to supply the army, and he proposed money taxes on the market economy along with in-kind taxes on the nonmarket economy. Finally, he again called for a national bank founded on public and private credit. In connection with his bank proposal, Hamilton discussed the origins of modern banking in Italy, the Bank of Amsterdam, the Bank of England, and the flaws in John Law's system in France. He especially admired the Bank of England, which united public authority and private credit to create a vast structure of reliable paper credit convertible into a specie base. The bank he outlined to Duane is similar to the Bank of the United States proposed in the earlier letter, but now Hamilton introduced a new feature by saying that the bank should have three branches, in Virginia, Philadelphia, and Boston.[9]

Hamilton's third important letter-essay of the war period, dated April 30, 1781, was to Robert Morris, shortly after Congress had appointed Morris to be its superintendent of finance. Hamilton took some credit in the letter for recommending that Congress appoint single executives to lead key departments. He then shared with Morris some ideas he had on financial administration, as well as a plan that while "crude and defective" might be a "basis for something more perfect." First, he said the revenue capacity of the country had to be estimated, and he did that. Next, he estimated necessary civil and military expenses. These greatly exceeded revenue capacity, leaving a shortfall that had to be financed. Foreign loans might help but could not provide all the needed means. Therefore, a more elaborate plan had to be devised.

Hamilton's plan, of course, called once again for establishing a national bank. He discussed for Morris the pros and cons of national banks, in theory and in history. Much of the remainder of the long letter-essay was devoted to proposing and discussing, point by point, 20 articles, "only intended as outlines," that would compose the bank's charter. The bank, for example, would be, like the Bank of England, in law a corporation with limited liability for shareholders, which—at a time when there were precious few corporations in America—seemed so obvious to Hamilton and perhaps to Robert Morris that he said it "needs no discussion." The letter ends with a brief discussion of the national debt once the war is over. It would not present a problem, Hamilton said, because the country's growth and a good financial administration would easily enable the United States to pay it. In fact, properly managed, the national debt would be "a national blessing."[10]

Morris replied to Hamilton that he had been thinking along similar lines, although the Bank of North America (BNA) that he soon would propose to Congress was much less ambitious in scale and scope than the bank Hamilton recommended.[11] Congress approved Morris's proposal, chartering the BNA as a corporation late in 1781, and the BNA opened for business in early 1782. It was the first U.S. bank of the modern variety. Although Morris had hoped that private investors would step forward to purchase the stock that would capitalize the BNA, such subscriptions were slow in coming. Interestingly, in view of Hamilton's proposals, Morris therefore used the proceeds of a recently negotiated foreign loan (from France) to subscribe on behalf of Congress for most of the BNA's capital stock.

When Hamilton a decade later became the first secretary of the Treasury of the new government created by the U.S. Constitution, the plans for financial reform that had begun to take shape in 1779 had become more refined.

In part the refinements came from additional experience. After Yorktown, Hamilton left the army and began the study of law. He was admitted to the New York bar within a year. Robert Morris in 1782 appointed him continental receiver of taxes for New York State. When the New York legislature did not provide much to be collected, the experience heightened Hamilton's appreciation of the imbecility of the Confederation's fiscal arrangements. He served in Congress in 1782–83, where he and a new acquaintance, James Madison, worked with Morris and others, but without much success, to improve fiscal and governmental underpinnings. In 1784, he helped found the Bank of New York and wrote its constitution. In 1786, he was a delegate to, and drafted the report of, the Annapolis convention, which called for the Philadelphia convention of 1787. Serving in the New York legislature, he was appointed as one of three New York delegates to the 1787 convention. After the new Constitution was adopted by the convention, he conceived of the so-called *Federalist Papers* to explain the constitution and encourage state conventions to ratify it. Hamilton wrote the majority of the 85 Federalist essays, recruiting Madison and John Jay to write the others. After ratification, Hamilton pressured Washington, the only leader known and respected throughout the country, to accept the presidency.

In 1789, when Washington appointed him secretary of the Treasury, Hamilton found himself in the key position to implement his decade-old plans for a stronger national government and what we now can say was a financial revolution. Implementation was not to prove easy because it involved passing several key pieces of legislation, and Bismarck's later observations about making sausage and legislation clearly were applicable. But implementation of the financial revolution happened during Hamilton's term, 1789–95, at the Treasury. The U.S. financial revolution of the early 1790s was neat and quick. It did not take the decades that were required in its Dutch and English antecedents. Hamilton's formulation and execution of a modernizing financial plan for the United States have to be regarded as a triumph of enlightened political economy. Given the formidable opposition the plan encountered, it was not an easy accomplishment.

The Political Economy of Financial Modernization

As mentioned earlier, in 1788 the United States had none of the key components of a modern financial system, whereas by 1795 it had every one of them. The change is summarized and amplified in Table 3.1.

How did all this change happen so quickly during Hamilton's years as secretary of the Treasury, 1789–95? As the finance minister of the new

TABLE 3.1
U.S. financial system, 1788 and 1795

	1788	1795
Public finances, national	Bankrupt	Thriving
Central bank	No	Yes, with 5 branches
Money	Fiat state paper, foreign coins	Convertible U.S. $
Banks	3, no system	20 state, 5 BUS branches, system
Securities markets	Trivial, sporadic	Several cities, organized
Business corporations	Few	Many more

federal government, Hamilton could exert direct influence only in three areas, namely, public finance, the central bank, and money. The first two were extremely controversial, so change was accomplished by "backroom" political deals.

The Treasury could exert only indirect evidence on the last three developments. Chartering banks (apart from the central bank) and business corporations was a jealously guarded prerogative of state legislatures. Because neither federal nor state governments took any overt actions to establish securities markets, it was left to private business incentives. Nonetheless, as discussed later, the impetus for these changes also emanated from the federal Treasury Department.

PUBLIC FINANCE AND THE NATIONAL DEBT

During the 1780s, the Confederation government's inability to provide for interest and principal payments on its domestic and foreign debts was one of the stronger arguments for constitutional reform. The new federal government finally obtained the power of the purse, which it implemented with duties on imports and tonnage in 1789. Shortly after Hamilton took over an empty Treasury in September 1789, Congress asked him to prepare a plan for reforming public credit. Congress received the report in January 1790.[12]

Hamilton's debt restructuring plan included a promise to pay interest on Congress's debt in hard money (or equivalents such as convertible banknotes) starting in 1791. It also called for assuming the war-related debts of the states and incorporating them into the national debt with interest commencing in 1792. These were bold gambles for a government with an empty Treasury and just beginning to build a revenue system. Indeed, they were Hamilton's boldest gambles, ones that occupied most of his attention during his term at Treasury. The problem he faced was that providing for ordinary federal expenses and paying interest on the national debt would require more than $5 million per year if interest on the full debt were paid at promised rates. No one could predict in 1789, for a new government that had almost no revenue, when it might be able to collect such an annual sum. In fact, it did not do so until 1794. So Hamilton proposed that domestic creditors voluntarily accept a reduced rate of interest—what today would be called a "haircut"—on a fully funded debt. That reduced the revenues required to operate the federal government and pay interest on the debt to about $3.6 million, a sum that would in fact be raised, just barely, in 1792. Hence, assuming Congress adopted Hamilton's plan, the years 1789–92 would require deft financial management, borrowing in one place to meet payments in another, and so on, to create and maintain the illusion that public credit was stronger than in fact it was.

But that is getting ahead of the story. James Madison, Hamilton's friend and collaborator during the 1780s, surprised Hamilton and leading Federalists in Congress in the initial debates in early 1790 on Hamilton's public credit proposals. Madison called for *discrimination* in the treatment of the original debt holders—those who had lent money and other resources to the government during the revolution—and subsequent purchases of those securities. Because the Confederation government was essentially bankrupt, many of the original holders had sold their securities at small fractions of face value. Enactment of Hamilton's plan would raise the value of public securities—indeed, values had been rising for more than a year in recognition of the possibility—and Madison thought (or at least argued) that "justice" required paying the current holders ("speculators") the highest market value below par that they had paid, with the remaining difference between par and that highest market value allocated to the original lenders.

The problem with Madison's proposal is that after the fact, and therefore probably unconstitutionally, it would have violated the terms of the debt contracts between securities holders and the government. Moreover, the proposal seemed inconsistent with Madison's earlier views, but it likely shored up his political base in Virginia, which he represented in the House.[13]

In any case, the proposal was quickly and easily defeated. But what if it had passed? Domestic and foreign holders of U.S. debt would have learned that they could not trust the new government of the United States to live up to its contracts, as in fact it had not done up to 1790. In that case, the overall plan for financial reform, if not stillborn, would have suffered a drastic setback before it could get off the ground. Consider what happens today when emerging-market countries for whatever reasons decide to alter the terms of their contracts with creditors. The results, whether or not the

International Monetary Fund (IMF) intervenes, are not usually happy ones for the creditors or the countries.

Assumption of state debts was a far more controversial feature of Hamilton's plan. Why not let the states provide for their own debts, as some were already doing, and let the federal government provide only for its debts? Later, after he had stepped down as Treasury secretary, Hamilton would write that this was "in truth the most plausible argument which was used against assumption," and if it had been adopted, his work as Treasury secretary would have been easier because the debt he had to manage would have been smaller. Hamilton says he rejected the idea for several reasons. The plan would have left citizens in different states with unequal debt burdens. It would have left the country with 15 different systems of finance, and if one or more states defaulted, the national character and credit would be stained—as actually happened half a century later after many states renewed borrowing on a large scale and then nine of them defaulted on their debts. It would have put the states and the federal government in competition for revenue bases and revenues. All of these outcomes would inevitably produce, in Hamilton's word, "collisions." Hamilton's assumption plan avoided that while at the same time lightening the financial burdens of states and expanding the financial responsibilities of the federal government. He regarded such expansions of federal responsibility as an advantage for the country's "defence and safety." [14]

Despite Hamilton's arguments, assumption came close to defeat. Many southern and some northern leaders and congressmen, jealous of eroding states' rights and enhancing federal responsibilities and powers, were adamantly opposed. One of the engaging stories of U.S. history is that assumption was saved at the last moment when Jefferson invited Madison and Hamilton to dinner at his house in New York, then the capital, in June 1790. At the dinner, in return for Madison agreeing to switch enough southern votes to pass assumption, Hamilton agreed to move the capital of the United States from New York to the banks of the Potomac, after it resided for a decade in Philadelphia (a feature of the deal that would garner support in Pennsylvania for assumption), allowing time for a new capital city to be built.

The whole deal may have been more complex than this simple version. A number of public characters, including Washington and Madison, would receive personal financial benefits from the move of the capital to the Potomac. The actual deal probably involved passage of a resolution saying that the House would refrain thereafter from discussing the emancipation of slaves. [15] And it almost certainly involved Virginia getting a sweetheart deal in the settlement of Revolutionary War state accounts that was under way at the time.[16] Madison comes through as a clever congressman and legislative strategist.

Why Jefferson, who had brokered at least part of the assumption deal, later said that it was one of great regrets of his life and that Hamilton had duped him has puzzled historians. Jefferson's friends, the state of Virginia, and the South as a whole gained a lot from the deal. Perhaps the acceptance of this first piece of Hamilton's financial plan, which dealt with an existing national problem that most agreed needed attention, did not yet suggest the changing balance of federal and state powers that would be evident a year later, by the middle of 1791, as implementation of the plan further unfolded. That change in balance would prove upsetting to proponents of powers reserved to the states in the new constitutional system.

Once the Potomac residence deal was done (or thought to be done—we revisit the issue later), several acts of Congress during the summer of 1790 endorsed virtually the whole of Hamilton's public credit plan. The voluntary exchange of old domestic securities for three new issues of Treasury bonds—the birth of the current Treasury debt market—commenced in the fall of 1790, as did quarterly interest payments on the new bonds in 1791. In New York, Philadelphia, and Boston, active secondary trading markets for the new securities emerged, providing financial historians with a good record of newspaper price quotations.

Despite his reputation as an advocate of energetic, even "big," government, and of constitutionally *implied* as well as *expressed* powers at the federal level, Hamilton on several occasions showed himself as proponent of what today would be called time-consistent financial policies. In the January 1790 "Report on the Public Credit," he propounded the principle that public credit could be made "immortal" if a government always connected to its borrowing a set of tax increases sufficient to pay not only the interest on the debt but also a little more that would allow the debt eventually to be redeemed. The idea first surfaced in his "Continentalist IV" essay published in 1781 as he was heading to Yorktown with the Continental Army.[17] And it was reiterated again in what some call his final major report to Congress as secretary of the Treasury in January 1795.[18] Related ideas are discussed by Adam Smith in *The Wealth of Nations*, although it is not clear that Hamilton had read Smith as early as 1781.[19] British practice by that time was to issue consols—perpetual debts funded only by taxes to pay interest with no thought of redemption. U.S. opinion and practice favored retiring public debts but seldom provided for debt retirement at the time new debt was issued. New York State, however, may have implemented a

Hamilton-type policy when it first borrowed to construct the Erie Canal; at the same time, New York levied taxes to pay interest on and ultimately redeem the debts.[20]

THE BANK OF THE UNITED STATES (BUS)

Because Hamilton by 1790 had been considering a national bank for at least a decade, it could hardly have been a surprise that it became a key component of his plan. He mentioned in the "Report on the Public Credit" of January 1790 that he soon would make a national bank recommendation. He did that in December 1790, and there is nothing in the records of 1790 to indicate that his cabinet colleagues and congressional leaders were against a national bank. The Senate passed the bill on January 20, 1791; the exact vote is not known, but judging by a vote the same day on an amendment to limit the charter to 10 rather than 20 years, the vote was on the order of 16–6, the vote against the shorter limit.

Given the earlier lack of controversy, it must again have been a surprise to many in the administration and Congress when Madison in the subsequent House debates over the bank bill suddenly rose to contend that the bank was unconstitutional. Madison argued that the Constitution had said nothing about such a bank, much less authorized the federal government to charter one. Despite Madison's constitutional concerns, the House passed the legislation by a vote of 39–20. But the president had to act on the bill, and a strong cast of characters—Madison, Secretary of State Jefferson, and Attorney General Edmund Randolph—advised him to make (or threaten to make) the bill his first veto on grounds of nonauthorization by the Constitution. Washington asked Madison to draft a veto message. He also referred the opinions of the two cabinet officers to Hamilton and asked for his opinion and response to theirs. Hamilton then produced one of his finest and most influential public reports, contending that constitutions have implicit as well as explicit powers, and that the bank legislation fell under the implicit category. He effectively demolished the strict-construction arguments of his cabinet colleagues. Washington read Hamilton's argument and approved the bill.

Once again, however, there may have been more to this than Hamilton simply carrying the day by dint of his powers of reasoning and persuasion. Why did Madison and Jefferson, after knowing of Hamilton's forthcoming plan for a bank for at least a year, suddenly come out to oppose it? Why did Washington contemplate vetoing the bank legislation? Forrest McDonald provides an intriguing political-economy interpretation missed by many scholars of the period. Jefferson and Madison, on returning to the new temporary capital at Philadelphia at the turn of 1791, discovered, according to McDonald, that Pennsylvanians were scheming to undo the residence deal of the previous summer and planned to keep the capital at Philadelphia permanently instead of having it move to the Potomac. The failed attempt in the Senate to limit the bank's charter to 10 years, so that it would come up for renewal when the capital was to move to the Potomac, was one response to such a scheme. Its failure was among the reasons for Madison's late-breaking opposition to the bank bill in the House.

Moreover, President Washington had a problem, since he had unilaterally intervened to move the site of the projected Potomac capital closer to his home at Mount Vernon and outside the Potomac range in which commissioners were supposed to select a site. All of these Virginians wanted to make sure that the capital moved to the Potomac in 1800, and Washington, to avoid potential personal embarrassment, wanted his unilateral decision to be retroactively approved by Congress. By threatening to torpedo the bank bill, the Virginians might be able to get what mattered more to them. A bill to approve the site Washington had selected, and ensure also that the capital would move to the Potomac, was introduced. McDonald persuasively argues that each bill was held hostage to the other, and that in the end, although it is not clear which side blinked first, Congress approved both bills on the same Friday in late February 1791.[21] Madison once again showed his skills at congressional maneuvering to promote Virginia's and southern interests. But Hamilton got his bank.

If the national bank had been aborted, so would the U.S. financial revolution. Given the precariousness of the country's finances, the Treasury needed to draw on the credit of a large bank as soon as it could. It took time to organize the BUS, so the Treasury would not be able to do this for a year. In 1792 and 1793, the Treasury did in fact receive four loans from the BUS totaling $1 million. The BUS became for the Treasury a reliable source of short-term credit, a depository for public revenues, and a mover of government funds through its nationwide branch network to where they were needed. It issued convertible dollar banknotes used throughout the country. It was even a modest source of income since the federal government owned 20 percent of the stock, and the dividends were greater than the interest on the loan from the BUS that had enabled it to buy BUS stock. The alternative of relying on state banks—collectively far smaller in capital and resources than the BUS in 1792—for these advantages would have been an inferior solution. Events were to prove this when the two central banks of early U.S. history were not rechartered. Moreover, the stimulus the BUS gave to bank and other corporate chartering by the states (discussed later) would have been lost.

MONEY — THE DOLLAR

Creating the convertible dollar was the least controversial aspect of the U.S. financial revolution at the national level. By the late 1780s, most national leaders were fed up with the inflationary experiences of state fiat paper money, which seemed to be a reprise of the bad experience with continental and state currencies during the War of Independence. The Constitution thus banned the states from further issues, although federal paper money was not explicitly prohibited. Congress was given the power to coin money and regulate its value. Some scholars of the debates at Philadelphia in 1787 nonetheless argue that banning the federal government from ever issuing inconvertible fiat paper money was intended by the delegates, and hence a part of "original" meaning or intent.[22]

It is evident that Hamilton, who was a member of the Philadelphia convention but not present at every debate, did not agree that this was original intent. He did, however, think it a good idea. In the "Report on a National Bank" of December 1790, he wrote:

> The emitting of paper money by the authority of Government is wisely prohibited to the individual States by the National Constitution. And the spirit of that prohibition ought not to be disregarded by the Government of the United States. Though paper emissions under a general authority might have some advantages, . . . yet they are of a nature so liable to abuse, and it may be affirmed so certain of being abused, that the wisdom of the Government will be shown in never trusting itself with the use of so seducing and dangerous an expedient.

Hamilton instead advocated, as did Robert Morris and most of the American merchant class, bank-issued paper currency convertible into a specie base, as was the practice of European financial leaders. He argued that the relative demands for banknotes and specie inherently limited overissue of bank paper, whereas "the discretion of the government is the only measure of the extent of the emissions by its own authority."[23] Once again, as in his advocacy of tying tax increases to service and redeem debts to every debt issue, Hamilton comes across as wanting the federal government to avoid the temptations of pursuing time-inconsistent financial policies.

In the "Mint Report" of February 1791, Hamilton recommended the gold and silver contents of the U.S. dollar, essentially defining it as a unit of account for the United States. His predilections were for a gold dollar, but he ended up recommending bimetallism as a way of increasing the money supply. He thought the market gold-silver ratio had been stable for a considerable period, allowing for bimetallism, but the ratio did not remain stable and bimetallism in practice could not be sustained. The broad outlines of the "Mint Report" drew on earlier writings of Jefferson, who got an advance copy of the report and was pleased with it. It was about the last time the two leaders saw eye to eye on an issue.[24]

BANKS AND BANKING SYSTEMS

In 1789, the United States did not have a banking system. It did have three banks, the BNA in Philadelphia, the Bank of New York in New York City, and the Massachusetts Bank in Boston. These were isolated institutions serving the mercantile communities of their respective cities. Two of the banks were corporations chartered by governments with privileges of limited shareholder liability. The Confederation Congress chartered the BNA at Philadelphia on Robert Morris's recommendation, as a measure to aid war financing. It opened in 1782 and soon received charters from several state governments as well. These were not acts of endorsement but the initial expressions of doubt about whether the national Congress had a right to charter a bank. Such expressions of doubt would arise again and again in 1791, and in later decades until they were ultimately settled in favor of such a right during the Civil War. When the BNA opened, the War of Independence was pretty much over, so the BNA quickly became an ordinary commercial bank of discount, deposit, and note issue.

Hamilton and others founded the Bank of New York in 1784. The founders applied for a charter of incorporation from the New York legislature, but—in another sign of state governments' doubts about banking corporations—they were rebuffed that year and in several later applications. The New York legislature finally granted the bank a charter in 1791, an event that is interesting in connection with the advantages of federalism in supporting financial development (discussed later). Massachusetts chartered its bank in 1784. Compared to the Philadelphia and New York banks, its early years were uneventful.

By 1795, the 2 incorporated banks of 1789 had become 20. One of these was the Bank of New York with its 1791 charter. Baltimore (which had no bank in 1789), Philadelphia, and Boston now had 2 state-chartered banks each. Rhode Island had 2, in Providence and Newport. Besides the Bank of New York, the state of New York had chartered banks in Albany and Hudson. Connecticut had banks in New London, New Haven, Hartford, and Middletown. New Hampshire had chartered a bank. The District of Columbia had 2 banks by 1795, well before the national capital would move there in 1800.

In addition to these state banks, by 1795 the BUS had not only its home office in Philadelphia, the temporary seat of the federal government, but branches ("offices of discount and deposit") in Boston, New York, Baltimore, and Charleston. Since the BUS carried on a commercial banking business along with being the federal government's bank, there were actually 25 corporate banks (including BUS branches) in 1795, compared to the 2 or 3 (counting the yet-to-be-chartered Bank of New York) of 1789.

By 1805, the Bank of the United States would have four more branches, in Norfolk, Savannah, New Orleans, and Washington, D.C. Albert Gallatin, President Jefferson's Treasury secretary, had specifically requested that the BUS establish the two latter branches. And the states by 1805 had chartered 51 more banks. There were thus 80 banks by 1805, including 9 offices of the BUS. The momentum of financial development established in the financial revolution of 1789–95 carried on thereafter in U.S. history.

Why were so many banks founded after 1790 and so few before? A peculiar consequence of the BUS (in both its first, 1791–1811, and second, 1816–36, manifestations) was to stimulate the growth of U.S. banking both when it appeared on the scene and when it departed from it. The latter is easy to understand: if federally sponsored banking facilities were removed (for political, not economic, reasons), states and individuals would act to replace them (for both political and economic reasons).

In 1791, when the BUS was chartered, it also stimulated the chartering of state banks. How did that happen? New York's experience is instructive. The New York legislature, after defeating several charter applications beginning in 1784, finally chartered the Bank of New York in 1791, shortly after President Washington approved the bill calling for creation of the BUS. The bill, drafted by Hamilton, allowed the BUS to open branches throughout the country. State political leaders knew that the BUS would open branches and that one of them would be in New York City. If New York State did not have a bank or banks beholden to it from having obtained a state charter, the state would be ceding the ground of banking to the new federal government, about which antifederalist politicians controlling the state's government continued to harbor suspicions. State legislator James Kent (later New York's Chancellor Kent) indicated how vertical competition in a federal system could favor financial development when he at that time told a correspondent, "It is as requisite to have a state bank to control the influence of a national bank as for a state government to control the influence of a general government."[25] Hence, not to be co-opted by the BUS, New York in 1791 finally granted the Bank of New York a charter of incorporation.

The episode illustrates the positive advantages of the federal structure for financial development. But it also exposes a potential flaw in federal structures: if either the states or the federal government could dominate outcomes, one level of government might undercut the other. This is what happened when state dominance in 1811 and 1832 prevented recharters for the BUS, and it is what nearly happened in the 1860s when federal dominance came close to eliminating state-chartered banking. These were reversals of financial development engendered by shifts in the relative powers of state and federal governments. They indicate that a federal structure of government by itself is no guarantee of good outcomes.

New York's chartering of the Bank of New York in 1791 was defensive. It was a measure designed to counter federal influence in the state. A more positive variation of the stimulus the BUS gave to state-chartered banking played out in Rhode Island. There the first state bank was chartered in 1791 in the hope—unrealized—that it would help attract a branch of the BUS to Providence.[26] That hope was unrealized possibly because Rhode Island earlier had been among the states most reluctant to support a federal union with expanded powers. The leadership of the BUS were mostly Federalist, and as such may have been reluctant to reward with a BUS branch a state that long opposed Federalist goals.

Tables 3.2 and 3.3 summarize the growth of state banking in the early decades of U.S. history. The banking system grew especially rapidly during 1791–95 (Table 3.2), and after the two BUS charters were not renewed (1810–15, 1830–35). Table 3.3 omits the two national banks, which with their 34 total branches gave the early United States nationwide branch banking, something it had for most of the period 1792–1836 and then would not have again until the 1990s.

Could the U.S. banking system have grown even more rapidly? Undoubtedly, as restrictions on the growth of state banking in these decades are well documented, and as the Rhode Island story indicates, the BUS could have opened more branches than it did. States sometimes favored limited banking growth for fiscal reasons. The states had lost the right to issue fiat paper money with its seignorage in the constitutional settlement, but they quickly discovered that they had not lost much because they could invest in and tax the banks they chartered. When states invested in banks, their fiscal interest (dividends) sometimes dictated that they charter new banks slowly to protect their investments.[27]

But there are always at least two ways to view such history. One is to compare the present with the past—what might be called the "time-series" approach—which almost always, certainly in U.S. history, leads to a con-

TABLE 3.2
The first U.S. banks, 1781–1801

Year of charter	Bank	State–place	Opened, if different from charter
1781 (1782, 1786, 1787)	North America	PA—Philadelphia	1782
1784	Massachusetts	MA—Boston	
1790	Maryland	MD—Baltimore	
1791	United States	US—Phila.; Bost., NY, Balt., Charleston, 1792; Norfolk, 1800; Wash. DC, 1801; Savannah, 1802; New Orleans, 1805	
	New York	NY—NYC	1784
	Providence	RI	
1792	New Hampshire	NH	
	Albany	NY	
	Hartford	CT	
	Union	CT—New London	
	Union	MA—Boston	
	New Haven	CT—New Haven	
	Alexandria	VA	
	Richmond	VA	(did not open)
1793	Columbia	NY—Hudson	
	Pennsylvania	PA—Phila.	
	Columbia	DC	
1795	Nantucket	MA	
	Merrimack	MA—Newburyport	
	Middletown	CT	
	Rhode Island	RI—Newport	
	Baltimore	MD	
1796	Delaware	DE—Wilmington	
	Norwich	CT	
1799	Portland	ME/MA	
	Essex	Salem	
	Manhattan Co.	NY—NYC	
1800	Gloucester	MA	
	Bristol	RI	
	Washington	Westerly	
1801	South Carolina	Charleston	1792

SOURCE: Davis (1917, vol. 2, appendix B).

clusion that the past, especially the distant past, was pretty backward and undeveloped compared to what came later. It sometimes leads also to a conclusion that history itself is irrelevant.

Another way of viewing history might be termed the "cross-section" or comparative approach. How did the United States compare with other countries in a given era? Canada did not have even 1 chartered bank until 1817. It had 6 banks in 1830 and 16 in 1840.[28] Compare those figures

TABLE 3.3

U.S. state-chartered banks: Numbers and authorized capital,
by region and national total, 1790–1835

(capital in millions of dollars)

Year	NEW ENGLAND		MID-ATLANTIC		SOUTH		WEST		U.S.	
	No.	Cap.	No.	Cap.	No.	Cap.	No.	Cap.	No.	Cap.
1790	1	0.8	2	2.3					3	3.1
1795	11	4.1	9	9.4					20	13.5
1800	17	5.5	11	11.9					28	17.4
1805	45	13.2	19	21.7	6	3.5	1	0.5	71	38.9
1810	52	15.5	32	29.4	13	9.1	5	2.2	102	56.2
1815	71	24.5	107	67.1	22	17.2	12	6.4	212	115.2
1820	97	28.3	125	74.4	25	28.6	80	28.4	327	159.6
1825	159	42.2	122	71.2	32	33.3	17	9.4	330	156.6
1830	186	48.8	140	73.8	35	37.3	20	10.5	381	170.4
1835	285	71.5	189	90.2	63	111.6	47	35.0	584	308.4

SOURCE: Sylla (1998).

with the U.S. figures listed in Tables 3.2 and 3.3. Mexico did not have a chartered bank until 1863. It had 8 banks in 1883 and 46 in 1911.[29] In contrast, the United States had 80 banks and branches in 1805 and 1,600 banks by 1860. By 1913, the United States would have tens of thousands of banks and roughly a third of the world's bank deposits, far more than any other country.[30] In England until 1825, all banks apart from the Bank of England had to be unlimited-liability partnerships with no more than six partners. There were several hundred such small partnerships. By 1825, the United States had 330 far larger and better-capitalized state banking corporations (mostly in the northeastern states) as well as a central bank with 25 branches—the Bank of England had no branches then—carrying on interstate banking throughout the country. Compared to that of its neighbors in Canada and Mexico and even to England, the development of banking in the early United States is impressive.

SECURITIES MARKETS

The federal debt restructuring of late 1790, including assumption of state debts, and the initial public offering of rights to purchase shares of the Bank of the United States in July 1791 together were seminal events in bringing modern securities markets to the United States. Three new federal debt securities, easily understood and hence relatively easy to value, replaced a wide variety of old national and state issues. One of the new securities was a standard 6 percent bond. The other two, a 3 percent bond and a deferred

6 percent bond (a zero coupon bond until 1801, when it would pay 6 percent interest) represented the "haircut" implicit in Hamilton's plan that was
necessitated by the time it would take to build up revenues after starting
in 1789 with an empty Treasury. Holders of domestic U.S. debts received
one package of the new securities, with interest payments commencing in
1791. Holders of assumed state debts got a different package of the three
new issues, and interest starting in 1792.

The exchange was voluntary, but virtually all securities holders took advantage of it. The alternative involved standing in line behind those who
exchanged old for new debt and hoping enough additional revenue would
come in to allow Congress and the states annually to appropriate interest payments according to the original contracts. As liquid markets were organized
in New York, Philadelphia, and Boston to trade the new issues, the disadvantages of standing in line were increasingly apparent. Roughly half of the domestic national debt was converted from old to new securities within a year
(by September 1791), and almost all the rest (including many state debts) by
the end of 1794.[31] That the massive conversion proceeded smoothly and all
interest due on the new securities was punctually paid speak well of the efficiency with which the Treasury Department was administered.

The Bank initial public offering (IPO) was more controversial because
it led to a speculative bubble. It began with "scrips"—rights representing
a down payment of $25 to purchase $400 full shares in the Bank in installments sequenced over two years—offered and selling out quickly on July 4,
1791. Speculation pushed scrip prices up to about $300 in roughly a
month, so IPO purchasers who sold at the top, before the market fell back,
could have multiplied their money 12-fold in that time. Such rampant
speculation in paper was something new in America. It was repeated in the
early months of 1792, when prices of U.S. 6 percent debt securities, which
could be tendered to make installment payments on Bank shares, rose to
well above par before crashing in March and April. The crash was felt most
severely in New York City, where numerous bankruptcies occurred.

New York's legislature reacted to the crash of 1792 by passing in April a
law banning public auctions of securities and making unenforceable in the
courts contracts for selling securities one did not own, that is, short sales.
Pennsylvania's legislature debated but failed to pass similar legislation. The
result was to drive securities trading indoors, into private clubs of brokers,
who would make and enforce their own rules. New York's most famous
club, the one that evolved into the New York Stock Exchange, began not
long after the April 1792 law. In May, a group of brokers met under a
buttonwood tree on Wall Street, according to legend, and formed such a

club. Philadelphia claims to have started even earlier, in 1790. Short sales continued in these clubs, enforced by private sanctions rather than the official court system. Legal historians demonstrate that judges in the official court system came gradually to recognize the customs of brokers as having the force of law. They suggest that this flowed from the obvious utility of securities markets, and perhaps because many judges themselves were investors in securities.[32]

However sustained, U.S. securities markets expanded steadily after the big bang of 1790–91. The markets were born with the creation of some $60 million of national debt securities in the form of three simple and liquid bond issues, and rights to $10 million in shares of the Bank of the United States. They were sustained when other corporations, most prominently (and befitting a financial revolution) state-chartered banks and insurance companies, used them to access capital. Initially, foreign investors provided a lot of that capital; in roughly a decade after 1790, European investors purchased about half of the U.S. national debt and BUS shares.[33] Not long after, state and local governments would enter the markets to raise money for a variety of public purposes by issuing securities.

The events of 1790–92 produced a political backlash that extended well beyond initial forays into securities-market regulation. The break between Hamilton and his colleagues Madison and Jefferson that began to appear in 1790–91 became complete in 1792. Securities speculation probably encouraged the break, particularly when it became clear that many members of Congress profited handsomely from rises in the prices of public debt securities and bank scrips and stock that they had voted to create. This smacked of "corruption," and there was an extensive body of eighteenth-century political writing about it emanating from English "country party" opposition to the "court party" financial policies of Walpole and other leaders that seemed to describe all too well the "corrupt" practices that suddenly appeared to be invading the United States. A similar literature quickly came from American pens, embodying the ideology of a new Republican political party led by Jefferson and Madison that arose to protest the allegedly "corrupting" policies of Hamilton. He and other supporters of those policies simultaneously formed a Federalist party to defend their financial reforms and nation building. For the rest of the 1790s, U.S. politics would not be pretty.[34]

Although the issues in the bitter political debates of the 1790s were many and complex, at their heart were supposed conflicts between two types of property, one old and one new. The Republican charge of "corruption" against the Federalists was that they had used government to create a new kind of artificial property, namely, public debt and corporate shares, and were using it to undermine republicanism and restore monarchy. How? One way was mentioned previously. Congressmen would support the creation of artificial forms of property and the political goals of its proponents because they themselves stood to benefit personally. Another way was also obvious. The wealthy owners of the new property and the speculators who dealt in it would both support the government and influence it in their own pecuniary interests. Further, the new property would create a mass of officeholders or, in the rhetoric of English eighteenth-century republicanism, "place-men," who would owe their jobs to a system organized to transfer wealth from the many to the few, and hence would support the nefarious goals of a government that provided them with those jobs.

Republicans said less about the old property, perhaps because it was obvious to all that it included what all were familiar with, namely, real property such as land and buildings. To a Republican theorist such as John Taylor of Caroline, these were "natural property" and not the "artificial property" being created to "corrupt" government and society.[35]

In the U.S. context, it is curious that the debates hardly ever mentioned another form of property, slaves, apart—ironically—from Republicans often using the term "slavery" to describe what would be the outcome for most Americans if the Federalists succeeded. Federalists, having learned that any notion of ending slavery would have torpedoed the Constitution and that, after the adoption of the Constitution, any further questioning of slavery at the national level would lead to moves for secession, seemed to conclude that to keep open the possibility of a unified nation, they had to keep shut their mouths and still their pens on slavery.

What makes this especially curious is that the human property of American slave owners in the 1790s had a market value approximately twice as great as the $70 million bonds and stocks at par value (market value was lower) created by the new federal government.[36] Moreover, the value of slave property naturally increased as time went on, unlike federally created securities.

Were not slaves a property interest to be defended? Of course they were. How best to defend that interest? Perhaps by attacking, in the name of states' rights, any new property interest that might arise to question the vested interest in slave property, and by attacking particularly a new and stronger federal government that might one day, if not kept in its place or co-opted by slave interests, threaten those interests.

In the modern United States, slaves are long gone, and the value of stocks and bonds vastly exceeds the value of land and buildings. That should not prevent us from seeing what the political economy of financial modernization was about two centuries ago, when the value of slaves alone greatly exceeded the value of stocks and bonds. It was not really about the corruption inherent in corporate stocks and public debts. That to a modern eye was a smokescreen to cover the underlying political and economic interests of slave owners. When the slave owners came to national power in 1801 and held it until 1861, further discussions about the corrupting nature of stocks and bonds suddenly became muted at the federal level, even as those financial instruments increased in number and value, right along with the number and value of slaves. Those who tend to take seriously the 1790s arguments about "corruption" need to confront that curious muting of corruption concerns once national political control shifted from Federalists to states' rights Republicans.

CORPORATIONS

The most distinctively "American" feature of the early U.S. financial development was the proliferation of corporations. The other features—restructured public finances, a new and stable currency, a central bank, a banking system, and securities markets—had appeared in the earlier Dutch and British financial revolutions. But those earlier financial revolutions produced nothing like the number of corporations that multiplied in the United States during the financial revolution of 1789–95, and continued to multiply thereafter. When European nations began to allow incorporation of business under general laws after the mid-nineteenth century, the United States had had such laws for two or more decades, and even before it had general incorporation laws there were thousands of corporations formed by special acts of state legislatures.

In large measure, the appearance of so many corporations in the United States before they appeared elsewhere has to be attributed to the federal structure of the country, which left virtually all chartering of corporations in the hands of state governments. This was another advantage of a federalist structure for financial development. The sovereign states of the American Union in competition with one another would charter vastly more corporations than more populous and politically centralized countries such as Britain and France.

Nonetheless, the record makes it clear that the impetus for increased corporate chartering came from the federally sponsored financial revolution. This is evident in Table 3.4, which shows when business corporations were chartered before 1801. There were only 7 charters in the colonial era. During the decade 1781–90, some 28 more companies received corporate charters. During the next decade, 1791–1800, when the financial revolution of the Federalists was accomplished, more than 10 times as many

TABLE 3.4
*Number of business corporations chartered in the U.S.,
eighteenth century*

Colonial era	7		
1781	1	1791	9
1782	0	1792	31
1783	1	1793	15
1784	3	1794	17
1785	3	1795	42
1786	2	1796	32
1787	6	1797	41
1788	5	1798	36
1789	3	1799	33
1790	4	1800	39
1781–90	28	1791–1800	295

SOURCE: Davis (1917, vol. 2, table 2, p. 26).

business corporations were chartered. In the midst of that revolution, more corporations were chartered in the United States in the two years 1791 and 1792 than had been chartered in all the previous years of American history up to 1790.

Increased corporate chartering by states was no coincidence. As noted earlier, after Congress chartered the BUS, states began to charter more banks for "defensive" and other reasons. That was easier to do because liquid securities markets, another creation of the financial revolution, created a 1790s securities "ownership culture" receptive to new-venture IPOs.

Representative government and frequent elections in states made extending corporate privileges to constituents a good strategy for getting into office and being reelected. Economic competition between states in a federal system encouraged neighboring states to emulate one another's chartering activities. Hence, the momentum established in the early 1790s carried on. The New England states chartered more than 1,700 business corporations between 1800 and 1830, without the benefit of general incorporation acts. In these three decades, New York chartered nearly 1,000 business corporations, Pennsylvania more than 400, New Jersey and Maryland nearly 200 each, and Ohio more than 100.[37] These are the states we know about from previous studies. We should learn more about them and the others. In corporate chartering, something different was happening in the United States from anything that had happened anywhere else in previous history. This explosion of corporation chartering began to happen during the financial revolution of the early 1790s, but it was implicit in the program Hamilton had begun to formulate a decade earlier. Old Europe with a considerable lag could only emulate it.

The Political Economy of Reversals

In the United States, the first and second central banks were killed, to the detriment of an efficient financial system and probably to the detriment of U.S. financial stability and economic growth, by the very forces of federalism and balances of power that had encouraged financial development.

The first central bank was killed despite a Republican administration of Madison and Gallatin that wanted it to continue. This was a case of weak leadership. Gallatin in 1809 argued strongly for the utility of the Bank to the government and the country and made a series of suggestions for amending the charter to address various concerns. The concerns included the Bank's then majority foreign ownership, the lack of a bonus payment to the government in the original charter, the lack of interest payments by the Bank on government deposits, and the lack of a provision requiring the Bank to lend the government three-fifths of its capital "whenever required." Gallatin said that all of these could be easily remedied in a new charter. He called for increasing the stock to $30 million, with $5 million of the additional $20 million reserved for citizens of the United States, and the remaining $15 million to be subscribed by states wishing to do so, with the promise that these states would get branches of the BUS if they wished. He also suggested that the federal government and subscribing states be allowed to appoint some of the Bank's directors. These were reasonable suggestions, and many of them found their way into the second BUS charter a few years later.[38]

In the 1811 debates over charter renewal, there were echoes of the constitutionality argument Madison himself had raised in 1791, an argument in which he no longer believed. But the determining factor was the interests of state politicians and state bankers, who were far more numerous by 1811 than in 1791. State politicians in the absence of a BUS could charter more banks and have more control of American banking. State-chartered banks, without a BUS, would be free of a competitor and a regulator, and they might well be able to take over the banking business of the federal government. Such interests determined the outcome, by the slenderest of margins, in 1811. George Clinton, the antifederalist vice president, had to break a tie vote in the Senate to prevent recharter of the BUS. The absence of the BUS was sorely felt in the War of 1812, and a second BUS was chartered in 1816 with the support of many of its 1811 opponents.

The second BUS, whose constitutionality was reaffirmed by the Supreme Court in the case *McCulloch v. Maryland* in 1819, was killed in 1832 by Andrew Jackson's presidential veto, an instance of strong but misguided leadership, after the House and Senate had decided that it should continue, by votes of 107–85 and 28–20.[39] The interests of state politicians and bankers were if anything even more important in 1832 than in 1811. There is also evidence that Jacksonian politicians at the federal level hoped with the veto to obtain a central bank that they would control after Director Nicholas Biddle's bank was gone. The bank veto of 1832 ushered in an era of financial and economic instability that bedeviled the United States for a decade, and an increasingly problematic currency system that would not be reformed until the 1860s, when the federal government once again assumed greater control over U.S. monetary and banking arrangements.[40]

The United States without a central bank, but with a number of less effective substitutes for a central bank, suffered more financial instability than other leading nations into the twentieth century. Financial crises, which hardly occurred in the years from 1789 to 1836, happened with some regularity in 1837, 1857, 1873, 1884, 1893, and 1907. The last of these crises was enough to bring about change. In 1913–14, the United States created the Federal Reserve System, which can be thought of as the Third Bank of the United States. The Fed corrected what might be regarded as design flaws in the first and second Banks. For example, the Fed did not compete with other banks, and it was effectively controlled by the U.S. government rather than its stockholders and managers appointed by stockholders. Unlike the First and Second Banks, the Fed has persisted.

In the 1990s, interstate banking—such as was once provided by the First and Second BUS—returned to the United States. One can thus argue that the original Hamiltonian architecture of the U.S. financial system, after suffering some damage in the financial reversals of the 1810s and 1830s, gradually has been restored. Key improvements came in the 1860s, the 1910s, and the 1990s.

Conclusion

The U.S. case surely affirms the idea that limited government, federalism, and separation of powers can be positive structural arrangements to foster rapid financial development, and therefore a higher rate of economic growth. In a comparative context, by the 1820s the United States may well have had the most "state-of-the-art" financial system of any nation, and its rate of growth, total and per capita, likely exceeded that of any other country.

Nonetheless, the United States suffered reversals of financial development in the 1810s and 1830s, and these reversals can be traced to the ways in which the limited government, federalism, and separation of powers operated in this early period of U.S. national history. Thus, the U.S. case may warn us not to jump too quickly to a conclusion that such political arrangements constitute "market-preserving federalism" and foster effective finance and economic growth, whereas others do not. The U.S. experience was more complex than that. If anything, it argues that leaders who understand finance and its relationship to growth, and who are also skilled in getting things done politically, may matter just as much as political structures in producing good outcomes. Hamilton was such a leader, and there were others before and after him in a variety of political systems. Examples are Walpole in eighteenth-century Britain, Matsukata in nineteenth-century Japan, and Goh Keng Swee in twentieth-century Singapore.[41] In the United States itself, one could also contrast, for example, the ineffective leadership of the Federal Reserve System during the Great Depression of 1929–33, and again in the Great Inflation of the 1970s, with its far more effective leadership in the 1950s and 1960s, and again from the 1980s to the present. Political structures matter, but so also does leadership within those structures.

Notes

1. See Weingast (1995). Weingast makes a good point. Federalism can help to preserve markets, but it also can hinder their extension (see Sylla 1991). And—equally important—federalism encourages experimentation and the discovery of best practice (see Sylla 2000). I think Weingast takes it too far, however, when citing the cases of Argentina, Brazil, and India as "federal systems but not market-preserving federal systems." He says, "In all of these countries, the political authority of the national government compromises the independence of local political authority" (1995, p. 28). At least in the case of Argentina, it is arguable that the independence of local political authority compromises the authority of the national government. This chapter, in the spirit of Alexander Hamilton, can be viewed as an argument that an imbalance in favor of local (state) authority, such as existed in the United States before the Constitution of 1787, and continued in some ways from 1801 to 1861, can be as damaging to markets, economic growth, and national security as an imbalance in favor of national authority.

2. Wright (2003); Haber (2004).

3. See Rajan and Zingales (2003).

4. Sylla (1998, 2002); and Rousseau and Sylla (2003, 2005).

5. For the Dutch case, see t'Hart et al. (1997); and de Vries and van der Woude (1997). For the British case, see Dickson (1967); and Brewer (1988). For the French case, see Murphy (1997).

6. Davis (2004) indicates a fairly steady expansion of industrial output at a rate of approximately 5 percent per year over the whole period. There was no gradual acceleration of this key component of the modern sector. The gradual accelerations often found in broad measures such as the gross domestic product (GDP) and gross national product (GNP) for modernizing economies appear to result from modern economic sectors, initially small, growing at high rates and gradually coming to dominate the economy.

7. A notable exception is Ferguson (1961, chap. 4).

8. Syrett's (1961–87) *Papers of Alexander Hamilton*, hereafter cited as PAH.

9. PAH, 2:400–418.

10. Ibid., 2:604–35.

11. Ibid., 2:645–46.

12. The full report, with editors' introductory notes and Hamilton's appendices, is in ibid., 6:51–181.

13. For accounts of the discrimination issue, see McDonald (1982, chap. 8); and Chernow (2004, chap. 15).

14. See "The Defence of the Funding System," an essay of July 1795 that was never finished, in PAH, 19:1–73.

15. Ellis (2000, chap. 3).

16. McDonald (1982, chap. 8).

17. PAH, 2:669–74.

18. Ibid., 18:46–148.

19. Smith (2000, book 5, chap. 3).

20. Wallis, Sylla, and Grinath (2004).

21. McDonald (1982, chap. 9).

22. Hammond (1957, chap. 4).

23. "Report on a National Bank" of December 1790, including editors' notes and drafts, is in PAH, 7:237–342.

24. "Mint Report" of January 1791, with editors' notes and drafts, is in ibid., 7:463–607. Jefferson's letter to Hamilton after his advance look at the report is on p. 451.

25. Quoted by Wright (1996, p. 144).

26. Davis (1917, vol. 2, chap. 2).

27. See Sylla, Legler, and Wallis (1987); and Wallis, Sylla, and Legler (1994).

28. Wright (2003).

29. Haber (2004).

30. Michie (2003).

31. Bayley (1884).

32. Banner (1998, chaps. 5, 7, 8).

33. Sylla, Wilson, and Wright (2006).

34. See Banning (1978).

35. Banner (1998, chap. 6).

36. Ellis (2000, chap. 3).

37. Banner (1998, chap. 6) summarizes the evidence on early nineteenth-century corporate chartering by U.S. states.

38. Albert Gallatin, "Report of the Secretary of the Treasury on the subject of a National Bank," made to the Senate, March 2, 1809, in Clarke and Hall (1967, pp. 116–20).

39. To say that Jackson was misguided in vetoing Congress's bill to recharter the BUS is, of course, a judgment. But it is a judgment supported by the advent in 1913–14 of the Federal Reserve System, which reversed Jackson's action by reinstituting a central bank chartered by Congress. Similarly, a conference commentator on an earlier version of this chapter argued that Hamilton failed to design a financial system that could be sustained politically. In the short run, yes. But in the long run, no, as the chapter now proceeds to argue.

40. Hammond (1957).

41. A conference commentator doubted that leadership mattered much. If, say, Hamilton had been killed leading the final bayonet charge at Yorktown, given that the United States had instituted "market-preserving federalism," someone else would have led a similar financial revolution. A response might be that Hamilton, of course, had a lot to do with creating market-preserving federalism in the United States and that federalism in nations such as Argentina, Brazil, and India did not preserve markets or produce a Hamilton-type financial innovator.

References

Banner, Stuart (1998). *Anglo-American Securities Regulation: Cultural and Political Roots, 1690–1860*. Cambridge, UK: Cambridge University Press.

Banning, Lance (1978). *The Jeffersonian Persuasion: Evolution of a Party Ideology*. Ithaca, NY: Cornell University Press.

Bayley, Rafael (1884). "History of the National Loans of the United States." In *Tenth Census of the United States, 1880*, vol. 7: *Wealth, Taxation, and Public Debt*. Washington, DC: Government Printing Office.

Brewer, John (1988). *The Sinews of Power: War, Money, and the English State, 1688–1783*. New York: Knopf.

Chernow, Ron (2004). *Alexander Hamilton*. New York: Penguin.

Clarke, Matthew St. Clair, and David A. Hall (1967). *Legislative and Documentary History of the Bank of the United States, Including the Original Bank of North America*. New York: A. M. Kelley.

Davis, Joseph H. (2004). "An Annual Index of U.S. Industrial Production, 1790–1915." *Quarterly Journal of Economics* 119: 1177–1215.

Davis, Joseph Stancliffe (1917). *Essays in the Earlier History of American Corporations*. 2 vols. Cambridge, MA: Harvard University Press.

de Vries, Jan, and Ad van der Woude (1997). *The First Modern Economy*. Cambridge, UK: Cambridge University Press.

Dickson, P. G. M. (1967). *The Financial Revolution in England*. London: Macmillan.

Ellis, Joseph J. (2000). *Founding Brothers: The Revolutionary Generation*. New York: Knopf.

Ferguson, E. James (1961). *The Power of the Purse: A History of American Public Finance, 1776–1790*. Chapel Hill: University of North Carolina Press.

Haber, Stephen (2004). "Political Institutions, Bankers, and Economic Growth: Evidence from the United States and Mexico." Working paper, Stanford University.

Hammond, Bray (1957). *Banks and Politics in America, from the Revolution to the Civil War*. Princeton, NJ: Princeton University Press.

McDonald, Forrest (1982). *Alexander Hamilton: A Biography*. New York: Norton.

Michie, Ranald (2003). "Banks and Securities Markets." In Douglas Forsyth and Daniel Verdier, eds., *The Origins of National Financial Systems: Alexander Gerschenkron Reconsidered*. London and New York: Routledge.

Murphy, Antoin Murphy (1997). *John Law: Economic Theorist and Policy-Maker*. Oxford, UK: Oxford University Press.

Rajan, Raghuam, and Luigi Zingales (2003). "The Great Reversals: The Politics of Financial Development in the Twentieth Century." *Journal of Financial Economics* 69: 5–50.

Rousseau, Peter L., and Richard Sylla (2005). "Emerging Financial Markets and Early U.S. Growth." *Explorations in Economic History* 42: 1–26.

——— (2003). "Financial Systems, Economic Growth, and Globalization." In M. Bordo et al., eds., *Globalization in Historical Perspective*. Chicago: University of Chicago Press.

Smith, Adam (2000). *The Wealth of Nations*. Modern Library Classics. New York: Modern Library.

Sylla, Richard (2002). "Financial Systems and Economic Modernization." *Journal of Economic History* 62: 277–92.

——— (2000). "Experimental Federalism: The Economics of American Government, 1789–1914." In S. L. Engerman and R. E. Gallman, eds., *The Cambridge Economic History of the United States*, vol. 2: *The Long Nineteenth Century*. Cambridge, UK: Cambridge University Press.

——— (1998). "U.S. Securities Markets and the Banking System, 1790–1840." *Federal Reserve Bank of St. Louis Review* 80: 83–98.

——— (1991). "The Progressive Era and the Political Economy of Big Government." *Critical Review* 5: 531–58.

Sylla, Richard, John Legler, and John Joseph Wallis (1987). "Banks and State Public Finance in the New Republic: The United States, 1790–1860." *Journal of Economic History* 47: 391–403.

Sylla, Richard, Jack Wilson, and Robert E. Wright (2006). "Integration of Trans-Atlantic Capital Markets, 1790–1845." *Review of Finance* 10: 613–44.

Syrett, Harold C., ed. (1961–87). *The Papers of Alexander Hamilton.* 27 vols. New York: Columbia University Press.

t'Hart, Marjolein, et al. (1997). *A Financial History of the Netherlands.* Cambridge, UK: Cambridge University Press.

Wallis, John Joseph, Richard Sylla, and Arthur Grinath III (2004). "Sovereign Debt and Repudiation: The Emerging-Market Debt Crisis in the U.S. States, 1839–1843." NBER Working Paper 10753.

Wallis, John Joseph, Richard Sylla, and John Legler (1994). "The Interaction of Taxation and Regulation in Nineteenth Century U.S. Banking." In Claudia Goldin and Gary D. Libecap, eds., *The Regulated Economy: A Historical Approach to Political Economy.* Chicago: University of Chicago Press.

Weingast, Barry R. (1995). "The Economic Role of Political Institutions: Market-Preserving Federalism and Economic Development." *The Journal of Law, Economics, and Organization* 11: 1–31.

Wright, Robert E. (2003). "Early U.S. Financial Development in Comparative Perspective: New Data, Old Comparisons." Paper presented at NBER Conference, "Developing and Sustaining Financial Markets, 1820–2000," Cambridge, MA.

——— (1996). "Banking and Politics in New York, 1784–1829." Ph.D. diss., SUNY–Buffalo.

Chapter 4

Answering Mary Shirley's Question, or

What Can the World Bank Learn from American History?

JOHN JOSEPH WALLIS

All successful modern economies are the result of 400 years of culture and history that shaped their development.

—Douglass C. North

Does that mean that developing countries today are doomed to wait 400 years before they get the right institutions and can develop?

—Mary M. Shirley

The conversation between Doug North and Mary Shirley took place at the conference in Traverse City, Michigan, in July 2003 that led to this book. Mary's question is as daunting as Doug's assertion is sweeping. This chapter focuses on a fragment of the answer to Mary's question: How important were British culture and history to financial developments in the early United States? The obvious answer is "very important." Yet financial sector development in the United States took a different path from that of Britain. A case can be made for the argument that American financial innovation led British innovation by the mid-nineteenth century (see Richard Sylla's chapter in this volume) and that institutional differences were the result of active government policy rather than the absence of government policy. Very quickly after independence Americans moved down a different path.

If America's path was determined by 400 (200?) years of history and culture, then we expect to see roughly similar institutions emerging throughout the United States. We don't. The interstate differences in American financial systems provide important clues about the inevitability of institutional development, or lack thereof, in the United States. Upon closer examination, the institutions that are similar across states tend to emphasize the bad, rather than the good, aspects of government policies for financial markets. The historical predisposition brought from England apparently predisposed Americans to pursue bad policies.[1] Not until 50 years after the second national constitution was written in Philadelphia did American state governments straighten out their financial institutions. As the subtitle of this chapter hints, the United States faced significant obstacles in developing modern financial systems, including their historical and cultural predispositions. Their British inheritance did not inevitably lead American states to adopt the right policies. The World Bank does have something to learn from American history, as nondeveloping countries around the world today still struggle with the problems that the United States had solved by 1850.

Answering Mary's question with regard to financial markets requires thinking about two framing issues. First, what are the nature of economic development and the government's role in promoting or retarding it? The following section lays out a general approach to economic development, stressing the importance of markets and the critical role of open access and free entry. This framework leads directly to the question of how the United States established free entry into financial markets. Second, what are the nature and functions of banks? The typical model of the banking system focuses on its role in intermediating capital markets to provide funds for long-term investments. There is nothing wrong with the model conceptually, but it doesn't describe well the functions banks actually performed in early nineteenth-century America. The second section examines the role of banks early in the development process, with a particular emphasis on the provision of short-term trade credit. Understanding how banks worked enables us to understand why states wanted banks and provides a framework for understanding some of the regional peculiarities of early American banking.

The third section traces the development of early American banking. States wanted banks, but that had little or no relationship to wanting free entry in banking. States began creating banks through special legislative charters. States tended to limit entry in order to maximize the amount of revenue extracted from the bankers. Limited entry created economic rents, and bankers were willing to pay states for access to the rents. Corporations received entry limits as an integral part of the enticement to provide the public service.[2] Although state banking policies were far from homogenous, the general trend was not toward the kind of open-access institutions that promote development.

The deliberate creation of economic rents as a tool of public policy was part of the New World's European cultural inheritance. The policy created enormous political difficulties for American governments. State constitutions, from 1776 onward, required state governments to implement an open-access political system based on republican representation and a broad suffrage. Empowered voters wanted economic development. Promoting economic development by creating privileged private corporations was fundamentally inconsistent with an open-access political system. Entry was open in the political system and closed in the economic system. Yet no other development model existed. States resolved the contradiction in the 1840s by requiring open-access economic institutions and embedding those requirements in constitutional mandates. The new policy produced "free banking" in the financial sector, where "free" refers to entry restrictions—free banks were still regulated. In the larger economic context, free entry was produced by general incorporation acts that allowed entry into the corporate form through an administrative procedure. Free banking systems were not the financial system that today's banking experts recommend. But the economic flaws in the free banking systems were of secondary importance. Free entry was a solution to a political, not an economic, problem.

The closing sections trace developments after the 1840s, in particular the failure of New England and the southern states to adopt constitutionally mandated free entry. Institutional developments were not uniform throughout the United States. In the case of the South, their peculiar institutions (to borrow a phrase) appear to have had significant long-run negative impacts on the development of their economies. Americans did have institutional options; 400 years of history did not determine the institutions they chose; and, as evidence, some states made the wrong choice.

A Theory of Economic Development: The Role of Limited Entry and Open Access

Every introductory economics class begins by teaching students how a price-making market allocates resources efficiently among producers and consumers.[3] The efficient operation of markets depends on competition, and competition depends on entry. Entry, or more generally, open access, is a fundamental property of efficient markets.[4] In premodern economies, and in most nondeveloping economies in the modern world today, entry is limited. The focus, therefore, is on how the United States came to mandate free entry into banking.

The focus on free entry may seem a bit odd. For most of the twentieth century, economic and financial historians criticized nineteenth- and early twentieth-century American states for producing too many banks.[5] Unit banking in some states and free banking in most states produced a plethora of small banks extremely susceptible to liquidity crisis. Banking panics are a persistent feature of American business cycles up to 1933, and much of the blame for them can be laid at the feet of the free-entry banking system.

Such criticisms are valid, but partial. The criticisms ignore the political and economic circumstances in which free banking came about. They implicitly assume that the United States would have gotten the "right" number of banks in the absence of free banking. They assume that entry into banking would *not* have been controlled by politicians for political ends. As we will see, the historical record suggests that entry into banking would have been limited, and limited for political purposes, had it not been for free banking.

On a larger scale, the movement to free entry in banking occurred simultaneously with a movement toward open entry in other areas of the economy. Although the famous Free Banking Act of New York was passed in 1838, the wave of free banking laws resulted from constitutional changes implemented in the 1840s.[6] States wrote new constitutions or amended old ones to require that state legislatures pass general incorporation acts that enabled firms to obtain a corporate charter through an administrative process. General incorporation took the creation of corporations out of the hands of legislatures and dramatically reduced the rents that could be created by a "special" charter. New York mandated general incorporation in its constitution of 1846 and then enacted "more than thirty general incorporation statutes between 1846 and 1857."[7]

Although it can be argued that the United States had de facto if not de jure free entry in many sectors of the economy before the 1840s, the history presented in the next section shows that free entry was not the default policy in banking. The American tendency to allow free entry emerges most strongly as an exercise of the right of individuals to assemble and thus to form cooperative associations at their pleasure. Free entry, however, did not happen automatically. The political and legal framework supporting free entry had to be deliberately constructed. The most formal form of support for private organizations was the corporation charter, but American state governments supported many types of organizations in many ways.[8]

It is critically important for economic historians and social scientists to appreciate that without free entry, markets do not work nearly as well as they do with free entry. On the other hand, we cannot expect that voters and politicians firmly grasped the concept in 1800. The intellectual appreciation of the powerful effect of free markets on economic performance was not well understood in the early nineteenth century. Adam Smith published the *Wealth of Nations* in 1776, but there is no doubt that neither American nor British culture immediately internalized Smith's lessons or the general notion that free markets conveyed enormous social benefits. Free entry was not adopted in the 1840s because Americans understood that laissez-faire economic policies would make them all better off.

Americans also understood that politicians could use restrictions on economic entry to create rents. These rents were then available to bind the interests of the rent recipients to the current government. Elsewhere I have defined the use of rent creation for political purposes as "systematic corruption." [9] The Americans fought a revolutionary war in part because they believed that the British government was systematically corrupt. The British Crown used the creation of economic privileges—through the national debt, the creation of private joint stock companies, and the Bank of England—to systematically purchase influence in the House of Commons and erode the constitutional protection of British liberties. [10]

The political debate that erupted in 1791 between Federalists like Washington, Hamilton, and Adams and the nascent Democratic-Republicans like Madison and Jefferson over chartering the Bank of the United States and the assumptions of state debts was precisely about systematic corruption. In the "Report on the Public Credit" Hamilton claimed: "If all the public creditors receive their dues from one source . . . their interests will be the same. And having the same interests, they will unite in support of the fiscal arrangements of the government." [11] Not surprisingly, many Americans interpreted Hamilton's claims as an attempt to reinstitute the corrupt British system in the United States: Prime Minister Hamilton sitting at the center of a web of influence held together by grants of economic privilege (limited entry).

Early Americans were faced with a difficult problem. They wanted to promote economic development, but promoting development required banks for finance and canals for transportation. Americans knew from their British inheritance that promotion could be accomplished through the creation of special-purpose private corporations whose owners would perform the required public services in return for their private rents. They also understood that the creation of these economic rents threatened the very open-access political system that they tried to create in their constitutions. They feared that systematic corruption in politics would bring their experiment in democracy to a tragic end. In the words of the time, democracy would end up producing tyranny and slavery. [12] As we will see, early attempts to promote financial sector development heightened those fears. Free entry was not adopted for economic reasons. It was an economic solution to a political problem.

What Do Banks Do?

We all know that banks gather the funds of small (and perhaps not so small) depositors who are risk averse, seek liquidity, and lack specialized information and then invest those funds in large, long-term, and perhaps risky, investments about which the banks have detailed information. "Financial intermediation" is the primary function of banks. In a growing industrial economy, manufacturing requires large infusions of capital in order to invest in fixed plant and equipment that may not yield a return for a substantial period. A growing financial sector aids economic development by providing investment capital that individual savers cannot. In a Solow growth framework, better financial intermediation enables a rise in the capital/labor ratio, increasing the productivity of labor, raising incomes, and promoting economic growth. It would be nice if the story were true, as it implies economic development simply requires capital accumulation. To see why this story is not true of the United States in the early nineteenth century, we need look no farther than the answers to two questions: Where did most of the capital in the United States go? What did banks actually do?

Beyond any reasonable doubt the three most capital-intensive nonfinancial sectors of the American economy by 1850 were agriculture, transportation, and housing.[13] Agriculture was far and away the most important, particularly if we include the value of land as capital.[14] No one ever claimed that a lack of capital held up the development of American agriculture. Indeed, more of the nation's capital was tied up in the nation's farms than in any other investment in 1850. Manufacturing comes in a distant fourth in capital intensity. A number of studies have shown that early manufacturing firms, whether in the United States or the United Kingdom, financed their early formation and expansion with funds borrowed from family and friends and subsequently out of retained earnings. Not until much later in the process of industrialization, late in the nineteenth century in America, did manufacturing firms begin to finance long-term investment with large amounts of external capital raised from banks and financial markets. Bond and equity markets, for example, began by trading national and state government debt; then the stock of banks, insurance companies, and public utilities; then the bonds of railroads; and then the stock of railroads. It was not until the 1880s and 1890s that manufacturing firms used stock markets to raise significant amounts of funds in the form of bonds or stocks. Bank loans were an important part of working capital for manufacturing firms, but investment capital was not.

If early nineteenth-century banks did not funnel depositors' money into manufacturing, what were they doing? Although most banks took deposits, the banking system as a whole should not be characterized as a "deposit banking system." In 1837, the U.S. treasurer's report on banks showed 632 banks, with paid-in capital of $291 million, loans and discounts (assets) of $525 million, circulation (banknote issues that were the liabilities of banks) of $149 million, and deposit liabilities of only $127 million.[15] Of total bank liabilities of roughly $660 million, only a quarter were deposits made by bank customers. Most of the deposits that were made represented corresponding deposits of businesses and large customers of the bank who simultaneously had borrowed money from the bank. The banking system's ability to provide loans to the economy did not depend on mobilizing the resources of small, risk-averse, liquidity-seeking depositors.

Nor was bank lending tied up in long-term, illiquid investments. Out of over $600 million in assets in the banking system as a whole, only $12 million were held in stocks, $19 million in real estate, and $10 million in "other investments." Table 4.1 breaks down the assets and liabilities of the Bank of the United States (BUS) in March of 1836 and two later dates when the bank was rechartered as the Bank of the United States of Pennsylvania (BUSP). The BUS was not a typical bank, but its assets reflect the common pattern of bank holdings. Out of $73 million in total assets, the bank held discounted bills (short-term financial instruments with maturity of less than 90 days) to the total of $58 million; $6 million in specie; and $7 million in obligations of state banks and their notes. All of these assets were short term and could easily be sold in the open market (except during a financial panic). Of the $73 million in bank assets, $71 million were either in cash, specie, or easily liquidated short-term commercial paper.[16]

Early nineteenth-century bankers did not borrow large amounts from many small depositors and then lend funds out in large, illiquid loans and thus make their profits on the difference in interest rates on deposits and loans. These bankers risked their own capital (and the capital of their investors); leveraged that capital by issuing banknotes that were the bank's liabilities; and invested the lion's share of their funds in short, quickly maturing, low-risk commercial loans to finance commerce. This was the model of early American banking. The primary function of banks was to make short-term loans to finance the movement of goods from producers to consumers.

Two question arise. If banks were not lending for long-term investment, why were Americans (and their state governments) so eager to have banks? What happened when banks, as they sometimes did, followed the textbook policy of making large, illiquid, long-term investments?

TABLE 4.1

Assets of the Bank of the United States, March 3, 1836;
April 1, 1839; and March 1, 1841

(in thousands of dollars)

	1836	1839	1841
Assets			
Bills discounted			
on personal security	20,148	12,991	14,404
on other security	17,386	18,815	3,071
on bank stock	3,061	296	0
Domestic bills of exchange	17,751	7,446	2,638
Bills receivable for post notes	0	306	0
Total bills	58,345	39,854	20,115
Stock accounts	0	12,043	10,842
State bonds	0	5,645	20,305
Specie	6,224	3,070	862
Due from state banks	4,376	6,662	7,912
State banknotes	2,351	2,085	972
Other	2,551	5,482	8,910
Total assets	73,847	74,841	69,918
Liabilities			
Circulation	20,114	6,680	3,870
Post notes	0	4,891	6,105
Foreign liabilities	372	13,702	17,009
Due state banks	3,412	3,675	1,868
Due to depositors	3,711	4,474	2,210
Other	3,024	2,071	2,183
Total liabilities	30,633	35,493	33,245

SOURCE: Congressional Report 226, 29th Cong., 1st sess., 1846, appendix E, p. 442.
NOTES: Estimates of state bond holdings are taken from elsewhere in the report. "Foreign liabilities" includes the balance on various foreign accounts, the foreign exchange account, loans in Europe, and bonds in Europe.

People wanted banks for a simple reason: to get their goods to market. The primary function of banks was to discount commercial paper, primarily bills of exchange and similar bills. Bills of exchange arose as a credit instrument to facilitate the physical movement of goods.[17] For example, think of wheat produced in Indiana to be sold in New York. There is considerable time involved in the shipment of wheat, a cost that neither the farmer nor the New York miller wants to bear. A bill is created in the exchange between the farmer, the miller, and their agents. A bank "discounts" the bill of exchange, purchasing the bill for banknotes, holding it until maturity, and in the process financing the sale and movement of the goods. Although financial costs are a small percentage of the New York price of wheat, they can be a substantial percentage of the profit that farmer makes from selling the wheat. A farmer who sells wheat for $1.00 a bushel that costs $.90 to grow can see all profits evaporate in transportation and financial costs if it takes \$.10 to get the wheat to New York. Even the small reduction in financial cost that ensued from having a local bank in Indiana could make an enormous difference to the profits of Indiana farmers. Increases in farm profits are reflected in the value of Indiana farmland. Rising land prices directly affect the public finances of the state of Indiana, whose primary source of revenue is a property tax on land. Not surprisingly, Indiana created a state bank to help farmers get their crops to market.[18]

The answer to the second question is also straightforward. "Putting all your eggs in one basket" is a risky investment strategy. Commercial banks did not invest in long-term, illiquid loans for precisely that reason. But there were occasions on which states created banks precisely for the purpose of making long-term, illiquid investments. Most often, these were land banks that invested in mortgages. Chartering a land bank involved several problems. First, unlike a commercial bank whose services were likely to benefit a large number of constituents (even while making a small number of bankers and stockholders rich), a land bank benefited only those who were able to obtain mortgages. Second, because of the inherent riskiness of land banks, state governments often were the primary investors. Land banks were more prevalent in the South (although there had been a number of land banks in colonial New England). So the answer to the question of what happened when states chartered investment banks hinges on the experience of southern land banks. As we will see, it wasn't pretty.

Developments in Early American Banking

The national government's experience in banking can be described quickly. Two Banks of the United States were chartered, one in 1791 and the other in 1816. The first bank's charter expired in 1811 and was not renewed. The second bank's charter expired in 1836. Although charter renewal passed Congress in 1832, President Andrew Jackson vetoed the charter bill. The national banks were important. They were the biggest single banks in the country, they were the financial agent of the national government, and they performed a central (but not irreplaceable) role in making a market in state banknotes throughout the country. They do not figure in our story, however. After the second bank lost its charter in 1836, it was rechartered as the Bank of the United States of Pennsylvania (BUSP). After 1836 there were no nationally chartered banks to contend with.

States began chartering banks in the 1790s.[19] By 1837 there were 632 banks in operation (according to the secretary of the Treasury), at least one in every state. States varied enormously in their policies toward banks. One generalization holds true, however: until Michigan entered the Union in 1837 and legislated free banking, no state's initial banking policy allowed free entry. In New England and the Northeast, states began chartering banks and typically reserved a block of stock in each chartered bank for the state. Massachusetts, New York, Pennsylvania, and Maryland all acquired bank stock by donation to the state at the time of the chartering.[20] In the Southeast, South Carolina, Georgia, and later Alabama also took blocks of stock in the banks they chartered. States who owned large blocks of bank stock stood to gain larger dividends if the banks were profitable. Limiting entry increased bank profits and increased the dividends the state received. The promotion of economic development through the creation of special privileges and limited entry immediately came into conflict with the stated constitutional goals of promoting open political and economic access.

In the 1800s and 1810s, the dynamics of the contradiction played out differently in each state. In Massachusetts, dividends from early banks led the state to create a large state bank, the Bank of the Commonwealth of Massachusetts. It was capitalized at $3 million and chartered in 1812. It was easily the largest bank in the state. In order to ensure the bank's profitability, Massachusetts imposed a tax on the capital stock of all banks. Within a few years, however, the state realized that it earned more on the tax on bank capital than it did on bank dividends. The state then sold off its bank stock and relied on the tax on bank capital for state revenues. By the 1820s, Massachusetts was receiving more than half of state revenue from the tax on bank capital, owned no bank stock, and had adopted de facto free entry into banking. Maximizing the number of banks was the easiest way for Massachusetts to maximize the amount of bank capital and its revenues from the capital tax. Connecticut, Rhode Island, and Maine (split from Massachusetts in 1820) also taxed bank capital. These states had a fiscal incentive to maximize the number of banks and the amount of bank capital. In 1837, these four states had 273 out of the nation's 626 banks.[21] By the early 1830s, New England states had de facto but not de jure free banking. Anyone who wanted a charter received one under the existing charter form.[22]

Pennsylvania and New York followed different paths. Pennsylvania came to rely on fees generated by issuing bank charters and bank dividends as a major source of revenue. The state deliberately limited the number of banks that received charters in order to maximize revenues from the sale of charters. In the 1820s and 1830s, Pennsylvania received over a quarter of state revenues from bank charter fees.[23] In New York, the state also regulated entry. In 1820, the state passed a general regulatory act, which

stipulated the form of bank charters. The Albany Regency, the political machine headed by Martin Van Buren, used bank chartering as a tool of political control. Only the Regency's friends could obtain charters; however,
the Regency lost control of the state government in the election of 1837.
New York adopted its famous free banking law in 1838, under a Whig-
dominated legislature.[24]

For a number of historical and geographic reasons, the northeastern part
of the country was more urban, was more oriented toward domestic and
international trade, and had more banks. Table 4.2 gives the number of
banks and paid-in bank capital by state in 1837. New England had 304 of
the 626 banks in the country, the Mid-Atlantic states had 205 banks, and
the remainder of the country only 118.

Banks in the South and West tended to be larger, more heavily capitalized
(although there is some question about how much of the capital was actually
paid in to the bank), and much more likely to be closely connected to the state.
Of the $115 million in bank capital in southern and western states in 1837,
perhaps as much as $60 million had been invested by state governments.[25]
There were monopoly, or near-monopoly, state banks in Indiana, Missouri,
Illinois, Alabama, and Arkansas.[26] Banks owned completely or largely by state
governments dominated the banking systems in Kentucky, Florida, Mississippi, and Tennessee—these four states also chartered other banks in which
the state did not invest. States throughout the West and South either prohibited entry altogether by creating a monopoly state bank(s) or created a few
banks with enormous advantages over their competitors because of the scale
of state investment and the state's financial patronage.

No American state before 1837 started with a free-entry banking policy,
and by 1837 only the New England states and Michigan had de facto or de
jure open entry. New York still restricted bank entry to the politically connected. Pennsylvania still limited entry to squeeze out charter fees. Indiana,
Illinois, Alabama, Missouri, and Arkansas established monopoly state banks.
Florida, Mississippi, Louisiana, Kentucky, and Tennessee invested substantial state funds in one or more banks. Although they granted charters to
other banks, the state banks dominated the financial system. Florida, Mississippi, Louisiana, and Arkansas had all established land banks.

The northwestern states were not noticeably more liberal in charter
policy than the southern states. Southern states were more likely to charter
land banks with state investment, but southern states were more willing to
charter other banks. The presence of land banks in the South proved to be
critical in the financial crisis that began in 1839. Whether the important
effects of land banks on state finance reflected ex ante or ex post influences

TABLE 4.2
Number of banks and paid-in bank capital by state, 1837

Region	State	No. of banks	Paid-in capital (in dollars)
New England	ME	55	5,226,700
	NH	27	2,839,508
	VT	6	510,000
	MA	123	37,074,690
	RI	62	9,837,171
	CT	31	8,744,697
Mid-Atlantic	NY	98	37,101,460
	NJ	25	4,142,031
	PA	49	23,750,338
	DE	4	818,020
	MD	21	10,438,655
	DC	7	2,204,415
South	VA	5	6,731,200
	NC	3	2,525,000
	SC	10	8,636,118
	GA	16	11,438,828
	FL	4	2,046,710
	AL	3	7,572,176
	LA	16	36,769,455
	AR		0
	MS	9	12,872,815
	TN	3	5,092,665
	KY	4	7,145,326
	MO	1	250,000
Northwest	IL	2	2,014,760
	IN	1	1,585,481
	OH	32	9,247,296
	MI	9	1,400,000
	BUS		35,000,000
	Total	626	293,015,515

SOURCE: Treasurer's Report of 1841, U. S. Congress, House Document 111, 26th Cong., 2d sess.

will be considered in a later section. The land banks are important enough that they deserve a closer look.

Horror Stories

We rarely read histories of how the Americans screwed up their institutions and made serious mistakes. But they did. Four southern states invested heavily in land banks: Mississippi, Florida, Arkansas, and Louisiana. Conditions were unique in each state; indeed, Louisiana was quite different, yet all four states gave state bonds to private banks. Within a few years, the banks violated the terms of their charters, although often in purely technical ways.

All four states ultimately repudiated the bonds they issued in order to invest in banks. This section details the history of southern land bank investment.

Almost all southern state borrowing in the 1820s and 1830s was invested in land banks.[27] Private stock in these banks was purchased by a mortgage on the lands of the stockholders; the stock purchased was usually limited to half the value of the lands mortgaged.[28] Stockholders were then able to borrow from the bank to buy new lands as well. The state purchased its share of stock by issuing bonds.[29] The bank's liquidity came from sale of the state bonds; their primary assets were the private mortgages. In every case, the banks themselves were responsible for debt service on the bonds, although the details of the arrangements differed between banks.[30] In no case was a state directly responsible for paying interest on state bonds. In contrast, every northern state that borrowed to finance transportation investment was immediately liable for interest payments.[31]

The bank charters all included clauses to the effect that "the faith of this state be, and is hereby pledged, both for the security of the capital and interest." The charters often included this clause: "That to secure the payment of the capital and interest of said bonds, the subscribers shall be bound to give mortgage, to the satisfaction of the directors, on property, to be in all cases equal to the amount of their respective stock." [32] The second provision effectively attached the land of the stockholders as collateral for the state bonds and was critical in Louisiana.

The way land banks were set up created three problems when the banks began failing in 1839. First, the benefits of land banks were highly concentrated in the hands of the few wealthy individuals who held stock in the banks: "What right had a few hundred stockholders to make the whole people . . . and their posterity . . . groan under a load of debt for these institutions?" These banks clearly served the interests of elites, corrupt or not. Popular sympathies were not on the side of the bankers and stockholders.[33] Second, because the states purchased their stock with bonds given to the banks, the banks actually marketed the bonds. State restrictions on bond sales—the requirement that bonds be sold at par or better, for example—were often not honored by the banks. The par sales clauses provided a legal pretext for subsequent repudiation. Third, the banks had an incentive to overvalue lands. Directors represented stockholders, whose ability to purchase stock and get additional loans depended on the appraised value of their lands. When loans were based on overvaluations in a rising market, and then land prices fell after 1839, many stockholders found that the face value of their mortgages was greater than the current market value of their lands. They defaulted on their mortgages.[34] The banks were then unable to service the bonds, and the bondholders came to the states for their interest payments. The overvaluation of stockholders' land also contributed to the popular perception that banks and bankers were corrupt.

Mississippi was the most notorious repudiator. Throughout the 1820s, there was only one bank in the state, the State Bank of Mississippi. In 1830, the state issued a charter to the Planters' Bank. The state issued bonds to purchase $2 million of the bank's authorized capital of $3 million. The State Bank of Mississippi curtailed its business and eventually surrendered its charter, and the Planters' Bank become the state's largest bank and its fiscal agent. As stipulated in its charter, the Planters' Bank paid interest on the state bonds out of the dividends paid on the state's stock. The state chartered 24 new banks between 1833 and 1836, most of them in 1836 and 1837.[35] The state did not acquire an interest in any of these banks or issue any new debt. Many of the chartered banks never began operation; the Treasury counted only 9 banks in operation in 1837 (see Table 4.2).

Both the banks and the state were hit hard by the Panic of 1837. In the midst of the turmoil, Mississippi considered plans for yet another land bank, the Union Bank, to be capitalized at $15.5 million financed by state bonds. The state constitution required that any law authorizing debt be passed at two consecutive sessions of the legislature. The original bill passed on January 21, 1837, and again on February 5, 1838.[36] The bill was then amended on February 15, 1838. The amended bill reduced the total state investment from $15.5 million to $5 million and stipulated that "said [state] bonds shall not be sold under their par value" (section 9). The act also reduced the amount that shareholders had to pay when they subscribed for their stock from $10.00 (10 percent of the $100.00 share value) to $2.50 in "current bills of the banks of undoubted solvency of this state" (section 19).[37] The amended bill passed the legislature only once, not twice. The state made over the bonds to the bank, which approached Nicholas Biddle, and on August 18, 1838, the whole lot was sold to the BUSP:

> In their eagerness to place their bank in operation the commissioners [of the Union Bank] either were hoodwinked by the shrewd financier or they connived with him in breaking their instructions. The contract specified that the bonds were to be paid in five equal installments; but that the interest began from the day of the sale. To make them negotiable abroad, they were made payable in England at the rate of four shillings six pence on the dollar.[38]

The constitutionality of the bond issue was already suspect because the amended act had not passed two sessions of the legislature and the contract reached with Biddle further put the bonds at risk. By selling bonds on credit, the state clearly did not receive par value, since interest began accruing from August 18, and the state did not receive payment until up to a year later. The sterling payment feature required the Union Bank to repay $2,189.92 in principal for every $2,000.00 it received.[39]

The loan commissioners representing the bank had hardly been hoodwinked; the bank received all five installments. Biddle, however, was under the impression that the Union Bank would use its resources "for the purpose of bringing back the state to a sound condition of currency."[40] The BUSP had acquired substantial holdings of stock in Mississippi and other southern banks in 1836 and 1837, and Biddle was quite interested in restoring the state of Mississippi banks.[41] When Biddle received the bonds in the fall of 1838, he quickly sent them to Europe, where some were sold and the rest hypothecated as security for loans raised by the BUS's agent, Samuel Jaudon.[42]

Instead of using its resources to relieve the situation of the existing banks, however, the Union Bank issued $2,600,000 in post notes payable in August 1839, that is, the Union Bank borrowed even more money. In 1839, the Union Bank refused to provide details about its financial condition to the state, in violation of its charter and Mississippi law. In July 1840, Governor McNutt proclaimed that the Union Bank had forfeited all of its banking powers and privileges because of its failure to pay specie, a proclamation the bank refused to acknowledge.[43] In December 1840, the bank provided information to the state indicating that it possessed $7,768,433.73 in assets, of which only $2,500,000.00 were providing any income to the bank; $1,280,000.00 of those assets were cotton notes. At that point the Bank had only $19,500 in demand notes in circulation and held mortgages of only $735,986.[44] Instead of acquiring $5,000,000 in mortgages to secure the state bonds, the Union Bank directors had spent $7,600,000 of borrowed funds (state bonds and post notes) with only $2,500,000 to show for it, and held almost no mortgages as security.

The Union Bank had been in operation for less than three years when it failed to meet the interest payment on the state bonds in 1841. The state never paid any interest on the Union Bank bonds and formally repudiated them on February 26, 1842. The reasons given by the state for repudiating were technicalities: the legislation had not been passed in a constitutional manner, the bonds were sold under a credit arrangement below par, and the final terms for paying interest in Britain in specie further violated the par sales provision.[45] These were truly technicalities, because the state's 11th amendment protections made it immune from creditors. But the real battle wasn't over technicalities; it began when the Union Bank refused to provide accurate information to the state: "The fact that the [bank] managers have smothered the important facts called for, proves that culpable mismanagement and selfish favoritism have characterized their operations."[46] In fact, the managers and directors of the Union Bank did steal from the state; they managed to turn $7,500,000 into $2,500,000 in just two years. The popular perception in Mississippi was that "we were robbed."[47] Interestingly, by 1845 Mississippi was collecting enough in property tax revenues to easily service the Union Bank bonds.[48] The state didn't repudiate because it was poor; it repudiated because the voters were mad.

In Florida, the bonds issued by the Union Bank of Florida were openly sold under par in Europe by the bank's agent, Colonel Gamble, and the bank's loan policies came under scrutiny immediately. Florida had been naive, it could never hope to service the bonds, and it too was probably robbed. The territory never paid any interest on the bonds and repudiated in 1842. When Florida repudiated, it claimed that, as a territory, it never possessed the legal power to issue the bonds in the first place.

In Arkansas, the state invested in two banks, the Real Estate Bank of Arkansas and the State Bank of Arkansas. Neither bank was a financial success, and both banks suspended payments on state bonds in 1841. After a lengthy lapse, Arkansas made some restitution on some of its bonds in 1869, but the state essentially repudiated the remainder of its debts.[49]

We know quite a bit about the operation of the Real Estate Bank. As a result of wrangling over repayment of the debt, the state accountants audited the bank's books in 1856; Worley has analyzed the *Report of the Accountants*.[50] In Arkansas, the Real Estate Bank was designed to benefit a small group of wealthy landowners. Stockholders had privileged borrowing rights at the bank: "The stockholder could not only borrow first but pay back last; stockholders could borrow for twenty years, nonstockholders for only ten. . . . Actually only 284 individuals became stockholders. The charter of the bank provided the legal foundation upon which a system of privilege was built which operated for the benefit of this small group."[51] In 1842, the stockholders owed the bank $1,499,671.90, and nonstockholders owed only $423,571.56.[52] There is clear evidence that the bank regularly allowed stockholders to purchase stock with mortgages based on overvalued assessments of land. The bank eventually foreclosed on mortgages for land that was appraised in 1837 at $856,335, which later sold for only $80,235.[53] Those stockholders were able to purchase 10 times as much bank stock as they could have had their lands been truly valued, and being stockholders enabled them to return to the bank for loans on new land purchases.

The evidence that the Real Estate Bank and the state government were controlled by a small group of interconnected families seems overwhelming. John Wilson was the Speaker of the House and first president of the Real Estate Bank.[54] The Sevier family provided a critical link: "Political control, and therefore bank control, was to a remarkable extent in the hands of a group of related families. The group's influence during the state banking period was centered in Sevier's political prestige. The related families were variously known as the 'Bourbon Dynasty,' 'Sevier's hungry kinfolks,' or simply as 'the family.'"[55] Just as in New York, bank chartering was a tool of political manipulation for the benefit of a small faction that controlled the political system. It was systematic corruption.

The ex ante corruption in the establishment of the Real Estate Bank played a critical role in the unwillingness of taxpayers to service the state debts ex post. In the wake of the state default, the *Arkansas State Gazette* commented: "We believe that the people of Arkansas would stand direct taxation *for State purposes* as cheerfully as any people in the Union; but that we should be taxed to pay the debts of the most *aristocratic* monopoly of land holders in the United States is unbearable."[56]

In Louisiana, on the other hand, the integrity of the banks was never called into question nor the methods by which the bonds had been marketed. The charter of the Bank of Louisiana included the clause pledging the credit of the state but not the clause securing the state bonds by the mortgages of the stockholders. The charters of the Consolidated Association of Planters, the Union Bank, and the Citizens Bank did include the security clause. When, in 1843, the banks were forced to suspend interest payments, Louisiana acknowledged its obligation to service the bonds issued on behalf of the Bank of Louisiana but required that all of the property of the stockholders in the Consolidated Association, the Citizens Bank, and the Union Bank be liquidated before the state meet its obligations to the bondholders.[57] The state enacted legislation in 1843 that enabled mortgagees to repay their mortgages with state bonds at face, rather than market, value. This enraged creditors outside Louisiana. Louisiana repudiated de facto rather than de jure; it never paid interest or principal on the $21,000,000 in bonds issued in favor of the three banks.

Two important implications can be drawn from the southern experience. First, just as the Albany Regency in New York used limits on entry in banking to create rents that were then used to keep a political faction in power, the Bourbon Dynasty in Arkansas used limited entry and abuse of the state's credit to keep a faction in political power. The Mississippi and Florida histories hint at similar patterns, but no one to my knowledge has unearthed a level of detail enabling us to see systematic corruption at work so clearly in those states. New York and Arkansas are states at one extreme of institutional developments in banking, but their examples are so tangible and concrete that it is inconceivable that people were not aware that systematic corruption posed a viable threat under the democratic constitutions adopted by American states. Martin Van Buren, architect of the Albany Regency, was secretary of state and vice president under Andrew Jackson and president from 1839 to1842. Van Buren, the "red fox of Kinderhook," was widely hailed as a political wizard, and it was impossible not to see the power of systematic political manipulation of the economy in his rise to power.

Second, the form of commercial banking adopted by most states produced banks focused on short-term commercial lending. Southern state land banks, however, failed in 1840 and 1841 because they invested state credit in one illiquid asset, land. When land prices fell after 1839, all these banks were in trouble. If we believe that the purpose of banks is to provide capital for long-term investment projects, and we advise the World Bank to advise governments to create banks to pursue specific lending strategies in narrowly defined industries or functions, those banks will inevitably fail just as southern land banks failed between 1839 and 1841.

The exception that proves the rule is the BUSP. After the bank lost its national charter in 1836 and was rechartered as a state bank, Nicholas Biddle, the bank's president, took the bank in a new direction. The BUSP began underwriting the issue of state debt, as described previously in Mississippi, and to take large positions in the stock of private corporations (mostly banks, railroads, and other transportation companies). Biddle even speculated in the cotton market. As Table 4.1 shows, by 1841 discounted bills fell to 29 percent of bank assets, whereas state bonds and private stocks rose to 44 percent of bank assets. The BUSP had become locked in to long-term, illiquid assets. When states' credit faltered after 1839 and states began defaulting on their debts in 1841, the BUSP found itself in possession of $20 million worth of illiquid state bonds that, in many cases, it could not legally sell for less than par! The market value of state bonds fell, and the BUSP went under.

The 1840s: Reaction and Constitutional Change

The default crisis of 1841 and 1842 engulfed the entire country. Florida, Mississippi, Louisiana, Arkansas, Illinois, Indiana, Michigan, Pennsylvania, and Maryland all suspended interest payments for a period of time. Florida, Mississippi, Louisiana, Arkansas, and Michigan repudiated all or part of their debts. New York, Ohio, and Alabama barely avoided default.[58] It was

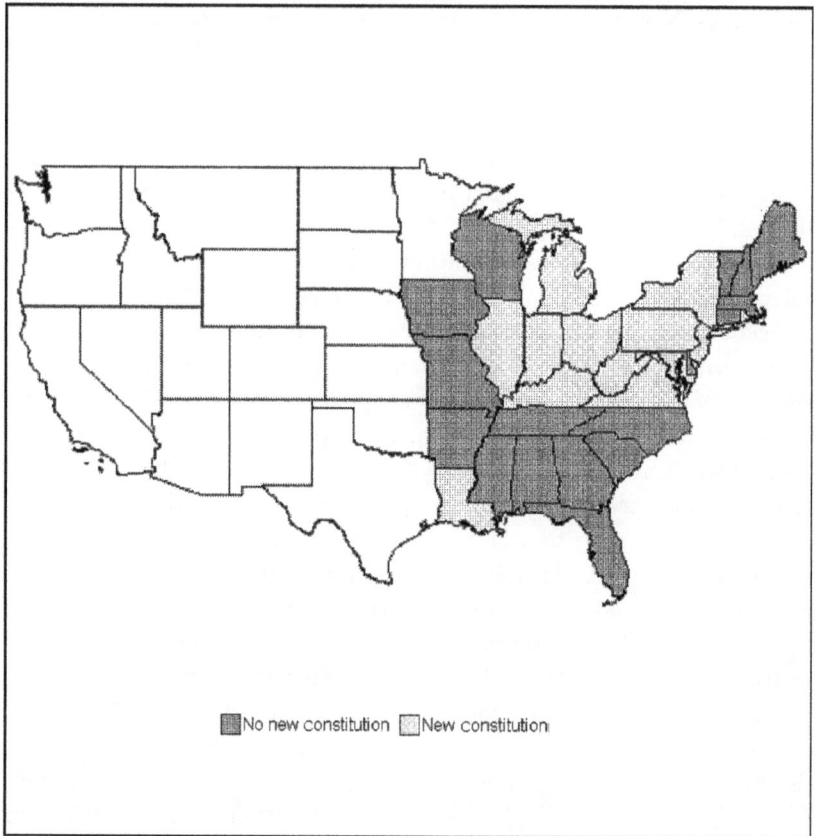

Figure 4.1   States with new constitutions, 1842–52

SOURCE: Wallis, John Joseph. NBER/University of Maryland State Constitution
Project. http://www.stateconstitutions.umd.edu.

an emerging markets financial crisis on the scale of the Asian crisis of the
1990s. The crisis was a turning point in American history, even though it is
usually overlooked in histories that focus on the national government. Between 1842 and 1852, 11 states wrote new constitutions, others amended
theirs, and the focus of constitutional change was the institutional structure
of the economy.[59] At the heart of the changes was the issue of entry, specifically, the creation of constitutional language mandating state legislatures to
pass general incorporation acts that allowed creation of corporations by an
administrative act. In banking, this produced free banking, but the change
was not limited to banking.

I have traced the constitutional changes and their causes elsewhere. I argue that the adoption of free entry was an explicit response to fears about systematic corruption.[60] State constitutional conventions adopted general incorporation in order to reduce rents. They saw the creation of economic rents as too tempting for a democratic political system, so they took the option off the table.

There is a curious geographic incidence of constitutional changes. Figure 4.1 maps the states that wrote new constitutions between 1842 and 1852. Writing a new constitution is defined as replacing an existing constitution. So Wisconsin and Iowa, who wrote their first constitutions, are not treated as writing new constitutions (Iowa did replace its constitution in 1857). Michigan, which wrote its first constitution in 1837, replaced it with a new constitution in 1850.[61] The figure exhibits a striking geographic pattern. Neither New England nor the South adopted new constitutions, with the exception of Rhode Island in New England and Louisiana in the South.

Not every state that adopted a new constitution adopted general incorporation. General incorporation laws were mandated in New Jersey, Louisiana, New York, Illinois, Michigan, Maryland, Indiana, Ohio, Iowa, California, and Wisconsin. Free banking was mandated in Illinois, Michigan, Indiana, Maryland, Wisconsin, and Ohio. Of course, it was already on the books in New York.[62] Why were constitutional change, mandated general incorporation, and free banking concentrated in a band of states from the Northeast to Northwest and not in the South or New England? There are a number of possible answers, which together form a consistent pattern.

NEW ENGLAND

New England states did not need to change their constitutions to mandate free entry. They had established de facto free entry in banking in the 1810s and 1820s. New England states had de facto general incorporation as well. As the Handlins' document in *Commonwealth* shows, by the 1830s Massachusetts had come to view widespread access to the corporate form, and associated free entry into most lines of business, as a function of responsible government. Kessler counts over 3,000 corporations in New England before 1837 and another 3,000 by 1860.[63] When Massachusetts finally adopted a free banking law in 1851, only one new bank was created; the state already had free banking. When New York adopted free banking in 1838, within two years 90 new free banks were chartered.

The New England states created free economic entry by legislation. Voters and politicians did not feel the need to guarantee free entry by constitutional means. In fact, as late as 1900 Massachusetts (and Rhode Island) still did not have constitutional mandatory general incorporation, the only states without constitutional mandates.[64]

THE REST OF THE NORTH

Unlike New England, which moved to de facto free entry in banking well before the Panic of 1837, states throughout the rest of the northern tier were still wrestling with the problem of promoting economic development through the creation of private privilege. Banking in New York was a political matter. Banking in Pennsylvania was a fiscal matter. Banking in Maryland was dominated by a handful of Baltimore banks. Banking in Indiana, Illinois, Missouri, Kentucky, Tennessee, and Arkansas was dominated by a state-financed and -owned bank. There was no evidence that democratic legislatures naturally produced free entry in banking, nor was there any evidence that legislatures would do so anytime soon.

New York, Pennsylvania, Maryland, Ohio, Michigan, Indiana, and Illinois were all in deep financial trouble in the early 1840s as the result of investments in canals and railroads.[65] All of them had reason to be suspicious of project promoters—whether it was for a bank, canal, or railroad—who claimed that the state could provide financial or transportation infrastructure without raising taxes if only a special corporation were created or state debt issued. Categorical distrust, however, the complete prohibition of state investment or promotion, was too expensive. Many projects had turned out to be good investments, like the Erie Canal, the Ohio canals, and many banks in the Northeast.

These seven states changed their constitutions to include the following requirements:

1. Procedural debt restrictions that prevented states from issuing bonds unless tax increases sufficient to service the bonds were approved by a majority of voters and put into place before bonds were issued
2. Mandatory general incorporation and, in many states, outright prohibition of special incorporation

These changes were made at the constitutional level; state legislatures were not free to reverse or ignore them.

THE SOUTH

The South was clearly different. Louisiana was the only state in the South that adopted mandatory general incorporation or procedural debt restrictions. Virginia wrote a new constitution in 1850, but the issue in Virginia was reapportionment and suffrage, and the new constitution said nothing about corporations or debts.

The reason for the lack of southern constitutional change appears to have roots in the pre-1837 pattern of state investment, almost all of which was in land banks, as well as in the post-1837 behavior of the banks in which states had invested. These patterns were clearly "southern" and can be associated with a politically dominant slaveholding class, but it is not clear that southern constitutional developments were driven solely by slavery. That is an issue for another, and larger, inquiry.

As described earlier, most American banks were commercial banks. Their primary purpose was to facilitate commercial exchange. Throughout the northern and southern states, commercial banks played a central role in getting agricultural goods to markets in the urban centers and manufactured goods and imports to consumers in agricultural areas. Cotton dominated southern agriculture, and marketing the southern cotton crop was the focus of southern and northeastern commercial bankers, as well as British bankers.

Why then did southern states invest in land banks? Land banks were risky. Their assets were the mortgages pledged by the stockholders, assets whose value was likely to rise and fall in concert with the price of cotton. There was no portfolio diversification to minimize risk. The beneficiaries of land bank lending were a relatively small group of wealthy individuals who bought stock in the bank. As we saw, in Arkansas the very limited lending to a social elite crippled the willingness of voters to raise taxes to service state bonds issued to found the banks. Unlike northern commercial banks, which, with exceptions in Indiana and Illinois, were not financed with state bonds, southern land banks created concentrated benefits to a political elite and spread the default risk widely over all the taxpayers in the state. Southern states appeared to be systematically corrupt. A group of politicians created a set of economic benefits available to a small portion of the population in return for the support of a critical elite.

Ex post, taxpayers legitimately complained that they had been robbed by corrupt politicians and bankers who fleeced the states out of millions of dollars. The evidence in Mississippi and Arkansas seems undeniable, and in Florida it is quite suggestive. Louisiana finessed the issue by requiring the bondholders to exhaust their remedies against the stockholders of the banks before the state would acknowledge its obligations. Mississippi and Florida, and later Arkansas, simply repudiated their bonds.

In the North, taxpayers, voters, and politicians deliberated and concluded that the debt crisis was not produced by corrupt individuals but

from a fundamental flaw in their democratic systems. They remedied the
flaw by changing their constitutions.

In the South, there are two alternative explanations of why states did not
alter their constitutions. The first is that voters and politicians decided their
predicament was due to the peculation of a few unscrupulous bank promoters who hoodwinked voters and politicians alike into opening the state
treasury for the benefit of a few. These states saw nothing to fix in their
constitutions; they simply resolved never to borrow money again. Borrowing was not a terribly attractive option for Mississippi, Florida, and Arkansas anyway. As long as they remained in default and repudiation, national
and international credit markets were unlikely to lend to them under any
terms. The test case is Louisiana, which did borrow again in the 1850s to
build railroads. Louisiana was the only southern state to implement constitutional changes, and it was able to borrow.

The second interpretation is that southern states were systematically corrupt, ex ante and ex post. A small group of politicians created a benefit for
a well-defined and identifiable elite: large landowners who owned slaves.
The politicians created an infrastructure investment that benefited only that
group and limited entry into the benefits by distributing stock in the bank
only to the politically connected. When the states repudiated the debts, ab-
solving taxpayers of the necessity to raise taxes, but also preventing the state
from reentering credit markets for the foreseeable future, they released the
political elites who had mortgaged their lands from being forced to redeem
their debts.

Southern states did not adopt free entry in banking or other lines of
business. To argue the fine points of whether the failure to adopt constitutionally mandated free entry crippled the southern economy is not the
subject of this chapter. The economies of southern states lagged behind
northern economies until the 1930s. Conclusions about causation are impossible to draw because slavery and the Civil War are co-linear with the
southern constitutional patterns.

Conclusions

We asked at the outset whether the inheritance of British institutions and
culture, particularly British traditions regarding incorporation and banking,
played a critical role in the formation of a financial system in the United
States. The evidence seems decisive, and the answer is no.

Regulation and chartering of banks quickly came under the control of
state governments. The national government played a role in banking, and

the first and second Banks of the United States were important financial institutions while they lasted. But banking policy was shaped decisively by state governments, not the national government. Even more important, the critical institutional element, controls on entry, always remained completely in the hands of state governments.

State banking policy was inconsistent with a strong cultural heritage from Britain. The British had, along with the Dutch, the world's best financial system in 1790. Many, though not all, Americans admired the British system and wished to emulate it. Initially, however, American states emulated the worst aspect of the British system: limited entry and political manipulation of entry for public financial gain. By the 1820s, New England states found a way to implement free entry that filled state coffers even faster than selling bank charters or collecting dividends. Other parts of the country were slow to follow. New York, Pennsylvania, and Maryland experimented with different ways to exploit the rents created by limiting entry into banking. In New York the result was a politically obnoxious manipulation of bank chartering to ensure the position of a political faction. In the West and South, states created monopoly state banks or heavily financed one or two state banks in competition with smaller private banks. American states did not inherit a predisposition to institutional financial structures destined to produce economic development.

In the 1840s, states throughout the northern part of the country reversed their course and adopted free entry into banking and into most lines of business. There is no indication they did this for economic reasons. Voters and politicians understood that allowing state legislatures to create private rents through limited entry posed serious problems for their democratic forms of government. General incorporation was an economic solution to a political problem. By eliminating the possibility of creating rents by mandating free entry, it was possible to short-circuit the process by which a political faction systematically corrupted the economy.

Southern states chose not to follow this path. Whether they chose not to because southern society was dominated by slave owners; or whether southern society was systematically corrupt; or whether southern society was systematically corrupt because of the presence of slave owners; or whether southerners simply chose not to interpret the events leading up to the default crisis of 1841 and 1842 in the same way that their northern brothers did is neither clear nor is it a question that we are capable of answering at this time. Nevertheless, the fact that southern states moved onto such a distinctive path raises serious questions about how determinative the British historical and cultural influences were in American financial development.

Institutional developments in the United States were the domain of state governments. If American states generally adopted institutions that promoted economic development because of our British heritage, then we have to explain why some American states did not develop those institutions. If one wishes to argue that British heritage mattered (as I do), but that distinct institutions developed out of that common heritage because conditions varied in different regions and states, then we find ourselves in the economic history equivalent of the nature/nurture debate. Regardless of how that argument is resolved, American history clearly shows that the starting point for an answer to Mary Shirley's question must be that 400 years of culture is not inevitably determinative. Of course, this leaves open the question of whether the British heritage was a prerequisite for any of the institutions that developed in the United States.

Can we answer Mary Shirley's question? Was Doug North right that economic growth only follows on 400 years of cultural and historical development? Does the World Bank have something to learn from American history about the institutional changes that encourage thriving markets and economic development? The American example points to four conclusions. First, although the British inheritance was important, it was not determinative. The influence of British institutions is certainly more subtle and complicated than the simple tests I have performed, but no clear American pattern emerges out of the British experience with respect to entry in banking. To the extent that state banking policies shared something from their common heritage, it was an antidevelopment policy: states tended to limit entry. Second, states quickly moved onto their own paths of institutional development. By the 1830s, state financial and banking systems varied widely. Third, the common response to the crisis of the 1840s was a uniquely American response. The response owed nothing to Britain. Americans moved to free entry in banking and every other substantial line of economic enterprise significantly before Britain did. When Americans got free entry, they took advantage of it, and the American economy took off.

Finally, there is hope in the American example. There are lessons to learn as well.

Notes

Doug North, Barry Weingast, Steve Haber, Dick Sylla, Karen Clay, and other participants at the conference, as well as the members of the Ohio State economic history seminar provided helpful comments.

1. That is "bad" in an ex post sense. The initial policies followed by

American states appear, in retrospect, to be ones that would have inhibited economic development had they continued in place for a long period of time. As we shall see, the policies changed.

2. Corporations sometimes received monopoly privileges in their charters. A government could still convey substantial market power through its chartering policy even if it did not formally grant a monopoly on entry to the chartered firm. The case of Pennsylvania, described in this chapter, is a clear case of limited entry, as described in Schwartz (1987) and Wallis, Sylla, and Legler (1994).

3. The ideas in this section are based on Wallis (2006) and the general framework developed in North, Wallis, and Weingast (2006).

4. Note that unlike zero transaction costs or well-defined property rights, entry is not just an assumption of the model. Entry is a deliberate policy choice that societies make.

5. See Redlich (1968) and Sylla's review article (1971) on the Soundness tradition.

6. For the history and chronology of free banking, see Shade (1972). For the constitutional changes that led to widespread general incorporation, see Wallis (2005).

7. Gunn (1988, p. 232). Gunn's entire chapter on general incorporation laws (see pp. 222–45), is relevant, as are Seavoy's (1982) and Hurst's (1970) entire books.

8. This is the theme of Handlin and Handlin (1969). For a consideration of public support for private organizations in early nineteenth-century America, see Wallis (2003b).

9. Wallis (2006).

10. For the general history of systematic corruption, see Bailyn (1967); Wood (1969); and Shalhope (1972). For the British system, see Robbins (1959); Weston (1965); and Pocock (1975).

11. See "Report on the Public Credit," in *American State Papers: Finance,* 1:15. See Ferguson (1961) for an analysis of how constitutional issues and the public debt interacted in Hamilton's thinking. For the events surrounding the emergence of competitive parties in the 1790s and the critical role played by the bank debate, see Banning (1978); McCoy (1980); and Wallis (2006).

12. The importance of the phrase "tyranny and slavery" is explained in its intellectual and historical context in Skinner (1998, pp. 36–57).

13. See Gallman (1992).

14. Including land as part of the capital stock is inappropriate for national income accounting. Only the value of land should be included. But when our goal is to understand the impact of financial intermediation on economic development, the value of land is critically important, because one function of banks may be to facilitate the transfer of land between owners, i.e., mortgage banking.

15. *Report from the Secretary of the Treasury,* 29th Cong., 1st sess., H. Doc.

226, 1846. Banks also held $37 million in specie and $12 million in "stock" (mostly state government bonds). The figures in the text are taken from the national summaries on pp. 1258–59.

16. As the table shows, by 1840 the BUSP had changed its asset portfolio and become heavily invested in loans to state governments and private corporations. The changing composition of the bank's assets played a central role in the bank's collapse in 1841.

17. See Rodgers (1995) and Neal (1991) for a description of how bills of exchange worked.

18. The fiscal interest of the state plays a key role in the adoption of specific government institutions. For an application of this idea specifically to Indiana in 1836, see Wallis (2003a), and more generally Heckelman and Wallis (1997). Wallis, Sylla, and Legler (1994) use the fiscal interest idea to explain the development of early nineteenth-century banking.

19. For a complete series on the dates at which states chartered individual banks and their authorized capital, see Fenstermaker (1965).

20. The bulk of this section is taken from Wallis, Sylla, and Legler (1994).

21. Ibid.

22. The New England states did not pass general incorporation acts, but they did pass general regulatory acts. A regulatory act specified the default structure of a corporation. The legislature could then create a new corporate charter by reference to the regulatory act. Regulatory acts did not prevent states from chartering special corporations with different privileges and structures, nor did it prevent states from limiting entry, as in the case of New York discussed later.

23. Wallis, Sylla, and Legler (1994).

24. The New York case has been studied in detail. See Benson (1961); Wallis, Sylla, and Legler (1994); and Bodenhorn (2006).

25. The $60 million is estimated simply by taking the amount of state debt issued to invest in banks. See Wallis, Sylla, and Grinath (2004).

26. The state was the primary owner/investor in both of the two banks in Illinois and the two banks in Arkansas (Arkansas is discussed in the next section). The state bank in Alabama dominated state finances and the banking system; see Brantley (1961).

27. See Sparks (1932, pp. 98–111) and the descriptions of individual states in McGrane (1935).

28. For a detailed description of land banks, see Sparks (1932, pp. 83–113).

29. In a few cases the state did not even own stock in the bank; it simply loaned the bonds to the bank in return for which the bank promised to service the bonds. This was the case in the most notorious case, the Union Bank of Mississippi.

30. For example, section 7 of the Mississippi charter of the Union Bank required that "both the capital and interest of the said bonds shall be paid by

said bank, at the times they shall severaly fall due." See *Laws of Mississippi*, Adjourned Session, January 21, 1837.

31. See the arrangements described in the charter of the Bank of Louisiana, *Laws of Louisiana*, 6th Legislature, 2nd sess., April 10, 1824, "An Act to incorporate the subscribers to the Bank of Louisiana," sections 7 and 8, pp. 100–102: "That if the dividends on the stock held by the state in the said bank, shall at any time be insufficient to pay the instalments of interests on the principal of said bonds, as the same may become due, that said bank shall supply such deficiency, and charge the same to the account of the state, and for the payment thereof the faith of the state is hereby pledged."

32. Both quotes are from the charter of the Union Bank of Mississippi, *Laws of Mississippi*, Adjourned session, January 21, 1837, the first clause quoted from section 5, p. 39, and the second clause from section 8, p. 40.

33. The quote is from the Florida territorial governor's address to the legislature recommending repudiation, *Florida Senate Journal*, 1841, pp. 12, 13, 17, as quoted in McGrane (1935, p. 238).

34. The apocryphal quote comes from a letter to Van Buren from Claiborne, dated April 10, 1837, which McGrane summarizes: "Mississippi was already engulfed in the throes of the panic of 1837; estates formerly valued at $30,000 were selling for $3,200; whole plantations were falling under the sheriff's hammer" (1935, p. 195). In Florida, "the lands which originally had been valued at $5 an acre and which all the time had remained totally unproductive, now were appraised at $15 and more an acre and the advance of the bank was raised to $10 per acre" (p. 227).

35. See Schweikart (1987, pp. 178–82); and Fenstermaker (1965, table A-17). Nine of the banks chartered were also railroad companies.

36. The original bill can be found on pp. 34–57 of *Laws of Mississippi*, 1837, and again on pp. 9–33 of *Laws of Mississippi*, 1838. The amendments to the 1838 bill can be found on pp. 33–45.

37. According to Kilbourne (2006), "current notes of the state" referred to the banknotes of banks outside Natchez; these notes were at a substantial discount by 1838 (p. 126).

38. McGrane (1935, p. 197).

39. The sterling price used in the agreement was the official exchange rate, not the prevailing market exchange rate, which was 9 percent higher than the official rate.

40. Nicholas Biddle to Samuel Jaudon, October 2, 1838, *Letterbooks*, Nicholas Biddle Papers, Library of Congress, p. 514, as quoted in Kilbourne (2006, p. 132).

41. Biddle claimed he had been "influenced entirely by a desire to assist the Banks of Mississippi in their effort to resume, and the plan by which it . . . [had been] proposed to accomplish this was, that the Union Bank, having a credit established at New Orleans, could draw on it for the notes of other Missis-

sippi Banks thus absorbing their circulation—making at the same time a large profit—and then, being a creditor of the other Mississippi Banks, settle with them gently and kindly." Nicholas Biddle to J. C. Wilkins, October 8, 1838, *Letterbooks*, Nicholas Biddle Papers, Library of Congress, as quoted in Kilbourne (2006, p. 135). Biddle's negotiations were predicated on the assumption that the Union Bank would assist the other Mississippi banks in resuming specie payments, and that would allow the BUSP to obtain specie for the large debts on the obligations of other Mississippi banks that the BUSP held. Wilkins was president of the Planters' Bank and a loan commissioner at the Union Bank.

42. Of the $5,000,000 in Mississippi bonds taken by Biddle, at least $3,008,000 were never sold but used by Jaudon to as security for loans in Europe in late 1839 and early 1840. All of the Michigan bonds taken by the BUSP ended up unsold and used as collateral for European loans. For the loans, see Smith (1955, p. 218).

43. Mississippi *House Journal*, 1841, pp. 84–85.

44. The bank had $1,573,335.50 in bills receivable (unpaid loans that had been converted into promises to pay), $1,117,337.78 in suspended debts, and $2,696,869.26 in suspended debts in suit. The figures are taken from Mississippi *House Journal*, 1841, pp. 82–83.

45. See, in particular, the detailed arguments laid out by Governor McNutt in his veto message of a bill acknowledging that Mississippi should honor the Union Bank and the Planters' Bank bonds, Mississippi *House Journal*, 1841, p. 491.

46. See McNutt's message to the legislature January 7, 1840, *House Journal*, p. 50. Here is how the bank president responded in July 1840 to the governor's proclamation that the Union Bank had forfeited its banking privileges: "I regret that the bank feels constrained from a sense of public duty to disregard the provisions of that act. The charter of the bank is a contract, and contains, in its own terms, the extent of the obligations of the parties to it." By 1840 the bank had brazenly violated several clauses of its charter. Also see McNutt's message to the legislature on January 8, 1839, detailing the bank's unwillingness to provide information to the state, in *House Journal*, 1839, p. 28.

47. The state recognized an obligation to pay the Planters' Bank bonds, but after making a small distribution to the bondholders in 1848, remained in default on them until 1852, when it finally repudiated the Planters' Bank bonds as well.

48. In the early 1830s, Mississippi never reassessed property, nor did it appear to add new property to the tax rolls: the assessed value of land was $4,775,584 in 1830 and only $5,013,553 in 1837. In the early 1840s, Mississippi overhauled its property tax. Assessed land values rose to $54,060,330 in 1845. Property tax revenues rose from $95,555 in 1836 to $268,573 in 1841 and to $413,777 in 1845. Interest payments on the Union Bank bonds were $250,000 per year.

49. In 1884 Arkansas amended its constitution to prevent payment of the outstanding bonds.

50. Worley (1950).

51. Ibid., p. 405.

52. See *Report of the Accountants*, p. 27 (Worley 1950, p. 414). I have been unable to obtain a copy of the *Report of the Accountants*, and so repeat Worley's citations and page numbers.

53. *Report of the Accountants*, p. 85 (Worley 1950, p. 406).

54. Wilson was forced to resign from both positions when he stabbed and killed Representative Joseph J. Anthony on the floor of the House on December 4, 1837. Anthony and others had challenged Wilson's method of apportioning shares in the stock of the bank. Wilson was charged with murder but was never convicted (Worley 1950, pp. 409–11).

55. Ibid., p. 413.

56. February 17, 1841, as quoted, with emphasis, in Worley (1950, p. 423).

57. See the charter for the Bank of Louisiana, *Laws of Louisiana*, 6th Legislature, 2nd sess. For the amended charter for the Consolidated Association of Planters, see *Laws of Louisiana*, 8th Legislature, 2nd sess., February 28, 1828, Act 19, Section 6, p. 32. For the Union Bank of Louisiana, see *Laws of Louisiana*, 10th Legislature, 3rd sess., April 2, 1832, Section 8, p. 50. For the Citizens Bank, see *Laws of Louisiana*, 11th Legislature, 1st sess., April 4, 1833, Section 7, p. 176. The state recognized the bonds issued on behalf of the Bank of Louisiana and the bonds it had issued for a railroad and public utilities in the mid-1830s.

58. The crisis is described in Wallis, Sylla, and Grinath (2004).

59. Figure 4.1 separates West Virginia from Virginia. In the 1840s, West Virginia was still part of Virginia. The figure also depicts Pennsylvania as having a new constitution. Pennsylvania's constitution was rewritten in 1839 and amended in the 1850s. So there were eleven new constitutions between 1842 and 1852, and Pennsylvania made changes to its constitution similar to those of other states.

60. Wallis (2005).

61. In the figure, Pennsylvania is regarded as writing a new constitution because it significantly amended the constitution it had written in 1837 to include a procedural debt restriction in 1857.

62. For details on constitutional changes with respect to corporations, see Wallis (2005).

63. Kessler (1948).

64. See Evans (1948) for the most complete history of constitutional and legislative incorporation law in the nineteenth century.

65. On the periphery of this group, Virginia, Kentucky, and Tennessee were about to launch larger internal improvement schemes in the 1850s.

Massachusetts had begun work on the Western railroad in the 1830s. But the Massachusetts railroad was small enough that the state could easily service its bonds by restoring the state property tax. New York, Alabama, and Georgia also reinstituted state property taxes that had been allowed to lapse in the 1820s and 1830s because of revenues from banks. Pennsylvania and Maryland had not had property taxes since the 1790s, and their slowness in implementing state property taxes is the reason they were forced to default. See Wallis, Sylla, and Grinath (2004).

References

Bailyn, Bernard (1967). *The Ideological Origins of the American Revolution.* Cambridge, MA: Harvard University Press.

Banning, Lance (1978). *The Jeffersonian Persuasion.* Ithaca, NY: Cornell University Press.

Benson, Lee (1961). *The Concept of Jacksonian Democracy: New York as a Test Case.* Princeton, NJ: Princeton University Press.

Bodenhorn, Howard (2006). "Bank Chartering and Political Corruption in Ante-bellum New York: Free Banking as Reform." In Claudia Goldin and Ed Glaeser, eds., *Corruption and Reform.* Chicago: University of Chicago Press.

Brantley, William H., Jr. (1961). *Banking in Alabama: 1816–1860.* 2 vols. Birmingham, AL: Birmingham Printing.

Evans, George Heberton (1948). *Business Incorporations in the United States, 1800–1943.* Baltimore: NBER/Waverly Press.

Fenstermaker, J. Van (1965). *The Development of American Commercial Banking 1782–1837.* Kent, OH: Kent State University, Bureau of Economic and Business Research.

Ferguson, James (1961). *The Power of the Purse: A History of American Public Finance, 1776–1790.* Chapel Hill: University of North Carolina Press.

Gallman, Robert (1992). "Capital Stock." In Robert Gallman and John Joseph Wallis, eds., *American Economic Growth and Standards of Living Before the Civil War.* Chicago: University of Chicago Press.

Gunn, L. Ray (1988). *The Decline of Authority: Public Economic Policy and Political Development in New York, 1800–1860.* Ithaca, NY: Cornell University Press.

Handlin, Oscar, and Mart Flug Handlin (1969). *Commonwealth: A Study of the Role of Government in the American Economy: Massachusetts, 1774–1861.* Cambridge, MA: Belknap Press.

Heckelman, Jac, and John Joseph Wallis (1997). "Railroads and Property Taxes." *Explorations in Economic History* 34: 77–99.

Hurst, James Willard (1970). *The Legitimacy of the Business Corporation in the*

Law of the United States, 1780–1970. Charlottesville: University of Virginia Press.

Kessler, William C. (1948). "Incorporation in New England: A Statistical Study, 1800–1875." *Journal of Economic History* 8: 43–62.

Kilbourne, Richard Holcombe, Jr. (2006). *Slave Agriculture and Financial Markets in Antebellum America: The Bank of the United States in Mississippi, 1831–1852.* London: Pickering and Chatto.

McCoy, Drew R. (1980). *Elusive Republic: Political Economy in Jeffersonian America.* Chapel Hill: University of North Carolina Press.

McGrane, Reginald C. (1935). *Foreign Bondholders and American State Debts.* New York: Macmillan.

Neal, Larry (1991). *The Rise of Financial Capitalism.* New York: Cambridge University Press.

North, Douglass C., John Joseph Wallis, and Barry R. Weingast (2006). "A Conceptual Framework for Interpreting Recorded Human History." NBER Working Paper No. 12795.

Pocok, J. G. A. (1975). *The Machiavellian Moment: Florentine Political Thought and the Atlantic Republican Tradition.* Princeton, NJ: Princeton University Press.

Redlich, Fritz (1968). *The Molding of American Banking: Men and Ideas.* New York: Johnson Reprint Corporation.

Robbins, Caroline (1959). *The Eighteenth-Century Commonwealthman.* Cambridge, MA: Harvard University Press.

Rodgers, James Steven (1995). *The Early History of the Law of Bills and Notes.* New York: Cambridge University Press.

Schwartz, Anna (1987). "The Beginning of Competitive Banking in Philadelphia." In Anna Schwartz, *Money in Historical Perspective.* Chicago: NBER/University of Chicago Press.

Schweikart, Larry (1987). *Banking in the American South from the Age of Jackson to Reconstruction.* Baton Rouge: Louisiana State University Press.

Seavoy, Ronald E. (1982). *The Origins of the American Business Corporation, 1784–1855.* Westport, CT: Greenwood Press.

Shade, William Gerald (1972). *Banks or No Banks: The Money Issue in Western Politics, 1832–1865.* Detroit: Wayne State University Press.

Shalhope, Robert E. (1972). "Toward a Republican Synthesis: The Emergence of an Understanding of Republicanism in American Historiography." *William and Mary Quarterly* 29: 49–80.

Skinner, Quentin (1998). *Liberty Before Liberalism.* New York: Cambridge University Press.

Smith, Walter B. (1955). *Economic Aspects of the Second Bank of the United States.* Cambridge, MA: Harvard University Press.

Sparks, Earl Sylvester (1932). *History and Theory of Agricultural Credit in the United States.* New York: Thomas Crowell.

Sylla, Richard (1971). "American Banking and Growth in Early Nineteenth Century America: A Partial Review of the Terrain." *Explorations in Economic History* 9: 197–227.

Wallis, John Joseph (2006). "The Concept of Systematic Corruption in American Economic and Political History." In Claudia Goldin and Ed Glaeser, eds., *Corruption and Reform: Lessons from America's Economic History*. Chicago: University of Chicago Press.

——— (2005). "Constitutions, Corporations, and Corruption: American States and Constitutional Change, 1842 to 1852." *Journal of Economic History* 65: 211–56.

——— (2003a). "The Property Tax as a Coordination Device: Financing Indiana's Mammoth System of Internal Improvements." *Explorations in Economic History* 40: 223–50.

——— (2003b). "Public Promotion of Private Interest (Groups)." In Jac Heckelman and Dennis Coates, eds., *Collective Choice: Essays in Honor of Mancur Olson*. London: Springer-Verlag.

Wallis, John Joseph, Richard Sylla, and Arthur Grinath (2004). "Sovereign Default and Repudiation: The Emerging Market Debt Crisis in the United States." NBER Working Paper W10753.

Wallis, John Joseph, Richard Sylla, and John B. Legler (1994). "The Relationship Between Taxation and Regulation of Banks in Early Nineteenth Century America." In Claudia Goldin and Gary Libecap, eds., *The Regulated Economy: A Historical Approach to Political Economy*. Chicago: University of Chicago Press.

Weston, Corinne Comstock (1965). *English Constitutional Theory and the House of Lords, 1556–1832*. London: Routledge & Kegan Paul.

Wood, Gordon S. (1969). *The Creation of the American Republic, 1776–1787*. Chapel Hill: University of North Carolina Press.

Worley, Ted. R. (1950). "Control of the Real Estate Bank of the State of Arkansas, 1836–1855." *Mississippi Valley Historical Review* 37: 403–26.

Chapter 5

Beyond Legal Origin and Checks and Balances

*Political Credibility, Citizen Information, and
Financial Sector Development*

PHILIP KEEFER

Government decisions ranging from prudential regulation to the security of property and contractual rights are at the center of financial sector development. A substantial body of research has emerged to explain why some governments support financial sector development and others do not, focusing largely on the role of political checks and balances and the legal institutions of countries. Substantial issues remain, however.

First, data limitations have made it difficult for researchers to test directly the role of political checks and balances in financial sector development and to distinguish the role of political checks from that of competitive elections. Most of the literature uses subjective measures that do not clearly identify the underlying formal institutions. Employing objective measures of political institutions, results shown in the following analysis support the argument that formal political checks and balances are a significant determinant of financial sector development, more so than competitive elections per se.

Second, the literature addresses only the formal institutions that shape the incentives of governments to support financial sector development. However, policies that support financial sector development have the characteristics of public goods, and political conditions beyond formal institutions have significant effects on such policies. In particular, public goods create benefits for all citizens that are difficult for governments to target to narrow constituencies. The following analysis shows that the political characteristics of countries that influence government incentives to provide public goods—specifically, where political competitors can make credible preelectoral promises to voters and where voters are well informed about the contribution of political decisions to their welfare—are also determinants of financial sector development and appear to dominate the effects of political checks and balances.

Third, there is broad agreement that secure property rights are key to financial sector development. However, the hypothesis that the political influences on financial sector development should operate in part through their effects on the security of property rights has not been directly tested. The work discussed here examines this hypothesis directly and finds results supportive of the argument.

Finally, the analysis here revisits the relationship between legal institutions and political influences. On the one hand, estimates in this analysis demonstrate that the political determinants of financial sector development are robust to controls for legal origin. More revealing, after controlling for the potential endogeneity of political influence, legal origin is found to have no significant impact on financial sector development. This contrasts with results in the literature, in which it is political checks and balances that have no significant influence on financial sector development when controls for legal institutions are included. The results in the following analysis suggest that legal origin is a proxy for the political attitudes of governments toward financial sector development; when those attitudes are properly modeled, legal origin loses significance.

Political and Legal Influences on Financial Sector Development

The prominence of political and legal institutions in the literature is rooted in the argument that governments prone to expropriation stifle financial sector development and that these institutions curb expropriatory tendencies. The threat of expropriation suppresses growth on the asset and liability sides of the balance sheet: deposits fall in the face of possible expropriation. Bankers are unwilling to lend to those who might abscond with the funds under the protective umbrella of a sympathetic government. And investors are unwilling to capitalize banks whose profitability is placed at risk by the prospect of government expropriation.

Competitive elections and political checks and balances give citizens the opportunity to block expropriation. Whether elections or checks and balances matter most in cementing the credibility of government decisions is unclear, however. Acemoglu, Johnson, and Robinson (2001, 2002) argue heuristically for both, but the analysis in Acemoglu and Robinson (2001) emphasizes the role of elections: the threat of replacement by citizens prevents governments from expropriating citizens. North and Weingast (1989), in contrast, argue that political checks and balances have significant economic effects even in the absence of competitive elections and a universal franchise. The role of checks and balances is also thoroughly documented in other areas in which government credibility is at issue (for example, in the case of monetary policy, by Keefer and Stasavage 2003).

The *necessity* of either competitive elections or checks and balances as a precondition for financial sector development and economic growth has been called into question by Haber, Razo, and Maurer (2003) and others. The Haber, Razo, and Maurer study of the autocratic Porfirio Díaz regime in Mexico demonstrates that autocrats can also stimulate financial sector growth and economic growth more generally by arranging self-enforcing or externally enforced contracts with privileged bankers and industrialists (crony capitalism).

The empirical findings in the following analysis are consistent with results in the cross-country empirical literature that political checks and balances are a robust determinant of financial sector development. The contribution here is novel in two respects. First, the evidence is based, for the first time, on objective indicators of political checks and balances in countries. Second, the empirical work demonstrates for the first time that political checks and balances operate in part through their impact on the security of property and contract rights in countries, a relationship that has been hypothesized but not directly tested.

The law and finance literature (see the seminal contribution by La Porta et al. 1998) advances similar arguments in the context of legal institutions: some legal institutions—particularly those in the English common law tradition—offer greater judicial protection of private actors relative to the state. Beck, Demirgüç-Kunt, and Levine (2001) summarize a key argument in the law and finance literature by arguing that "English common law evolved to protect private property owners against the crown" (p. 2). In fact, substantial evidence suggests that countries of English, German, or Scandinavian legal origins perform significantly better on numerous dimensions than countries with legal systems rooted in French or socialist legal traditions. Beck et al. (2001) conclude that legal origin offers a substantially stronger explanation of financial development than political checks and balances.

Particularly among legal scholars, these arguments have sparked considerable controversy. On the one hand, scholars dispute whether the posited differences in French and German systems (for example, with respect to their dynamism) or between civil and common law systems (for example, with respect to their acceptance of judge-made law) are correct. On the other, although the result that legal origin matters has proved to be highly robust, it is less clear that the evidence matches the specific hypotheses regarding the ranking of legal traditions outlined in the literature.

For example, Beck et al. (2001) compare the financial sector development of countries with British, French, and German legal origins to that of countries with socialist or Scandinavian legal origins. Theory suggests that English common law heritage should have the strongest effect on financial sector development since it is argued to be both adaptable to new economic and market conditions and more protective of the private sector. The German/Scandinavian civil law systems enjoy only the advantage of being more efficient and more adaptable than the French civil law system. Beck et al. (2001) find, in contrast, that British legal origin is significantly less conducive than the German to financial sector development (credit to the private sector) and often not significantly different from the French.

The following analysis, which examines additional political hypotheses and employs different political variables, reaches conclusions that diverge from those in Beck et al. (2001). The dynamics of political competition and political checks and balances matter significantly for financial sector development, whether or not legal origin is taken into account, in the estimates here. Moreover, measures of legal origin are insignificant in specifications that control for the possibility that both political variables and financial sector development are influenced by unobserved factors.

Economic Interests, Politics, and Financial Sector Development

The cross-country empirical literature focuses on political and legal institutions, and the analysis here extends this to political factors, such as voter information and the credibility of preelectoral political promises. A large body of country-specific research also looks at the economic interests of political decision makers and their constituencies. For example, revisiting the evidence presented in North and Weingast (1989) and Stasavage (2003) points out that the Whigs cared more about the cost of capital than the Tories did. Only when the Whigs controlled the British Parliament did interest rates paid by England on sovereign loans begin to drop. Looking at the politics of financial sector legislation in the United States, Kroszner and Strahan (1996), Kroszner and Stratmann (1998), Broz (2002), and many others have shown that economic interests within congressional districts are significant determinants of legislator voting behavior with respect to financial legislation.

The interest group approach to political economy is hard to extend to the question of why financial sector development is greater or faster in some countries than in others, for two reasons. First, the U.S. literature suggests that the influence of interest groups depends on their representation in the constituencies of key veto players. Unfortunately, the identification of interest groups and their importance in key constituencies is not possible in cross-country comparisons. At the same time, however, there is little qualitative evidence that policy differences across countries are purely a reflection of differences in the types and alignments of economic interests. More persuasive is the argument that the important political differences across countries are those that shape government incentives to serve the interests of private or narrow interests at the expense of broad public interests. Two characteristics are, in particular, prominent in the literature: citizen information about the actions of political decision makers and the credibility of preelectoral political promises. These are the focus of attention in the analysis below.

Public Goods, Political Competition, and Financial Sector Development

The political economy and legal origin literatures typically portray the security of property rights as the product of institutions that allow governments to credibly commit not to expropriate. However, secure property rights can also be regarded as a public good (and expropriation as a public bad). In the typical case of expropriation, the government takes the assets of one economic actor and distributes them to others. If expropriation were nothing more than the struggle of one narrow interest of society against another, political checks and balances would resolve the struggle as long as each special interest controlled at least one of the veto gates in the political structure.

This depiction of expropriation ignores substantial social costs that are at the center of concern about the security of property rights, however. The risk of expropriation threatens all assets in a country. Similarly, an act of expropriation imposes costs on all citizens and not only the target of expropriation. The asset values and employment opportunities of all citizens depend on the rate of return that investors expect as a condition of placing fixed assets in a country. That rate of return must rise when expropriation risks increase. A policy of nonexpropriation can therefore be seen as a public good that benefits all citizens in the same way that national defense does.

Similarly, the regulatory decisions of governments have attributes of public goods. Regulatory failure in the financial sector leads to the economic disruption of a banking crisis or the costs of a slow-growing financial sector. These are felt broadly throughout an economy.

Taken together, these arguments suggest that financial sector development should depend on the incentives of government decision makers to provide public goods.[1] Competitive elections are certainly one factor contributing to these incentives. Absent competitive elections and an enfranchised citizenry, the costs to "average" citizens of removing nonperforming governments rise. Unelected governments should therefore confront fewer political costs when they privilege themselves or narrow interests with private goods at the expense of citizens generally. In fact, Keefer (2004) finds that competitive elections are a strong and significant determinant of the magnitude of government fiscal transfers in the event of crisis. That is, elected governments face greater political costs from allowing insolvent banks to socialize the risks of imprudent lending. Ultimately, elected governments face greater political costs when they attempt to make fiscal transfers to special interests (delinquent borrowers, careless depositors, imprudent bankers) at the expense of citizens generally.

Elections often fail to generate accountability, however. In 1997 expropriation risk was the same or higher in 35 percent of countries exhibiting competitive elections than in 60 percent of the countries that did not.[2] Although the literature identifies several explanations for this, two are the focus here. First, political competitors strive to gain electoral advantage by making claims to voters about what they will do if they take office. If those promises are not credible, however, they do not affect the election, and politicians have no reason to abide by them once they take office. One precondition of credibility is that government actors confront a cost from reneging. Such a cost might come in the form of damaged reputation. A second source of low credibility is voters' lack of information about government policy actions and their connection to citizen welfare. Without this information, it is not possible for citizens to verify whether politicians have taken the actions promised prior to their election. Absent verifiability, political promises are not credible.

The analysis of information in the literature generally takes for granted the credibility of agreements and asks how imperfect voter information distorts outcomes. Besley and Burgess (2002) do this, asking how imperfect voter information about politician type or actions allows worse outcomes than would otherwise prevail. Grossman and Helpman (1996) argue that if voters are uninformed about candidate characteristics, candidates can spend money to persuade the voters of their qualities. As in the credibility story, citizens in general suffer as politicians obtain resources to finance information campaigns by providing favors to special interests. They assume, however, that candidate promises to citizens and to special interests are credible.

If politicians are entirely noncredible and can do nothing about it, two outcomes are possible. One is that politicians provide nothing to anyone. A second, introduced by Ferejohn (1986), is that voters are able to co-ordinate on a performance threshold below which they expel the poor-performing incumbents and above which they reelect them, independently of challenger characteristics, since challengers are not credible. Keefer and Vlaicu (2004) argue, however, that politicians in fact try to overcome their credibility problems. As they do so, they rely on clients and personalized transfers, provide little in the way of public goods, and are able to engage in substantial corruption. Insecure property rights and lack of attention to prudential regulation of the financial sector are consistent with, though not directly predicted by, these analyses. The intuition is straightforward: politicians who cannot make credible promises to the whole population try to make promises at least to a few. These few do not internalize the costs of expropriation or risky financial sector regulation.

Each of these—voter information and politician credibility prior to elections—influences whether agreements between voters and politicians are credible. Credibility in this case does not refer to the credibility of gov-ernment commitments to continue particular policies in the future—for example, promises to bankers not to expropriate rents from financial trans-actions. Instead, it refers to promises that politicians make to voters prior to elections.

This is an unusual way to frame the political economy of financial sector issues. On the one hand, government credibility is not usually conceived of as a public good. On the other, much of the political economy literature concerns conflict between special interests (large versus small banks, banks versus insurance companies, healthy banks versus insolvent ones). The in-troduction of a conflict between narrow and broad interests and of the incentives of governments to provide public or private goods nevertheless contributes in two ways to our understanding of financial sector develop-ment. It provides a single explanation for two phenomena usually treated separately (the security of property rights and the efficiency of regulation); and it helps to illuminate why countries with similar formal institutions exhibit such different levels of financial development.

Empirical Approach

The empirical investigation that follows examines financial sector development over two periods: medium-term growth in the financial sector over the period 1975–2000; and long-run growth, using the size of the financial sector in 2000. This mirrors the growth literature, most of which uses medium-term growth (for example, 1975–2000), but one branch of which examines the very long run (Hall and Jones 1999; Acemoglu, Johnson, and Robinson 2001, 2002). These are appropriate time periods not only for growth but for any fundamental determinant of growth, such as financial sector development.

To test the hypotheses linking political factors to financial sector development, therefore, we employ the following two base empirical specifications:

$$\textit{Growth of the financial sector}_i \ (1975–2000) = \beta_1 + \beta_2 \ln(\textit{initial financial sector})_i \\ + \beta_3 \, (\textit{initial political / institutional variable})_i + X_i' \beta_4 + \varepsilon_i \quad (1)$$

and

$$\textit{Size of the financial sector}_i \ (2000) = \beta_1 + \beta_2 \, (\textit{initial political / institutional variable})_i \\ + X_i' \beta_3 + \varepsilon_i. \quad (2)$$

Equation (1) allows medium-term growth of the financial sector to vary with the initial size of the financial sector, analogous to medium-term growth regressions in which growth varies with the level of initial income per capita. In the second equation, the initial size of the financial sector is omitted in order to preserve the long-run character of the investigation.[3]

These specifications raise numerous issues, the most important of which are, what should be in X, and how should one should address the potential endogeneity of the political and institutional variables? With respect to the first question, the base specification in equations (1) and (2) is parsimonious, following Beck et al. (2001) in the financial literature and many others in the growth literature. The argument behind parsimony is simple: the effects of political institutions on financial sector development are likely to be both direct and indirect. As a first approximation we would like to know the aggregate effects of both.

As always, endogeneity is a concern: economic variables might drive political outcomes, or omitted factors might determine both. The first possibility is taken into account through the use of initial values of political institutions. Instrumental variable estimates are used to address omitted variable bias. Unfortunately, among the entire range of instruments typically used to control for the endogeneity of institutions in the literature, none are valid for the entire range of specifications examined here. However, colonial origin (whether a country is of British, French, or Spanish colonial origin) turn out to be valid for most specifications.

Data

The following regressions require data on financial sector development and the political characteristics of countries. For the first, estimates rely on *private credit*, total credit extended to the private sector by banks and other financial institutions. This variable is the preferred measure of financial sector development in Beck et al. (2001) and is taken from the Financial Structures Database of the World Bank (see Beck, Demirgüç-Kunt, and Levine 2000). Beck et al. describe this as the preferred measure of financial sector development.

Four different measures of political institutions or competition are evaluated here. All are taken from the *Database of Political Institutions (DPI)* (Beck et al. 2001), running from 1975 to 2000. In contrast to the measures used in much of the literature, those here are all objective and easily replicable by others. The *checks* indicator is an objective counterpart to a subjective measure often used to capture checks and balances, *Executive Constraints* from the Polity IV database. It measures how many political actors can block proposed legislation, therefore tracking whether formal institutions exist that potentially impose constraints on arbitrary behavior by the executive branch.[4]

The *checks* variable captures the two ingredients identified by many as essential for secure property rights: elections and checks on the executive branch. However, unlike the *Executive Constraints* Polity IV measure, *checks* captures only the formal constraints on the executive that theory predicts should protect property rights, not whether those formal constraints are in practice binding. It therefore constitutes a better test of theories of the role of institutions.

The *DPI* also contains two variables assessing the competitiveness of elections, the *Legislative* and *Executive Indices of Electoral Competitiveness* (*LIEC, EIEC*). The executive index, *EIEC*, is used here. This reaches its highest score (7) when multiple parties can and do compete for executive election and no party gets more than 75 percent of the vote. A 6 means that one party receives more than 75 percent of the vote; a 5, that only one party ran for office though others could have; and so on until 1, indicating no elections were held. Since most scholars would agree that only the most competitive category of *EIEC* is a reasonable approximation to elections, a dummy variable is used in the regressions here, equaling 1 when *EIEC* is 6.5 or greater, and 0 otherwise. The effect of checks and balances net of competitive elections can then be assessed by controlling for *EIEC* in regressions that include *checks*.

The remaining two democracy variables capture distortions in the market for political office. The first distortion is the lack of credibility of pre-electoral political promises. The evidence in Keefer (2005) indicates that the performance of democracies with fewer continuous years of competitive elections is starkly different from that of older democracies: the younger democracies are more corrupt; spend more on public investment and government jobs; and exhibit lower secondary school enrollment, rule of law, and bureaucratic quality—relations that are robust to a variety of specifications and endogeneity controls. These policy differences can be best explained by the greater difficulties that competitors in younger democracies confront in making impersonal credible commitments to voters prior to elections. From the *DPI*, one can calculate how many years a country has continuously held competitive elections (where both the *Legislative* and *Executive Indices of Electoral Competitiveness* equal 7). The value of this variable (*continuous years of competitive elections*) in 1975 is therefore used in the following regressions.[5]

A large literature has also argued that voter information is critical to the effects of elections on incumbent behavior. Following the empirical research in this literature (see, for example, Adserà, Boix, and Payne 2003), *newspaper circulation* from the *World Development Indicators* is therefore used as a proxy for the extent of voter information and its effect on growth. The 1975 (initial) values of all political variables are used here, with the exception of newspaper circulation. To counter spotty coverage in any given year, we employ the average of newspaper circulation over the period 1975–2000.

INSTRUMENTS

The literature uses a variety of instruments to identify the effects of institutions: distance from the equator (Hall and Jones [1999] use this instrument for their index of social infrastructure), colonial heritage, years since the creation or independence of a country (Persson, Tabellini, and Trebbi 2003), and settler mortality and urbanization in 1700 (Acemoglu, Johnson, and Robinson 2001, 2002). In all cases, each of these instruments has been introduced into the literature as a measure of underlying political institutions rather than as a direct estimate of property rights. As a consequence, to the extent that they are valid instruments for property rights in growth equations, one would expect them also, logically, to be reasonable instruments for institutions of various kinds in the growth equations. In the current context, however, only colonial origin variables are (generally) valid.

OTHER CONTROLS

The specification here is parsimonious, allowing the estimates of institutional variables to reflect both their direct and indirect effects. Two controls are always included, land area and total population. These capture exogenous variation across countries in the size of the market, which in turn might have a significant impact on the development of the financial sector. Some specifications also control for income per capita in 1975. This is a challenging test for the political hypotheses under consideration here, since there is a well-known correlation between income and variables related to democracy. Finally, extensions of the base regressions encompass other variables, including the legal origin of countries.

Results

A number of questions motivate the analysis in this chapter. Do objective measures of political checks and balances matter? What is the relative contribution of political checks and balances and competitive elections? Do noninstitutional political factors, voter information, and the credibility of preelectoral political promises have a significant effect on financial sector development? Does the influence of political factors operate through the security of property rights, as theory predicts? And how robust are these findings in the presence of controls for legal institutions? The results reported here address each of these questions.

POLITICAL CHECKS AND BALANCES, ELECTIONS,
AND FINANCIAL SECTOR DEVELOPMENT

Tables 5.1a–c revisit the issue of whether political checks and balances and competitive elections support financial sector development. Tables 5.1a and 5.1b, using, respectively, ordinary least squares and two-stage least squares estimates of equations (1) and (2), show that objective measures of political checks and balances and, to a lesser extent, competitive elections have a significant influence on financial sector development. These results contrast with those reported by Beck et al. (2001) but are consistent with the evidence in, for example, North and Weingast (1989).[6] Controlling for endogeneity strengthens the results: both magnitudes and statistical significance rise; and the *F-* and *J*-statistics reported in Table 5.1b support the claim, in

TABLE 5.1A
Competitive elections, checks and balances, and lending to the private sector

POLITICAL VARIABLE:	COMPETITIVE ELECTIONS (1975)			CHECKS AND BALANCES (1975)		
Dependent variable: Lending to the private sector by banks and nonbank financial institutions	Growth in lending 1975– 2000 (OLS)	Level of lending 2000 (OLS)	Level 2000 (OLS)	Growth 1975–2000 (OLS)	Level 2000 (OLS)	Level 2000 (OLS)
Political variable	.012	.066	.34	.006	.05	.12
	(.16)	(.51)	(.00)	(.02)	(.09)	(0.0)
Land (thousands of square miles)	0.0	−.000097	.000013	−.000002	−.000011	.000010
	(.912)	(.63)	(.59)	(.89)	(.60)	(.69)
Average population (millions)	−.000095	.000078	.0003	−.00002	.000734	.00034
	(.45)	(.05)	(.43)	(.17)	(.08)	(.46)
Log real income/ capita (1975)		.21			.19	
		(0.0)			(0.0)	
Private sector lending (1975)	−.03			−.04		
	(.07)			(.03)		
R^2	.04	.36	.20	.07	.38	.24
N	78	93	116	78	93	116

SOURCE: See text.
NOTES: *p*-values are reported in parentheses, based on robust standard errors. Constants not reported.

five of six regressions, that the colonial heritage dummy variables are valid instruments.

The magnitude of the effects is large. On average, the two-stage least squares estimate in Table 5.1b suggests that financial sector growth over the period 1975–2000 was 3.3 percentage points per year as fast with every unit increment in checks and balances; and 10 percentage points as fast in countries with competitive elections in 1975 than in countries without. These estimates seem implausibly large, but are not because the initial size of the financial sector was much larger in countries exhibiting competitive elections and political checks and balances in 1975 (twice as large in countries with competitive elections than those without, for example). The initial size of the financial sector has a significant negative effect on subsequent growth (similar to the convergence effect that leads initial income per capita to be negatively associated with subsequent income growth) so that fast growth because of political institutions is somewhat offset by slow growth because of large initial financial sectors. Moreover, there is a large divergence between yearly growth rates of the financial sector across countries: a 14 percentage point difference separates the yearly growth rates of the fastest- and slowest-growing financial sectors in the sample.

TABLE 5.1B
Two-stage least squares estimates of Table 5.1a

POLITICAL VARIABLE: Dependent variable: Lending to the private sector by banks and nonbank financial institutions	COMPETITIVE ELECTIONS (1975)			CHECKS AND BALANCES (1975)		
	Growth 1975–2000 (IV)	Level 2000 (IV)	Level 2000 (IV)	Growth 1975–2000 (IV)	Level 2000 (IV)	Level 2000 (IV)
Political variable	.10	.83	.91	.033	.27	.30
	(0.0)	(.02)	(0.0)	(.001)	(.004)	(0.0)
Land (thousands of square miles)	−.00003	−.00008	−.00001	−.00002	−.0002	−.0002
	(.22)	(.78)	(.61)	(.41)	(.60)	(.53)
Average population (millions)	−.0005	.004	.004	−.00007	.004	.004
	(.10)	(.60)	(.59)	(.01)	(.57)	(.61)
Log real income/ capita (1975)		.004			.02	
		(.97)			(.76)	
Private sector lending (1975)	−.12			−.03		
	(.005)			(.001)		
F-statistic on instruments (first stage)	3.52	1.64	6.2	4.39	3.53	7.3
Hansen J-statistic (chi-squared p-value)	.66	N/A	.42	.55	.68	.83
N	78	91	103	78	91	103

SOURCE: See text.

NOTES: p-values are reported in parentheses, based on robust standard errors. The instruments are three dummy variables indicating whether a country has British, French, or Spanish colonial origins. It is inappropriate to calculate the J-statistic in the second regression, given the low significance of the instruments in the first-stage regression. Constants not reported.

TABLE 5.1C
The effect of checks and balances, controlling for elections

Dependent variable: Lending to the private sector by banks and nonbank financial institutions	Growth 1975–2000 (OLS)	Level 2000 (OLS)	Level 2000 (OLS)
Checks and balances	.006	.067	.09
	(.12)	(.10)	(.03)
R^2	.07	.38	.25
N	78	93	116

SOURCE: See text.

NOTES: Table 5.1c uses the same specification as in the first three columns of Table 5.1a, with the addition of competitive elections. Other controls and constants not reported. The values in parentheses are p-values, based on robust standard errors.

The checks and balances variable in Tables 5.1a and 5.1b takes into account the competitiveness of elections: countries lacking competitive elections are automatically assigned a 1 for this variable. It is possible, therefore, that the estimated effects of checks and balances reflects the impact of competitive elections rather than political checks and balances per se. Table 5.1c reports estimates from regressions that add the competitiveness of elections in 1975 to the specifications of Table 5.1a. Political checks and balances continue to exhibit a strong effect on financial sector development.

VOTER INFORMATION, POLITICAL CREDIBILITY,
AND FINANCIAL SECTOR DEVELOPMENT

The central argument of this chapter is that the effects of politics on financial sector development extend beyond the formal institutions of competitive elections and political checks and balances. The evidence in Tables 5.2a and 5.2b supports this contention, and Table 5.2c suggests that the effects of political checks and balances reported in Table 5.1a may be due to the omission of these political variables. The ordinary least squares estimates in Table 5.2a indicate large effects of both the continuous years of competitive elections and average newspaper circulation. A one standard-deviation

TABLE 5.2A

Continuous years of elections, newspaper circulation, and lending to the private sector

POLITICAL VARIABLE:	CONTINUOUS YEARS OF COMPETITIVE ELECTIONS (1975)			AVERAGE NEWSPAPER CIRCULATION (1975–2000)		
Dependent variable: Lending to the private sector by banks and nonbank financial institutions	Growth 1975– 2000 (*OLS*)	Level 2000 (*OLS*)	Level 2000 (*OLS*)	Growth 1975–2000 (*OLS*)	Level 2000 (*OLS*)	Level 2000 (*OLS*)
Political variable	.0006	.005	.013	.00008	.001	.002
	(.01)	(.09)	(0.0)	(.01)	(0.0)	(0.0)
Land (thousands of square miles)	−.000002	−.00002	−.00008	−.0000002	.00002	.0002
	(.28)	(.32)	(.66)	(.88)	(.90)	(.20)
Average population (millions)	.000001	.00026	−.00015	−.00004	.006	.004
	(.92)	(.37)	(.71)	(.76)	(.06)	(.12)
Log real income/ capita (1975)		.21			.12	
		(0.0)			(.003)	
Private sector lending (1975)	−.02			−.05		
	(.15)			(.02)		
R^2	.08	.36	.29	.11	.45	.43
N	66	73	88	78	94	115

SOURCE: See text.

NOTES: *p*-values are reported in parentheses, based on robust standard errors. Constants not reported.

TABLE 5.2B

Two-stage least squares estimates of Table 5.2a

POLITICAL VARIABLE:	CONTINUOUS YEARS OF COMPETITIVE ELECTIONS (1975)			AVERAGE NEWSPAPER CIRCULATION (1975–2000)		
Dependent variable: Lending to the private sector by banks and nonbank financial institutions	Growth 1975–2000 (IV)	Level 2000 (IV)	Level 2000 (IV)	Growth 1975–2000 (IV)	Level 2000 (IV)	Level 2000 (IV)
Political variable	.002	.02	.03	.0003	.002	.002
	(.004)	(.006)	(0.0)	(.002)	(.007)	(0.0)
Land (thousands of square miles)	−.00005	−.00038	−.0004	−.00001	.0002	.0002
	(.03)	(.15)	(.13)	(.48)	(.34)	(.29)
Average population (millions)	−.00001	−.0025	−.0025	−.02	.004	.005
	(.96)	(.63)	(.61)	(.20)	(.17)	(.09)
Log real income/ capita (1975)			.01			−.008
			(.91)			(.93)
Private sector lending (1975)	−.06			−.12		
	(.04)			(.004)		
F-statistic on instruments (first stage)	6.2	4.2	4.7	7.3	4.5	12.5
Hansen J-statistic (chi-squared p-value)	.04	.02	.09	.05	.04	.05
N	66	71	79	78	92	104

SOURCE: See text.

NOTES: *p*-values are reported in parentheses, based on robust standard errors. Instruments for the fourth and eighth regressions are three dummy variables indicating whether a country has British, French, or Spanish colonial origins. Constants not reported.

increase in the initial number of continuous years of competitive elections is associated with an increase in the rate of growth of the financial sector of 0.6 percentage points per year and with an increase in the size of the financial sector in 2000 of as much as 25 percent of gross domestic product (GDP). Results for newspaper circulation are still larger. These findings are robust to controls either for initial financial sector development or initial income, despite the fact that both are highly correlated with the two political variables. They imply that government actions supportive of financial sector development, including the security of property rights, are sensitive to government incentives to provide public goods.

If these variables accurately proxy the credibility of preelectoral political promises and voter information, respectively, the results in Tables 5.2a and 5.2b underline the importance of a different kind of credibility for financial sector development. When average citizens do not believe the promises of political competitors to provide such public goods as secure property rights

TABLE 5.2C
*The effects of political credibility and voter information, controlling for
political checks and balances*

POLITICAL VARIABLE: *Dependent variable*: Lending to the private sector by banks and nonbank financial institutions	CONTINUOUS YEARS OF COMPETITIVE ELECTIONS (1975)			AVERAGE NEWSPAPER CIRCULATION (1975–2000)		
	Growth 1975–2000 (OLS)	Level 2000 (OLS)	Level 2000 (OLS)	Growth 1975–2000 (OLS)	Level 2000 (OLS)	Level 2000 (OLS)
Political variable	.0003	.003	.01	.00007	.001	.002
	(.13)	(.31)	(0.0)	(.04)	(0.008)	(0.0)
Checks and balances	.004	−.035	.06	.003	.04	.05
	(.20)	(.36)	(.05)	(.19)	(.13)	(.03)
R^2	.10	.36	.32	.12	.43	.42
N	66	73	88	78	93	114

SOURCE: See text.

NOTES: Table 5.2c uses the same specification as in Table 5.2a, with the addition of political checks and balances. p-values are reported in parentheses, based on robust standard errors. Constants and conditioning variables not reported.

or are unable to monitor the fulfillment of such promises, financial sector development slows.

Table 5.2b investigates the sensitivity of these results to the potential endogeneity of the political variables to financial sector development. Although the political variables remain highly significant, this exercise is less successful than in Table 5.1b. The F-statistics confirm that the colonial heritage dummies reported here are significant predictors of the political variables. However, the Hansen J-test rejects the assumption that these (or any other of the usual instruments) can be excluded from the second-stage regressions, so it is not possible to eliminate the possibility that omitted variables drive the results reported in Table 5.2a. However, once legal origin variables are taken into account, as in Tables 5.4 and 5.5, the same instrumental strategy succeeds in four of six of the regressions, and the political variables remain strongly significant.

One key robustness issue surrounding the results in Tables 5.1 and 5.2 concerns the measure of the size of the financial sector. One alternative measure that is sometimes used is liquid liabilities as a fraction of GDP (currency plus demand and interest-bearing liabilities of bank and non-bank financial intermediaries). Liquid liabilities are an inferior measure of financial sector development since they do not tell us the extent to which financial intermediaries actually channel funds to the private sector, as the private credit variable does. Nevertheless, when the two-stage least square regressions in Tables 5.1b and 5.2b are repeated using liquid liabilities as the dependent variable, results are at least as strong as when the private sector credit variable is used. The political variables are generally not significant in the ordinary least squares regressions of Tables 5.1a and 5.2a using liquid liabilities. This, however, is consistent with the fact that liquid liabilities are a noisier measure of financial sector development, making regression estimates more sensitive to the noisiness of the independent variables. Since instrumental variables reduce the noise in the potentially endogenous independent variable, results improve in the two-stage least squares estimates.

The results in Tables 5.2a and 5.2b indicate that when average citizens do not believe the promises of political competitors to provide such public goods as secure property rights or are unable to monitor the fulfillment of such promises, financial sector development slows. Once again, however, one might argue that these two variables, meant to capture the dynamics of political competition, may instead reflect the influence of the excluded institutional variables, political checks and balances, and elections.

To examine whether this is the case, we replicate in Table 5.2c the regressions reported in Table 5.2a, controlling in addition for checks and balances. This variable, as the earlier discussion indicates, takes into account both the presence of competitive elections and the number of veto players in government. As the results in Table 5.2c indicate, there is little evidence that institutions drive the results in Table 5.2a. On the contrary, the magnitude of the effect of political checks and balances drops significantly in comparison with Table 5.1a, suggesting that the results in Table 5.1a are affected by the omission of other political characteristics of countries. The reported magnitude of the effects of the political variables in Table 5.2c, on the other hand, is little changed by the inclusion of checks and balances, and in most cases the political variables are statistically significant.

Politics, Property Rights, and Financial Sector Development

The arguments in the foregoing analysis echo the literature in claiming that the link from politics and political institutions to financial sector development passes through the security of property rights. The difference here is that secure property rights are a consequence both of the political checks and balances that enhance the credibility of government policies, as in the literature, but also of the willingness of governments to provide public goods. Regardless of the underlying dynamics of the link, however, the empirical links in this chain have not been explicitly estimated. One

way to address these links is to estimate the system of equations (3a) and
(3b), which indicate whether the component of secure property rights explained by political institutions is a significant determinant of financial sector development.

Most of the literature on financial sector development gives prominence
to the argument that the security of property and contract rights is key.
The argument here is that a variety of political attributes of countries contribute to the security of property rights by influencing the willingness of
governments to provide public goods generally. These different arguments
all imply the following hypothesis, which is directly tested for the first time
in the analysis here: that component of secure property rights explained by
political institutions, legal origin, or the characteristics of political competition is a significant determinant of financial sector development.

$$\textit{Security of property rights}_i(1975) = \beta_1 + \beta_2 \ln(\textit{initial financial sector})_i \\ + \beta_3 \textbf{(political/institutional variable)}_i + X_i'\boldsymbol{\beta}_4 + \varepsilon_i, \quad \textbf{(3a)}$$

$$\textit{Growth of the financial sector}_i(1975-2000) = \alpha_1 + \alpha_2 \ln(\textit{initial financial sector})_i \\ + \alpha_3(\textbf{predicted security of property rights}) + X_i'\boldsymbol{\alpha}_4 + \mu_i, \quad \textbf{(3b)}$$

or

$$\textit{Size of the financial sector}_i(2000) = \alpha_1 + \alpha_2 \textbf{(predicted security of} \\ \textbf{property rights)} + X_i'\boldsymbol{\alpha}_3 + \mu_i. \quad \textbf{(3b')}$$

These regressions simply ask whether the component of secure property
rights that can be explained by politics or political institutions is a significant determinant of financial sector development. The measure of property
rights follows Knack and Keefer (1995) and is the sum of four variables
from the *International Country Risk Guide* (Political Risk Services): the risk
of expropriation, the enforceability of contracts with government, corruption, and bureaucratic quality. The earliest value of this variable, from
1984, is used here.

Table 5.3 presents several sets of results. Columns 1 and 3 confirm the
well-known connection between the security of property rights and financial sector development. These estimations are based on the specifications
in columns 1 and 2 in Table 5.1a, with the initial value of the property
rights variable substituted for the political variable.

Columns 2 and 4 in Table 5.3 present the more novel results showing
that the component of secure property rights explained by each of the political variables is a significant determinant of financial sector development.
They summarize the results of eight separate estimates of the system of
equations (3), using in turn each of the four political variables analyzed in

TABLE 5.3
*Does the effect of politics on financial sector development
go through the security of property rights?*

Dependent variable: Lending to the private sector by banks and nonbank financial institutions	Growth 1975–2000	Level 2000
Security of property rights (1984)	.0009 (.06)	.12 (.001)

Results from estimates of equations 3b, 3b': the effect on financial development
of the component of property rights predicted by

Competitive elections (1975)	.0017 (.12)	.012 (0.68)
F-statistic from first stage	13.47	2.28
Checks and balances (1975)	.002 (.01)	.018 (.07)
F-statistic	36.89	15.73
Continuous years of competitive elections (1975)	.002 (.004)	.018 (.08)
F-statistic	68.25	18.03
Newspaper circulation (average 1975–2000)	.002 (0.01)	.036 (0.0)
F-statistic	36.5	22.44

SOURCE: See text.
NOTES: Columns 1 and 3 use the specifications of columns 1 and 2 in Table 5.1a, substituting the property rights measure for the political variables. Columns 2 and 4 report the results from estimating equations (3b) or (3b') in the main text, using the predicted value of the security of property rights from equation (3a) in the main text. The control variables in columns 1 and 2 and in columns 3 and 4 are the same as in columns 1 and 2 of Table 5.1a, respectively; neither estimates of these nor control variables are reported. The p-values are reported in parentheses, based on robust standard errors.

Tables 5.1 and 5.2. From equation (3a), Table 5.3 reports only the F-statistic (values above approximately 2.5 reject the null hypothesis that the political variable does not add explanatory power to the estimation of the security of property rights). From the estimates of equations (3b) or (3b'), columns 2 and 4 report only the coefficient on that component of property rights predicted by equation (3a) using the respecting political variable.

In almost all cases, the F-statistics reported in columns 2 and 4 and the (unreported) t-statistics on the estimates of the coefficients of the political variables in equation (3a) confirm that the 1975 values of the political variables are significant determinants of the security of property rights in 1984. The results in columns 2 and 4 of Table 5.3 first confirm the prediction in the literature that political checks and balances accelerate financial sector development through their effect on the security of property rights. However, consistent with the previous results showing the more fragile relationship between competitive elections and financial sector development, that component of secure property rights predicted by competitive elections does not have a significant impact on financial sector development.

The remaining results in columns 2 and 4 support the new predictions of this chapter, that the security of property rights is also a public good, the provision of which is influenced by the conditions of political competition. The continuous years of competitive elections (the credibility of political promises) and newspaper circulation (voter information) are both determinants of the security of property rights, and as columns 2 and 4 indicate, that component of secure property rights that they determine is a significant determinant of financial sector development. These results are not driven by the omission of the institutional variables and their possible correlation with the noninstitutional political variables: in three of the four cases, these results are robust to the inclusion of *checks*.

The results in Table 5.3 underline the need to broaden the analysis of how secure property rights emerge. Although the theoretical and empirical literature has emphasized the existence of competitive elections and of political checks and balances (for example, North and Weingast 1989; Acemoglu, Johnson, and Robinson 2002), other political factors turn out to be at least as important, related to the characteristics of political competition in countries.

Legal Origin, Politics, and Financial Sector Development

The role of legal origin is ignored in the foregoing estimations. Implicitly, though, the role of politics in financial sector development is present in many of the debates regarding the influence of legal institutions. Some scholars argue that legal traditions are the direct product of political forces (La Porta et al. 1998; Glaeser and Shleifer 2000), for example, emerging from the different choices rulers made to control bureaucratic malfeasance or recalcitrant barons. At the same time, modern studies of judicial performance in the United States and elsewhere (for example, Gely and Spiller 1990) demonstrate unambiguously the dependence of judicial decision making on the preferences of political decision makers, just as other literature has demonstrated the influence of politics on other government institutions, even when they enjoyed de jure independence from politicians (for example, central banks, as in Keefer and Stasavage 2003). Those same political forces might be expected to influence political institutions and the dynamics of political competition over the periods under consideration here.

In fact, there is a significant relationship between legal origin variables and each of the political variables under consideration here. An easy way to see this is to group together those legal origins regarded in the literature as being more conducive to the protection of private property rights, the English, German, and Scandinavian. A variable that takes a value of 1 if a country has English, German, or Scandinavian legal origins and a 0 otherwise is highly associated with whether countries exhibit competitive elections, political checks and balances, more continuous years of competitive elections, and greater newspaper circulation, controlling for the logarithm of per capita income in 1975. The literature contains no arguments suggesting that the legal characteristics of countries determine their political institutions and the nature of political competition; in view of the demonstrated influence of politics on judicial decisions, such an argument would be implausible. These results suggest instead that historical forces may determine both—for example, political forces that determined legal institutions in the past also influenced more contemporary political characteristics of countries.

Evidence presented in Beck et al. (2001) indicates that legal origin is the predominant determinant of financial sector development. Table 5.4 substitutes legal origin variables for the political variable in the specifications of Table 5.1a. The first three columns follow their approach in controlling for British, German, and French legal origins. The second three

TABLE 5.4
Legal origin and financial sector development

Dependent variable: Lending to the private sector by banks and nonbank financial institutions	Growth 1975–2000 (OLS)	Level 2000 (OLS)	Level 2000 (OLS)	Growth 1975–2000 (OLS)	Level 2000 (OLS)	Level 2000 (OLS)
British legal origin	.008	.23	.24	.02	.21	.26
	(.43)	(.12)	(.03)	(.06)	(.02)	(.003)
German legal origin	.017	.64	.90	.03	.62	.93
	(.113)	(.001)	(0.0)	(.02)	(0.0)	(0.0)
French legal origin	−.01	.04	.002			
	(.31)	(.76)	(.98)			
Scandinavian legal origin				.01	.10	.48
				(.31)	(.35)	(0.0)
R^2	.09	.46	.26	.09	.47	.31
N	78	94	117	78	94	117

SOURCE: See text.
NOTES: Specifications are as in the first three columns of Table 5.1a, substituting the legal origin for the political variables. *p*-values are reported in parentheses, based on robust standard errors. Constants and other conditioning variables not reported.

columns substitute the Scandinavian legal dummy for the French so that all of the legal traditions that are thought to be most conducive to financial sector development, the British, French, and German traditions, can be compared more easily to those that are thought to be less conducive.

Results in the first three columns of Table 5.4 verify that the effects of legal origin variables in the particular specifications used here are similar to those found by Beck et al. (2001). The last three columns of Table 5.4 also replicate the findings in Beck et al. that countries with Scandinavian and especially German legal origin perform not only better than the French but also better than that of countries with British legal origin. In fact, most specifications show that financial sector development under German legal origin was as much as three times as conducive as British legal origin to financial sector development, despite the theoretical arguments pointing to the superiority of countries with common law legal systems.

Beck et al. (2001) also find that, whether or not one controls for legal origin, political variables have little impact. The variables they use to test their political hypotheses are subjective indicators from the Polity IV database. The results presented earlier already indicate that political measures different from the ones they employ are highly significant determinants of financial sector development. There remains the question, however, of whether these political results survive the introduction of controls for legal origin.

TABLE 5.5A

Competitive elections, checks and balances, and lending to the private sector

Dependent variable:	COMPETITIVE ELECTIONS (1975)			CHECKS AND BALANCES (1975)		
Lending to the private sector by banks and nonbank financial institutions	Growth 1975– 2000 (OLS)	Level 2000 (OLS)	Level 2000 (OLS)	Growth 1975– 2000 (OLS)	Level 2000 (OLS)	Level 2000 (OLS)
Political variable	.01	−.03	.20	.005	.03	.08
	(.26)	(.34)	(.01)	(.04)	(.26)	(0.001)
British legal origin	0.017	.18	.19	.015	.15	.18
	(.08)	(.04)	(.03)	(.10)	(.08)	(.03)
Scandinavian legal origin	.004	.13	.34	.005	.12	.36
	(.70)	(.25)	(0.0)	(.56)	(.25)	(0.0)
German legal origin	.024	.65	.80	.025	.63	.78
	(.06)	(0.0)	(0.0)	(.05)	(0.0)	(0.0)
R^2	.10	.47	.36	.12	.48	.40
N	78	93	116	78	93	116

SOURCE: See text.

NOTES: *p*-values are reported in parentheses, based on robust standard errors. Constants not reported. Specifications based on Table 5.1a, with the addition of legal origin variables.

TABLE 5.5B
Two-stage least squares estimates of Table 5.5a

First-stage regressions

Dependent variable: Lending to the private sector by banks and nonbank financial institutions	COMPETITIVE ELECTIONS (1975)			CHECKS AND BALANCES (1975)		
	Growth 1975– 2000 (IV)	Level 2000 (IV), with GDP/capita	Level 2000 (IV), no GDP/capita	Growth 1975– 2000 (IV)	Level 2000 (IV), with GDP/capita	Level 2000 (IV), no GDP/capita
British legal origin	.019	.13	.19	−.03	.34	.28
	(.91)	(.34)	(.15)	(.96)	(.45)	(.51)
Scandinavian legal origin	.50	.42	.70	.19	−.34	.96
	(.04)	(.07)	(.001)	(.78)	(.64)	(.16)
German legal origin	.29	.46	.72	−.17	.08	1.42
	(.27)	(.04)	(.001)	(.83)	(.91)	(.04)
British colonial heritage	.013	.11	.003	−.31	−.10	−.17
	(.94)	(.80)	(.98)	(.54)	(.84)	(.70)
French colonial heritage	−.40	−.09	−.31	−1.6	−.66	−1.28
	(.042)	(.54)	(.02)	(.006)	(.15)	(.004)
Spanish colonial heritage	.06	.13	.12	−1.07	−.90	−.80
	(.72)	(.30)	(.38)	(.04)	(.03)	(.06)
F-statistic on instruments	2.55	1.02	3.43	2.92	1.84	3.23

Second-stage regressions

	COMPETITIVE ELECTIONS (1975)			CHECKS AND BALANCES (1975)		
Political variable	.09	.19	.66	.036	.22	.27
	(0.003)	(.66)	(0.004)	(.018)	(.13)	(0.005)
British legal origin	.008	.13	.05	−.002	−.01	.018
	(.55)	(.35)	(.72)	(.93)	(.93)	(.90)
Scandinavian legal origin	−.04	.04	−.05	−.025	.09	.019
	(.17)	(.82)	(.83)	(.34)	(.42)	(.93)
German legal origin	−.006	.56	.40	.01	.53	.36
	(.80)	(.019)	(.094)	(.68)	(.01)	(.21)
Hansen J-statistic (chi-squared p-value)	.29	N/A	.19	.58	.48	.71
N	78	91	103	78	91	103

SOURCE: See text.
NOTES: *p*-values are reported in parentheses, based on robust standard errors. Instruments for the fourth and eighth regressions are three dummy variables indicating whether a country has British, French, or Spanish colonial origins. Constants and conditioning variables not reported. Specifications, with the addition of the three legal origin variables, are as in Table 5.1. It is inappropriate to calculate the *J*-statistic in the second regression, given the low significance of the instruments in the first-stage regression.

To the extent that legal origin is a proxy for the early political conditions of countries, it is not appropriate to examine the robustness of political determinants of financial sector development to controls for legal origin. Political variables may be insignificant in the presence of legal origin variables simply because the latter embed political circumstances that more directly capture political incentives toward the financial sector than the political variables themselves. With this significant caveat in mind, Tables 5.5

and 5.6 replicate the specifications in Tables 5.1a, 5.1b, 5.2a, and 5.2b, with the addition of the legal origin controls. Following these earlier tables, Tables 5.5a and 5.6a present the results of ordinary least squares regressions, and Tables 5.5b and 5.6b the instrumental variable estimates, using colonial heritage variables as instruments.

From Tables 5.5a and 5.6a, it is clear that controls for legal origin reduce somewhat the estimated effects of some political variables. However, in contrast to the results found elsewhere in the literature using different political variables, the political hypotheses considered here are not rejected in 10 of 12 specifications, even when controlling for legal origin and even recognizing that legal origin itself captures political effects. The specification does not drive these results, since in these same tables the pattern of results of the legal origin variables is similar to that found in Beck et al. (2001): German legal origin is significantly better for financial sector development than all other legal traditions, whereas British legal origin is frequently significant but of much lower magnitude.

Two-stage least square results, using the colonial heritage variables as instruments, are reported in Tables 5.5b and 5.6b. Results from the first-stage regressions confirm the close relationship between legal origin and political variables. For example, Scandinavian and German legal origins are

TABLE 5.6A

Continuous years of elections, newspaper circulation, and lending to the private sector

Dependent variable: Lending to the private sector by banks and nonbank financial institutions	CONTINUOUS YEARS OF COMPETITIVE ELECTIONS (1975)			AVERAGE NEWSPAPER CIRCULATION (1975–2000)		
	Growth 1975–2000 (OLS)	Level 2000 (OLS)	Level 2000 (OLS)	Growth 1975–2000 (OLS)	Level 2000 (OLS)	Level 2000 (OLS)
Political variable	.0006	.003	.011	.0001	.001	.002
	(.009)	(.32)	(0.0)	(0.0)	(0.0)	(0.0)
British legal origin	0.014	.22	.15	.014	.16	.18
	(.18)	(.05)	(.15)	(.10)	(.05)	(.01)
Scandinavian legal origin	−.01	−.016	−.0004	−.04	−.28	−.21
	(.42)	(.91)	(0.998)	(.03)	(.08)	(0.18)
German legal origin	.02	.62	.75	−.006	.34	.37
	(.16)	(0.001)	(0.0)	(.67)	(0.09)	(0.02)
R^2	.14	.50	.45	.21	.52	.51
N	66	73	88	78	94	115

SOURCE: See text.

NOTES: *p*-values are reported in parentheses, based on robust standard errors. Constants not reported. Specifications based on Table 5.1a, with the addition of legal origin variables.

Two-stage least squares estimates of Table 5.1a

First-stage regressions

Dependent variable: Lending to the private sector by banks and nonbank financial institutions	CONTINUOUS YEARS OF COMPETITIVE ELECTIONS (1975)			AVERAGE NEWSPAPER CIRCULATION (1975–2000)		
	Growth 1975–2000 (IV)	Level 2000 (IV), with GDP/capita	Level 2000 (IV), no GDP/capita	Growth 1975–2000 (IV)	Level 2000 (IV), with GDP/capita	Level 2000 (IV), no GDP/capita
British legal origin	3.6 (.57)	5.65 (.29)	5.03 (.37)	-4.39 (.89)	52.47 (.08)	41.90 (.20)
Scandinavian legal origin	24.2 (.005)	22.56 (.002)	33.58 (0.0)	331.91 (0.0)	292.44 (0.0)	336.92 (0.0)
German legal origin	-1.23 (.89)	.33 (.96)	10.81 (.15)	216.77 (0.0)	211.61 (0.0)	264.96 (0.0)
British colonial heritage	-5.51 (.42)	5.27 (.34)	1.47 (.80)	-10.73 (.32)	-45.24 (.14)	-59.2 (.08)
French colonial heritage	-16.55 (.033)	1.34 (.80)	-8.39 (.16)	-103.91 (.008)	-42.21 (.19)	-122.61 (0.0)
Spanish colonial heritage	-14.73 (.03)	-4.52 (.29)	-7.0 (.15)	-33.68 (.32)	-44.85 (.12)	-57.30 (.09)
F-statistic on instruments	2.06	1.21	1.15	2.66	1.26	4.72

Second-stage regressions

	CONTINUOUS YEARS OF COMPETITIVE ELECTIONS (1975)			AVERAGE NEWSPAPER CIRCULATION (1975–2000)		
Political variable	.003 (0.05)	.02 (.20)	.04 (0.016)	.0006 (0.0)	.003 (.20)	.003 (0.0)
British legal origin	-.009 (.68)	.05 (.79)	-.16 (.51)	.003 (.13)	.05 (.69)	.099 (.27)
Scandinavian legal origin	-.09 (.11)	-.41 (.32)	-1.07 (.11)	-.21 (.002)	-.98 (.26)	-.70 (.05)
German legal origin	.008 (.79)	.58 (.003)	.32 (.41)	.12 (.03)	.19 (.79)	-.03 (.94)
Hansen J-statistic (chi-squared p-value)	N/A	N/A	N/A	.84	N/A	.55
N	66	71	79	78	92	104

SOURCE: See text.

NOTES: *p*-values are reported in parentheses, based on robust standard errors. Instruments for the fourth and eighth regressions are three dummy variables indicating whether a country has British, French, or Spanish colonial origins. Specifications are as in Table 5.2, with the addition of the three legal origin variables. Constants and other conditioning coefficients not reported. It is inappropriate to calculate the *J*-statistic in the second regression, given the low significance of the instruments in the first stage regression.

significantly associated with competitive elections and newspaper circulation; Scandinavian legal origin predicts continuous years of competitive elections in 1975.

The second-stage regressions reveal that among the 12 regressions in Tables 5.5b and 5.6b, in only 6 is even one of the three legal origin variables significant (almost always German legal origin), and in none is more than one significant. In all cases, the estimated magnitudes of the political variables are only slightly lower than the large magnitudes reported in Tables 5.1b and 5.2b, and in 8 of the 12 regressions, the political variables are significant. In 6 of these 8 cases, the J-statistic supports the validity of the instruments, and we can exclude the possibility that the results are driven by omitted variable bias.

It is instructive to ask why the political results here stand in such stark contrast to those in Beck et al. (2001). The answer is likely twofold. First, the subjective measures of political phenomena that they use may overweight the presence of competitive elections. As the evidence here suggests, among all political determinants, competitive elections by themselves form a weaker basis for financial sector development.

Second, although they are careful to test the role played by special interests both in theory and in their empirical work, the variables used here may be more apt for the task. They use the variable *special* from the *DPI*, which records whether parties in government are committed to a nationalist, rural, regional, or religious agenda. Despite the variable label, its best use is likely as a measure of the ideological orientation of governments rather of government willingness to reward narrow interests in society. This is the case with the nationalist and religious categories, for example, which are not traditional dimensions by which one evaluates the extent to which narrow groups in society seek economic benefits from government at the expense of society at large.[7] The political variables in the analysis here capture more directly the political incentives for politicians to cater to special interests.

Finally, one can ask what Tables 5.5 and 5.6 imply for the effects of legal origin on financial sector development. As discussed previously, the results in Tables 5.5a and 5.6a, as in Beck et al. (2001), raise questions about why German legal institutions are superior to the British common law tradition when theory predicts the superiority of the latter. In addition, the insignificance of legal origin in Tables 5.5b and 5.6b literally means that legal institutions have no independent effect on financial development after controlling for the component of political conditions predicted by colonial heritage. This, in turn, has two possible interpretations.

The first is more consistent with theory and evidence regarding the relationship between legal institutions and politics, which support the assumption that legal institutions can be changed by politicians. If this is the case, variables capturing legal institutions are actually proxies for political attitudes toward financial sector development. Those attitudes are shaped by political characteristics of countries. However, political variables are likely noisier indicators of political attitudes than actual political choices regarding legal institutions. Instrumenting political variables with colonial heritage lessens noise. Once political characteristics are properly identified, as in Tables 5.6a and 5.6b, legal origin ceases to have an independent impact on financial sector development.

Alternatively, one can assume that fundamental political institutions do not influence legal origin and that legal institutions have a direct effect on financial sector development unmediated by political considerations. According to this interpretation, the instrumental variable results in Tables 5.5b and 5.6b are spurious because colonial heritage jointly determines the (independent) legal and political evolution of countries. The use of colonial heritage to instrument for political variables attributes all of the joint variation in political and legal institutions to the political variables alone, leaving little variation in legal institutions to explain financial sector development. It is not possible to empirically separate the two alternatives. However, the second is the less plausible alternative, since it relies on the counterfactual assumption that political influence on the judiciary is limited.

Conclusion

Three conclusions emerge from this analysis. First, consistent with much of the literature, political checks and balances are important to the development of the financial sector. This chapter is the first to show this systematically with objective data and, more important, to demonstrate explicitly that the effect of checks and balances passes through the security of property rights. Second, financial sector development depends on the willingness of governments to provide public goods, ranging from hospitable regulation to secure property rights. Given that, we would expect that political characteristics of countries that affect government incentives to provide public goods would also significantly determine financial sector development. Strong evidence is found for this: the continuous years of competitive elections and newspaper circulation, proxies for the credibility of preelectoral political promises and voter information, are both significant determinants of financial sector development. Indeed, they seem to dominate political checks and balances as determinants of financial sector development. This analysis demonstrates explicitly, and for the first time, that all of these political influences operate through their influence on the security of property rights.

Finally, this chapter has revisited the debate concerning politics, legal origin, and finance. In contrast to earlier work, the new and more objective political variables used here are found to be robust to controls for legal origin. Moreover, some evidence presented here suggests, though tentatively, that legal origin is likely to be a proxy for underlying political factors that reflect the willingness of governments to favor broad over narrow interests in society. When this willingness is directly modeled, and one controls for the potential endogeneity of political effects, legal origin variables are no longer significant determinants of financial sector development.

Notes

1. Incentives to provide public goods are also influenced by formal political and electoral institutions. However, in a cross-country setting such institutions as voting rules (proportional representation versus plurality voting) and political systems (presidential versus parliamentary) do not generally have a systematic influence on provision of public goods (see Keefer 2004). Theoretically, the specific political arrangements that give rise to political checks and balances may or may not encourage provision of public goods (see, e.g., Persson and Tabellini 2000).

2. The expropriation risk measure is from Political Risk Services' *International Country Risk Guide*, and the measures of competitive elections from the *Database on Political Institutions*. These are discussed later. There was no difference at all between countries with and without competitive elections on another commonly used measure of property rights, the rule of law measure from the same source.

3. Including 1975 financial sector size in equation (2) would render it nothing more than an investigation of growth over the period 1975–2000.

4. Beginning from a value of 1 (meaning that there is only one veto player and no checks and balances), this variable increments by 1 if countries have potentially competitive elections of the executive; by 1 in presidential systems if the legislature and presidency are controlled by different parties; in parliamentary systems, the value is incremented by the number of parties in the government coalition whose departure would cause the government to lose a majority; and in all systems by 1 for each party supporting the government in the legislature with an ideological stance strongly differing from that of the executive's party (see the *DPI* codebook for more details).

5. The 1975 value of this variable in the *DPI* is actually taken from Clague et al. (1996); values subsequent to 1975 are updated according to the method-

ology explained in the text. The use of values of *persistence* averaged over the 1975–2000 period does not change the results reported.

6. Beck et al. (2001) show that initial values of subjective measures of democracy from the Polity III database are not significant determinants of financial sector development. They also use *current*, not initial, values of the checks and balances measure used here and find it has a significant impact on financial sector development.

7. Governments entirely driven by clientelist or patronage motives are often indifferent to religious or regional interests. Governments recorded as religious in the *DPI*, such as the Christian Democratic Party of Germany, are surely more driven to provide public goods than the major political parties of Bangladesh, which are not recorded as exhibiting any of these four biases. In contrast, the variables used here, particularly the continuing years of competitive elections and newspaper circulation, are linked in the literature to all government actions that favor narrow interests at the expense of broad social interests.

References

Acemoglu, Daron, Simon Johnson, and James A. Robinson (2002). "Reversal of Fortune: Geography and Institutions in the Making of the Modern World." *Quarterly Journal of Economics* 117: 1231–94.

——— (2001). "The Colonial Origins of Comparative Development: An Empirical Investigation." *American Economic Review* 91: 1369–1401.

Acemoglu, Daron, and James A. Robinson (2001). "Inefficient Redistribution." *American Political Science Review* 95: 649–61.

Adserà, Alícia, Carlos Boix, and Mark Payne (2003). "Are You Being Served? Political Accountability and Governmental Performance." *Journal of Law, Economics and Organization* 19: 445–90.

Beck, Thorsten, George Clarke, Alberto Groff, Philip Keefer, and Patrick Walsh (2001). "New Tools in Comparative Political Economy: The Database of Political Institutions." *World Bank Economic Review* 15: 165–76.

Beck, Thorsten, Asli Demirgüç-Kunt, and Ross Levine (2001). "Law, Politics and Finance." The World Bank, Policy Research Working Paper.

——— (2000). "A New Database on Financial Development and Structure." *World Bank Economic Review* 14: 597–605.

Besley, Tim, and Robin Burgess (2002). "The Political Economy of Government Responsiveness: Theory and Evidence from India." *Quarterly Journal of Economics* 117: 1415–52.

Broz, Lawrence (2002). "Domestic Politics of International Financial Rescues: Congressional Voting on Bailouts in the 1990s." Mimeo, Department of Political Science, University of California, San Diego.

Clague, Christopher, Philip Keefer, Stephen Knack, and Mancur Olson (1996). "Property and Contract Rights Under Democracy and Dictatorship." *Journal of Economic Growth* 1 (June): 243–76.

Ferejohn, John (1986). "Incumbent Performance and Electoral Control." *Public Choice* 50: 5–26.

Gely, Rafael, and Pablo Spiller (1990). "A Rational Choice Theory of Supreme Court Statutory Decisions with Applications to the *State Farm* and *Grove City Cases*." *Journal of Law, Economics and Organization* 6: 263–300.

Glaeser, Edward, and Andrei Shleifer (2000). "Legal Origins." Mimeo, Department of Economics, Harvard University.

Grossman, Gene, and Elhanan Helpman (1996). "Electoral Competition and Special Interest Politics." *Review of Economic Studies* 63: 265–86.

Haber, Stephen, Armando Razo, and Noel Maurer (2003). *The Politics of Property Rights: Political Instability, Credible Commitments, and Economic Growth in Mexico, 1876–1929*. Cambridge, UK: Cambridge University Press.

Hall, Robert E., and Charles I. Jones (1999). "Why Do Some Countries Produce So Much More Output Than Others?" *Quarterly Journal of Economics* 114: 83–116.

Keefer, Philip (2005). "Democratization and Clientelism: Why Are Young Democracies Badly Governed?" Mimeo, Development Research Group, The World Bank.

——— (2004). "Elections, Special Interests and the Fiscal Costs of Financial Crises." The World Bank, Policy Research Working Paper.

Keefer, Philip, and David Stasavage (2003). "The Limits of Delegation: Veto Players, Central Bank Independence, and the Credibility of Monetary Policy." *American Political Science Review* 97: 407–23.

Keefer, Philip, and Razvan Vlaicu (2004). "Democracy, Credibility, and Clientelism." The World Bank, Policy Research Working Paper.

Knack, Stephen, and Philip Keefer (1995). "Institutions and Economic Performance: Cross-Country Tests Using Alternative Institutional Measures." *Economics and Politics* 7: 207–28.

Kroszner, Randall S., and Philip E. Strahan (1996). "Regulatory Incentives and the Thrift Crisis: Dividends, Mutual-to-Stock Conversions, and Financial Distress." *Journal of Finance* 51: 1285–1320.

Kroszner, Randall S., and Thomas Stratmann (1998). "Interest Group Competition and the Organization of Congress." *American Economic Review* 88: 1163–87.

La Porta, Rafael, Florencio López-de-Silanes, Andrei Shleifer, and Robert W. Vishny (1998). "Law and Finance." *Journal of Political Economy* 106: 1113–55.

North, Douglass C., and Barry Weingast (1989). "Constitutions and Commitment: The Evolution of Institutions Governing Public Choice in Seventeenth-Century England." *Journal of Economic History* 49: 803–32.

Persson, Torsten, and Guido Tabellini (2000). *Political Economics: Explaining Public Policy.* Cambridge, MA: MIT Press.

Persson, Torsten, Guido Tabellini, and Francesco Trebbi (2003). "Electoral Rules and Corruption." *Journal of the European Economic Association* 1: 958–89.

Stasavage David (2003). *Public Debt and the Birth of the Democratic State: France and Great Britain 1688–1789.* New York: Cambridge University Press.

Chapter 6

The Microeconomic Effects of Different Approaches to Bank Supervision

JAMES R. BARTH, GERARD CAPRIO,

AND ROSS LEVINE

Introduction

A large and growing body of research finds that cross-country differences in banking sector development influence national rates of long-run economic growth (Levine 1997, 2006). Banks mobilize savings and allocate those resources to productive ends. Opportunities for economic development are enhanced if banks conduct this intermediation task efficiently and allocate capital effectively. These findings highlight the substantial social welfare benefits of developing public policies that enhance bank operations. These findings also stress that banking system stability is not the only criterion for defining well-functioning bank operations: the efficiency of intermediation and the effectiveness with which banks identify, fund, and monitor firms are critical for fostering long-run economic growth.

Yet only with the creation of a new international database on bank regulatory and supervisory policies have researchers begun to assess which banking sector policies promote sound financial intermediation around the world (Barth et al. 2001a, 2001b, 2004, 2006). This new database includes detailed data on as many as 275 regulatory and supervisory practices in over 150 countries. Thus, these data permit researchers to examine the effects of individual regulatory and supervisory powers. These data also allow researchers to aggregate information on individual regulations and statutes to assess the effects of broad approaches to bank regulation and supervision.

This chapter reviews and presents microeconomic evidence on the impact of two broad approaches to bank regulation and supervision on the efficiency with which banks intermediate savings (Demirgüç-Kunt et al. 2004) and the degree to which corruption distorts bank lending decisions (Beck et al. 2006a). Strategically, we follow Barth et al. (2004, 2006), who show that national approaches to bank supervision fall along a spectrum. Some countries adopt an overall approach to bank supervision that focuses on direct official supervision of banks, whereas other countries place comparatively greater emphasis on adopting regulations that empower private sector monitoring of banks. We argue that countries do not select individual regulations and statutes in isolation; rather, individual country policies reflect broad public policy approaches to bank supervision. By adopting this strategy of aggregating individual regulatory and supervisory powers into aggregate indexes, one loses the specificity associated with examining individual laws. The advantage of this aggregate approach is that it provides evidence regarding which broad regulatory and supervisory strategies promote well-functioning bank operations.

The public interest approach to bank regulation and supervision stresses that market failures—information and contract enforcement costs—interfere with the incentives and abilities of private agents to monitor banks effectively. Given the severity of market failures, a powerful supervisory agency that directly monitors and disciplines banks can, in theory, reduce corruption in lending and thereby enhance the efficiency of capital allocation, and encourage a sufficient degree of competition to boost the efficiency of intermediation. The public interest approach assumes that (1) there are market failures; (2) official supervisors have the capabilities to ameliorate those market failures by directly overseeing, regulating, and disciplining banks; and (3) official supervisors have the incentives to fix market failures and promote the development of banks that foster national economic prosperity (Stigler 1971, 1975).

The private interest view, however, questions whether official supervisory agencies have the incentives and ability to fix market failures and enhance the socially efficient operation of banks. Although market failures, such as information and enforcement costs, may impede private monitoring, government failures may be so large that empowering official supervisors produces socially counterproductive results (Hamilton et al. 1788; Shleifer and Vishny 1998; Haber et al. 2003). From this perspective, politicians and government supervisors do not maximize social welfare; they maximize their own welfare. Thus, official supervisors may not have the incentives to fix market failures. Indeed, supervisors may use their positions of power to funnel credit to connected firms, or banks may capture supervisory agencies and use the agencies to protect and enrich bankers. Strengthening official oversight of banks may therefore reduce banking efficiency and intensify corruption in lending.

According to the private interest view, the most efficacious approach to bank supervision relies on using government regulations and institutions to empower private monitoring of banks. Specifically, the private monitoring approach advocates effective information disclosure rules and sound contract enforcement systems so that private investors can exert appropriate corporate governance over banks with positive ramifications on bank efficiency and the integrity of lending. This is not a laissez-faire approach. Indeed, the private interest approach stresses that strong legal and regulatory institutions are necessary for reducing information and contract enforcement costs.

Extensions and mergers of the public and private interest views stress that the impact of strengthening official supervisory power or promoting information disclosure depends critically on legal and political institutions. For instance, one can partially define "sound" political and legal systems in terms of the degree to which they induce politicians and government officials to act in the best interests of society. From this perspective, empowering official supervisors will have a greater chance of boosting banking performance and lowering corruption in sound institutional environments than in political and legal environments that do not hold politicians and public officials accountable to society at large. Similarly, more information transparency—which is a key component of the private interest view of bank regulation—is unlikely to materially improve bank operations if legal and political institutions do not allow private investors to use this information to exert effective governance over banks. From this perspective, bank regulatory and supervisory practices—whether based on public or private interest foundations—depend on the operation of legal and political systems. Therefore, we also discuss the roles of legal and political institutions in determining the effectiveness of different banking sector policies.

To assess empirically the impact of the public and private interest approaches to supervision on bank operations, we use two microeconomic measures of the efficient operation of banks. First, across a broad cross section of countries, we use bank-level data of the ratio of each bank's overhead costs to its total assets. Although these data are imperfect, high overhead costs can signal excessive managerial perquisites and market power that contradict the notions of sound governance of banks and efficient intermediation. As a second measure of bank efficiency, we use firm-level survey data across a large number of countries regarding the degree to which firms need corrupt ties with banks to obtain loans. Again, these data are imperfect, but the need for corrupt ties with bank officials to obtain funds may signal a socially inefficient form of allocating bank credit. Using these measures, we provide empirical evidence on which broad approaches to bank supervision promote the efficient functioning of banks.

To measure policies that empower official supervisors, we use the Barth et al. (2004) indicator of official power, which aggregates information on whether bank supervisors can take specific actions against bank management, bank owners, and bank auditors both in normal times and times of distress. Supervisory agencies can use these powers to improve the governance of banks as emphasized by the official empowerment view. Alternatively, the supervisory authority can use these powers to induce banks to funnel credit to favored ends as emphasized by the private empowerment view. Thus, the degree to which and the institutional conditions under which empowering the supervisory authority improves the functioning of banks are empirical questions.

To measure policies that empower private monitoring of banks, we use the Barth et al. (2004) indicator of private monitoring, which includes information on the degree to which bank regulations force banks to disclose accurate information to the public. The private interest view holds that regulations, laws, and enforcement mechanisms that improve private governance of banks will boost the functioning of banks. In contrast, the public interest view holds that market imperfections in banking are so substantive and pervasive that strengthening information disclosure laws will not materially improve banking operations. Again, sound theories support both sides of the debate. By assessing empirically the impact of the official supervisory power and the private monitoring indicators on bank efficiency and the integrity of bank-firm relations, we provide evidence on which supervisory approach is associated with better-functioning banks.

Although we have stressed differences between the public and private interest approaches, there may be complementarities at the level of individual regulations and statutes. Countries could adopt regulations that force banks to disclose accurate information to the public, while also creating official supervisory agencies that directly oversee bank activities. Conceptually, however, these approaches reflect different attitudes toward the role of government in monitoring banks. Indeed, differences in the degree of emphasis on empowering private monitoring of banks may represent a particularly useful litmus test of different national attitudes toward the role of government in the economy. Empirically, if the official power and private monitoring indicators are highly correlated, then we will observe multicollinearity in the regressions. Alternatively, if it is useful to classify bank supervisory approaches in terms of official empowerment versus private empowerment, then we will not observe multicollinearity and will instead observe that the official power and private monitoring indicators yield distinct results.

Methodologically, we use two distinct data sets, different econometric procedures, and different definitions of "better-functioning banks." First, we use a pooled bank-level, cross-country database and employ a generalized least squares random effects estimator to assess which supervisory strategies lower bank overhead costs. We use microeconomic data to minimize the possibility that reverse causality biases the results. Nevertheless, bank overhead costs are an imprecise measure of bank efficiency. Thus, we control for other bank-specific characteristics and use alternative measures of bank performance in assessing bank supervisory approaches. Second, we use a pooled firm-level, cross-country database and employ an ordered probit procedure to assess which supervisory strategies lower the tendency for firms to report that corruption in banking is a serious hindrance to obtaining credit. These survey data offer a unique insight into bank-firm relationships. Nevertheless, these survey data reflect each firm's subjective evaluations of constraints on firm growth, which underscores the need to control for potential biases and use caution in interpreting the results. Since each of these measures of bank performance and corresponding methodologies has strengths and weaknesses, there are advantages to employing both; if these different methodologies produce consistent results regarding the public and private interest approaches to bank supervision, this raises the level of confidence in the overall conclusions.

It is important to emphasize an important limitation to interpreting these analyses. This chapter, unfortunately, does not formally identify a logical chain running from truly exogenous factors, to the political and institutional setting, to bank supervisory approaches, to the functioning of banks, and on to the operation of firms and national rates of economic growth. As we emphasize throughout, bank supervision does not occur in a vacuum. Rather, as documented in great detail for the case of Mexico by Haber et al. (2003) and as illustrated in a cross-country context by Barth et al. (2006), bank regulations reflect an array of societal forces. Thus, this chapter does not explain how a country could implement an improvement in its supervisory regime, nor does it address whether a country's supervisory regime is socially optimal given other political and institutional constraints. In moving to a book-level study, Barth et al. (2006) provide an assessment of

(1) the determinants of different bank supervisory and regulatory policies and (2) the impact of different bank supervisory and regulatory approaches on bank development, efficiency, corruption, fragility, and governance. Nevertheless, by using different instrumental variables to extract the exogenous component of bank supervision, we provide information on the impact of different supervisory strategies on the functioning of banks, which is an important prerequisite for understanding what makes financial markets work effectively.

This chapter is related to two recent studies. First, Demirgüç-Kunt et al. (2004) study the relationship between bank net interest margins and a wide array of bank supervisory and regulatory indicators. Using the same database, we examine overhead costs instead of net interest margins to focus on a broad measure of bank governance and managerial perquisites and examine two broad approaches to bank supervision instead of examining many individual measures of bank regulation and supervision (also see Barth et al. 2006). Second, Beck et al. (2006a) examine the impact of different bank regulatory and supervisory practices on corruption in lending. Using a unified set of control variables, we examine the relationship between bank regulatory and supervisory strategies on both overhead costs and corruption in lending.

Furthermore, this chapter fits into an emerging body of cross-country evidence on the impact of bank supervision and regulation. Barth et al. (2004) conduct a pure cross-country analysis and find that financial development is (1) positively associated with supervisory approaches that force information disclosure and (2) negatively associated with powerful supervisors that directly monitor and discipline banks. We use microeconomic data to examine the relationship between bank supervisory approaches and bank efficiency. Also, to assess the linkages between banking sector policies and the corporate governance of banks, Caprio et al. (2003) examine whether different bank regulations and supervisory practices influence the market valuation of banks. Rather than examine bank valuations, we present microeconomic evidence on the impact of different approaches to bank supervision on the efficiency of bank operations as measured by overhead costs and the integrity of bank-firm relations. Finally, Barth et al. (2004) and Beck et al. (2006b, 2006c) study the impact of different regulations and different approaches to bank supervision on bank fragility. They show that official supervisory power does not reduce the probability that a country suffers a systemic banking crisis. In this chapter, we do not consider fragility. We examine the effect of bank supervisory approaches on bank efficiency and the degree of corruption of bank lending.

The remainder of the chapter is organized as follows. We first present the data, then the analyses on overhead costs, an examination of the impact of bank supervisory strategies on the degree of corruption in bank lending, and the conclusions.

Data

To examine the microeconomic effects of different approaches to bank supervision, we need measures of the different approaches to bank supervision and microeconomic measures of the functioning of banks. This section presents these data along with various conditioning variables.

APPROACHES TO BANK SUPERVISION: PROXY MEASURES

We use two indicators of approaches to bank supervision from Barth et al. (2004). The underlying data to construct these indexes were collected between late 1998 and early 2000 for 107 countries. Barth et al. (2001a) describe the data and how they were collected.

Official Power is constructed from 14 dummy variables that indicate whether bank supervisors can take specific actions against bank management, bank owners, and bank auditors both in normal times and in times of distress. This includes information on whether the supervisory agency can force a bank to change its internal organizational structure, suspend dividends, stop bonuses, halt management fees, force banks to constitute provisions against actual or potential losses as determined by the supervisory agency, supersede the legal rights of shareholders, remove and replace managers and directors, obtain information from external auditors, and take legal action against auditors for negligence. The exact definition of Official Power is provided in Table 6.1, and Table 6.6 provides the values for each country. We use the first principal component indicator of these variables, which varies between −3.05 (Singapore) and 1.14 (United States) with a mean of −0.11, and higher values indicating wider authority for bank supervisors.

In terms of theory, the public interest view stresses that supervisors will use these official powers to ameliorate market imperfections, improve the governance of banks, and thereby boost bank efficiency and lower the need for firms to have corrupt ties with bank officials to obtain loans. Thus, the public interest view predicts that higher values of Official Power will lower overhead costs and reduce corruption in bank-firm relations.

Alternatively, the private interest view stresses that powerful supervisors do not necessarily have incentives to reduce market imperfections. Rather, powerful supervisors will have the incentives, and tools, to maximize their own welfare, with potentially detrimental implications for overall bank efficiency and the integrity of bank lending. Thus, the private interest view predicts that Official Power will tend to (1) hurt the efficient functioning of banks and (2) increase corruption.

Modified versions of the private interest view would predict a nonlinear relationship between Official Power and bank operations that depends on the political and institutional environment. Specifically, although politicians and government officials maximize their own utility, they do so subject to various constraints. If political and legal institutions constrain the ability of politicians and government officials to extract private rents from their positions of power and instead create incentives for them to maximize social welfare, then increases in Official Power will tend to improve the efficient operations of banks. We focus on assessing the first-order impact of banking policies on bank operations and discuss recent work by Beck et al. (2006a) that tests these nonlinear effects.

Private Monitoring measures the degree to which bank supervision forces banks to disclose accurate information to the public and induces private sector monitoring of banks. Private Monitoring is constructed from nine dummy variables that measure whether bank directors and officials are legally liable for the accuracy of information disclosed to the public, whether banks must publish consolidated accounts, whether banks must be rated and audited, whether banks must be audited by certified international auditors, whether subordinated debt is allowable (which may create a class of private monitors), and whether there is both no explicit deposit insurance and no actual insurance paid the last time a bank failed (as a measure of the existence of an implicit deposit insurance regime). Private Monitoring is constructed as a principal component indicator, with higher values indicating more tools and incentives for private bank creditors to monitor banks. Again, Table 6.1 provides a more rigorous definition, and Table 6.6 lists the values for each country, with values ranging from −1.56 (Ghana) to 1.46 (United Kingdom).

In terms of theory, the private interest view holds that supervisory policies that force accurate information disclosure and give private creditors appropriate incentives can ameliorate market failures without increasing the likelihood of political/regulatory capture. Thus, the private empowerment view holds that Private Monitoring will be negatively associated with (1) overhead costs and (2) the degree to which firms need corrupt ties with banks to obtain credit. As stressed by Beck et al. (2006a), the private interest view presupposes the existence of sufficiently sound legal institutions that

TABLE 6.1
Variable definitions and sources

Variable name	Variable definition	Source
Dependent variables		
Bank Development	For each country, measures bank credit to the private sector as share of GDP, 2000–2001. Specifically, it equals $\{(0.5)[F(t)/P_e(t) + F(t-1)/P_e(t-1)]\} / [GDP(t)/P_a(t)]$, where F is credit by deposit money banks to the private sector (line 22d), GDP is line 99b, P_e is end-of-period CPI (line 64), and P_a is the average CPI for the year.	International Financial Statistics (IMF)
Overhead Costs	For each bank, this equals overhead costs divided by total assets, 1995–99 bank officials	Bankscope Database
Bank Corruption	For each firm, this equals the response to the question, "Is the corruption of for the operation and growth of your business: (1) an obstacle, (2) a minor obstacle, (3) a moderate obstacle, or (4) a major obstacle?" Thus, bigger numbers imply the corruption of bank officials is a bigger obstacle to obtaining financing. (2000)	World Business Environment Survey (WBES)
Supervisory variables		
Official Power	Measure of legal power of the supervisory agency. Principal component indicator of 14 variables: (1) Does the supervisory agency have the right to meet with external auditors? (2) Are auditors legally required to communicate directly to the supervisory agency any illicit activities, fraud, or insider abuse? (3) Can supervisors take legal action against external auditors for negligence? (4) Can the supervisory authority force a bank to change its internal organization? (5) Are off–balance sheet items disclosed to supervisors? (6) Can the supervisory agency order the bank's directors/managers to constitute provisions to cover actual/potential losses? (7) Can the supervisory agency suspend (a) dividends? (b) bonuses? (c) management fees? (8) Can the supervisory agency legally supersede the rights of shareholders and declare a bank insolvent? (9) Does the Banking Law give authority to the supervisory agency to intervene in a problem bank? (10) Regarding restructuring, can the supervisory agency (a) supersede shareholder rights? (b) remove and replace management? (c) remove and replace directors? (1999)	Barth, Caprio, and Levine (2004)
Private Monitoring	Measures regulations that empower private monitoring of banks. Principal component indicator of nine variables of whether (1) bank directors and officials are legally liable for the accuracy of information disclosed to the public, (2) banks must publish consolidated accounts, (3) banks must be audited by certified international auditors, (4) 100% of the largest 10 banks are rated by international rating agencies, (5) off–balance	Barth, Caprio, and Levine (2004)

sheet items are disclosed to the public, (6) banks must disclose their risk management procedures to the public, (7) accrued, though unpaid interest/principal enters the income statement while the loan is still nonperforming, (8) subordinated debt is allowable, and (9) there is no explicit deposit insurance system and no insurance was paid the last time a bank failed. (1999)

Country-level control variables

Activity Restrictions	Index of regulatory restrictions on the ability of banks to own nonfinancial corporations and to engage in securities market, insurance, and real estate activities.	Barth, Caprio, and Levine (2004)
Capital Index	An index of the stringency of capital regulations based on the following questions: Is the minimum capital-asset ratio requirement risk weighted in line with the Basel guidelines? Does the minimum ratio vary as a function of market risk? Is market value of loan losses not realized in accounting books deducted? Are unrealized losses in securities portfolios deducted? Are unrealized foreign exchange losses deducted? What fraction of revaluation gains is allowed as part of capital? Are the sources of funds to be used as capital verified by the regulatory/supervisory authorities? Can the initial disbursement or subsequent injections of capital be done with assets other than cash or government securities? Can initial disbursement of capital be done with borrowed funds? (1999)	Barth, Caprio, and Levine (2004)
Corruption	Corruption in government index. Low ratings indicate that government officials are likely to demand special, illegal payments. (1995)	Political Risk Services
Deposit Insurance	An aggregate index of the generosity of the deposit insurance regime. Specifically, it is the first principal component based on the following deposit insurance design features: existence of co-insurance, coverage of foreign currency and interbank deposits, type of funding (unfounded, callable, or funded), source of funding (banks only, banks and government, or government only), management (private, joint, or public), membership (compulsory or voluntary), and the level of explicit coverage (coverage limit divided by deposits per capita).	Demirgüç-Kunt and Detragiache (2002)
Entry Index	Extent of legal submissions required to obtain a banking license. (1999)	Barth, Caprio, and Levine (2004)
Foreign Banks	A measure of the degree of government ownership of banks, measured as the fraction of the banking system's assets that is in banks that are 50% or more foreign owned. (1999)	Barth, Caprio, and Levine (2004)

(continued)

TABLE 6.1 (*continued*)

Variable name	Variable definition	Source
GDP Growth	Growth rate of GDP, average 1995–99.	World Development Indicators
GDP per Capita	Real GDP per capita, averaged over 1995–99.	World Development Indicators
Government Banks	A measure of the degree of government ownership of banks, measured as the fraction of the banking system's assets that is in banks that are 50% or more government owned. (1999)	Barth, Caprio, and Levine (2004)
Political Violence	Indicator of the degree of political stability and absence of violence, which is constructed from numerous survey indicators.	Kaufmann, Kraay, and Zoido-Lobaton (1999)
Political Voice and Accountability	Indicator of the degree to which citizens have a voice in the political process and the extent to which politicians can be held accountable for their actions. This is constructed from numerous survey indicators.	Kaufmann, Kraay, and Zoido-Lobaton (1999)
Firm-level controls		
Competitors	Equals the logarithm of the number of competitors that the firm faces.	World Business Environment Survey
Exporter	Takes on the value 1 if the firm exports goods or services.	World Business Environment Survey
Firm Obstacles	Equals the response to the question, "How problematic is financing for the operation and growth of your business?" Answers vary between 1 (no obstacle), 2 (minor obstacle), 3 (moderate obstacle), and 4 (major obstacle).	World Business Environment Survey
Foreign Firm	Takes on the value 1 if a foreign entity owns any percentage of the firm.	World Business Environment Survey
Government Firm	Takes on the value 1 if the government owns any percentage of the firm.	World Business Environment Survey
Manufacturing	Takes on the value 1 if the firm is in the manufacturing sector.	World Business Environment Survey
Sales	Equals the log of sales in U.S. dollars as indicator of size.	World Business Environment Survey
Services	Takes on the value 1 if the firm is in the service sector.	World Business Environment Survey
Bank-level controls		
Bank Equity	Bank equity divided by total assets, year 1995.	Bankscope Database
Bank Size	Logarithm of total individual bank assets in millions of U.S. dollars, year 1995.	Bankscope Database

Variable	Description	Source
Liquidity	Liquid bank assets divided by total bank assets, year 1995.	Bankscope Database
Market Share	Individual bank assets over total commercial bank assets, year 1995.	Bankscope Database
Instrumental variables		
Independence	Percentage of years since 1776 that the country has been independent.	Easterly and Levine (1997)
Initial Political Openness	Measures the openness, competitiveness, and democracy in the first year of independence or 1800, whichever comes first. Specifically, it is the first principal component of five indicators: (1) Polity measures the degree of democracy–autocracy, e.g., institutions through which citizens express preferences, constraints on executive, the guarantee of civil liberties, the lack of suppression of political participation, the openness to nonelites. (-10 to $+10$). (2) XROPEN measures the openness of executive recruitment and ranges from hereditary succession (0) to competitive election (4). (3) XRCOMP measures the degree of competitiveness of executive recruitment and ranges from unopposed elections (0) to multiparty, competitive elections (3). (4) XCONST measures institutional constraints on executive decisions and ranges from unlimited authority (1) to institutional arrangements where a legislature has equal/greater authority (7). (5) PARCOMP measures the competitiveness of political groups and ranges from (a) repressed (no significant opposition outside ruling party) (1) to (b) highly competitive (enduring groups regularly compete for influence) (5).	Marshall and Jaggers (Polity IV Project)
Latitude	Absolute value of the latitude of the country.	Beck, Demirgüç-Kunt, and Levine (2003)
Religion	Percentage of the population of each country that belongs to the following religions: (1) Roman Catholicism, (2) Protestantism, (3) Islam, (4) Other religion.	Beck, Demirgüç-Kunt, and Levine (2003).

allow private investors to use greater information disclosure to improve governance of banks. Thus, the private interest view relies on well-functioning governmental and legal institutions in conjunction with regulatory requirements on the dissemination of accurate, comparable information to improve the operation of banks.

In contrast, the public interest view stresses the importance of market failures and is skeptical that information disclosure rules will substantively improve the governance of banks. Put differently, the public interest view rejects the presumption that many countries have sufficiently well-functioning legal institutions such that greater transparency will allow private investors to improve the governance of banks substantively. Thus, the public interest view holds that Private Monitoring will not be strongly linked with measures of bank efficiency and the integrity of bank-firm relations.

BANK EFFICIENCY: OVERHEAD COSTS
AND CONTROL VARIABLES

Overhead Costs equals bank overhead costs divided by total assets. We average the data over the period 1995–99 to abstract from business-cycle influences. However, we obtain the same results when using Overhead Costs in 1999. Overhead Costs may reflect cost inefficiency as well as market power. Thus, we use Overhead Costs to assess the microeconomic efficiency effects of different approaches to bank supervision, where lower levels of Overhead Costs signal greater efficiency. In robustness tests, rather than examine Overhead Costs, we studied Net Interest Margin, which equals interest income minus interest expense divided by total interest-earning assets. This alternative measure of bank efficiency produced the same results.

In terms of theory, the official supervision approach stresses that powerful official supervisors will improve the governance of banks, promote competition, and therefore lower overhead costs. In contrast, the private monitoring approach to bank supervision holds that powerful official supervision may actually breed bank inefficiencies as supervisors and bankers collude to achieve their goals to the detriment of overall bank efficiency. The private monitoring approach instead argues that stronger private monitoring will be more effective at reducing excessive overhead costs.

As listed in Table 6.4, the sample includes overhead cost data on over 1,400 banks across 75 countries. Nigeria has the highest average overhead costs across its banks, whereas Singapore has the lowest. There is considerable cross-bank variation in overhead costs such that the sample mean is 3.00 and the sample standard deviation is 1.64.

In the Overhead Cost analyses, we use a number of bank-level controls. **Market Share** equals the bank's assets divided by total bank assets in the economy. A bank that dominates the national market may enjoy larger overhead costs than a bank that does not control much of the market. **Bank Size** equals the logarithm of total bank assets in millions of U.S. dollars. Size may be an important determinant of overhead costs if there are increasing returns to scale in banking. In particular, larger banks may require lower overhead expenditures as a share of total assets. **Liquidity** equals the liquid assets of the bank divided by total assets. We use this indicator to control for differences in bank assets. In some cases, banks with considerable market power may hold a high ratio of liquid government assets and also enjoy high overhead costs. **Bank Equity** equals the book value of equity divided by total assets. Some theories suggest that well-capitalized banks face lower expected bankruptcy costs and hence lower funding costs. Thus, higher bank equity implies greater opportunities for larger overhead costs when loan rates do not vary much with bank equity. We obtained all of the bank-level data, including overhead cost data, from Demirgüç-Kunt et al. (2004), who constructed the indexes from the Bankscope Database. Table 6.4 lists the values for these bank-level control variables.

BANK EFFICIENCY: CORRUPTION IN LENDING AND CONTROL VARIABLES

To examine the relationship between bank supervisory strategies and the degree of corruption in bank lending, we use data from the World Business Environment Survey (WBES). The WBES contains information on almost 2,300 firms across 33 countries for which we also have data on bank supervision from Barth et al. (2004). The WBES surveyed firms of all sizes; small firms (between 5 and 50 employees) represent 40 percent of the sample, medium-sized firms (between 51 and 500 employees) are 40 percent of the sample, and the remaining 20 percent are large firms (more than 500 employees).

In this chapter, we focus on one question from the WBES that measures the degree to which firms need corrupt ties with banks to obtain bank credit.

Bank Corruption equals the response to this question: "Is the corruption of bank officials an obstacle for the operation and growth of your business: (1) no obstacle, (2) a minor obstacle, (3) a moderate obstacle, or (4) a major obstacle?" Thus, higher numbers imply that corruption of bank officials is a bigger obstacle to obtaining financing. Table 6.5 lists the average values of Bank Corruption across the firms in each of 48 countries in the sample. As shown, the sample includes about 4,700 firms. There is considerable cross-firm variation. The average firm has a value of Bank Corruption of 1.62, and the standard deviation is 0.97.

Again, in terms of theory, the public interest approach holds that powerful supervisors will improve the oversight of banks and reduce the need for corruption with beneficial effects on overall bank efficiency. The private interest approach instead stresses government failures: Official power will increase corrupt ties between supervisory officials and banks and thereby increase the need for firms to have corrupt ties with banks to obtain credit. The private interest approach emphasizes that private monitoring rather than official supervisory power will reduce bank corruption.

In analyzing the relationship between Bank Corruption and different approaches to bank supervision, we control for a number of firm-level traits. Specifically, the WBES comprises firms from the manufacturing, construction, and services sectors, so we include dummy variables for each firm's sector. The WBES also provides information on whether each firm is government owned, foreign owned, or privately owned, and whether the firm is an exporter. Again, we include 0–1 dummy variables for whether each firm is a government firm or a foreign firm, where private firms are the omitted category. We also include a dummy variable for whether the firm is an exporter. Finally, we include data on each firm's sales and the number of competitors that each firm reports it faces. Table 6.5 lists averages across firms in each country of these firm-level control variables.

Using data based on self-reporting by firms may produce concerns that a firm facing the same obstacles will respond to questions differently in different institutional and cultural environments. If this were pure measurement error, it would bias the results *against* finding a relationship between bank supervision and bank corruption.

Although problems with survey data may bias the results against the conclusions we draw from the empirical results, we do control for different institutional and cultural environments and control for the firm's response to another question regarding external financing. Thus, we assess the link between bank supervision and the integrity of the bank-firm relationship while controlling for the individual firm's view of external financing obstacles. Specifically, we control for the firm's response to the following question: "How problematic is financing for the operation and growth of your business?" Answers vary between 1 (no obstacle), 2 (minor obstacle), 3 (moderate obstacle), and 4 (major obstacle). Controlling for this more general question about firm financing obstacles reduces the likelihood that reporting biases or interpretation differences drive the results on the relationship between bank supervisory approaches and corruption in bank lending.

COUNTRY-LEVEL CONTROL VARIABLES

In examining the microeconomic effects of different approaches to bank supervision across many countries, we control for an assortment of country-specific factors. Table 6.1 provides detailed definitions of these country-specific control variables. Here we simply define the variables and note why they are included.

Activity Restrictions is an index of regulatory restrictions on bank activities in the areas of security underwriting, insurance, real estate, and owning nonfinancial firms (Barth et al. 2001b). We include this variable because we want to assess the links between broad approaches to bank supervision and bank efficiency while controlling for specific regulatory differences. Table 6.6 lists values for each country. Barth et al. (2004) provide a rigorous definition of this variable.

GDP Growth equals the growth rate of the economy over the period 1995–99. GDP Growth is included to control for business-cycle forces that may influence overhead costs and bank corruption. **GDP per Capita** equals real per capita gross domestic product (GDP) averaged over the 1995–99 period. We include this variable to control for the overall level of economic development. GDP per Capita is a summary measure of the impact of natural resources, capital accumulation, human capital accumulation, and institutional factors on economic development.

Political Violence is an indicator of political stability and the absence of violence, so higher values imply *less* violence. **Political Voice and Accountability** is an indicator of the degree to which the average citizen has a voice in the political process and the extent to which politicians can be held accountable for their actions through elections. We include these to control for differences in the political environment. Table 6.6 presents values for each country. **Corruption** is an index of the overall level of corruption in the country's government. Lower values imply that government officials are more likely to demand illegal payments. We include this variable for two reasons. In the Overhead Costs regressions, we include Corruption to control for the overall institutional environment in assessing the link between approaches to supervision and bank efficiency. In the Bank Corruption regression, we use Corruption to control for overall corruption and thereby provide a particularly rigorous test of whether there is a link between supervisory strategies and corruption in bank-firm relations.

Government Banks equals the fraction of the banking system's assets held by banks that are more than 50 percent owned by the government. Since government ownership may distort the application of different supervisory approaches, it is important to control for the degree of state-owned banks.

Overhead Costs and Bank Supervisory Approaches

METHODOLOGY

To assess the impact of bank supervisory approaches on bank efficiency while controlling for bank-specific and country-specific factors, we estimate regressions of the following form:

$$\text{Overhead Costs}_{i,k} = \alpha + \beta_1 S_i + \beta_2 B_{i,k} + \beta_3 C_i + \varepsilon_{i,k}, \tag{1}$$

where i indexes country i, and k indexes bank k; S_i represents the two measures of bank supervision—Official Power and Private Monitoring—in country i; $B_{i,k}$ is a vector of bank-specific characteristics for bank k in country i; C_i is a vector of country-specific control variables; and $\varepsilon_{i,k}$ is the residual. Thus, the unit of observation is an individual bank k in country i. Since the model includes country-specific variables, we use a generalized least squares estimator with random effects. Since the dependent variable in the regressions is an individual bank's Overhead Costs, it seems unlikely that an individual bank's efficiency drives national approaches to bank supervision. Nevertheless, as a robustness check, we used instrumental variables and confirmed this chapter's findings.

RESULTS

Table 6.2 presents regression results that indicate that Private Monitoring tends to exert a negative influence on Overhead Costs. There exists no statistical connection between Official Power and Overhead Costs. Table 6.2 provides regressions of Overhead Costs on the supervisory indexes, plus bank-specific controls, while also controlling for various country-level variables. Official Power does not enter any of the regressions significantly. Private Monitoring enters all of the regressions significantly and negatively, except the regression including all of the country-control variables, including GDP per Capita. There is a high correlation between the level of economic development and countries with approaches to bank supervision that

TABLE 6.2
Overhead costs and supervisory strategy: Bank-level evidence

OVERHEAD COSTS

	(1)	(2)	(3)	(4)	(5)	(6)	(7)
Official Power	-0.121	-0.203	-0.148	-0.151	-0.084	-0.123	-0.117
	(0.442)	(0.185)	(0.355)	(0.364)	(0.611)	(0.510)	(0.534)
Private Monitoring	-0.713	-0.743	-0.631	-0.744	-0.576	-0.642	-0.554
	(0.001)***	(0.002)***	(0.004)***	(0.009)***	(0.013)**	(0.046)**	(0.107)
Market Share	0.748	0.787	0.704	0.436	0.730	0.170	0.119
	(0.136)	(0.120)	(0.162)	(0.494)	(0.173)	(0.798)	(0.859)
Bank Size	-0.135	-0.134	-0.133	-0.118	-0.117	-0.090	-0.089
	(0.000)***	(0.000)***	(0.000)***	(0.000)***	(0.000)***	(0.001)***	(0.001)***
Liquidity	0.006	0.006	0.006	0.008	0.005	0.006	0.006
	(0.022)**	(0.031)**	(0.029)**	(0.007)***	(0.050)*	(0.029)**	(0.031)**
Bank Equity	0.025	0.025	0.025	0.026	0.029	0.030	0.030
	(0.000)***	(0.000)***	(0.000)***	(0.000)***	(0.000)***	(0.000)***	(0.000)***
Activity Restrictions	0.154	-0.187	-0.006	0.473	0.207	0.539	0.577
	(0.573)	(0.517)	(0.984)	(0.137)	(0.503)	(0.152)	(0.131)
GDP Growth	-0.166	-0.131	-0.162	-0.215	-0.160	-0.248	-0.268
	(0.019)**	(0.118)	(0.024)**	(0.046)**	(0.044)**	(0.068)*	(0.055)*
Political Violence		-0.591				-0.933	-0.677
		(0.017)**				(0.034)**	(0.212)
Political Voice / Accountability			-0.281			0.108	0.142
			(0.242)			(0.851)	(0.807)
Corruption				-0.030		0.338	0.461
				(0.878)		(0.273)	(0.181)
Government Banks					0.553	-0.360	-0.552
					(0.523)	(0.731)	(0.611)
GDP per Capita							-0.295
							(0.409)
Constant	4.281	5.272	4.792	3.701	3.815	2.298	2.157
	(0.000)***	(0.000)***	(0.000)***	(0.008)***	(0.000)***	(0.179)	(0.214)
Number of banks	1383	1376	1383	1214	1208	1063	1063
Number of countries	70	67	70	48	62	42	42

SOURCES: See Table 6.1.

NOTES: p-values are in parentheses. *Significant at 10%; **significant at 5%; ***significant at 1%. Estimated using generalized least squares with random effects. Variables are defined in Table 6.1.

rely on information disclosure and facilitation of private monitoring. Thus, even when we control for bank-level factors, regulatory restrictions on bank activities, economic growth, the degree of political violence, the extent of voice and accountability in the political process, the level of corruption in the government, and the extent of state ownership of banks, Private Monitoring enters negatively and significantly in the Overhead Costs regression.

The economic size of the relationship is not inconsequential. For instance, the regression coefficients (from regression [1]) suggest that if Mexico had the same level of Private Monitoring as the United States (0.97 instead of −0.43), the average value of Overhead Costs of Mexican banks would be reduced from 6 percent to about 5 percent. This would substantively reduce the difference in average Overhead Costs between Mexico and the United States, where Overhead Costs average a little over 3 percent. It is important to be cautious about these types of conceptual experiments: they do not incorporate information on the source of reform in Mexico's approach to bank supervision, and this experiment involves a nonmarginal change in Private Monitoring. Nevertheless, the regression coefficient suggests that successful changes in a country's approach to bank supervision may have nontrivial effects on bank efficiency.

The finding that the negative relationship between Private Monitoring and Overhead Costs becomes insignificant when controlling for GDP per Capita indicates that GDP per Capita summarizes features of the economy associated with the country's approach to bank supervision. Apparently, bank supervision does not occur in isolation and reflects deep political and institutional characteristics that also influence the overall level of economic development. Note, however, that even when we control for an array of country-specific factors, the link between Private Monitoring and Overhead Costs holds. It is only when including a particularly broad summary index of the country's economic success, GDP per Capita, that the relationship between bank supervision and bank efficiency loses significance. Moreover, contrary to the predictions of the public interest view, there is no evidence to support the contention that official supervisory power enhances bank efficiency.

In sum, Table 6.2 provides no support for the public interest approach to bank supervision. In contrast, the analyses suggest that regulations facilitating private monitoring of banks tend to increase bank efficiency. This relationship between private monitoring and bank efficiency holds when controlling for an array of bank-specific and country-level controls. At the same time, the results indicate a private monitoring approach to bank supervision is closely associated with the overall level of GDP per Capita.

These results are also robust to using different measures of bank operations. Barth et al. (2006) show that an approach to bank supervision that stresses stronger private monitoring tends to reduce bank net interest margins, but public policies that instead focus on official supervisory power do not boost bank efficiency. Observers may note, however, that the goal of strengthening official supervisory power may be to reduce banking system fragility, not to increase efficiency. Research by Barth et al. (2004, 2006) and Beck et al. (2006b, 2006c) shows that official supervisory power does not reduce bank fragility. Thus, the data tend to favor the private interest approach to bank supervision over the public interest view.

Bank Corruption and Bank Supervisory Approaches

METHODOLOGY

To assess the impact of bank supervisory approaches on the degree of corruption in bank-firm relations while controlling bank-specific and country-specific factors, we estimate regressions of the following form:

$$\text{Bank Corruption}_{j,i} = \alpha + \beta_1 S_i + \beta_2 F_{j,i} + \beta_9 C_i + \varepsilon_{j,i}. \tag{2}$$

The j and i subscripts indicate firm and country, respectively. S_i represents the two measures of bank supervision—Official Power and Private Monitoring—in country i; $F_{j,i}$ is a vector of firm-specific control variables; C_i is a vector of country-specific control variables; and $\varepsilon_{j,i}$ is the residual. Thus, the unit of observation is an individual firm j in country i.

Unlike the underlying assessment of bank corruption, the observed variable Bank Corruption is a polychotomous dependent variable with a natural order. Specifically, each firm chooses Bank Corruption as 1, 2, 3, or 4 if the underlying assessment of bank corruption falls between α_{k-1} and α_{k+1}, with the α-vector being estimated together with the coefficient vector β. We therefore use the ordered probit model to estimate equation (2). We employ a standard maximum likelihood estimator with heteroskedasticity-robust standard errors. When the estimation is done using clustering at the country level, the results do not change, as shown in Barth et al. (2006). Furthermore, when instrumental variables are used to identify bank supervisory strategies, the results hold (Beck et al. 2006a). The coefficients, however, cannot be interpreted as marginal effects of a one-unit increase in the independent variable on the dependent variable, given the nonlinear structure of the model. Rather, the marginal effect is calculated as $\phi(\beta'x)\beta$, where ϕ is the standard normal density at $\beta'x$.

RESULTS

The Table 6.3 regression results strongly reject the public interest view. Besides the bank supervisory indicators, the regressions include an array of firm-specific traits and country-specific factors. Official Power never enters the Bank Corruption regressions with a significant and negative coefficient. Indeed, Official Power enters positively and significantly in all eight regressions. These results directly contradict the public interest view, which predicts that powerful supervisory agencies will reduce market failures with positive implications for the integrity of bank-firm relations.

The economic magnitude of Official Power is substantial. As noted previously, the coefficients in Table 6.3 on Official Power from an ordered probit do not yield information on the impact of a change in Official Power on the probability that a firm reports that Bank Corruption is 1, 2, 3, or 4, where higher values signify a greater need for corrupt ties with bankers to obtain loans. We computed the impact of a change in Official Power from one standard deviation below the sample mean to one standard deviation above the mean. The estimates from regression (8) in Table 6.3 indicate that this would almost double the probability that a firm reports that the corruption of bank officials is a major obstacle for the operation of the business (that is, it almost doubles the probability that a firm reports a value of Bank Corruption of 4). Similarly, the estimates indicate that this change in Official Power would reduce the probability that a firm reports that the corruption of bank officials is no obstacle by 15 percent of the value when Official Power is one standard deviation below the sample mean. Although this type of experiment is subject to the same qualifications noted previously, the coefficients suggest an economically relevant impact of official supervisory power on Bank Corruption.

Two results from Table 6.3 support the private interest view. First, as predicted by the private monitoring view, Official Power always enters the Bank Corruption regressions positively. These results are consistent with fears that powerful supervisors further their own interests by inducing banks to lend to politically connected firms, so empowering official supervisors tends to increase corruption in bank lending. Importantly, these results hold even when controlling for the overall level of corruption in society. Thus, Official Power positively influences Bank Corruption even when controlling for aggregate corruption, which suggests that there is a strong, positive, independent link between official supervisory power and bank corruption.

The second result from Table 6.3 supporting the private interest view is that Private Monitoring enters negatively and significantly in all of the

Bank supervisory strategy and corrupt firm-bank relations, firm-level evidence

	BANK CORRUPTION							
	(1)	(2)	(3)	(4)	(5)	(6)	(7)	(8)
Official Power	0.144 (0.000)***	0.131 (0.000)***	0.161 (0.000)***	0.076 (0.005)***	0.172 (0.000)***	0.143 (0.000)***	0.117 (0.006)***	0.144 (0.002)***
Private Monitoring	-0.271 (0.000)***	-0.231 (0.000)***	-0.106 (0.013)**	-0.174 (0.000)***	-0.298 (0.000)***	-0.232 (0.000)***	-0.136 (0.002)***	-0.295 (0.000)***
Government Firm	-0.044 (0.684)	-0.052 (0.640)	-0.079 (0.493)	-0.109 (0.333)	-0.031 (0.779)	-0.005 (0.963)	-0.086 (0.464)	-0.072 (0.540)
Foreign Firm	-0.192 (0.003)***	-0.191 (0.003)***	-0.188 (0.004)***	-0.204 (0.002)***	-0.207 (0.002)***	-0.121 (0.070)*	-0.152 (0.031)**	-0.138 (0.049)**
Exporter	-0.085 (0.149)	-0.095 (0.109)	-0.079 (0.185)	-0.105 (0.074)*	-0.046 (0.449)	-0.092 (0.123)	-0.038 (0.535)	-0.036 (0.564)
Manufacturing	0.075 (0.350)	0.077 (0.337)	0.100 (0.215)	0.082 (0.304)	0.022 (0.792)	0.127 (0.113)	0.137 (0.113)	0.113 (0.194)
Services	0.148 (0.063)*	0.159 (0.046)**	0.179 (0.026)**	0.182 (0.023)**	0.117 (0.159)	0.221 (0.006)***	0.248 (0.004)***	0.210 (0.015)**
Sales	-0.039	-0.030	-0.017	-0.022	-0.037	-0.031	-0.019 (0.003)***	-0.019 (0.005)***
Competitors	0.241 (0.016)**	0.198 (0.053)*	0.113 (0.265)	0.073 (0.472)	0.220 (0.036)**	0.234 (0.023)**	0.021 (0.850)	0.077 (0.492)
GDP Growth	-12.052 (0.000)***	-8.183 (0.001)***	-0.582 (0.794)	-4.153 (0.038)**	-13.104 (0.000)***	-9.854 (0.000)***	-5.402 (0.000)***	-4.181 (0.084)*
Political Violence		-0.137 (0.012)**						
Political Voice/ Accountability			-0.403 (0.000)***				-0.674 (0.000)***	-0.735 (0.000)***
Corruption				-0.245 (0.000)***	0.226 (0.066)*		-0.165 (0.001)***	-0.179 (0.000)***
Government Banks						0.262 (0.000)***	0.320 (0.029)**	0.499 (0.002)***
Firm Obstacles							0.230 (0.000)***	0.225 (0.002)***
GDP per Capita								0.160 (0.001)***
Number of firms	2259	2259	2259	2259	2124	2259	2124	2124
Number of countries	33	33	33	33	31	33	31	31

SOURCES: See Table 6.1.

NOTES: *p*-values are in parentheses. *Significant at 10%; **significant at 5%; ***significant at 1%. Estimated using an ordered probit. Variables are defined in Table 6.1.

regressions. Thus, firms in countries with stronger private monitoring tend to have less need for corrupt ties to obtain bank loans. This is consistent with the hypothesis that laws that enhance private monitoring will improve corporate governance of banks with positive implications for the integrity of bank-firm relations. Again, these results hold when controlling for these factors: (1) firm-specific traits and a range of country-level controls, including GDP per Capita; (2) aggregate corruption; and (3) the firm's answer to the question regarding how hard it is to obtain financing. Thus, even when we control for general financing obstacles, the aggregate level of corruption, the level of economic development, the political system, and firm traits, the data still indicate a strong, negative link between Private Monitoring and Bank Corruption.

The economic impact of Private Monitoring on Bank Corruption is substantial. We calculated the impact of a change in Private Monitoring from one standard deviation below the sample mean to one standard deviation above the mean using the estimates from regression (8) in Table 6.3. The results indicate that this would cut in half the probability that a firm reports that the corruption of bank officials is a major obstacle for the operation of the business (that is, it reduces by 50 percent the probability that a firm reports a value of Bank Corruption of 4). Similarly the estimates indicate that this change in Private Monitoring would increase the probability that a firm reports that the corruption of bank officials is no obstacle by more than 25 percent of the value when Private Monitoring is one standard deviation below the sample mean. To give a specific country example, the estimates suggest that if Mexico had the same level of Private Monitoring as the United States, this would reduce by 40 percent the probability that a firm reports that the corruption of bank officials is a major obstacle (Bank Corruption = 4) and increase by 17 percent the probability that a firm reports that corruption is no obstacle to firm growth (Bank Corruption = 1) from the current estimates for Mexico.

Conclusions

The microeconomic evidence that is emerging from a number of studies is inconsistent with the public interest approach to bank supervision and regulation and broadly consistent with the private interest view (Demirgüç-Kunt et al. 2004; Barth et al. 2006; Beck et al. 2006a). The data do not suggest that strengthening the ability of official supervisors to monitor and discipline banks directly improves bank efficiency or the integrity of

TABLE 6.4
Summary of bank-level statistics across countries

Country	Overhead Costs	Market Share	Bank Size	Liquidity	Bank Equity
Australia	2.94	0.07	9.09	12.54	7.17
Austria	2.51	0.01	6.62	16.09	7.73
Bahrain	1.93	0.16	7.06	11.82	14.67
Bangladesh	2.07	0.08	4.72	44.51	6.30
Belarus	5.82	0.18	5.18	37.29	1.12
Belgium	2.55	0.02	7.07	23.08	6.47
Bolivia	3.85	0.09	4.50	19.85	14.90
Botswana	4.31	0.25	5.48	11.46	10.44
Burundi	5.20	0.50	4.16	20.74	10.12
Canada	1.93	0.00	6.59	22.46	7.12
Cayman Islands	1.21	0.21	4.72	22.47	25.45
Chile	3.04	0.07	6.72	26.16	12.48
China	1.40	0.07	8.65	40.44	8.70
Croatia	5.48	0.05	5.12	24.56	19.64
Cyprus	2.39	0.36	7.66	21.80	7.13
Czech Republic	2.41	0.07	7.11	13.12	7.84
Denmark	3.87	0.02	5.98	19.58	10.78
Egypt	1.89	0.02	6.90	—	7.74
Estonia	5.24	0.50	5.58	6.88	9.14
Finland	1.90	0.23	9.38	14.14	5.20
France	3.10	0.00	7.11	12.05	7.38
Germany	2.89	0.00	6.76	30.25	9.04
Ghana	7.68	0.31	5.52	49.18	11.59
Greece	3.22	0.11	8.04	32.16	6.15
Guatemala	5.84	0.04	4.50	23.72	10.33
Honduras	5.14	0.10	4.71	32.68	9.76
Hungary	4.26	0.06	6.26	9.25	9.18
Iceland	4.07	0.32	6.95	9.83	7.16
India	2.58	0.02	6.81	39.38	7.30
Indonesia	2.89	0.00	5.47	22.47	11.92
Ireland	2.73	0.25	9.49	29.44	6.51
Israel	3.16	0.08	7.53	12.27	10.36
Italy	3.64	0.01	7.57	29.76	8.22
Jamaica	7.04	0.27	5.37	32.91	9.25
Japan	1.56	0.01	9.80	11.80	3.76
Jordan	2.61	0.16	6.86	41.29	7.95
Kenya	4.79	0.07	4.58	35.57	10.08
Latvia	7.03	0.07	3.44	11.75	14.14
Lebanon	2.83	0.02	5.02	54.26	8.86
Liechtenstein	1.87	0.56	8.94	59.50	7.44
Lithuania	6.73	0.98	5.66	8.48	−0.77
Luxembourg	1.38	0.01	6.92	45.02	5.54
Macau	2.03	0.14	6.41	48.19	6.20
Macedonia	5.33	0.44	5.67	52.57	10.90
Malta	1.71	0.23	6.33	13.37	6.30
Mauritius	2.31	0.19	5.35	34.77	11.41
Mexico	5.98	0.04	4.38	38.26	31.84
Moldova	6.96	0.18	2.55	50.69	11.07
Morocco	2.09	0.17	7.82	28.60	10.36

(continued)

TABLE 6.4 (*continued*)

Country	Overhead Costs	Market Share	Bank Size	Liquidity	Bank Equity
Namibia	4.26	0.25	5.95	15.08	5.91
Nepal	2.45	0.25	4.39	37.21	8.08
Netherlands	1.95	0.04	7.51	34.01	6.83
New Zealand	2.49	0.19	8.53	9.08	6.09
Nigeria	7.79	0.12	6.31	64.46	7.60
Norway	1.87	0.09	7.94	5.96	6.48
Panama	1.95	0.02	5.55	21.93	9.15
Peru	5.79	0.10	5.83	26.89	10.58
Philippines	3.61	0.05	7.19	26.37	14.41
Poland	3.89	0.03	5.63	13.08	14.65
Puerto Rico	2.90	0.18	7.69	7.10	8.51
Romania	5.82	0.05	4.09	34.13	20.77
Russia	6.61	0.07	5.54	53.78	12.94
Rwanda	4.61	0.44	4.27	43.61	3.33
Singapore	1.18	0.19	8.78	13.36	15.23
Slovenia	4.23	0.08	5.61	16.10	13.29
South Africa	4.90	0.08	6.05	19.37	14.30
South Korea	2.66	0.06	9.69	11.03	5.84
Spain	2.98	0.02	7.70	23.97	8.88
Sri Lanka	3.05	0.25	5.66	27.75	13.28
Sweden	2.29	0.15	10.11	50.37	7.32
Switzerland	2.41	0.01	6.02	25.82	12.99
Taiwan	1.39	0.03	8.91	13.25	9.09
Thailand	2.22	0.21	9.36	8.53	7.49
Trinidad & Tobago	3.93	0.20	6.26	37.15	7.60
United Kingdom	2.57	0.02	7.53	30.52	12.08
United States	3.17	0.00	7.32	12.61	8.71
Average across banks	3.00	0.04	7.05	22.14	9.20
Standard deviation	1.64	0.10	2.02	16.53	6.97
Number of banks	1,457	1,457	1,457	1,402	1,456

SOURCES: See Table 6.1.
NOTE: Variables are defined in Table 6.1.

bank-firm relations. Rather, there is a positive association between empowering official supervisors and corruption in lending. The data further indicate that empowering official supervisors has little impact on the efficiency of intermediation as measured by bank overhead costs. In extensions, Beck et al. (2006a) test whether official supervisory power reduces bank corruption in countries with well-functioning legal and political institutions. They find that the answer is no. They never find a positive impact of supervisory power on the integrity of bank lending.

In contrast, the results support the view that empowering private monitoring of banks tends to enhance the efficiency of intermediation and enhance the integrity of bank-firm relations. Thus, regulations that focus

TABLE 6.5
Summary of firm-level statistics across countries

Country	Bank Corruption	Government Firm	Foreign Firm	Exporter	Sales (log of sales in U.S. dollars)	Competitors (logarithm of number of competitors)
Argentina	1.57	0.03	0.34	0.29	16.93	0.61
Belarus	1.26	0.30	0.07	0.27	0.46	1.03
Bolivia	1.64	0.00	0.23	0.38	14.63	0.61
Botswana	1.19	0.18	0.43	0.52	15.01	0.90
Brazil	1.26	0.02	0.27	0.32	16.75	0.58
Canada	1.03	0.03	0.26	0.49	16.98	0.63
Chile	1.20	0.02	0.35	0.46	16.94	0.66
Croatia	1.81	0.47	0.13	0.67	1.61	0.90
Czech Republic	1.88	0.16	0.17	0.33	0.77	0.96
Egypt	2.59	0.00	0.30	0.65	14.25	1.00
El Salvador	1.64	0.03	0.21	0.36	15.92	0.63
Estonia	1.35	0.21	0.21	0.57	1.20	0.93
France	1.27	0.06	0.30	0.44	16.73	0.57
Germany	1.52	0.08	0.30	0.35	17.47	0.57
Ghana	1.81	0.13	0.40	0.57	15.24	1.02
Guatemala	1.48	0.00	0.20	0.33	16.65	0.64
Honduras	2.05	0.00	0.21	0.41	18.60	0.63
Hungary	1.48	0.19	0.07	0.32	1.12	1.00
India	1.58	0.13	0.30	0.65	6.00	1.03
Indonesia	2.47	0.06	0.17	0.26	18.22	1.01
Italy	1.16	0.11	0.36	0.36	20.69	0.64
Kenya	1.45	0.10	0.41	0.88	15.23	0.97
Lithuania	2.24	0.07	0.06	0.29	0.83	0.96
Malawi	1.37	0.07	0.37	0.52	15.18	0.96
Malaysia	1.88	0.05	0.14	0.27	17.95	0.59
Mexico	2.18	0.00	0.19	0.44	15.55	0.65

(continued)

TABLE 6.5 (*continued*)

Country	Bank Corruption	Government Firm	Foreign Firm	Exporter	Sales (log of sales in U.S. dollars)	Competitors (logarithm of number of competitors)
Moldova	2.03	0.26	0.02	0.23	0.30	0.92
Namibia	1.11	0.17	0.29	0.69	15.25	0.90
Nigeria	1.92	0.03	0.17	0.38	15.32	1.02
Panama	1.45	0.05	0.18	0.46	17.08	0.58
Peru	2.23	0.01	0.24	0.28	16.27	0.60
Philippines	2.18	0.02	0.23	0.32	15.45	0.66
Poland	1.38	0.20	0.08	0.42	1.23	1.05
Portugal	1.47	0.06	0.29	0.23	19.67	0.75
Romania	1.96	0.22	0.16	0.20	0.62	0.90
Russia	1.88	0.14	0.02	0.08	0.56	0.98
Singapore	1.26	0.04	0.36	0.48	17.62	0.62
Slovenia	1.23	0.40	0.14	0.74	1.61	0.87
South Africa	1.14	0.08	0.35	0.86	18.25	0.98
Spain	1.27	0.08	0.23	0.39	15.55	0.62
Sweden	1.06	0.06	0.23	0.53	15.91	0.64
Thailand	3.14	0.01	0.20	0.38	18.96	1.05
Trinidad & Tobago	1.77	0.07	0.19	0.59	14.59	0.57
Turkey	2.31	0.18	0.09	0.41	1.59	0.95
United Kingdom	1.03	0.01	0.16	0.30	16.34	0.69
United States	1.45	0.04	0.10	0.31	16.99	0.65
Venezuela	1.48	0.06	0.31	0.46	17.25	0.55
Zambia	1.39	0.15	0.38	0.35	14.46	0.89
Average across firms	1.62	0.12	0.19	0.38	10.03	0.83
Standard deviation	0.97	0.32	0.39	0.49	8.20	0.32
Number of firms	4,712	4,712	4,712	4,712	4,712	4,712

SOURCES: See Table 6.1.
NOTE: Variables are defined in Table 6.1.

TABLE 6.6
Summary of country-level variables

Country	Official Power	Private Monitoring	Activity Restrictions	Political Violence (higher values signify LESS violence)	Political Voice and Accountability	Corruption	Government Banks
Argentina	−0.30	1.13	7.00	0.51	0.48	2	0.30
Australia	0.73	1.04	2.00	1.18	1.63	5	0.00
Austria	0.90	−0.43	1.25	1.38	1.45	5	0.04
Bahrain	1.00	0.77	2.25	−0.08	−1.04	—	0.04
Bangladesh	0.44	−0.82	3.00	−0.40	−0.01	—	0.70
Belarus	−2.24	−1.55	3.25	−0.37	−0.52	—	0.67
Belgium	0.38	0.69	2.25	0.82	1.44	5	—
Bolivia	0.22	0.06	3.00	−0.14	0.39	3	0.00
Botswana	0.82	0.97	2.50	0.74	0.78	4	0.02
Brazil	1.00	0.97	10.00	−0.32	0.55	3	0.52
Burundi	−0.35	−0.63	3.00	—	−1.29		0.63
Canada	−2.15	1.05	1.75	1.03	1.36	6	0.00
Chile	0.05	0.29	2.75	0.45	0.62	4	0.12
China	0.28	1.05	3.50	0.48	−1.30	—	—
Croatia	0.17	0.29	1.75	0.41	−0.32		0.37
Cyprus	1.00	−0.35	2.00	0.38	1.11	5	0.03
Czech Republic	1.00	−0.03	2.00	0.81	1.20		0.19
Denmark	−1.80	0.29	2.00	1.29	1.63	6	0.00
Egypt	0.38	−0.13	3.25	−0.07	−0.67	3	0.67
Estonia	0.27	0.29	2.00	0.79	0.79		0.00
Finland	−1.74	1.46	1.75	1.51	1.60	6	0.22
France	−1.16	0.69	1.50	0.65	1.15	5	—
Germany	−0.91	0.97	1.25	1.32	1.49	6	0.42
Ghana	−0.09	−1.56	3.00	−0.10	−0.43	4	0.38
Greece	−0.43	0.69	2.25	0.21	1.07	5	0.13
Guatemala	−0.42	−1.14	3.25	−0.75	−0.56	3	0.08
Honduras	0.82	−0.42	2.25	−0.33	−0.06	2	0.01

(continued)

Table 6.6 (continued)

Country	Official Power	Private Monitoring	Activity Restrictions	Political Violence (higher values signify LESS violence)	Political Voice and Accountability	Corruption	Government Banks
Hungary	1.00	−0.43	2.25	1.25	1.20	—	0.03
Iceland	−2.20	0.29	2.75	1.25	1.45	6	0.64
India	−0.36	−0.42	2.50	−0.04	0.50	3	0.80
Indonesia	0.74	0.25	3.50	−1.29	−1.17		0.44
Ireland	−0.54	0.37	2.00	1.43	1.50	5	—
Israel	−0.35	0.35	3.25	−0.46	1.08	5	0.17
Italy	−1.66	1.27	2.50	1.16	1.29	4	0.56
Jamaica	0.77	−0.69	3.00	−0.34	0.75	3	0.01
Japan	1.13	0.97	3.25	1.15	1.16	5	0.00
Jordan	−1.91	0.29	2.75	−0.06	0.15	4	—
Kenya	1.00	−1.00	2.50	−1.10	−0.70	3	0.00
Kuwait	0.22	1.04	2.50	0.68	0.00	—	0.04
Latvia	−1.04	−0.42	2.00	0.46	0.62	—	0.44
Lebanon	0.67	1.46	2.75	−0.25	−0.40	3	0.05
Liechtenstein	—	—	2.25	—	—	—	0.01
Lithuania	−0.34	0.29	2.25	0.35	0.77	—	0.01
Luxembourg	0.77	0.29	1.50	1.40	1.46	6	0.49
Macau	—	—	2.25	—	—	—	0.00
Macedonia	—	—	3.25	—	—	—	0.00
Malawi	−0.10	−1.25	13.00	0.04	0.06	3	0.00
Malaysia	−0.25	0.55	10.00	0.55	−0.14	4	0.25
Malta	−0.30	0.35	2.50	1.32	1.41	4	0.07
Mauritius	−1.52	0.29	3.25	1.14	1.01	—	0.24
Mexico	−0.17	−0.43	3.00	−0.35	−0.11	3	—
Moldova	−0.18	−1.83	1.75	−0.20	0.16	—	0.20
Morocco	0.59	0.39	3.25	0.09	−0.24	3	0.06
Namibia	−0.54	−0.13	2.75	0.71	0.47	5	—
Nepal	−0.73	−2.23	2.00	—	0.05	—	0.20
Netherlands	−0.94	0.37	1.50	1.48	1.61	6	0.06

New Zealand	0.49	1.44	1.00	1.42	1.46	6	0.00
Nigeria	0.61	0.39	2.25	-1.05	-1.23	—	0.13
Norway	—	—	2.50	—	—	6	—
Panama	1.14	-0.13	2.00	0.15	0.66	2	0.12
Peru	0.09	0.29	2.00	-0.53	-0.69	3	0.03
Philippines	0.95	-0.63	1.75	0.27	0.61	3	0.12
Poland	0.58	0.29	2.50	0.84	1.07	—	0.44
Portugal	1.00	0.97	9.00	1.39	1.48	5	0.21
Puerto Rico	—	—	3.50	—	—	—	0.00
Romania	-0.71	0.42	3.25	0.02	0.41	—	0.70
Russia	-0.40	-1.25	2.00	-0.69	-0.31	—	0.68
Rwanda	0.73	-2.95	3.25	—	-1.17	—	0.50
Singapore	-3.05	0.35	2.00	1.39	0.04	4	0.00
Slovenia	1.00	-0.43	2.25	1.09	1.07	—	0.40
South Africa	-2.95	0.77	2.00	-0.53	0.99	5	0.00
South Korea	0.38	1.46	2.25	0.16	1.00	4	0.30
Spain	-0.32	0.97	1.75	0.58	1.34	5	0.00
Sri Lanka	0.61	0.35	1.75	-1.63	-0.16	4	0.55
Sweden	-1.55	0.69	2.25	1.41	1.63	6	0.00
Switzerland	0.90	0.77	1.25	1.69	1.69	6	0.15
Taiwan	-0.66	0.42	3.00	0.94	0.71	4	0.43
Thailand	0.72	-0.42	2.25	0.25	0.22	3	0.31
Trinidad & Tobago	-0.91	-0.43	2.25	0.32	0.95	4	0.15
Turkey	-0.30	0.69	12.00	-0.94	-0.86	2	0.35
United Kingdom	0.59	1.46	1.25	0.92	1.49	5	0.00
United States	1.14	0.97	3.00	1.10	1.50	5	0.00
Venezuela	1.14	-0.43	10.00	-0.25	0.18	3	0.05
Zambia	0.51	-0.13	13.00	0.00	-0.05	3	0.23

SOURCES: See Table 6.1.
NOTE: Variables are defined in Table 6.1.

on information transparency are positively associated with improved bank operations. Beck et al. (2006b, 2006c) also examine whether empowering this private interest approach requires sound legal institutions. They show that information transparency works best in countries with efficient legal systems. For the bottom third of their sample, as ranked by the efficiency of the legal system, they find that information has no significant effect on corruption. For the remaining two-thirds of the sample, greater information transparency implies lower corruption in lending. In sum, the data provide strong support for the private interest view of bank regulation.

Without ignoring methodological and measurement concerns, the results have clear policy implications. As discussed in Barth et al. (2006), international institutions, including the Basel Committee on Banking Supervision, the International Monetary Fund, and the World Bank, have increasingly stressed the importance of strengthening official supervisory oversight of banks. The evidence presented in this chapter, however, provides cautionary evidence regarding this approach. Not only is strengthening government oversight of banks ineffective in reducing bank overhead costs but strengthening official supervisory powers is generally associated with an increase in corruption in bank lending. Rather, emerging microeconomic evidence on bank overhead costs and corruption in lending highlights the benefits and effectiveness of supervisory policies that promote information disclosure that facilitates private sector monitoring of banks. Simply forcing information disclosure is certainly not a panacea for all the complications and problems associated with overseeing banking systems, and merely disseminating information will not necessarily work in countries with dysfunctional legal and political systems. Nevertheless, these early efforts at exploiting the Barth et al. (2004, 2006) database on banking policies around the world provide no support for strengthening direct official oversight of banks and instead suggest that regulatory, legal, and political reforms that foster private monitoring of banks work better.

References

Barth, James R., Gerard Caprio Jr., and Ross Levine (2006). *Rethinking Bank Supervision and Regulation: Till Angels Govern*. Cambridge, UK: Cambridge University Press.

———— (2004). "Bank Supervision and Regulation: What Works Best?" *Journal of Financial Intermediation* 13: 205–48.

———— (2001a). "The Regulation and Supervision of Banks Around the World: A New Database." In Robert E. Litan and Richard Herring, eds., *Brooking-Wharton Papers on Financial Services*. Washington, DC: Brookings Institution.

———— (2001b). "Banking Systems Around the Globe: Do Regulations and Ownership Affect Performance and Stability?" In Frederic S. Mishkin, ed., *Prudential Supervision: What Works and What Doesn't*. Chicago: University of Chicago Press.

Beck, Thorsten, Asli Demirgüç-Kunt, and Ross Levine (2006a). "Bank Supervision and Corruption in Lending." *Journal of Monetary Economics* 53: 2131–63.

———— (2006b). "Bank Concentration, Competition, and Crises: First Results." *Journal of Banking and Finance* 30: 1581–1603.

———— (2006c). "Bank Concentration and Fragility: Impact and Mechanics." In Mark Carey and Rene Stulz, eds., *Risk of Financial Institutions*. Cambridge, MA: National Bureau of Economics Research.

———— (2003). "Law, Endowments, and Finance." *Journal of Financial Economics* 70: 137–81.

Caprio, Gerard, Jr., Luc Laeven, and Ross Levine (2003). "Governance and Bank Valuation." National Bureau of Economic Research, Working Paper 10158.

Coase, Ronald H. (1960). "The Problem of Social Cost." *Journal of Law and Economics* 3: 1–44.

Demirgüç-Kunt, Asli, and Enrica Detragiache (2002). "Does Deposit Insurance Increase Banking System Stability? An Empirical Investigation." *Journal of Monetary Economics* 49: 1373–1406.

Demirgüç-Kunt, Asli, Luc Laeven, and Ross Levine (2004). "Regulations, Market Structure, Institutions, and the Cost of Financial Intermediation." *Journal of Money, Credit, and Banking* 36: 593–622.

Easterly, William, and Ross Levine (1997). Africa's Growth Tragedy: Policies and Ethnic Divisions. *Quarterly Journal of Economics* 112: 1203–50.

Haber, Stephen H., Armando Razo, and Noel Maurer (2003). *The Politics of Property Rights: Political Instability, Credible Commitments, and Economic Growth in Mexico*. Cambridge, UK: Cambridge University Press.

Hamilton, Alexander, John Jay, and James Madison (1788). *Federalist Papers*. In Clinton Rossiter, ed., *The Federalist Papers*. Repr., New York: New American Library, 1961.

Kaufmann, D., A. Kraay, and P. Zoido-Lobaton (1999). "Governance Matters." The World Bank, Policy Research Working Paper 2196.

Levine, Ross (2006). "Finance and Growth: Theory and Evidence." In P. Aghion and S. Durlauf, eds., *Handbook of Economic Growth*. Amsterdam: North-Holland Elsevier Publishers.

———— (1997). "Financial Development and Economic Growth: Views and Agenda." *Journal of Economic Literature* 35: 688–726.

Shleifer, A., and R. W. Vishny (1998). *The Grabbing Hand: Government Patholo-gies and Their Cures*. Cambridge, MA: Harvard University Press.

Stigler, G. (1975). *The Citizen and the State: Essays on Regulation*. Chicago: University of Chicago Press.

——— (1971). "The Theory of Economic Regulation." *Bell Journal of Economics and Management Science* 2: 3–21.

Chapter 7

Political Drivers of Diverging Corporate Governance Patterns

PETER GOUREVITCH AND JAMES SHINN

Can governments protect investors in the shareholder management relationship, beyond the standard provision of ordinary contract enforcement
via courts? Recent literature on corporate governance answers in the af-
firmative: countries with strong investor protections have deeper financial markets than those where protections are weak.[1] The well-known La
Porta et al. (LLSV) work on corporate and securities law argues that "law
matters":[2] effective shareholder protection increases the depth of financial
markets and investments, and strong law and regulation contribute might-
ily to effective shareholder protection. Corporate governance systems vary
around the world because minority shareholder protections (MSPs) vary
greatly. Where MSP is high, shareholder diffusion takes place; where MSP
is low, blockholding or shareholding concentration prevails. Thus, the provision of MSP is key to strong financial markets. What then explains the
supply of MSP? In this chapter we stress political factors.

That law and regulation about MSP influence corporate governance is
an important finding. It suggests that a combination of private bonding
and standard tort law about contracts is not sufficient and that more active
regulation about corporate governance and securities is required—without
at the same time having a government so powerful it can trample on property rights.[3] Indeed, a well-known paradox arises: most specialists in law
and finance, though not all, think the shareholder diffusion model is superior to the blockholder model; yet, suspicious of big government, they

mostly see that diffusion models rely more heavily on effective regulation (to protect external investors) than do the blockholder models (which protect inside investors by internal mechanisms of monitoring, without enforcement by courts). Freer markets may indeed require more regulation.

If MSPs and their effective enforcement are important, what provides them? LLSV provide the most well-known answer—legal family: common law supports high MSP, whereas civil law supports low MSP. We join critics of this interpretation in arguing that the legal family distinction does not fully capture the political processes at work that influence the content and enforcement of regulation relevant to corporate governance.[4] It does not explain variance within countries over time where legal family remains the same (the "Great Reversals" noted by Rajan and Zingales),[5] nor variance across countries within the same legal family.

Understanding the politics of corporate governance regulation can be improved by looking directly at political variables—interest groups, partisan political conflict, and political institutions—familiar parameters long applied to political economy, and only recently to corporate governance.[6] That politics shapes law should not be surprising to anyone. Corporate governance determines who has the authority to allocate the firm's cash flow: does the cash go to the owners as profit, to the managers as the most powerful employees, to the middle-rank cadres, to the workers at the bottom, to the suppliers and distributors that form part of the larger network of which the firm is a part, or to the government as taxes?

Governance systems confer benefits. There may be several ways to govern a firm efficiently. The rules reflect considerations not only of efficiency but of distribution. The choice of rules that structure the struggle for power inside the firm is settled by the struggle for power outside the firm, in the political system that determines the rules. Naturally enough, groups in any society will push (or oppose) the system of corporate governance that helps (hurts) them the most. They will work through politics to create the public policy regime that reflects their preferences in corporate governance. Any convincing account of corporate governance systems must include accounts of the politics that produces the laws and regulations that have a bearing on corporate governance.

We can stylize the political process as the interaction of preferences with political institutions. On the side of preferences, we examine the coalitions that form among workers, managers, and owners in differing combinations in support of alternative policies. On the side of institutions, we examine the impact of consensus vs. majoritarian institutions in influencing the outcome of competition for primacy among competing coalitions.

Alternative Systems of Corporate Governance

The comparison of corporate governance systems focuses most frequently on the degree of shareholder concentration. The major distinction is between shareholder diffusion and blockholding. The dominant tradition in finance economics poses the core issue as overcoming the problem of managerial agency costs: how can the interests of managers and owners be reconciled so that managers have enough authority to take the requisite risks and initiatives to maximize returns but not exploit their insider knowledge by diverting cash to themselves at the expense of owners?[7] Blockholding solves this problem by direct supervision of managers by concentrated owners, who have the means (the shares) and the incentive (substantial stakes) to do so. The capacity of blockholders to monitor directly has the disadvantage for external investors that the firm could be managed to the benefit of the insiders, at the cost of the outsiders.

The diffusion model solves this problem by fragmenting share ownership so that no blockholder manipulation can take place. It envisions monitoring to be done by a board elected by the shareholders. It requires management to provide substantial information to the outsider shareholders, forbids insider trading, and creates a market for control of the firm—a series of rules and regulations known broadly as MSPs.

These two poles—diffusion shareholding vs. concentrated blockholding—define the range of systems we observe around the world. There are, of course, variants of each. The blockholding pattern is often broken down further into those that rely on extensive family or ethnic networks (notably in East Asia), those that rely on state bureaucracies (until quite recently France, now China), those that rely on financial institutions like banks as blockholders, and those with extensive cross-shareholding that nullifies the impact of shareholder diffusion. To simplify the comparisons, we lump these variants together under blockholding.

Countries vary substantially in the degree of ownership concentration. Table 7.1 lists countries along a continuum of concentration, conceived as a percentage of total shares owned by the largest blockholders (see our book for details on definitions).[8] Our sample of 39 countries accounts for 99.5% of the total world equity markets by value and covers countries from around the world.[9]

TABLE 7.1

Ownership concentration

Concentration	Country
4.1	Japan
5	China
15	United States
20	Netherlands
23.6	United Kingdom
24.6	Ireland
27	New Zealand
27.5	Australia
27.5	Canada
31.8	South Korea
37.5	Denmark
38.6	Norway
42.6	Malaysia
43	India
44.8	Singapore
45.5	Taiwan
46.4	Philippines
46.9	Sweden
48.1	Switzerland
48.8	Finland
49	Venezuela
51.5	Belgium
51.9	Thailand
52	South Africa
52.8	Austria
55	Israel
55.8	Spain
58	Turkey
59.6	Italy
60.3	Portugal
63	Brazil
64.6	Germany
64.8	France
66	Mexico
67.3	Indonesia
71.5	Hong Kong
72.5	Argentina
75	Greece
90	Chile

SOURCE: Gourevitch and Shinn (2005, chap. 2, appendix, table 2.1).

INTERVENING VARIABLES: MSP AND
DEGREES OF COORDINATION

Shareholder Protection (MSP)

What explains this variance? Since at least LLSV, researchers have focused on legal protections of shareholders from exploitation by managers or inside blockholders.[10] With high MSP, investors will accept a minority position in firms, and blockholders will sell down without fear of allowing the arrival of another blockholder; with low MSP, blockholding will remain. There is no canon in economic theory of precisely what practices constitute minority shareholder protections, but many codes exist of so-called best practice. For our purposes of constructing an aggregate index we employ a broad definition of corporate governance practices, including information, oversight, control, and managerial practices.[11]

Information practices include accounting rules and audit procedures.
Oversight practices include boards of directors and the rules governing their fiduciary responsibilities.
Control practices include voting rights and procedures: voting caps on minority or outside votes; equality of voting or its lack; notice information on voting; antitakeover practices like poison pills, dead hand, staggered boards, stock transfer restrictions, and "golden shares" triggered only in a contest, all of which shelter (or expose) managers and blockholders to a market for control.
Managerial incentives are modes of remunerating managers, including the use of stock options, and modes of setting and evaluating compensation.

Our version, a composite of information drawn from several sources using various definitions, is contained in Table 7.2; see our book for more detail on measurements.[12]

As in the index of blockholder concentration, there is considerable variation in minority shareholder protections, around the mean of 45 for this sample. Most of the sample countries fall between 20 and 50 on our index. On average, developed economies score higher than emerging markets.[13]

What is the relationship between MSP and shareholder diffusion? For our sample of 39 countries (see Figure 7.1),[14] there is indeed, as expected, a negative correlation between blockholding and shareholder protections, −33 for the whole sample and −44 for the developed countries (defined as gross domestic product [GDP] per capita greater than $10,000),[15] but there is an exuberant scattering of countries away from a simple linear relationship between blockholding and shareholder protections.[16]

The United States and the United Kingdom (GB) anchor the lower right-hand side of the distribution, with high protections and low concentration, as predicted by the conventional wisdom; and countries such as Italy (IT) anchor the upper left-hand side of the distribution, with low protections and high concentration. Yet there are many prominent outliers, such as Chile (CL), Hong Kong (HK), and France (FR), with high concentration of ownership and high shareholder protections.

TABLE 7.2
Minority shareholder protections index

Country	Information	Oversight	Control	Incentive	Total MSP	
United States	86	100	100	100	97	US
Singapore	89	71	80	97	84	SIN
Canada	83	71	100	78	83	CAN
United Kingdom	81	60	100	53	74	UK
Australia	75	71	80	59	71	AUS
Hong Kong	85	14	100	81	70	HK
Ireland	69	71	80	59	70	IRE
Malaysia	84	36	80	69	67	MAL
South Africa	73	43	100	41	64	SAF
Chile	35	14	100	66	54	CHIL
France	64	37	60	47	52	FRA
New Zealand	56	71	80	0	52	NZ
Argentina	48	0	80	72	50	ARG
Spain	57	14	80	50	50	SPN
Israel	74	29	60	31	48	ISR
Norway	66	29	80	16	48	NOR
Sweden	67	36	60	22	46	SWD
Finland	60	36	60	16	43	FIN
Venezuela	49	14	20	81	41	VEN
India	50	7	100	0	39	IND
Switzerland	59	36	40	16	38	SWT
Japan	66	0	80	0	37	JPN
South Korea	65	21	40	22	37	SK
Denmark	44	43	40	16	36	DEN
Netherlands	57	0	40	47	36	NED
Philippines	74	7	60	0	35	PHL
Taiwan	74	7	60	0	35	TAI
Belgium	43	32	0	59	34	BEL
Germany	44	29	20	41	33	GER
Thailand	78	7	40	6	33	THA
Brazil	27	0	60	41	32	BRZ
Austria	40	36	40	6	30	AUT
Greece	53	14	40	0	27	GRC
Mexico	59	14	20	9	26	MEX
Portugal	43	0	60	0	26	POR
Italy	69	7	20	0	24	ITAL
Turkey	51	0	40	0	23	TURK
Indonesia	45	0	40	0	21	INDO
China	25	0	20	0	11	CHIN

SOURCES: Gourevitch and Shinn (2005, table 3.1); La Porta et al. (2000, 2002); Davis Global Advisors (2002); Tokyo Stock Exchange (2001); Tenev and Zhang (2002); and Lefort and Walker (1999).

Conversely, Japan (JP) and the Netherlands (NL) are outliers in the other direction, with low concentration and low shareholder protections. China has even lower blockholder concentration, insofar as the state controls 95% of listed firms, and very low shareholder protections. Finally, the slope of a fitted ordinary least squares (OLS) regression line to this sample is −.25, not −1, as would be the case in a simple 45-degree line; in any case, the

Ownership concentration (y-axis, 0 to 100)

Minority shareholder protections index (x-axis, 0 to 100)

Data points: CL, GR, AR, HK, ID, MX, DE, FR, PL, BR, IL, TR, IT, AT, BE, ES, TH, VE, ZA, FI, PH, CH, SE, TW, JN, MY, SG, DK, NO, KR, NZ, AU, IE, GB, CA, NL, US, CN, JP

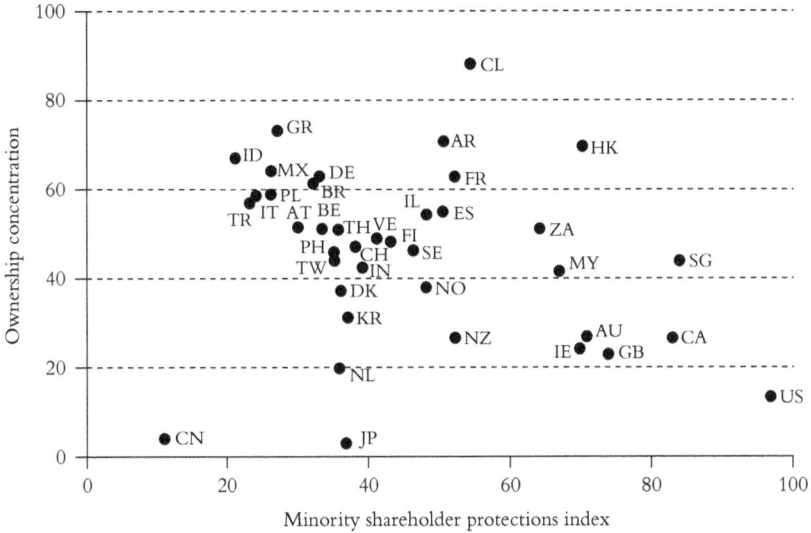

Figure 7.1 Blockholding and shareholder protections
SOURCE: Gourevitch and Shinn (2005, fig. 3.1).

relationship is not statistically significant.[17] Clearly, something more complex is going on here than a simple negative covariance of protections and ownership. Too many countries don't fit.[18]

Varieties of Capitalism: Degrees of Coordination (DoC)
Within Market Economies
We think the exclusive focus on MSP restricts too severely the range of laws and regulations that may affect corporate governance patterns. Roe has shown that shareholder diffusion correlates with income equality and employment protection rules. Hall and Soskice extend the connection to include welfare systems, labor training practices, and price-setting mechanisms—a range of measures that are familiar to specialists on the "varieties of capitalism." LLSV have expanded their initial interest only in "corporate law" now to include securities law, labor law, and more variables.[19] We explore these factors with a measure of DoC of market economies.

Apparently, MSP encourages ownership diffusion under some country conditions but not others. For example, Sweden and Malaysia rank high in MSP, but not high in shareholder diffusion. Corporate governance patterns vary substantially with other features of the economy, among them, job protections, product market competition, education and training systems, price and wage-setting mechanisms, financial structures, and income inequality. These countrywide economic features exhibit what Milgrom and Roberts called "institutional complementarity"[20]—a logic of fit that causes each to contribute to the other.

For example, in comparing Japanese and American firms, Aoki noted that the high job security pattern characteristic of Japan was possible only because cross-shareholding shielded firms from the pressure of having to lay off workers in the face of fluctuating demand in order to conform to external shareholder demands for profitability.[21] Conversely, where governance models push managers toward maximizing share prices and dividends, pressure grows for flexibility in all relationships, from labor contracts, to wages and prices, to suppliers and distributors, to finance and research. Zingales notes that as human capital grows in importance, the vital assets of the firm shift, with implications for corporate governance.[22]

A number of researchers have been exploring the degree of "fit" among economic practices.[23] Measuring institutional complementarity for countries leads to a dichotomous result. Hall and Soskice's *Varieties of Capitalism* volume, an important synthetic statement of this line of research, sorts countries into two groupings according to the degree of coordination that takes place: Liberal Market Economies (LMEs) and Coordinated Market Economies (CMEs).[24] In LMEs, firms coordinate through formal contracting in arm's-length relationships operating in highly competitive markets. In CMEs, firms coordinate though information sharing, repeated interactions, and long-term relationships, all sustained by institutional arrangements that make the stability of these commitments credible. In CMEs, managers invest in worker training to sustain manufacturing that demands high skill levels, and workers have incentives to engage in that training; in LMEs, managers prefer flexibility, hence lack motive to invest in skill development, and workers lack incentives to upgrade.[25] Firms in LMEs have the diffuse shareholder governance model; firms in CMEs have the blockholder model.[26]

Institutional complementarity implies that we need to know policy outcomes in related areas in order to know the impact of any given variable. Corporate governance outcomes are influenced by what happens in other elements of the system. Knowing corporate law, MSP, and private bonding mechanisms is important, but not sufficient. We need to know as well what happens in those other areas of the economy that have a functional relationship with corporate governance practices.

We use a measure of institutional complementarity developed by Hall and Gingerich, which they term the Coordination Index (CI).[27] It is constructed from country scores on six values: shareholder power (drawn on

TABLE 7.3
Coordination index

Austria	1
Germany	0.95
Italy	0.87
Norway	0.76
Belgium	0.74
Japan	0.74
Finland	0.72
Portugal	0.72
Denmark	0.7
France	0.69
Sweden	0.69
Netherlands	0.66
Spain	0.57
Switzerland	0.51
Australia	0.36
Ireland	0.29
New Zealand	0.21
Canada	0.13
United Kingdom	0.07
United States	0

SOURCE: Gourevitch and Shinn (2005, chap. 3).

LLSV), dispersion of control (an LLSV measure of concentration), stock market capitalization, level of wage coordination (the level at which wages are set: local, intermediate, or national), degree of wage coordination, and labor turnover (a proxy for job security). This index, shown in Table 7.3, was calculated for 20 of our sample countries for the period 1990–95.[28]

The logic of the coordination argument is that the CI should vary positively with Ownership Concentration, negatively with MSP. The correlation between Ownership and CI is positive (+.61). The same correlation between Ownership and MSP is strongly negative (−.89). This is demonstrated graphically in the following two plots. In Figure 7.2, Denmark and Austria are in the upper right-hand corner, with high levels of coordination and correspondingly high levels of ownership concentration. The United States anchors the lower left-hand quadrant, as expected. Two of our corporate governance outliers, Japan and the Netherlands, lie in the upper left-hand quadrant, both combining relatively high coordination with low ownership concentration. Figure 7.3 reveals the opposite relation between CI and MSP, as predicted by our interpretation of capitalist economic policies (CEP).

In this scatter plot the country sample falls much more closely along the 45-degree line (as the high negative correlation coefficient indicates), with Japan and the Netherlands much less different from the rest of the pack. This

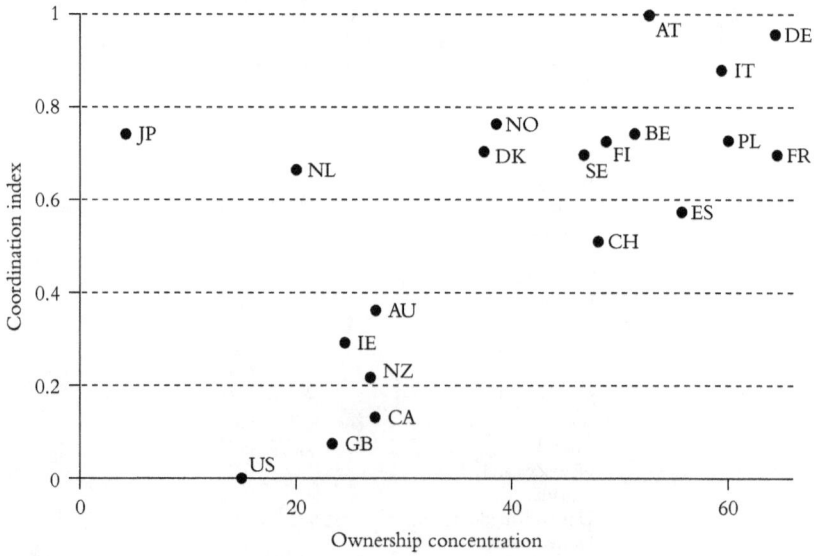

Figure 7.2   CI and ownership concentration

SOURCE: Gourevitch and Shinn (2005, chap. 3).

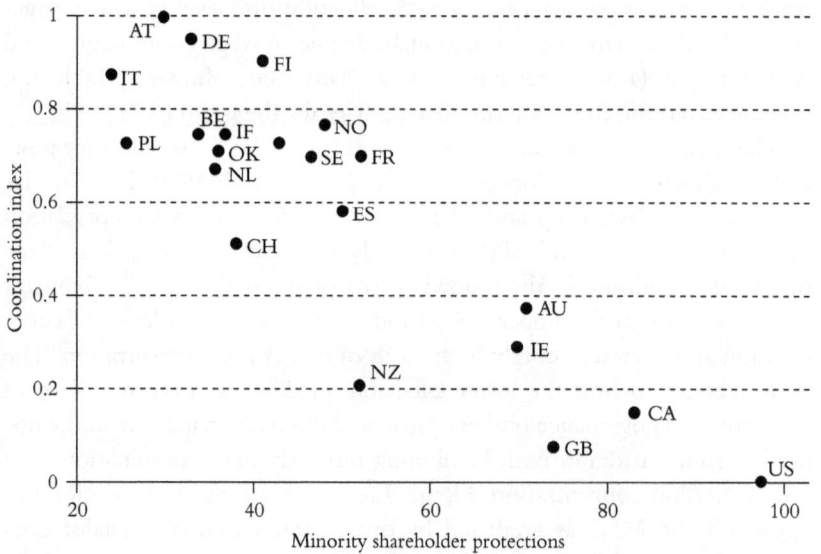

Figure 7.3   CI and MSP

SOURCE: Gourevitch and Shinn (2005, chap. 3).

suggests that the effect of CEP variables such as CI has a more direct effect on MSP and a somewhat more attenuated effect on Ownership (though still of the predicted sign), consistent with our overall causal schema. The positive correlation of CI with Concentration and negative correlation with MSP is supported by data of other researchers.[29] From this we infer some prima facie evidence that MSP as an explanation can be strengthened by reference to the economic policy context (DoC) in which it operates.

A Simple Causal Model

Policy shapes the incentives that produce corporate governance patterns. Policy is, in turn, shaped by the interaction of preferences aggregated through political institutions.[30] Holding preferences constant reveals the power of institutions in explaining outcomes; holding institutions constant reveals the power of preferences. Most of our data here look at the comparative statics—what can be explained by looking at preferences, and what by looking at institutions. The dynamic element—the feedback loop whereby the pattern of corporate governance itself shapes preferences and how a change of either institutions or preferences impacts the outcome—is less directly testable because we lack data points over time for change of the outcome (degrees of shareholder concentration). We can explore change by process tracing—case studies, analytic narratives of country patterns; we do this in our book but can do so only briefly here. We sketch out this simple model in Figure 7.4.

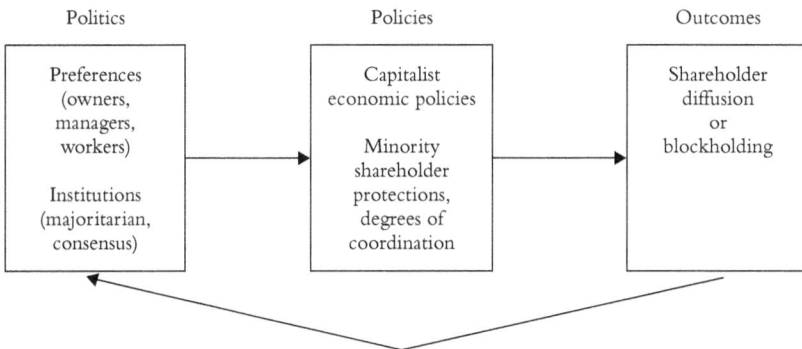

Politics	Policies	Outcomes
Preferences (owners, managers, workers) Institutions (majoritarian, consensus)	Capitalist economic policies Minority shareholder protections, degrees of coordination	Shareholder diffusion or blockholding

Figure 7.4 A simple model of causality

SOURCE: Gourevitch and Shinn (2005, p. 16, fig. 2.1).

MSPs, supplemented by DoC, explain variance in corporate governance systems. What explains the supply of MSP and of the specific version of DoC variables that reinforce MSPs? We examine first the preferences of major actors and the possible coalitions that can form among them in support of or opposition to different policy regimes. We then examine the role of political institutions in shaping the winners among these coalitional combatants.

PREFERENCES — THE PLAYERS: OWNERS, MANAGERS, AND WORKERS

We begin with the actors within the firm identified by finance theory— owners, managers, and workers—and the preferences for corporate governance practices of each group.[31] Each set of actors has a range of preferences that set up trade-offs with the other players, thus a set of alignments.

Owners prefer to minimize all the forms of agency costs paid to managers and workers, fearing that each of these is able to divert resources from profits and thus require the firm to pay them above-market prices. Owners may be concentrated or diffused. Concentrated owners incur a portfolio risk of exposure to a single firm; diffuse owners can spread out the risk of their equity investment over a variety of firms and assets. On the other hand, blockholders can help themselves to a variety of expropriation costs at the expense of minority shareholders. Diffuse owners don't share in expropriation costs; they focus on getting the best risk-adjusted rate of return on their investment, and a diversified equity portfolio. Some subset of owners may have common interests with workers against the expropriation claims of blockholders, whereas in other situations, blockholders may make common cause with managers and workers.

Managers seek income, job security, and managerial autonomy. They will want high payments of various kinds, from salary to options, and the greatest autonomy in directing the resources of the firm—which also gives them the greatest leeway to shirk. They dislike expropriation costs at the expense of the firm, for reasons similar to those of workers. Thus, they have common interests with workers against some kinds of owner action, and common interests with owners against worker claims.

Workers seek good wages; job stability in the face of layoffs, even at the expense of profitability; and protection of their pension claims on the firm. They are in conflict with managers and owners over wages and with managers over the issues of agency costs—workers have their own elements of "incomplete contract," thus bargain over its resolution.[32] They may be relatively indifferent to expropriation costs that help one set of shareholders at the expense of other shareholders—but they will oppose them—unless self-dealing by a blockholder threatens the financial viability of the firm, thus jobs, and its ability to cover its pension claims.

These groups can combine in different ways. Each group can make a bargain with another, stressing different objectives. Or more accurately, each group can divide, one faction going in one direction, another faction in the other.[33] This helps us understand "coalitional potential," the possible alliance combinations of the intrafirm players as they move outside to politics. With three groups, owners, managers, workers, we can identify three combinations of pairs, and two outcomes for each, depending on who wins. We list them in Table 7.4.

One pair of coalitions pits workers against owners/managers. In this "class conflict" concept of cleavages,[34] owners push for strong MSP to assure their investment. The flow of investment funds puts pressure on firms and governments to respond, at the risk of having investment go elsewhere. Thus, competition leads to a "race to the top."[35] Conversely, labor pushes against strong MSP to protect jobs and wages from the whiplash of market forces. Where labor is politically strong, MSP will be low, and where the right is strong, MSP will be high. This argument has been most extensively developed by Mark Roe. His data show that his political model (left vs. right) provides stronger correlations with diffusion/blockholding than does legal family (civil vs. common law). We agree with his conclusions on the primacy of political variables but find less robust his left vs. right findings; in extending the years covered and using somewhat different measures of governance outcomes, our data show a weaker result. We also do not find strong connection between investment flows and MSP, something the "investment" side of this argument would predict.[36]

Sweden and other Scandinavian countries are the most cited examples of the labor pattern, as labor-affiliated Social Democratic governments have been in office there for several decades. The Scandinavian countries rank in the middle on shareholder diffusion, somewhat higher on MSP, but low on market for control, as cross-shareholding agreements keep blockholding stable. The United States and the United Kingdom have had long periods of center-right governments: diffusion is high, MSP ranks high, and the market for control is relatively active.

An alternative political model of cleavage allies a cross-class coalition of workers, managers, and inside blockholders against external investors.[37] Here coalition partners defend the institutions of blockholding as part of a "corporatist compromise"—supplanting class conflict with accommoda-

TABLE 7.4
Preference theories: Political coalitions and governance outcomes

Coalition lineup	Winner	Political coalition label	Predicted outcome
Pair A: Class conflict			
Owners + managers vs. workers	Owners + managers	Investor	Diffusion
Owners + managers vs. workers	Workers	Labor	Blockholding
Pair B: Sectoral			
Owners vs. managers + workers	Managers + workers	Corporatist compromise	Blockholding
Owners vs. managers + workers	Owners	Oligarchy	Blockholding
Pair C: Property and voice			
Owners + workers vs. managers	Owners + workers	Transparency	Diffusion
Owners + workers vs. managers	Managers	Managerism	Diffusion

SOURCE: Gourevitch and Shinn (2005, chap. 2).

tions to sustain the firm, its employees, the security of managerial position, and autonomy of the firm from pressure of the market in favor of patient capital. This has also been called the "stakeholder model" in contrast to the stockholder model.[38] Indicators of such coalitions include measures of corporatism: institutions that build representation of business, labor, and other producer groups into mechanisms of consultation and governance. Corporatist institutions are created by cross-class coalitions to protect the system from class pressures. Our research supports the findings of other authors that cross-class bargains correlate strongly with MSP and with diffusion/blockholding outcomes.[39] These policy coalitions can be found in Germany, Austria, the Netherlands, and Italy. Indeed, it is possible to read the Scandinavian pattern as reassembling the cross-class coalition bargains, rather than placing them on the left, as labor dominated.[40]

A third cleavage pits workers and outside investors against managers and inside blockholders, in favor of greater transparency (hence the label) and shareholder protections. Instead of being the foes of investors, workers here side exactly with those groups the class conflict model posits as their enemies. Höpner sees the motive as protecting jobs: in Germany, the demand for accountability makes co-determination more effective. We stress the role of pension assets in aligning worker incentives with those of external investors. Where national pension systems have large shareholding, there is greater lobbying by labor-related groups on behalf of MSP and transparency; where pension systems are largely public PAYGO measures of defined benefits from special tax funds, there is less pressure for MSP. The United States and the United Kingdom are examples of countries with high pension ratios in stocks and high MSP.

Germany has a low percentage of pensions in financial markets but has seen in recent years some changes in public policy toward transparency. The Social Democrats and the Free Democrats have supported reform measures against the opposition CDU. This contradicts the left-right predictions of the class conflict model and provides a contrast with the corporatist version of the cross-class model. The CDU seems to defend the position of traditional "Rhineland" capital. This would fit Höpner's interpretation concerning co-determination as a motive for worker groups. It could also support the notion that "owners" are more deeply split: the finance side (the Free Democrats) interested in greater flexibility; some firms wanting higher stock values as levers for mergers in the integrated EU vs. manager/ blockholders heavily invested in the CME mode of production seeking to preserve their high investment in specific assets connected to it.

In the United States, some evidence for the transparency coalition can be found in the politics that created the Sarbanes-Oxley (SoX) bill in 2002 and conflicts in the SEC over implementation. The Democrats pressed for more MSP, whereas the GOP preferred to do little or to focus on penalties upon conviction; the Democratic appointees at the SEC push for stronger powers for the institutional investors and strict enforcement of the SoX bill, and the GOP members oppose both. The United Kingdom has stronger rights for institutional investors than does the United States.[41]

We have outlined several possible support patterns for or against high MSP, with competing coalitions contending to shape legislation. Which coalition prevails? We have already explored one channel to the answer—the different strengths of the various groups in political activities: votes, money, organizational strength, as measured by electoral outcomes and the political complexion of governments. National differences are explained by variance in the political strength of the various coalition members: strong labor left vs. strong business groups and various combinations in between.

POLITICAL INSTITUTIONS

A second channel for explaining which policy coalition prevails lies with political institutions: the set of rules that determine the processes of legislation and enforcement.[42] Institutions can affect outcomes. If preferences are assumed to be constant, varying the institutions will produce different policy outputs. Since countries differ in their political institutions, it may well be that differences in corporate governance structures reflect differences in political institutions. We explore this relationship here by correlating corporate governance outcomes with political form. Following a substantial political science literature, we sort country institutions into majoritarian and consensus types.[43] High levels of MSP and a liberal production regime will, we predict, correlate with majoritarian political institutions. Low levels of MSP and an organized or regulated production regime will correlate with consensus institutions. We analyze first the classification of political systems and then the causal mechanisms that produce a relationship.

Mechanisms of Interest Aggregation

Majoritarian systems magnify the impact of small shifts of votes, thus allow large swings of policy; consensus systems reduce the impact of vote shifts by giving leverage to a wide range of players through coalitions, thus have lesser swings of policy. Consensus systems have many "veto points"; majoritarian ones have few. In a consensus system, a wide range of opinion has to be included in decisions. The coalition nature of the government assures this, as all participants in the cabinet have to agree to important decisions. In a majoritarian system, large blocks of opinion can be overridden by a narrow majority; thus small shifts of votes can have big consequences. In analyzing these systems, researchers focus on the way institutions define the capacity to block or to pass legislation, thus to exercise a "veto." Although different terms are used to articulate this concept, we focus on veto "points" rather than two common alternatives, veto "gates" and veto "players."[44] Majoritarian systems have fewer veto players than consensus ones, so governments are able to make important decisions on a narrower base of support. Because consensus systems contain more veto points, governments depend on a broader base of support. We would expect therefore narrower policy swings in consensus systems, compared to majoritarian, on the same swing of votes in an election.

Measuring Institutional Differences

To quantify the countries in our sample in terms of consensus or majoritarian politics, we use an Index of Political Cohesion (see Table 7.5) derived from and modified from the Beck et al. World Bank database of political indicators (DPI).[45] In our index, 0 equals a unified presidential or one-party parliamentary government; 1 equals a divided presidential government, or a two-party coalition parliamentary government, or minority party parliamentary government; and 2 equals a multiparty coalition parliamentary government, measured over a longitudinal range of years in the DPI. Since

TABLE 7.5
Modified index of political cohesion

Canada	0.043478
New Zealand	0.130435
United Kingdom	0.130435
India	0.391304
Philippines	0.478261
Spain	0.565217
Australia	0.608696
Austria	0.608696
Greece	0.608696
Portugal	0.608696
South Korea	0.608696
Venezuela	0.608696
United States	0.652174
Argentina	0.695652
Japan	0.695652
Turkey	0.695652
Brazil	0.73913
Ireland	0.826087
Malaysia	0.956522
Chile	1
Denmark	1.086957
Norway	1.086957
Sweden	1.173913
Netherlands	1.304348
France	1.347826
Thailand	1.391304
Israel	1.521739
Italy	1.521739
Belgium	1.652174
Germany	1.652174
Finland	1.913043
Switzerland	2
Number of observations	38
Std. dev.	.5772191
Mean	.771167

SOURCES: Gourevitch and Shinn (2005, chap. 4); Beck et al.
(2001, chap. 4). We also thank Michael Hawes for assistance with
the data.

the number of veto players can change with each election, these scores are
the average across all the years available in the DPI. Table 7.5 shows the 32
countries in our sample for which we have data with which to calculate this
index, ranked from most majoritarian (lowest value) to most consensual
(highest value).

The Scandinavian countries are predictably grouped together, toward
the consensual end of the spectrum. But there are some counterintuitive
results. Japan, for example, often considered an archetypal consensus political system, in fact falls quite close to the United States on the cohesion

index. France and Thailand, both with a reputation for a strong executive, are actually more consensual than the Netherlands, by this measure.

ESTABLISHED DEMOCRACIES

For the sample as a whole (both democratic and authoritarian regimes), consensual political systems tend to have higher ownership concentration and lower shareholder protections; and majoritarian countries have the reverse, being correlated with lower concentration and higher shareholder protections, as shown by Figures 7.5 and 7.6.[46] Thus, the consensus/majoritarian distinction is strong among the well-established, well-institutionalized industrial democracies—those places where effective markets in both politics and the economy operate, where the actors in the firm are able to mobilize resources for political action in society.

Other treatments of political institutions stress the relationship among the variables differently. Pagano and Volpin show that proportional representation encourages blockholding, whereas plurality systems correlate with diffusion.[47] This goes very much in the direction of our analysis, as electoral law contributes to the political cohesion pattern we analyze. On its own, however, the impact of electoral law is muted by partisanship. Countries that code as plurality electoral systems are the United States,

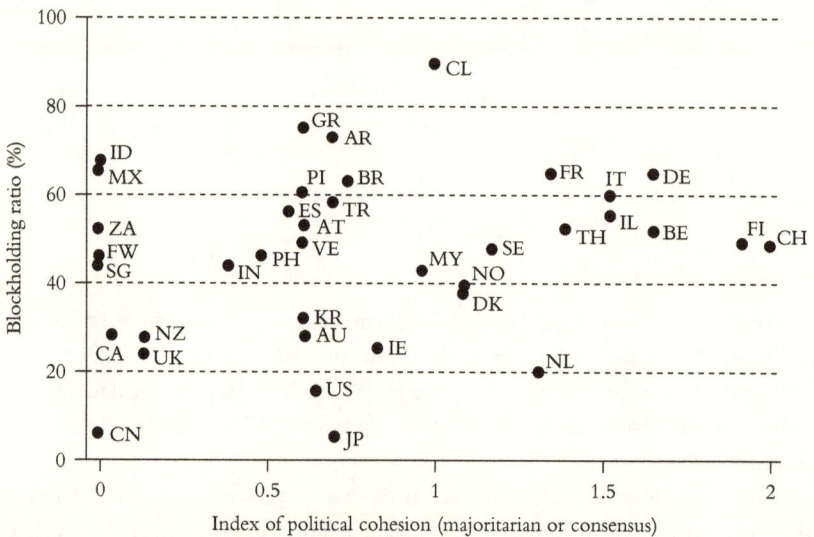

Figure 7.5   Political cohesion and blockholding

SOURCE: Gourevitch and Shinn (2005, chap. 4).

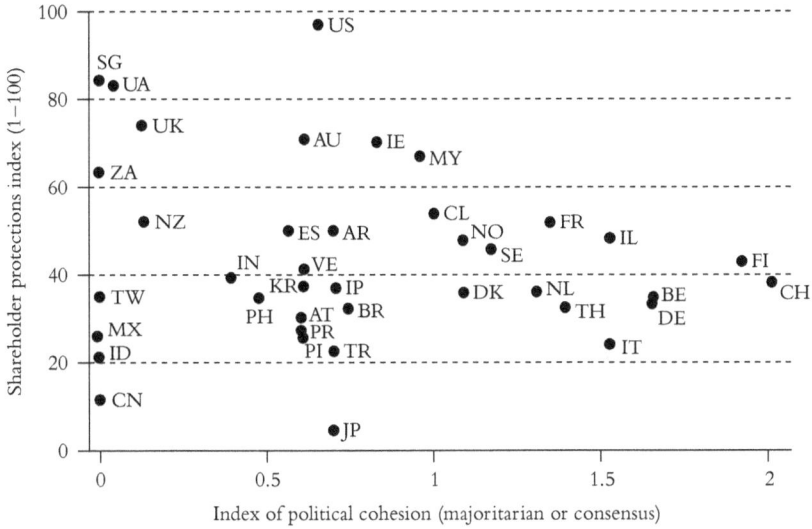

Figure 7.6 Political cohesion and shareholder protections

SOURCE: Gourevitch and Shinn (2005, chap. 4).

United Kingdom, Canada, Australia, and France. If we look at all the rest, with proportional representation or mixed-member districts, we note that they spread rather widely on the left-right variable. The "work" of the correlation is thus being done by the clumping of the diffusion countries on the strong "right"' indicators. We note as well that the impact of the left-right marker on the degree of diffusion is strong—the United States, United Kingdom, and Canada are quite strongly above the clumping of the other countries toward the bottom of the diffusion index. Thus, the partisan spread is greater among the blockholding countries.

Similar effects appear when we look at the number of political parties. The United States, United Kingdom, Canada, and Australia are all on one side of the party indicator and the diffusion indicator—few parties, high diffusion—whereas there is a big spread of party variable among the countries that concentrate toward low diffusion.

Electoral law interacts with societal preferences and the fractionalization of issue space to generate the number of political parties, and this is, in turn, quite important in shaping how formal institutional arrangements operate. Thus, in our view electoral law and number of political parties work through the political cohesion mechanisms to generate the pattern of majoritarian and consensus systems. Electoral law influences number of parties, which in turn enters into the cohesion index. The variables produce their results by their impact on the diffusion cases. The blockholding countries vary more greatly in type of political institution.

The Causal Mechanism of Credibility in the Institutional Argument
We have established a correlation between majoritarian and consensual political institutions and outcomes on corporate governance, at least for the advanced democracies. What is the causal mechanism at work?

The logic is this: The organized production regime rests on a high degree of interdependence among the various players in the firm—it rests on an arrangement among the stakeholders, managers, blockholders, and workers to preserve the institution of the firm against outsiders. The CME production systems rest on extensive interdependent investment in specific assets among members of a production "network"—workers with job-specific skills rather than general ones; managers in manufacturing that requires highly skilled stable workers; suppliers to technology that connects them to other members of a value chain. The LME systems specialize in flexibility of shifting resources; they don't invest in interdependent, specific assets and skills.

CME systems seek a high degree of policy stability around the policy regime that favors this outcome—to protect their stake in the high level of specific assets they have invested in that regime. Consensus systems are more likely to do that than majoritarian systems, as they give a "veto" to all players on the shape and rate of change. CME systems have blockholding governance patterns. Thus, consensus political systems protect blockholding/ stakeholder corporate governance systems.

Conversely, majoritarian institutions undermine the incentives of producers to commit to specific assets. These political systems have greater policy variance than do consensus ones. As a result, firms want flexibility, the ability to hire and fire, cut production, shift assets, sell, close, and move as market conditions require in the immediate time frame. They prefer policies that support the liberal governance model, hence policies that stress the primacy of the external shareholder, not the various stakeholders.[48]

The driving force is the capacity of consensus institutions to make credible commitments among coalition partners that a particular policy bargain will be durable. "Credible commitment" indicates the probability partners think the other side will hold to an agreement. The capacity of a coalitional system to make credible the corporatist compromise sustains blockholding. The workers, managers, and blockholders cement a deal that excludes minority shareholders. Systems with low credibility of commitment to political bargains cause policy variance, which undermines the arrangements all participants demand. This creates privatizing incentives, which induces blockholders to defect from the worker-manager corporatist alliance in favor of practices that protect minority shareholders.

Thus, in the worker-manager-blockholder alignment against minority owners, a high-credibility system leads to the corporatist understanding, whereby managers and workers smooth over the differences in their joint incentives in a corporatist deal; whereas a low-credibility system would make the elaborate cross-sector deals of corporatism unsustainable because of the risk of change or defection.

It is not that consensus systems necessarily produce an organized market economy (OME), though that may be likely as well, but once in place, for historically contingent reasons, they are more likely to preserve it. Several countries developed blockholding governance systems before they evolved their current political systems. The issue of genesis is different from persistence: a variety of variables shaped earlier development of governance patterns, with formal political institutions but one of these. We are not making an argument about "origins" here, but persistence. Once these coalitions jell, we suggest, political institutions sustain or undermine them. Majoritarian institutions undermine blockholding: policy variance corrodes confidence that the investment in the specific assets of the blockholding system is secure. Investors, managers, and workers will all be tempted to shift to the diffusion system, where assets move more freely. In our view, blockholding is the default beginning of market economies: all countries began that way, including the United States; over time, some of them moved, because of politically induced policy change, toward the diffusion model.

AUTHORITARIAN AND TRANSITIONAL COUNTRIES

The political argument we have developed so far—the interaction of political preferences and institutions—has been worked out for a specific set of countries: the economically advanced OECD countries, with stable democratic institutions. Despite the variance in governance patterns, all the countries in the market democracies have relatively good protection of property rights; the differences among the governance systems in those countries impact the type of production regime (coordinated vs. neoliberal arm's length), but effective market economies can be found in both systems, with different dimensions of focus and specialization.

As we move away from countries in this set, the argumentation becomes more difficult. Lower levels of wealth reduce the size of capital markets, weaken financial institutions, and keep limited the class of investors and the prosperity of workers. Weaker democracies reduce the impact of elections and democratic methods of preference aggregation. Property rights are uncertain. Market economies work poorly in some cases of authoritarian regimes (North Korea, Myanmar) but show periods of rapid growth in others (China, Singapore, Indonesia).

Corporate governance systems reflect some of these political differences. Overall, the more authoritarian the political system, the weaker are minority shareholder protections and the more likely we are to find blockholding patterns of ownership. Political transparency as well as firm-level transparency is a crucial ingredient of investor confidence. Without political transparency, property rights are in doubt. Whatever the formal legislation on the books, the rules may be administered in a biased way, and investors will be wary. Some minimum degree of external political transparency is a necessary (though not sufficient) condition for effective corporate governance, and particularly for protection of external minority shareholders. There are limits to the effectiveness of private ordering in providing for corporate governance.[49]

But political process is not absent from authoritarian regimes. Rulers in nondemocracies are not immune from social pressures. They do need support to govern. Even the most authoritarian rulers need soldiers, secret police, administrators, and party members. In exchange these supporters are given special privileges, such as money, access to schools, housing, and medical care. One-person rule is not possible; even it relies on a cadre of supporters.

That set of supporters has been called by some analysts the "selectorate"—the set of people upon whom the ruler relies for support.[50] The ruler is able to some degree to select the support base, excluding most people, while rewarding a few. Democratic rulers have more difficulty excluding people from power, though they may try to broaden or limit political participation.

Authoritarian systems can be classified by the nature of the selectorate, the degree of power dispersion, and power sharing. North Korea and Myanmar are extremes at one end of centralized power. China no longer fits that model despite one-party rule. It has opened up parts of the economy to the market. This makes the state dependent on investors, consumers, and workers for economic support, even if these are not able to vote in competitive elections to select the rulers. Economic actors can refuse to invest, buy, or work, and that means rulers have to follow policies that induce some kind of acceptance or support.

To that extent, nondemocratic rulers who seek market support have to provide some minimal protections to investors, to provide assurances of capital repatriation and other basic exercises of property rights of investors. The challenge for authoritarian rulers is how to make such guarantees credible in the absence of political mechanisms that can sanction them for noncompliance. Authoritarianism always leaves the possibility of interference, thus greater uncertainty to investors than occurs in stable democracies with predictable rules that are followed. Investors may still invest in these countries, of course, but with a high risk premium and a shorter time horizon.

Democracies, it must be noted, are by no means always stable or effective. Weak democracies have formalized elections and means of leadership succession but are quite vulnerable to manipulation by elites and special groups. Money, guns, poverty, weak civil service systems, and ignorance can all contribute to systems unable to enforce their rules and regulations. Again, law on the books is not the same as law in practice. The diffusion shareholding model of governance depends on effective public regulation, on a vigorous system of regulation and enforcement to make sure players of the complex game play their part. In a corrupt democracy, investors will feel insecure, and diffusion will not take place.

Governmental authority may thus pose a trade-off between adaptability and effectiveness with regard to corporate governance. McIntyre suggests a U-shaped curve.[51] Governments with many veto gates can be stable in policy because groups are able to inhibit substantial change, but ineffective because they cannot respond to crises. Conversely, authoritarian governments with few veto gates can respond quickly but are not consistent because their leaders can switch direction with little restraint.

An interesting contrast with the European experience may be noted: there we found that majoritarian systems encouraged diffusion because they undermined the policy stability that the highly interlocked production system of the blockholding countries required; policy volatility there breaks the bonds among actors, leading to production strategies that prefer flexibility, in turn, undermining the logic of blockholding. This may be an effect that happens only where there is substantial protection and confidence in the regulatory system. In many countries, of which Malaysia may be an example, the regulatory process may not be stable enough to provide those protections. There, policy volatility may also threaten the adequacy of shareholder protection. If shareholder protection is in question, blockholding retains support. Thus, centralized institutions can be too powerful, leading to blockholding.

The impact of consensus/majoritarian and veto gate models may, thus, vary according to the degree, length, and duration of democratic regimes.

In long-standing democracies, consensus regimes with low policy variation have in the past produced coalitions around blockholding. Majoritarian systems with higher policy variation may produce diffusion. Conversely, in less established democracies or in authoritarian regimes, policy variance may lessen confidence in shareholder-protecting regulation and, at the same time, high veto gate patterns may lesson confidence in the effectiveness of government. In both cases we will find blockholding.

Investor confidence may thus be highest at the bottom of the U shape—some important balance between the capacity to act and limits on arbitrary rule—the goal of democratic theorists for centuries. For example, McIntyre pairs Malaysia with Indonesia as having few veto points; in contrast with Thailand, lying at the other end, with many veto points; and the Philippines, in between but closer to Thailand. Even though Thailand also has a multiparty system, there the parties fight during the election and form volatile coalitions afterward; in Malaysia, "the parties divide the electoral map among themselves before each election to avoid competing with each other."[52] Politically, Malaysia has the capacity to take decisive action in policy change if the leaders find it useful to do so. In this respect Malaysia lies with the majoritarian countries of Europe—policy change can be sharp. This can be threatening to investors, as they cannot be sure of the stability of the policy regime. It can also mean strong response to problems and crises: McIntyre classifies Malaysia as having taken decisive action in response to the Asian financial crisis because its institutions allowed it.

Figure 7.7 from our emerging countries in the sample provides a graphical hint (although no statistical evidence) that a U-shaped curve may exist with respect to corporate governance outcomes in authoritarian or weak democratic states, with blockholding still high at the upper and lower ends of the Index of Political Cohesion on the x-axis, and lower in the middle of the distribution.

We are less sure about how to measure the impact of political institutions in other types of systems. Much of the research in institutions has looked only at processes in relatively well-established democracies, generally in wealthy countries. We need ways of thinking about what happens in authoritarian regimes or poorly functioning democracies. We expect that in those cases, the quality of law is weak. Governments are able to intervene without adequate restraint by the rule of law. Property rights are thus suspect and courts vulnerable to political interference. Under those conditions, the external monitoring model for corporate governance will not function well, and investors will not feel reassured. The result will be blockholding. This may often take place with strong "ascriptive" mechanisms—family,

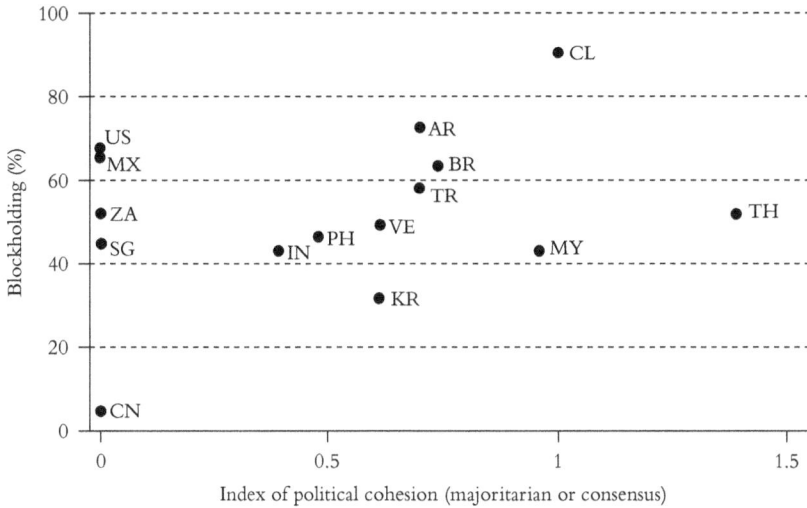

Figure 7.7   State strength and blockholding U-curve

SOURCE: Gourevitch and Shinn (2005, p. 82, fig. 4.4).

religion, and ethnicity providing ties that function something like reputational bonding mechanisms among the members of a production network.

Authoritarian regimes do have constituency pressures, so there is a politics to their policy. If they engage in trade and seek foreign investment, they have to worry about the views of those investors. They will generate domestic constituencies that can have influence—not an electorate, but a selectorate, key actors who control or administer various resources. Even authoritarian regimes can credibly commit to some kind of market discipline if they extend themselves politically to rely on markets for employment and prosperity. Some of these countries are transitional, from authoritarian to democratic, or have democracies that function at different levels. Something can be learned by comparing these institutions and by comparing processes of transition. Our work here is tentative. In our book we place alongside the statistical comparison a set of "process-tracing" case studies of several countries.

South Korea is a strong example of the impact of institutional change. The authoritarian regime favored the *chaebols*, the highly concentrated networked firms. Democratization broadened the influences at play: smaller firms kept out of the chaebol system, trade unions hitherto repressed, and dissident voices from various regions and religious groups. The broader coalition was antagonistic to the chaebol system and supported a variety of changes that broke up the old system. Banks and firms lost state subsidies, finance became more transparent, and various MSPs were introduced. The result has been a shift toward more shareholder diffusion. Chile is another example of institutional change: under Pinochet, social security was privatized, though quite highly regulated (the institutions that managed the pensions were obligated to buy only government bonds, for example). Russia is another case of institutional change, but of weak democracy; ownership oligarchy appears to prevail there in the absence of effective counterbalancing political forces. In the other countries of our sample, policy change has expressed shifts in the balance of political forces and change of preferences, rather than formal institutional changes.

The Legal Family Argument—Is This Politics?

Although the legal family school provides an intriguing stylized fact that compels attention—the correlation between MSP and legal family—it is not in our view convincing or at least is insufficient. If civil law is more regulatory, why does that regulation appear to favor blockholding rather than supply effective shareholder protection? Strong regulation per se could favor MSP as blockholding. The fact of higher regulation does not establish by itself the content thereof.

The legal family school is not clear about the status of legislation: what explains the actual regulations enacted by governments and enforced by them? Common law countries can pass legislation that suffocates markets, and civil law countries can pass laws that protect MSP if they so choose. Common law Britain became more interventionist under a Labor government in 1945, whereas civil law France became less regulatory after 1985. Common law countries can have effective rule of law, or weak rule where the common law legacy does not protect against extensive political interference with markets and courts—Pakistan, for example, and several countries in Africa.

Legal tradition can evolve in different directions, depending on the politics that shapes legislation and enforcement. LLSV note that although it may be true that "political factors affect corporate governance through channels other than the law itself[,] . . . the law remains a crucial channel through which politics affects corporate governance."[53] Indeed, law is a channel, but this confirms the point about the centrality of politics: politics picks the law and shapes its enforcement.

Pistor and colleagues note the importance of the transplantation effect: how law moved from one country to another—thus how common and civil law moved from France and the United Kingdom to their former colonies or related empires—turned on local conditions. We interpret the "transplant" effect as an argument calling attention to politics—the way in which receiving societies want to use the legal family legacy depends on local politics, institutions, and cultures.[54] Legal family interpretations seem to leave countries trapped in their initial founding moment. It cannot explain "the great reversals," the changes that have taken place within one country over time. It has odd policy implications: does it mean no civil law country can develop effective MSP? If not, then legal family cannot be so decisive in its impact.

We agree with LLSV that law and regulation matter, but legal family is not a convincing interpretation of why countries have the law they do. The more likely explanation of the correlation is that the application of legal family and the character of institutional development are both driven by other variables, such as the interaction of settlers with native populations in extractive industries.[55]

Conclusion

Corporate governance has become an important object of analysis in evaluating the impact of public policy on economic development. It is no longer the black box safely ignored. At least since the Mexican financial crisis of the 1980s and the Asian financial crisis of the 1990s, and more recently the Enron crisis in the United States, researchers have come to appreciate its importance. LLSV have made a vigorous case for the importance of law and regulation in shaping variance on corporate governance outcomes.

We build on this work to push at the politics of the supply of law and regulation. Countries vary substantially in the laws they have on key aspects of corporate governance—directly on the MSP, indirectly in laws pertaining to labor markets, welfare systems, antitrust, and economic competition. Public policy shapes laws that influence these systems. High MSP and strongly neoliberal economic policy are more likely to create shareholder diffusion models than are low MSP and highly "coordinated" economic policy. What creates high MSP and neoliberal coordination structures? We examine several variables—partisan voting, cross-group bargains, and political institutions. Changing economic conditions alter incentives (the pattern of pension holdings, rewards in the world economy), and institutional patterns influence the strategic interaction among coalition partners. We offer this as contribution to the integration of laws and regulation about corporate governance, securities, and finance into political accounts of the formation and enforcement of law.

Is one system superior to another? This is strongly debated and somewhat unsettled. Diffusion systems generate deeper capital markets, as in the United States and the United Kingdom. But it is not clear that over time and at all times that they produce superior growth, and productivity, and they may produce greater income inequality and social uncertainty.[56] It may be that each has a comparative advantage with the terms of trade between them shifting with technology (rapid technological change favors the diffusion models, which shift resources more rapidly; stable technology may work well in blockholding, where lowering transactions costs may be an advantage).

Notes

Our thanks to Christina Chan for help in preparing the manuscript and to the conference participants for their helpful comments.

1. For a comprehensive review of the debates on these relationships, see Becht, Bolton, and Roell (2003).

2. See LLSV (1997, 1998, 1999, 2000, 2002, 2006).

3. In "Coase vs. the Coasians," Glaeser, Johnson, and Shleifer (2001) explore disagreement among Coasians on the sufficiency of private bonding mechanisms in supplying protections without explicit regulations on corporate governance broadly defined.

4. Rajan and Zingales (2003); Kroszner (2000); Roe (2003); Perotti and von Thadden (2003); Berkowitz, Pistor, and Richard (2003b); and Pagano and Volpin (2001).

5. Rajan and Zingales (2003). See also their more recent book, *Saving Capitalism from the Capitalists* (2004).

6. See references in note 4 above.

7. As Zingales (2000) notes, other theories of the firm lead to different understandings of the governance problem.

8. Table 7.1 is drawn from Table 2.1 in Gourevitch and Shinn (2005, chap. 2, appendix). It is a composite of information drawn from several sources, with varying definitions of concentration.

9. Japan and China are seen as having essentially blockholding management patterns despite the low shareholder concentration; in Japan, cross-shareholding counteracts diffusion to prevent an effective market for control and minority shareholder rights; in China, the government owns 95% of firms listed in exchanges.

10. The logic of the MSP argument is this: If a nation's law poorly protects minority stockholders, a potential buyer may fear that the majority stockholders will shift value to themselves and away from the buyer. See Roe (2003, pp. 165–66).

11. Among these practices, some are formal, embedded in statute or regulatory procedures, whereas others are informal, a matter of convention or "norm." The mix of formal and informal practices varies from country to country, as does the latitude for innovation that is granted to firms by the regulatory authorities. Further muddying the waters, some practices are complements—for example, formal protections for minority shareholder voting rights can be overridden by takeover rules in several countries in this sample—whereas others may act as substitutes; there is a considerable (and inconclusive) academic literature on the notion of complements and substitutes. The empirical evidence on the effectiveness of corporate governance practices in protecting the interests of minority shareholder is surprisingly thin; as Mayer observed, "Corporate governance has become a subject on which opinion has drowned fact" (1996, p. 3).

12. Table 7.2 is drawn from Table 3.1 in Gourevitch and Shinn (2005).

13. As with the index on concentration, these data must be interpreted with caution. The accounting index is dated, almost a decade old; things have changed since then. The disclosure index is much more recent but is based on required disclosures, usually by stock exchanges; it says nothing about the actual compliance or enforcement of this disclosure. The data on nonexecutive directors (NEDs) is also suspect, since true independence is hard to verify, and again, the enforcement of fiduciary duties toward minority shareholders is not picked up by this index. Finally, the incentive compensation data are based on a limited sample of firms in each country, biased toward larger and multinational firms.

14. Figure 7.1 is drawn from Gourevitch and Shinn (2005, fig. 3.1).

15. The countries in our sample account for 99.6% of the MSCI Standard ACWI Free Index (99.8% of the index reweighted for free float)—virtually the entire global equity market.

16. Gourevitch and Shinn (2005, appendix; table 4 contains the statistics used to develop this figure).

17. Gourevitch and Shinn (2005, appendix, tables 5 and 6).

18. As with the blockholding data, these minority protections data are a static snapshot. There have been recent, significant changes in these areas of minority protections in several sample countries that will not be picked up by this index. Moreover, we have weighted all four groups of practices—information, oversight, control, and compensation—equally in creating our overall synthetic index of minority shareholder protections. A small survey of institutional investors performed by the authors in a previous study suggested that not all protections are equally important to foreign portfolio investors, and that their priority was (in descending order) information, compensation, control, and—at the bottom of the list—oversight (Shinn and Gourevitch 2002). Given the wide standard deviation in the oversight values, rescaling the numbers to reflect the notional priorities of portfolio investors would generate quite different ratings and would eliminate some of the anomalies in this index.

19. Roe (2003); Hall and Soskice (2001); and LLSV (2006).

20. As Gingerich and Hall note, "In general, two sets of institutions can be said to be complementary to each other when the presence of one set raises the returns available from the other" (2002, p. 4). Gingerich and Hall derive the idea from Milgrom and Roberts (1990, 1992, 1995). See also Jaikumar (1986). The logic of institutional complementarity underlies the overall argumentation of the "varieties of capitalism" literature as developed in Hall and Soskice (2001).

21. Aoki (1990, 1994).

22. Zingales (2000).

23. See Porter (1990); Boyer (1989); Amable (2002); Amable, Ernst, and Palombarini (2005); Boyer and Durand (1997); and Ernst (2002).

24. Hall and Soskice (2001); See Martin Höpner (2003a); Gingerich and Hall (2002).

25. See Amable (2002).

26. Roe notes the same pattern, that the "world's wealthy democracies have two broad packages: (1) competitive product markets, dispersed ownership, and conservative results for labor; and (2) concentrated product markets, concentrated ownership, and pro labor results. The three elements in each package mutually reinforce each other" (2003, p. 140).

27. Hall and Gingerich (2001).

28. We are wary of the endogeneity between the CI and both our MSP and Ownership data sets, because CI incorporates values reflecting similar calculations (our data sets draw on some LLSV values and roughly correlate with those measures). For that reason (among others) we rely more on correlations between our own MSP index and the Ownership data rather than on the CI data.

29. See Höpner (2003b, p. 35, table 1). Gingerich and Hall (2002, p. 34, fig. 1) show a similar relationship (included as a measure in Höpner's table) presented graphically.

30. See Frieden (1999); Gourevitch (1999); and Rogowski (1999).

31. The basic formulation of the agency problem looks at owners and managers only, on the grounds that there is no problem of incomplete contract with workers. Concern with "human capital" undermines that distinction, and thus we include workers (Zingales 2000).

32. Finance theory traditionally sees the issue of the incomplete contract as lying largely between owners and managers. Some theorists explore its existence in the labor issues, where workers acquire specific assets of value to the firm (Zingales 2000).

33. Having laid out this coalition pattern, we alert the reader to an important complication: each of our three major actors — owners, managers, and workers — turns out to be a composite. The interest in these actors derived from a realization that the firm is not a monolithic whole but a composite of underlying units. Not all members of each category behave in lockstep with their

fellow category members, especially across firms. For example, owners cleave into insider blockholders and external minority shareholders. Both are owners; indeed, both are shareholders. "Old money" blockholders and "new money" entrepreneurs have different preferences (including very different stakes in equity markets) and behave differently in the corporate governance arena.

Similarly, workers face possible conflicts between concern for their jobs and concern for their pension investments. Without substantial savings in the firm, workers' major assets are their jobs; thus, they will worry about job preservation. That may motivate them to worry about a voice in the firm so as to preserve jobs. Historically that has motivated worker representatives toward the corporatist stakeholder bargain with managers and blockholders for stability in the firm and weak protection of outsiders. Conversely, where workers have substantial savings invested in the firm or in shares generally, they acquire the concerns of minority shareholders. The greater their savings, the more worried they are about managerial actions that could threaten those assets. As investors in the firm, they care about profitability—like other investors. But as minority shareholders they care about managerial agency costs.

Managers divide along choice of strategies. Some managers prefer the security and predictability of dealing with "patient" blockholders; others prefer the autonomy of dealing with diffused shareholders in financial markets. Some are willing to commit to high MSP exchange for high remuneration (through stock options, among others); others prefer job security to remuneration and will do anything to avoid a contest for control.

We alert readers to these distinctions among owners, workers, and managers to bear in mind as we develop the argumentation and particularly in the country case studies.

34. This model of political economy derives from many sources: the Stolper-Samuelson model of trade based on labor, capital, and land; and on Marx's view of struggle between the owners and workers.

35. See Hansmann and Kraackman (2000); and Cheffins (2001, 2002).

36. Gourevitch and Shinn (2005, chap. 5, fig. 5.2).

37. The cross-class cleavage is well known to specialists on the political economy of trade disputes. See applications by Rogowski (1989); Magee, Brock, and Young (1989); Gourevitch (1986, 1977); Frieden (1988); and Hiscox (2001).

38. See Dore (2000, 2004).

39. Gourevitch and Shinn (2005, chap. 6). See also Höpner (2003a); Gingerich and Hall (2002); Hall and Soskice (2001); and Swank and Martin (2001).

40. See country case studies in Gourevitch and Shinn (2005, chaps. 6–7). These include Chile, China, France, Germany, Japan, South Korea, Malaysia, the Netherlands, Russia, Singapore, Sweden, the United Kingdom, and the United States.

41. On Sarbanes-Oxley, see Romano (2004); and Cioffi (2005).

42. Our usage of institutions here is that of political scientists speaking largely of "parchment institutions," the documents more or less formal; this is different from the usage found often in sociology, in which institutions means "established practices," separate from any formalism. See Gourevitch (2005).

43. See Lijpart (1999); Beck et al. (2001); and Shugart and Carey (1992, chap. 9).

44. The phrase *veto gates* refers to formal institutional points where legislation can be blocked, such as a presidential veto, or a legislative committee, or the Supreme Court. A *veto player* is any person or group who has the capacity to block legislation (a specific committee chair, or party leader, or interest group). A *veto point* combines the notion of institution (a de jure concept) and individual or group; it is thus any point in a political system where legislation can be blocked, be it veto gates or veto players.

Thus, a presidential system with a bicameral legislature would have three veto gates, but the number of veto players depends on the division of government and the degree of party unity. If such a system had a strong party system, and the same party controlled all three veto gates, there would be only one veto player. But, if there was divided government, there could be two or three veto players (depending on the organization of the parties controlling the two chambers of the legislature).

Similarly, a unicameral parliamentary system would have only one veto gate but could have any number of veto players depending on how many parties are included in the governing coalition. So majoritarian and consensus systems could both have any number of veto gates. What distinguishes them is that consensus systems have many veto players, whereas majoritarian systems have few veto players. Consensus systems, by having multiparty coalition government, have many groups that can veto legislation, whereas majoritarian systems lack these multiple de facto veto players.

45. The index of political cohesion used here is a recoding of the Beck et al. (2001) material, done to measure our definition of veto players. We recoded the instances of minority parliamentary government from 3 to 1, i.e., from the highest score on the list to the same score as two-party parliamentary government. The justification for this is that though minority governments are forced to find support from other parties in order to pass legislation, they have the ability to shop around for that support, and usually need only one other party to get things through. Thus, they are coded by us as equivalent to two-party government (IPCOH = 1), rather than multiparty (IPCOH = 2), or even higher as they had initially been (IPCOH = 3). There are several other potential variables from the Beck DPI database that we probed for use as a measure of consensus or majoritarian institutions, including, for example, type of election and political fractionalization. We believe that the measure of veto players captured by our index is the most effective.

46. For the sample as a whole, a bivariate regression of blockholding against both the Index of Political Cohesion and the tenure variable is significant at $t = 2.42$ with an adjusted $r^2 = 24$. Similarly, regressing the minority shareholder protections index against both the Index of Political Cohesion and the tenure variable is significant at $t = 2.24$, adjusted $r^2 = 25$. See Gourevitch and Shinn (2005, appendix, table 8).

47. Pagano and Volpin (2005).

48. Huber and Powell (1994).

49. See discussion in Gourevitch and Shinn (2005, chap. 3).

50. See, for example, Shirk (1993); and Roeder (1993).

51. McIntyre (2001).

52. Ibid.

53. LLSV (2000).

54. Berkowitz, Pistor, and Richard (2003a).

55. See the vigorous literature on this trajectories debate, including Acemoglu and Johnson (2005); Acemoglu, Robinson, and Johnson (2001); Acemoglou and Robinson (2005); Acemoglu, Johnson, and Robinson (2004); Robinson and Sokoloff (2003); and Laeven and Woodruff (2005).

56. Rajan and Zingales (2004) strongly disagree.

References

Acemoglu, Daron, and Simon Johnson (2005). "Unbundling Institutions." *Journal of Political Economy* 113: 949–95.

Acemoglu, Daron, Simon Johnson, and James Robinson (2004). "Institutions as the Fundamental Cause of Long-Run Growth." National Bureau of Economic Research Working Paper 10481.

Acemoglou, Daron, and James Robinson (2005). *Economic Origins of Dictatorship and Democracy.* Cambridge, UK: Cambridge University Press.

Acemoglu, Daron, James A. Robinson, and Simon Johnson (2001). "The Colonial Origins of Comparative Development: An Empirical Investigation." *American Economic Review* 91: 1369–1401.

Amable, Bruno (2002). "Institutional Complementarity and Diversity of Social Systems of Innovation and Production." *Review of International Political Economy* 7: 645–87.

Amable, Bruno, Ekkehard Ernst, and Stefano Palombarini (2005). "How Do Financial Markets Affect Industrial Relations: An Institutional Complementarity Approach." *Socio-Economic Review* 3: 311–30.

Aoki, Masahiko (1994). "The Japanese Firm as a System of Attributes: A Survey and Research Agenda." In Masahiko Aoki and Ronald Dore, eds., *The Japanese Firm: Sources of Competitive Strength.* Oxford, UK: Clarendon Press.

——— (1990). "Toward an Economic Model of the Japanese Firm." *Journal of Economic Literature* 28: 1–27.

Becht, Mario, Patrick Bolton, and Ailsa Roell (2003). "Corporate Governance and Control." In C. Constantinides, M. Harris, and R. Stulz, eds., *Handbook of Economics and Finance*. Amsterdam: North-Holland.

Beck, Thorsten, George Clarke, Alberto Groff, Philip Keefer, and Patrick Walsh (2001). "New Tools in Comparative Political Economy: The Database of Political Institutions." *World Bank Economic Review* 15: 165–76.

Berkowitz, Daniel, Katharina Pistor, and Jean-Francois Richard (2003a). "Economic Development, Legality, and the Transplant Effect." *European Economic Review* 47: 165–95.

——— (2003b). "The Transplant Effect." *American Journal of Comparative Law* 51: 163–201.

Boyer, Robert (1989). *The Regulation School: A Critical Introduction*. New York: Columbia University Press.

Boyer, Robert, and J. P. Durand (1997). *L'Après-fordisme*. Paris: Syros.

Cheffins, Brian (2002). "Corporate Law and Ownership Structure: A Darwinian Link." *University of New South Wales Law Journal* 25: 346–78.

——— (2001). "Does Law Matter? The Separation of Ownership and Control in the United Kingdom." *Journal of Legal Studies* 30: 459–84.

Cioffi, John (2005). "Irresistible Forces and Political Obstacles: Securities Litigation Reform and Sarbanes-Oxley's Structural Regulation of Corporate Governance." Mimeo, Conference on Corporate Governance, University of California, San Diego.

Davis Global Advisors (2002). *Leading Corporate Governance Indicators* (November).

Dore, Ronald (2004). "Pros and Cons of Insider Governance." REITI Working Paper.

——— (2000). *Stock Market Capitalism: Welfare Capitalism, Japan and Germany Versus the Anglo-Saxons*. Oxford, UK: Oxford University Press.

Ernst, Ekkehard C. (2002). "Financial Systems, Industrial Relations, and Industry Specialization: An Econometric Analysis of Institutional Complementarities." OECD Report.

Frieden, Jeffrey (1999). "Actors and Preferences in International Relations." In David A. Lake and Robert Powell, eds., *Strategic Choice and International Relations*. Princeton, NJ: Princeton University Press.

——— (1988). "Sectoral Conflict and U.S. Foreign Economic Policy, 1914–1940." *International Organization* 42: 59–90.

Gingerich, Daniel W., and Peter A. Hall (2002). "Varieties of Capitalism and Institutional Complementarities in the Political Economy: An Empirical Analysis." Paper presented to Workshop on Comparative Political Economy, Cornell University.

Glaeser, Edward, Simon Johnson, and Andrei Shleifer (2001). "Coase vs. the Coasians." *Quarterly Journal of Economics* 3: 853–99.

Gourevitch, Peter (2005). "Politics, Institutions and Society: Seeking Better Results." Paper prepared for World Bank Conference Legal Forum, Washington, DC.

——— (1999). "The Governance Problem in International Relations." In David Lake and Robert Powell, eds., *Strategic Choice and International Relations*. Princeton, NJ: Princeton University Press.

——— (1986). *Politics in Hard Times: Comparative Responses to International Economic Crises*. Ithaca, NY: Cornell University Press.

——— (1977). "International Trade, Domestic Coalitions and Liberty: Comparative Responses to the Crisis of 1873–1896." *Journal of Interdisciplinary History* 8: 281–313.

Gourevitch, Peter A., and James P. Shinn (2005). *Political Power and Corporate Control: The New Global Politics of Corporate Governance*. Princeton, NJ: Princeton University Press.

Hall, Peter, and Daniel W. Gingerich (2001). "Varieties of Capitalism and Institutional Complementarities in the Macroeconomy: An Empirical Analysis." Paper presented to the annual meetings of the American Political Science Association, San Francisco.

Hall, Peter, and David Soskice, eds. (2001). *Varieties of Capitalism: The Institutional Foundations of Comparative Advantage*. New York: Oxford University Press.

Hansmann, Henry, and Reinier Kraackman (2000). "The End of History for Corporate Law." *Georgetown Law Journal* 89: 439–67.

Hiscox, Michael (2001). "Class Versus Industry Cleavages: Inter-industry Factor Mobility and the Politics of Trade." *International Organization* 50: 1–46.

Höpner, Martin (2003a). "European Corporate Governance Reform and the German Party Paradox." Max Planck Institute for the Study of Societies Working Paper.

——— (2003b). "What Connects Industrial Relations and Corporate Governance? Explaining Institutional Complementarity." Max Planck Institute for the Study of Societies Working Paper.

Huber, John D., and G. Bingham Powell Jr. (1994). "Congruence Between Citizens and Policymakers in Two Visions of Liberal Democracy" *World Politics* 46: 291–326.

Jaikumar, Ramchandran (1986). "Postindustrial Manufacturing." *Harvard Business Review* 64: 69–76.

Kroszner, Randall S. (2000). "The Economics and Politics of Financial Modernization." *Federal Reserve Bank of New York Economic Policy Review* 6(4): 25–37.

Laeven, Luc, and Christopher Woodruff (2005). "The Quality of the Legal

System, Firm Ownership, and Firm Size." The World Bank, Policy Research Working Paper.

La Porta, Rafael, Florencio López-de-Silanes, Andrei Shleifer, and Robert Vishny (LLSV) (2006). "What Works in Securities Law?" *Journal of Finance* 61: 1–32.

———— (2002). "Investor Protection and Corporate Valuation." *Journal of Finance* 57: 1147–70.

———— (2000). "Investor Protection and Corporate Governance." *Journal of Financial Economics* 58: 3–27.

———— (1999). "Corporate Ownership Around the World." *Journal of Finance* 54: 471–517.

———— (1998). "Law and Finance." *Journal of Political Economy* 106: 1113–55.

———— (1997). "Legal Determinants of External Finance." *Journal of Finance* 52: 1131–50.

Lefort, Fernando, and Eduardo Walker (1999). "Ownership and Capital Structure of Chilean Conglomerates: Facts and Hypotheses for Governance." *Revista Abante* 3: 3–27.

Lijpart, Arend (1999). *Patterns of Democracy: Government Forms and Performance in Thirty-six Countries*. New Haven, CT: Yale University Press.

Magee, Stephen P., William A. Brock, and Leslie Young (1989). *Black Hole Tariffs and Endogenous Policy Theory in General Equilibrium*. Cambridge, UK: Cambridge University Press.

Mayer, Colin (1996). "Corporate Governance, Competition, and Performance." OECD Working Paper 164.

McIntyre, Andrew (2001). "Institutions and Investors: The Politics of the Financial Crisis in Southeast Asia." *International Organization* 55: 81–122.

Milgrom, Paul, and John Roberts (1995). "Complementarities, Industrial Strategy, Structure and Change in Manufacturing." *Journal of Accounting and Economics* 19: 179–208.

———— (1992). *Economics, Organization and Management*. Englewood Cliffs, NJ: Prentice Hall.

———— (1990). "The Economics of Modern Manufacturing: Technology, Strategy and Organization." *American Economic Review* 80: 511–28.

Pagano, Marco, and Paolo F. Volpin (2005). "The Political Economy of Corporate Governance." *American Economic Review* 95: 1005–30.

———— (2001). "The Political Economy of Corporate Governance." Centre for Economic Policy Research Working Paper 2682.

Perotti, Enrico, and Ernst-Ludwig von Thadden (2003). "The Political Economy of Bank and Market Dominance." European Corporate Governance Institute Finance Working Paper 21/2003.

Porter, Michael (1990). *The Competitive Advantage of Nations*. New York: Free Press.

Rajan, Raghuram, and Luigi Zingales (2004). *Saving Capitalism from the Capitalists*. New York: Crown Business.

———— (2003). "The Great Reversals: The Politics of Financial Development in the Twentieth Century." *Journal of Financial Economics* 69: 5–50.

Robinson, James, and Kenneth Sokoloff (2003). "Historical Roots of Latin American Inequality." *The World Bank 2003 LAC Flagship Report*, chap. 5. Washington, DC: World Bank.

Roe, Mark (2003). *Political Determinants of Corporate Governance: Political Context, Corporate Impact*. New York: Oxford University Press.

Roeder, Philip G. (1993). *Red Sunset: The Failure of Soviet Politics*. Princeton, NJ: Princeton University Press.

Rogowski, Ronald (1999). "Institutions as Constraints on Strategic Choice." In David Lake and Robert Powell, eds., *Strategic Choice and International Relations*. Princeton, NJ: Princeton University Press.

———— (1989). *Commerce and Coalitions: How Trade Affects Domestic Political Alignments*. Princeton, NJ: Princeton University Press.

Romano, Roberta (2004). "Sarbanes-Oxley Act and the Making of Quack Corporate Governance." New York University, Law and Economics Research Paper 04-032.

Shinn, James, and Peter Gourevitch (2002). *How Shareholder Reforms Can Pay Foreign Policy Dividends*. New York: CFR.

Shirk, Susan (1993). *The Political Logic of Economic Reform in China*. Berkeley: University of California Press.

Shugart, Matthew S., and John M. Carey (1992). *Presidents and Assemblies: Constitutional Design and Electoral Dynamics*. New York: Cambridge University Press.

Swank, Duane, and Cathie Jo Martin (2001). "Employers and the Welfare State: The Political Economic Organization of Firms and Social Policy in Contemporary Capitalist Democracies." *Comparative Political Studies* 34: 889–923.

Tenev, Stoyan, and Chunlin Zhang (2002). *Corporate Governance and Enterprise Reform in China: Building the Institutions of Modern Markets*. Washington, DC: World Bank.

Tokyo Stock Exchange (2001). *Survey on Directors*.

Zingales, Luigi (2000). "In Search of New Foundations." *Journal of Finance* 55: 1623–53.

Chapter 8

Credible Commitment and Sovereign Default Risk

Two Bond Markets and Imperial Brazil

WILLIAM R. SUMMERHILL

The new institutional political economy stresses heavily the role of formal political institutions in securing the financial development required for modern economic growth.[1] Three central propositions regarding political organization and economic development occupy the new institutional political economy. First, limiting discretion by the sovereign is indispensable for creating secure rights in financial property. Establishing a limited, and usually representative, government involves the creation of multiple veto points over policymaking. Multiple veto points make for policy stability and help protect the interests of political minorities.[2] Multiveto player institutions thereby reduce the risk of arbitrary interventions by any single political actor or social group and help the state to credibly commit to honor its obligations.

Second, the delegation of authority over specific elements of economic policy to private agents can significantly enhance credibility by further reducing government discretion.[3] Third—and a major implication of the first two propositions—is that by securing financial property, limited government results in a double-barreled financial revolution: the state can issue debt as needed, under good terms, and private financial markets can develop unhindered by fear of sequestration or inflationary erosion. Consistent with the findings of the burgeoning literature on modern finance and growth, financial development has profound consequences for the real economy.[4] In short, getting the political institutions right makes it possible to get the economic institutions right, which in turn affects incentives, thereby getting relative prices right. A better alignment of the private and social returns on investments results in economic growth.

As attractive as this story is, detailed historical studies of the fiscal and economic impact of formal political institutions in countries outside the set of canonical cases are in woefully short supply. In light of the purported implications that institutions hold for financial development, this chapter focuses on the first two propositions of the new institutional political economy: the role of institutions in establishing credibility, and the role of delegation in enhancing it. It does so by reference to nineteenth-century Brazil.[5] Brazil serves as an especially insightful case for three reasons. First, the question of how to create and sustain long-term sovereign debt in a newly emerging market continues to occupy considerable interest among economic investigators. Brazil's public finances stood out among those of nineteenth-century Latin American nations for the success with which the country issued debt. Second, Brazil consistently honored its foreign obligations when its neighbors did not. As early as 1825 every newly independent nation of Latin America had defaulted on its foreign debt, with the exception of Brazil.[6] These defaults were repeated at several intervals during the nineteenth century.[7] Third, Brazil succeeded in issuing a large amount of long-term domestic debt. It did this in an era when every other Latin American country was regularly in default to its domestic creditors.[8] Brazil thus escaped the strong form of what modern international finance researchers have labeled "original sin."[9] Brazil's burgeoning domestic debt was denominated in domestic currency, and it even listed a home-currency loan in London (albeit with an exchange clause). The long-term domestic debt accounted for most of the government's funded obligations as early as the 1850s.

Shortly after independence Brazil successfully implemented the classic solution to the debt dilemma, forging institutional arrangements that established the basis for limited government. The Constitution of 1824, bolstered by the Additional Act of 1834, emplaced multiple veto points in the policymaking arena. The creation of Parliament eliminated the sovereign's ability to unilaterally tax, spend, borrow, or default. Moreover, the Parliament's lower chamber was responsive to the enfranchised elite, making it possible for debt holders to exercise influence over a veto point. The result of these institutional changes was the creation of a long-term funded debt that actively traded in domestic secondary markets, and which became the largest component of the central government's obligations by the middle of the nineteenth century. As the public debt expanded, yields on long-term government bonds fell. Sovereign credit risk varied considerably over time, in response to an array of political factors and policy innovations.

Prominently, the delegation of monetary policy to the Banco do Brasil in the 1850s and 1860s further enhanced credibility. This institutional basis for the public debt endured until the military coup in 1889. The ensuing republican government severely weakened the legislative branch. Inflationary policies in the early 1890s destroyed the value of the domestic debt and undermined the government's ability to raise new funds at home. In contrast to its admirable nineteenth-century record, Brazil embarked on a path of serial default in the twentieth century.

The remainder of the chapter proceeds in five sections. The first takes up the origins of credible commitment in imperial Brazil by analyzing the country's political-institutional changes in the aftermath of independence. It also documents the expansion of the public debt, and in particular the domestic component, following the adoption of the Constitution of 1824. The second section turns to empirics, creating measures of Brazil's sovereign credit risk in the form of yield series on sovereign debt, both at home and in London. The third section searches systematically for structural breaks in these yield series, in an effort to identify events and processes impacting the government's credit risk after it had created the public debt. The fourth section supplements the search for structural breaks, testing a number of hypotheses regarding systematic determinants of credit risk, taking into account multiple factors simultaneously. The final section concludes by discussing briefly how Brazil's credible commitment was undone in the 1890s.

Credible Commitment in Imperial Brazil

The problems confronted by governments in establishing and maintaining credibility among potential lenders are well known. Lenders cannot compel governments to honor loan agreements, barring some sort of absolute advantage in violence (and even then they may not find it worthwhile to do so). The theory of sovereign debt shows that under a variety of settings, no matter what terms the sovereign agreed to initially, the incentives for default in the future can be overwhelming.[10] This creates a commitment problem. In light of this problem, lenders withhold funds in the first period of the lending game, and the sovereign cannot borrow. To obtain an outcome with positive lending, lenders must have a way to impose a sufficient and credible penalty on a defaulting sovereign.[11] The greater the penalty, the larger the amount of debt the sovereign can take on. Penalty mechanisms are difficult to come by. Threats by lenders to cut off future lending in case of default are not sufficient to enable lending. As the value of additional borrowing by the sovereign approaches zero, so does the cost to the sovereign of selectively defaulting. Should the sovereign default, the attractiveness to at least one creditor of the possibility to recoup some of its loss creates sufficient leverage for the sovereign to then selectively arrange new lending, and the problem of credibly penalizing the sovereign persists.[12] The amount a sovereign can borrow is limited by the size of the penalty that lenders can impose if the sovereign fails to perform. Additionally, if the sovereign can establish a credible penalty, government may be able to elicit savings from the domestic economy that otherwise would not be available at all.[13]

There are significant financial and economic consequences, of both a direct and indirect character, if the sovereign can credibly commit to honor debts and successfully borrow. In the case of exogenous shocks to revenues (or costs), borrowing rather than increasing taxes can smooth revenues and avoid efficiency-degrading distortions in the economy. Potential indirect consequences of credible commitment are several. In the case where an exogenous shock is in the form of war or domestic rebellion, the ability to borrow sufficiently can mean the difference between victory and disaster. Where borrowing leads to the establishment of rights in financial property, it can have large positive externalities, leading to the florescence of private capital markets.[14] Where the need to borrow results in the delegation of authority to a legislative body, establishing the debt can give rise to representative government and lay the groundwork for democracy.[15]

In light of the fiscal and military advantages of borrowing, sovereigns may find it in their self-interest to establish a penalty that lenders can impose. Such was the case in Brazil, where independence from Portugal was declared in 1822 by Pedro I, son of the Portuguese sovereign. Proclaimed emperor of Brazil, Pedro confronted a long-brewing military conflict with Spanish Americans to the south. In 1823 he convened a constituent assembly to draw up a constitution for the country. Disbanding the assembly in 1824, in part because of its slow pace of progress, Pedro had his councillors complete the draft of the constitution, which was then distributed throughout the country for ratification by local officials. Under the constitution Pedro, an heir to an absolutist, divided his authority over policymaking with a bicameral Parliament. The Constitution of 1824 served as the coordinating device for national governance that endured with only modest modifications for more than six decades. It specified the inviolability of property, including the public debt.[16] It further assigned the responsibility for the budget and taxation, along with the borrowing, to the Parliament.[17] Brazil's franchise was restricted (limited to adult free males with an income), but no more so than in most Western European parliamentary systems at the time, and was sufficient to provide a basis of representative government. Importantly, the franchise was restricted by wealth, and wealthy Brazilians figured prominently among those who held government debt.

The institutional arrangements codified in the constitution increased the potential penalty for sovereign default in two ways. The first was by better aligning the interests of policymakers with debt holders. Since policymakers in the Parliament's lower house, the Chamber of Deputies, were office-holding politicians, they had to be concerned with the preferences of their constituents. If the median deputy (or an otherwise sufficiently influential deputy) in the lower chamber was responsive to domestic debt holders, he would suffer at the very least a severe electoral penalty if the Parliament permitted the government to default. Moreover, even if the median deputy was not especially responsive to debt holders, cross-issue coalitions within the chamber could accomplish the same result.[18] Less formally, but more severely, the promise to honor the debt was part of a broader package of expectations that, if violated, could result in the withdrawal of support for the emperor.

Events in 1831 provide a revealing natural experiment, as both of these institutional arrangements proved binding. In the case of potential sanctions against the emperor, the penalty was realized in April, though not directly in relation to the debt. Pedro I came to be seen as beholden to Portuguese-born advisors, and politically powerful nativists viewed him increasingly with suspicion, fearing an eventual return to absolutism and Portuguese domination. When the armed forces in Rio de Janeiro withdrew their support, Pedro I was forced to abdicate.[19] The system, however, remained intact, and a series of elected regents ruled Brazil for nine years until Dom Pedro II ascended the throne in 1840.

Two months after Pedro I's abdication, the minister of finance brought forward to the Chamber of Deputies two linked proposals. One was to retire a large amount of copper money (much of it counterfeit) from circulation to try to improve the quality of the monetary base. The second was to authorize the cabinet to suspend service on the foreign debt for five years, to provide funds for the redemption of copper and other needs. The proposal was defended by the government's allies, but vigorously opposed by a majority.[20] The possibility of even a selective default, targeted at bondholders in London, was seen as putting the credibility of all government obligations at risk. To make sure the next packet boat to Europe did not carry news of the minister's proposal without information on its resolution, the Chamber of Deputies accelerated the required study and deliberation of the cabinet proposal, defeating it by a vote of 59 to 23. Debt-holder interests were clearly represented in the Chamber of Deputies.

In short, three features of independence-era institutional changes made it possible for the government to honor debts: the assignment of authority over budgets, taxation, and borrowing to the Parliament; the enfranchised elite's prominent role as holders of the domestic debt, which made default politically costly; and the risk that the sovereign could be deposed (with the system held intact) in case of a transgression against the core interests of the Brazilian elite. Together, these raised the penalty that could be applied to both politicians and the sovereign in case of default.

A principal consequence of credible commitment was a profound shift in the composition of the government's obligations, on two margins. First, funded obligations came to quickly outweigh unfunded debt. By 1829 Brazil's funded debt had attained 60 percent of its total obligations. That share rose steadily through 1862. Between 1862 and 1868 the portion of debt that was funded was set back to its 1844 level, as a result of the rapid issue of short-term treasury notes to help finance the war against Paraguay. The share of funded debt increased thereafter, and by 1885 had nearly returned to its prewar ratio. Overall, Brazil's funded debt exceeded its unfunded obligations by a wide margin.

Second, the long-term effect of the domestic penalty made a major difference to the structure of the debt. Although Brazil enjoyed success in raising foreign funds that was unrivaled in Latin America through the 1880s, the domestic component of the debt grew even more quickly. The domestic share increased through the 1850s, was set back somewhat during the Paraguayan war by heavy borrowing abroad, and then returned to preeminence thereafter. Domestically issued debt attained its highest level in 1889, when apólices (notes issued by the Treasury and traded in domestic money markets) and national loans combined had represented long-term obligations totaling nearly 435 million milréis (more than 46 million pounds sterling) in circulation. In short, the Constitution of 1824 provided a political foundation for a large domestic public debt, whereas the nature and degree of the penalty that the government confronted meant that Brazil elicited from its own relatively underdeveloped capital markets an unusually large amount of savings, with a growing share of the debt accounted for by domestic issues.[21]

Sovereign credit risk is reliably indicated by yields on government bonds.[22] To the extent that investors believe that a government is likely to default, they charge an extra premium to hold its securities. Though the risk of sovereign default was low enough to allow Brazil to borrow affordably, the government's credit risk varied considerably between 1825 and 1889. In short, political institutions that permitted the imperial government to borrow overseas and at home were not the sole determinant of credit risk. Exogenous events, internal disorder, economic conditions, and financial policy measures all influenced perceptions of government's credit worthiness. Because Brazil's colonial government did not place securities in bond markets, it is not possible to use bond yields to test for macro-institutional changes related to the advent of the empire and the Constitution of 1824.[23] Bond yields and measures of risk premia do, however, permit a search for critical events, or "turning points," in Brazil's financial history.

Measuring Sovereign Credit Risk

Institution-based credible commitments to honor sovereign debt had salutary effects on both the volume of Brazil's borrowing and its costs, but such effects were in no way irreversible. Sustaining credibility, thereby permitting the government to enjoy low-cost, long-term credit, further depended on events and government actions. Debt markets constantly reassessed the government's willingness to repay. Institutional changes, policy measures, political events, and wars all could alter the sovereign's credit risk (for the better or for the worse) long after initial credibility had been established.[24] The best available continuous measure of credibility used to indicate changes on government default risk is the yield on sovereign debt in secondary markets. Since Brazil almost completely partitioned its domestic and foreign debt markets, yields on sovereign debt instruments in both markets are examined in this chapter to both chart changes in credit risk and to search for their proximate determinants. Gauging the determinants of the financial markets' perception of the imperial government's risk of default provides insights into factors that impacted sovereign credibility at the margin.

For Brazil's domestic debt the analysis relies on end-of-month measures of the current yield on apólices that paid an annual 6 percent coupon in domestic currency. Secondary-market price quotes become available only in 1829. The 4 percent and 5 percent apólices made up only a small share of the debt, were relatively illiquid, and were so infrequently quoted as to rule out their use. The national loans that appeared in 1868 and 1879 cover only a portion of the period of interest. Apólice prices are available continuously from 1829 through the end of the monarchy in 1889, making them the preferred asset for constructing the domestic yield series.

Perpetuities for all intents and purposes, apólices had no fixed date of redemption. At any given point in time the price of an apólice equaled the net present value of the future stream of coupon payments into infinity. The apólice's yield to maturity was the internal rate of return that satisfies

$$P = \sum_{t}^{\infty} \frac{coupon_t}{(1 + r)^t},$$

where P is the net present value of the bond given by its market price, *coupon* is the annual coupon rate, t is the year, and r is the internal rate of return. With a perpetual-interest-bearing security the yield to maturity at time t simplifies to the current yield:

$$r_t \cong \frac{coupon_t}{price_t}.$$

End-of-month apólice price quotes came from two primary sources. The first is Rio de Janeiro's leading business daily, the *Jornal do Commércio*, which regularly published the recent transaction prices and quotes for government securities.[25] The transaction account books, in manuscript form, of the Rio de Janeiro stock exchange provide most of the apólice prices from 1850 through 1895.[26] Occasionally, when the account books did not report a transaction, the *Jornal do Commércio* listed a price (either as a quote, or based on a transaction in the curb market) that could be used. In some instances no quote was available for the end of the month or within two weeks before or after the end of the month. When no quote was available, linear interpolation filled the gap. Of 796 monthly observations from 1829 through 1895, only 10 were obtained in this manner, and only 3 were quotes from outside the ±two-week interval at the end of the month. The result is the first, and to date the only, monthly time series of Brazilian domestic interest rates in existence.

The yield series for Brazilian bonds in London is compiled by first calculating the yield to maturity for various overlapping issues.[27] The component series were selected based on data availability and the time remaining until redemption.[28] Not every Brazilian issue was regularly quoted in London. The bond issues that were most frequently quoted had, in some cases, differing coupon rates. The yields on bonds with different coupons could be linked to create a single, consistent yield series by calculating the yield to maturity. The time span for each component series was selected to avoid using observations "too close" to the maturity date, when prices of bonds that had been trading at discount converge on the redemption value.

The yield to maturity is simply the expected internal rate of return on the bond when purchased at time t, given by

$$P_t = \sum_t^T \frac{coupon_t}{(1 + r)^t} + \frac{P_R}{(1 + r)^T},$$

where P_t is the market price of the bond at purchase, which is equal to the discounted stream of remaining future coupon payments and the redemption price (P_R) of the bond at maturity in year T. The yield to maturity is given by r.

End-of-month prices for Brazilian bonds in London come from three sources: the *Times* of London, the *Course of the Exchange*, and the *Economist* magazine.[29] The breadth of coverage by these three sources for Brazilian bond issues differed over time. On many occasions one source would provide greater detail on price quotes than did the others. All three sources were scrutinized for the entire period of interest to identify which provided the best coverage at any given moment.

The component series of bond prices, selected in accordance with the best available price quotations, draw on price quotes for six different issues at two different coupon rates. From 1825 through 1852 the prices are for the Brazilian 5 percent bonds that made up Brazil's initial issue in 1824–25. From 1853 through mid-1859 prices are for the Brazilian $4\frac{1}{2}$ percent issue of 1852. From 1859 through 1862 the prices are for the $4\frac{1}{2}$ percent issue of 1858. From 1862 through 1865 the price used is a composite reported for 1852, 1858, and 1860. All of these bore $4\frac{1}{2}$ percent annual coupon rates, but each had a different maturity. Since none of the sources distinguished among these three issues in this four-year period, nor provided more complete prices on any other issue in circulation, the yield to maturity for this interval uses the reported composite 1852/58/60 price with the redemption date for the 1858 issue. From late 1865 through early 1875 prices come from the 5 percent loan of 1865. The 5 percent loan of 1875 serves as the basis of the series through 1889.

The prices of Brazilian bonds in London varied in accordance with two influences. One was the market's assessment of Brazil's creditworthiness, which is of interest here. The other was general, marketwide conditions impacting bond yields not only of the Brazilian government but also of other sovereign borrowers and private firms. As a result Brazil's bond prices could rise or fall for reasons having nothing to do with Brazil per se, which contemporaries understood well.[30] Default risk on Britain's consolidated annuities was very nearly zero, and changes in their prices reflected fundamental shifts in the relative scarcity of capital. To isolate the Brazil-specific component of sovereign risk, subtract the yield on consols in London (analogous to Brazilian apólices) from the Brazil yield-to-maturity time series. The residual provides the desired measure of the Brazilian government's sovereign risk.[31] Figures 8.1 and 8.2 present the Rio yield series and the London risk-premium series.

What is clear from Figures 8.1 and 8.2 is that the yields on Brazilian issues declined, on average, over time. Increases in yields were intermittent,

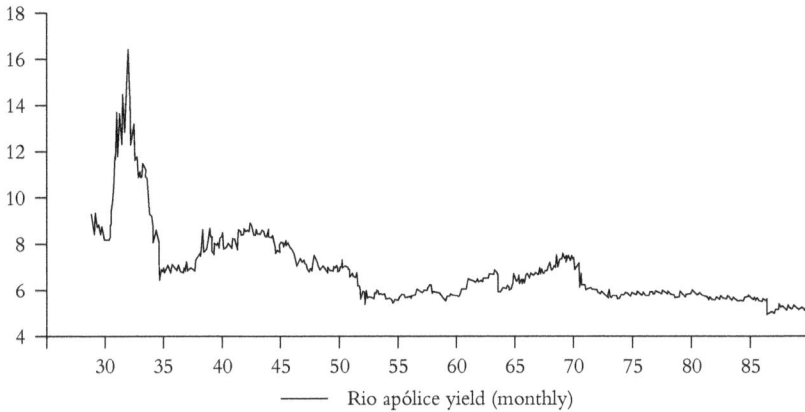

Rio apólice yield (monthly)

Figure 8.1 Monthly yield on Brazilian apólices, 1829–89

SOURCE: See pp. 232–235.

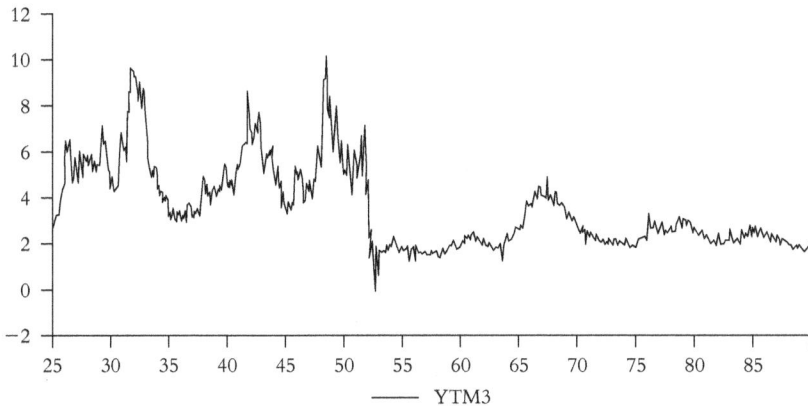

YTM3

Figure 8.2 Monthly risk premium on Brazilian bonds in London, 1825–89 (yield to maturity net of yield on 3% consols)

SOURCE: See pp. 232–235.

nonpermanent, and a predictable response to unpredictable events. Figure 8.1 presents the current yield on apólices in Rio de Janeiro, based on end-of-month spot observations. The most dramatic change in yields came with the political instability of the First Reign (1822–31). Nativist, anti-Portuguese sentiment was the defining feature of early national Brazilian politics. Emperor Pedro I, despite having declared independence and establishing the relatively liberal Constitution of 1824, came to be viewed as increasingly beholden to Portuguese influences and advisors. Under pressure to return to Portugal because of the succession crisis, Pedro I abdicated the Brazilian throne in April 1831.[32] The big run-up in yields came during this political storm. Yields increased before and after abdication but dropped precipitously soon thereafter; as the regency was emplaced, it became clear that the core institutions of the constitutional monarchy were not threatened, and that the public debt would not be repudiated. Yields again rose some 200 basis points from 1835 to 1844, as a well-known series of local uprisings and separatist revolts erupted in various parts of Brazil. The decline in yields in the mid-1840s appears closely related to the pacification of the longest-running separatist revolt in Brazil's far south. Declining yields were also due in part to new tariffs in 1844, which raised rates on British goods to those paid by products from other nations, resulting in a near balancing of the budget.[33]

Rio yields hovered below 6 percent for much of the 1850s, during the government of the "conciliation" cabinet. Yields rose gradually, and even at the height of the war with Paraguay in the 1860s did not attain the levels seen in the early 1840s. Hefty new issues of debt both at home and overseas did not prevent yields from falling again below 6 percent, where they stayed for most of the 1870s and 1880s. The conversion of Brazilian apólices from 6 percent to a 5 percent basis had been authorized by the Parliament in the early 1880s. It did not have much of a visible impact on yields, nor in the financial press, when it was implemented in April 1886.

Brazilian apólices were not necessarily more risky than the government's bonds in London. Visual inspection is sufficient to show that yields in the secondary markets of Rio de Janeiro and London moved in tandem, with a couple of notable exceptions. The comparison in Figure 8.3 shows that yields in Rio de Janeiro were distinctly higher than those in London during much of the politically turbulent transition from the 1820s to the 1830s. These differences had nothing to do with the lower coupon rates on the London issues, since lower dividends were simply priced into the bond and the yield adjusted accordingly. Yield gaps between the two markets had much to do with expectations about the exchange rate. Dividend obliga-

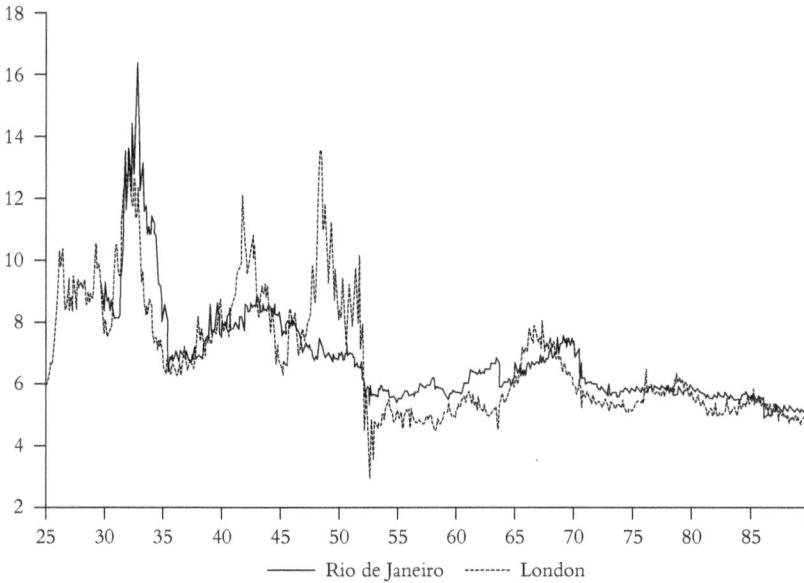

Figure 8.3 Apólice yields in Rio de Janeiro and yield to maturity on Brazilian bonds in London, 1825–89

SOURCE: See pp. 232–235.

tions denominated in sterling were going to continue to be paid in sterling, barring an exchange-rate meltdown. Dividends and the values of bonds in Rio de Janeiro, however, were vulnerable to local inflation. Yields in Rio were distinctly lower than those in Rio in the late 1840s, as the milréis ended its long slide against the pound sterling. Yields climbed more sharply in London later in the war against Paraguay than they did in Brazil.[34]

Turning Points: Critical Events and Brazil's Credit Risk

Changes in bond yields that are persistent, in a statistically significant way, indicate market-moving events. Several techniques have evolved to try to distinguish such structural breaks from random variation.[35] Here the procedure created by Bai and Perron is applied both to the Brazil risk-premium series in London and the apólice yield series in Rio de Janeiro. The procedure identifies structural breaks in the data series that result in regime shifts that take the form of persistent changes in the average yield. The approach locates structural breaks in the time series without imposing any prior expectations on the data and has the advantage of simultaneously locating multiple breaks

TABLE 8.1

Break points in the risk-premium series for Brazilian bonds
in London, February 1825 to December 1889

INTERVAL LENGTH $(h) = 38$ (MONTHS); MAXIMUM NUMBER OF STRUCTURAL BREAKS
$(m) = 9$

BREAK MONTHS (T_i)	BOUNDARY MONTHS FOR 95% CONFIDENCE INTERVAL	
November 1830	June 1826	January 1831
January 1834	December 1833	February 1834
October 1837	July 1836	July 1838
December 1840	February 1839	March 1841
February 1844	July 1843	September 1845
September 1847	June 1841	December 1847
February 1852	January 1852	March 1852
June 1865	February 1865	August 1865
December 1869	June 1869	May 1870

Parameter	β_i	t-statistic
β_1	5.05	57.7
β_2	7.27	61.2
β_3	3.52	32.28
β_4	4.46	37.6
β_5	6.27	52.8
β_6	4.36	39.0
β_7	6.16	61.3
β_8	1.87	32.2
β_9	3.75	37.6
β_{10}	2.28	48.1
$R^2 = 0.84$	$F = 415.4$	
$n = 778$		

SOURCE: See pp. 232–235.
NOTE: SupF tests support nine breaks vs. zero breaks, at the 1.0% level. Both the UD max
and WD max tests support the existence of breaks vs. the alternative of no breaks. The number of
breaks selected by BIC is nine.

(when they are present) in a single series. The procedure estimates a system
of linear equations of the form

$$y_t = \alpha_i + \beta_i t + \varepsilon_t \text{ for } t = T_m + 1, \ldots, T$$

in which y is the bond yield, α is the intercept, β is slope of the trend, and
ε is an error term. The system provides consistent estimates of the number
of break points (m), the break-point dates (T), and coefficients for each
break (β). The number of break points and their dates depends in part on
the minimum interval (h) permitted between breaks. There is naturally a
trade-off involved, since very short intervals risk picking up very short-
term shifts, whereas long intervals risk missing potentially important break

TABLE 8.2

*Break points in Brazilian apólice yield series in Rio de
Janeiro, September 1829 to December 1895*

INTERVAL LENGTH (h) = 39 (MONTHS); MAXIMUM NUMBER OF STRUCTURAL BREAKS (m) = 8

BREAK MONTHS (T_i)	BOUNDARY MONTHS FOR 95% CONFIDENCE INTERVAL	
November 1834	September 1834	September 1835
December 1838	February 1838	June 1840
October 1846	June 1846	June 1847
January 1852	October 1851	April 1852
February 1861	August 1859	June 1861
April 1867	July 1866	June 1868
August 1870	May 1870	November 1870
April 1886	November 1885	September 1886

Parameter	β_i	t-statistic
β_1	10.67	57.7
β_2	7.11	61.2
β_3	8.11	32.28
β_4	6.92	37.6
β_5	5.74	52.8
β_6	6.40	39.0
β_7	7.11	61.3
β_8	5.76	32.2
β_9	5.08	37.6
R^2 = 0.80	F = 345.6	
n = 796		

SOURCE: See pp. 232–235.
NOTE: SupF tests support eight breaks vs. zero breaks, at the 1.0% level. Both the UD max and WD max tests support the existence of breaks vs. the alternative of no breaks. The number of breaks selected by BIC is eight.

points. Given the monthly basis of the yield series, the minimum interval is set at the shortest length permitted by the procedure and the length of the overall series.

Structural breaks are present both in the London risk-premium series from 1825 to 1889 and in the Rio apólice yields from 1829 to 1895. Tables 8.1 and 8.2 present the break points and confidence intervals. In both cases the number of breaks is selected using Bayes Information Criterion (BIC). In practice the BIC indicates more structural breaks than the sequential method, though almost every break indicated by the sequential procedure is also indicated using BIC. All test statistics indicate the presence of statistically significant structural breaks in both series. The shortest possible span between breaks (the length of each regime) is employed, which for the London series corresponds to 38 months and for the Rio series is 39 months. In the case of the London series the BIC indicates nine different break points, and for the Rio yields, eight break points. Since the Rio yield series begins only in 1829, the procedure likely misses a break point like that in the London series around 1830.

Between the two series there are only three break points that are closely related. This difference is due not only to the markets for these bonds being segmented but also to the fact that events or news that created a structural shift for one market did not necessarily do so for the other. Most of the break points have ready explanations, though in some cases there are several candidates, and there is no reason to believe ex ante that break points whose confidence intervals cover a period of several months or even several years were necessarily due to a sole event.

In the London risk-premium series the first break point (November 1830) has a confidence interval nearly five years long and thus includes nearly all of the political turmoil of the last half of Emperor Pedro I's reign. As seen in Figure 8.4, which charts both the break points and the mean risk premia by regime, the risk premium increased with the evolving political crisis that resulted in the forced abdication of Pedro I.[36] The second break point (January 1834), after which risk declined, does not correspond to any particular event and likely reflects a positive shift in sentiment toward the viability of the Brazilian state under the regency. The third break point (October 1837), raising the risk premium anew, was most likely the result of the Sabinada revolt, a local uprising in Salvador, Bahia.[37] The fourth break (December 1840), which saw an additional increment added to Brazil's credit risk, came during a period of several critical events: the partisan political struggles behind the end of the regency and the ascension to the throne by the adolescent emperor Dom Pedro II; and considerable advances by Farroupilha rebels in the south.[38]

The confidence interval around the fifth break point (February 1844) includes the final defeat of the Farroupilha rebellion and is naturally accompanied by a fall in the risk premium.[39] It also encompasses the new Alves Branco tariff that went into effect in November 1844. The tariff significantly raised duties, including those on British imports, and demonstrated a willingness by the state to raise taxes, taxes that could then be used to service the debt.[40] The sixth break point (September 1847) has no obvious interpretation; it comes too early for the outbreak of the Praieira revolt in Pernambuco, although it may be a response to the building tensions in the region during 1847. However, the confidence interval around it is so large

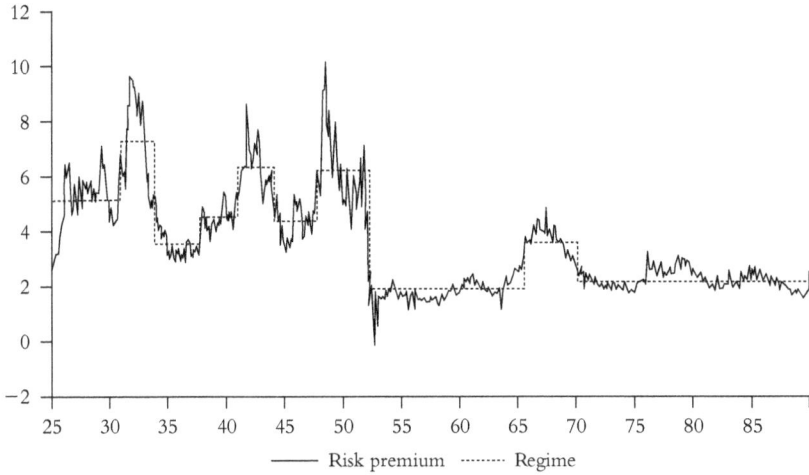

Figure 8.4 London risk premium and yield regimes

SOURCE: See pp. 232–235.

(running from June 1841 through December 1847) that it could include a wide variety of events.

The seventh break in the series (February 1852), which exhibits a relatively narrow two-month confidence interval, involved the largest enduring decline in the government's risk premium under the empire. Two factors were at work here. First, between November 1851 and March 1852 the imperial government resumed regular amortization of its London bonds.[41] The turning point also corresponds directly to the military defeat of the Argentine leader Rosas, a strategic campaign in which Brazil emerged on the winning side.

The most likely and obvious interpretation of the eighth break, which raised the average risk premium in June 1865, is a response to the worsening of hostilities with Paraguay. In April Paraguay had successfully invaded Corrientes in Argentina. By May the Triple Alliance Treaty had been signed by Brazil, Argentina, and Uruguay, confirming the gravity of the conflict. Paraguayan forces then invaded Rio Grande do Sul in Brazil in June. These, along with losses suffered by the Brazilian navy in their victorious engagement at Riachuelo in June, further suggested that the war would not end quickly.[42] The final break point (December 1869) brought yields back down. The confidence interval encompasses the last major battle of the war in 1869, at Campo Grande/Acosta Ñú, and the death of Solano López at the hands of Brazilian forces in 1870.[43]

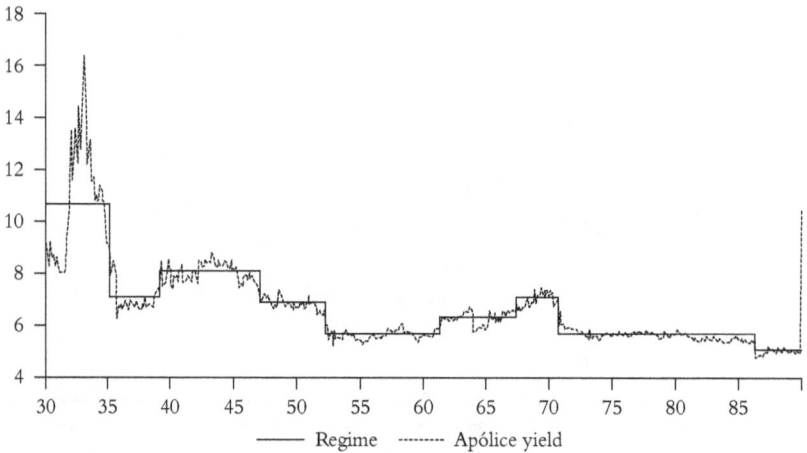

Figure 8.5   Rio apólice yield regimes

SOURCE: See pp. 232–235.

Most of the eight turning points detected in the Rio yield series similarly correspond to prominent events, mainly political or policy related in
nature. Figure 8.5 charts the different yield regimes that result from the
eight breaks. The first break in the series (November 1834) comes only
one month after the resumption of service on the Portuguese loan, which
Brazil had suspended during the succession crisis in Portugal. Its confidence
interval includes the death of Pedro I in Portugal, which eliminated the
risk, much feared by the nativists, that the ex-emperor might return to
Brazil.[44] Although not strictly inside the confidence interval, it also came
only three months after the passage of the Additional Act in August 1834.
This measure was effectively a constitutional amendment that checked the
authority of the emperor, reducing excessive centralization by the national
government. Given that it was adopted under the regency, during which
no emperor ruled, it had the effect of vesting the Chamber of Deputies
with supreme constitutional authority. For the first time the institutions
established by the Constitution of 1824 visibly rested completely on con-
sent, free of pressure and influence from the throne.[45] The act significantly bolstered the multiveto player character of the institutions of 1824.
The break here corresponded to a decrease of nearly 300 basis points in the
government's mean credit risk and was the largest single regime shift of the
nineteenth century.

The second break in the Rio de Janeiro yield series (December 1838)
is quite similar to the fourth break in the London risk-premium series:

the period was one of turmoil in the late 1830s, culminating in the early arrival of Pedro II to the throne. The third break (October 1846) does not correspond to any widely known event. It comes too early to be explained by the Praieira revolt in Pernambuco, is followed by a period of reduced mean yield, and is possibly a lagged response to the end of the long-running Farroupilha rebellion, though the confidence intervals are too narrow to include the conclusion of the conflict. The fourth break (January 1852) has a confidence interval that is consistent with the interpretation of the coeval break in the London series, with two prominent factors at work. First was the resumption of debt amortization in London. Second was the defeat of Rosas in Argentina, which brought about the end of a potentially long-term and costly conflict in the Rio de la Plata region, reducing Brazil's credit risk even further. The fifth break (February 1861) corresponds to the fall of the cabinet of the "10th of August," headed by Silva Ferraz.[46] Under Silva Ferraz the commercial code was modified in 1860 to restrict banks from issuing notes without full backing in specie.[47] The demise of the cabinet did not alter this policy but did usher in the first upward shift in yields in more than 20 years.

Although the outbreak of hostilities with Paraguay does not register as a break point in Rio, the sixth break (April 1867) appears at a particularly difficult moment of the military campaign. Between March and May 1867 more than 4,000 Brazilian soldiers died in the cholera epidemic that broke out first among the allied troops and then later spread to the Paraguayan forces.[48] In May Brazilian forces were forced to retreat after penetrating Paraguayan territory. The confidence interval around the break point also includes the allies' most important battlefield defeat of the war, at Curupaiti in September 1866. These events set back the campaign to seize Humaitá, the linchpin of the Paraguayan defenses, by a year. The confidence interval around the seventh break (August 1870) encompasses the death of Solano López (March 1870), the acceptance by Paraguay of the Triple Alliance Treaty (June 1870), and the establishment of the new Brazil-dominated Paraguayan government and constitution (November 1870).[49] The final break point (April 1886) most likely has a trivial explanation: Brazil successfully converted the 6 percent apólices to a 5 percent basis.

Two general implications emerge from the results of the break-point estimations. First, every identifiable market-moving event that resulted in a persistent change in the mean level of credit risk had a political or geopolitical basis. For the case of Brazil the market's perception of risk was driven more by the government's willingness to pay—that is, political factors—than its ability to service the debt. The structural-break results also confirm what is suggested by visual inspection of Figures 8.1 and 8.2: though a baseline level of credibility had been established by the Constitution of 1824 that permitted the government to issue long-term debt, the credit-risk consequences of that credibility were not irreversible, and sovereign default risk proved quite variable over time.

Delegation, Debt, and Disorder: Determinants of Sovereign Risk

Political institutions, like the Constitution of 1824, that create multiple veto points over policy changes enhance the credibility of sovereign debt. But they do not completely guarantee that debt will be honored. Unless debt holders exercise considerable influence over one of the veto points, creating multiple veto points alone is not a sufficient condition for credibility.[50] The interests of government creditors were well represented in the lower house of the Brazilian Parliament. Delegation of control over key aspects of economic policy may further enhance credibility, in the same way that delegation of authority over taxing, spending, and borrowing by the sovereign to a legislature improves credibility.[51] Specifically, the delegation of authority to manage aspects of the debt to independent bureaucracies or even private entities can reduce sovereign credit risk by insulating decisions that impact the debt from the vagaries of day-to-day political temptations.[52]

The imperial government implemented a modest form of delegation. In 1853 the government arranged for the creation of the privately financed third Banco do Brasil. From 1853 to 1866 the government delegated to the bank rights of issue and responsibility for managing the exchange rate.[53] The Treasury refrained altogether from new issues of currency. In return for its issue privileges, the bank made an implicit loan to the government by agreeing to retire each year a fixed amount of notes left in circulation by the first Banco do Brasil decades earlier. The goal, consistent with legislation of 1846 that established the sterling parity of the Brazilian currency, was to attain convertibility. The bank's monopoly of issue was weakened for a brief spell in 1857 as several competing banks—most of them outside Rio de Janeiro—were allowed by the government to issue notes for a few years.[54] As the largest, and uniquely privileged, of Brazil's commercial banks the Banco do Brasil was thus tasked with an often impossible goal: maintaining the quality of the currency while also keeping the local money market in good health.

Successful delegation would yield low inflation and provide exchange-rate stability. This in turn would bolster the value of the debt, reduce the government's credit risk, and lower borrowing costs. One weakness of delegation is that it can be undone. However, in a multiveto point setting, once authority has been delegated, stripping it away is more difficult if it requires the assent of all veto players.[55] In the Brazilian case this was an extraordinarily weak form of delegation. Although the bank had a board composed of directors elected by its shareholders, the government named both the president and vice president.

The hypothesis that the delegation of monetary decisions to the Banco do Brasil reduced sovereign risk must be tested jointly with other variables that likely impacted credibility. A number of intuitive factors, namely, economic-financial variables, rebellions, and other key events, also account for variation in government credit risk. First, increased obligations, indicated by either the stock of debt or the size of the current deficit, potentially raise the sovereign's credit risk by weighing more heavily on the sovereign's ability and/or willingness to pay its debt. Two debt variables are included in the analysis: DEBTSTER, the total sterling value of Brazil's funded debt, and DIFDBT, a measure of the budget deficit derived by differencing the debt series. Neither monthly nor quarterly figures exist for these. Moreover, the date at which the foreign debt is reported each year differs from that for the domestic debt. Both dates vary at times during the nineteenth century. As a result, monthly estimates of the debt and the deficit are generated by linear interpolation between annual figures.

Second, an array of domestic political factors, including internal disorder and the partisan character of the government, may register an impact on bond yields. Brazil had a large number of armed uprisings from independence until the late 1840s. Most of these were of a small, local, and transitory nature. Indeed, by the time news of them arrived in London, or even Rio de Janeiro, the news that the uprising had been suppressed or was otherwise inconsequential might also be already known. Rebellions on a larger scale (or of longer duration) that called into question the central government's ability to maintain national integrity, or that raised the cost of governance, are of special interest. Moreover, the partisan basis of politics could influence credit risk by several mechanisms. One is by partisan revolt, best illustrated by the 1842 Liberal uprisings in Minas Gerais and São Paulo. Another channel of partisan influence would be if one party were seen as especially likely to default or suspend payments on debt.

To control for the impact of major revolts and partisan politics on credit risk, we included in the analysis dichotomous variables for several key regional political conflicts, along with party effects in the cabinet. The variable CABANAGEM takes on the value of 1 in the months of the revolt in Brazil's north that began in 1834.[56] The variable FARROP measures the impact of the Farroupilha rebellion in Brazil's south that ran from September 1835 to March 1845. The Liberal revolts from May 1842 through August 1842 in São Paulo and Minas Gerais are measured with the variable SPMGREV. The impact of the partisan identity of the cabinet is indicated by the variable GPDUM, which takes on the value of 1 when the Liberal party controls the government.[57]

A government's reputation for debt payment (or conversely, for poor payment) figures prominently in the literature on sovereign debt. With one exception (that of the Portuguese loan) Brazil regularly made its interest payments during the entire imperial era, and visual inspection of the yield series for both Rio de Janeiro and London reveals a downward trend over the long term. The hypothesis is that with each successive period of debt payment the market's assessment of Brazil's quality as a borrower grows more positive. TREND, a monthly time index, should capture this effect. The one exception to Brazil's record on repayment was introduced in the previous section: a loan it assumed from Portugal in return for recognition of its independence. Brazil halted service during the period in which the pretender Miguel challenged control of the Portuguese throne by Pedro I's daughter. PORTLOAN is a dummy variable specifically for the period in which Brazil was technically in default on the Portuguese loan.[58] The hypothesis is that, due to either risk of international conflict between Brazil and Portugal, or to concern that Brazil's halt on payments might become more generalized, during this period credit risk was higher.

Other forms of international conflict impact sovereign credit risk. PARAWAR is a dummy for the period of the Paraguayan war, from November 1864 to July 1870. Brazil's major external conflict in the nineteenth century, the war is predicted to raise credit risk. Ideally this variable would indicate the change in credit risk strictly resulting from concern that Brazil might lose the conflict. However, co-linearity between this and other variables potentially complicates interpretation. Domestic and foreign borrowing increased dramatically during the war, short-term debt ballooned, and the Treasury resumed its control over currency issue, greatly expanding the money supply. These simultaneous changes would likely all work in the same direction as the war itself in raising credit risk.

Finally, BB is a dummy variable for the period in which the government delegated monetary policy to the quasi-independent Banco do Brasil.[59] Since in practice this only occasionally resulted in outright convertibility, a second variable, CONVERTIBLE, is included for periods of full convertibility both during the 1853–66 period and again when convertibility was briefly established in 1889.[60]

TABLE 8.3

Determinants of Brazil's risk premium in London, 1825–89

DEPENDENT VARIABLE: YTM3
METHOD: LEAST SQUARES
SAMPLE (ADJUSTED): 1825:02 1889:11
INCLUDED OBSERVATIONS: 778 AFTER ADJUSTING END POINTS
NEWEY-WEST HAC STANDARD ERRORS & COVARIANCE (LAG TRUNCATION = 6)

Variable	Coefficient	Std. error	t-statistic	Prob.
C	5.344005	0.333569	16.02068	0.0000
TREND	−0.002162	0.001414	−1.529215	0.1266
CABANAGEM2	−1.661362	0.345489	−4.808730	0.0000
FARROP	0.884903	0.400415	2.209964	0.0274
SPMGREV	1.544631	0.340599	4.535036	0.0000
PARAWAR	0.603139	0.318750	1.892198	0.0588
DEBTSTER	−3.10E-08	1.77E-08	−1.749736	0.0806
DIFDBT	−8.10E-08	2.74E-07	−0.295917	0.7674
GPDUM	0.181236	0.208472	0.869356	0.3849
PORTLOAN	1.299935	0.550372	2.361921	0.0184
BB	−1.808164	0.417425	−4.331707	0.0000
CONVERTIBLE	−0.423075	0.185250	−2.283802	0.0227

R-squared	0.665573	Mean dependent var.		3.545315
Adjusted R-squared	0.660771	S.D. dependent var.		1.839430
S.E. of regression	1.071347	Akaike info criterion		2.991014
Sum squared resid.	879.2023	Schwarz criterion		3.062840
Log likelihood	−1151.504	F-statistic		138.5896

SOURCE: See pp. 232–235.
NOTES: Variable definitions for Tables 8.3 through 8.6: TREND is an annual time trend; DEBTSTER, the total sterling value of Brazil's funded debt; DIFDBT, a measure of the budget deficit derived by differencing the debt; CABANAGEM1 (not shown) takes on the value of 1 in the months of the revolt from January 1835 to May 1836 for the early period in which rebels were successful; CABANAGEM2 covers the entire conflict from January 1835 to June 1840; FARROP is a dummy for the Farroupilha rebellion from September 1835 to March 1845; SPMGREV is a dummy for the Liberal revolts from May 1842 to August 1842; GPDUM takes on the value of 1 when the Liberal party controls the cabinet; PORTLOAN is a dummy variable for May 1828 to September 1834 during which Brazil was in default on the Portuguese loan; PARAWAR is a dummy for the period of the Paraguayan war, from November 1864 to July 1870; BB is a dummy variable for the period in which the government delegated monetary policy to the quasi-independent Banco do Brasil, namely July 1853 to July 1866; CONVERTIBLE is a dummy variable for full convertibility to gold: April 1854 to November 1857; August 1858 to January 1859; October 1862 to September 1864; and June 1889 to December 1889.

Tables 8.3 through 8.6 provide ordinary least squares (OLS) results for four specifications of the determinants of credit risk, two variants each for the determinants of yields in London and Rio de Janeiro. Other specifications, not reported here, allowed for seasonality by using monthly dummy variables. None of these were significant and had no impact on the results.

Though it is plausible that reputation mattered, in only one of the specifications does TREND take on statistical significance, although in all specifications it has the predicted sign. Brazil's reputation for repayment (controlling for the disputed Portuguese loan) was widely discussed among financial commentators in the nineteenth century. In the end it may not

TABLE 8.4
Determinants of Brazil's risk premium in London, 1825–89

DEPENDENT VARIABLE: YTM3
METHOD: LEAST SQUARES
SAMPLE (ADJUSTED): 1825:02 1889:11
INCLUDED OBSERVATIONS: 778 AFTER ADJUSTING END POINTS
NEWEY-WEST HAC STANDARD ERRORS & COVARIANCE (LAG TRUNCATION = 6)

Variable	Coefficient	Std. error	*t*-statistic	Prob.
C	5.114630	0.340214	15.03355	0.0000
TREND	−0.001469	0.001447	−1.015579	0.3101
FARROP	0.141649	0.410014	0.345475	0.7298
SPMGREV	2.424345	0.315915	7.674041	0.0000
PARAWAR	0.558880	0.327622	1.705868	0.0884
DEBTSTER	−3.65E-08	1.81E-08	−2.014052	0.0444
DIFDBT	−8.11E-09	2.70E-07	−0.030067	0.9760
GPDUM	0.314501	0.198839	1.581692	0.1141
PORTLOAN	1.514072	0.553272	2.736577	0.0064
BB	−1.837640	0.425119	−4.322647	0.0000
CONVERTIBLE	−0.386199	0.184008	−2.098819	0.0362
R-squared	0.630590	Mean dependent var.		3.545315
Adjusted *R*-squared	0.625774	S.D. dependent var.		1.839430
S.E. of regression	1.125253	Akaike info criterion		3.087931
Sum squared resid.	971.1717	Schwarz criterion		3.153772
Log likelihood	−1190.205	*F*-statistic		130.9285

SOURCE: See pp. 232–235.

have had much of an impact. Indeed, also widely discussed at the time were nonreputational issues, such as worries over the current deficit, Brazil's reliance on inconvertible paper money, and the size of the funded debt. Based on the one significant parameter on TREND, a good reputation could have reduced Brazil's credit risk on apólices by about 3 basis points per year. Compounded over the entire imperial era, 180 basis points represented a considerable improvement in credit risk. It is not possible, however, to assign the entire TREND effect to reputational consequences alone. Over the course of the nineteenth century it is possible, and even probable, that the supply of funds investors were willing to employ in assets like those of Brazilian bonds increased. Any supply shifts are also captured by TREND, and disentangling the two effects is not possible.

The period in which Brazil suspended payments on the Portuguese loan (PORTLOAN) clearly had a major impact on the risk premium and Rio yields, raising them anywhere from 130 to 370 basis points. It also encompasses considerable instability in Brazil, including the abdication of Pedro I and the early period of the regency, effects that may be picked up as well by this variable.

TABLE 8.5

Determinants of domestic bond yields, 1829–89

DEPENDENT VARIABLE: RIOAPOLICEYIELD
METHOD: LEAST SQUARES
SAMPLE (ADJUSTED): 1829:09 1889:12
INCLUDED OBSERVATIONS: 724 AFTER ADJUSTING END POINTS
NEWEY–WEST HAC STANDARD ERRORS & COVARIANCE (LAG TRUNCATION = 6)

Variable	Coefficient	Std. error	*t*-statistic	Prob.
C	7.557201	0.340491	22.19499	0.0000
TREND	−0.001442	0.001169	−1.233595	0.2178
FARROP	0.586484	0.263334	2.227153	0.0262
SPMGREV	0.777561	0.169057	4.599403	0.0000
PARAWAR	0.663294	0.113476	5.845222	0.0000
DEBTSTER	−2.02E-08	9.12E-09	−2.217808	0.0269
DIFDBT	3.65E-07	1.22E-07	3.005297	0.0027
GPDUM	0.151428	0.082180	1.842649	0.0658
PORTLOAN	3.667108	0.755886	4.851404	0.0000
BB	−0.752013	0.148828	−5.052899	0.0000
CONVERTIBLE	−0.065820	0.141150	−0.466311	0.6411

R-squared	0.781609	Mean dependent var.		6.793022
Adjusted *R*-squared	0.778546	S.D. dependent var.		1.653736
S.E. of regression	0.778230	Akaike info criterion		2.351487
Sum squared resid.	431.8223	Schwarz criterion		2.421145
Log likelihood	−840.2382	*F*-statistic		255.1790

SOURCE: See pp. 232–235.

Conflict, especially the domestic variety, registers an impact on credit risk. But here the problem of multicollinearity among dummy variables rears its head. Inclusion of a variable for the Cabanagem revolt in two specifications yields a significant parameter of the wrong sign and changes the significance of other variables. In three of the four specifications the Farroupilha rebellion (FARROP) raises credit risk in London by as much as 88 basis points, and in Rio de Janeiro by between 58 and 84 basis points. The short-lived Liberal revolts of 1842 (SPMGREV) raised credit risk as well, though much more so in London than in Rio.[61] The war with Paraguay (PARAWAR) predictably raised yields, but for a major war did so only modestly. In only one specification is the partisan identity of the cabinet significant, with Liberal control raising yields slightly. It is not surprising that there does not appear to be much of an effect. There is no indication in the historiography that Liberals were in any way hostile to servicing the debt or that Conservatives uniquely represented any sort of a "moneyed" interest.

Increases in the deficit raise the yield only in Rio, but not in London. In three of the specifications the level of the debt is significant, but with

TABLE 8.6
Determinants of domestic bond yields, 1829–89

DEPENDENT VARIABLE: RIOAPOLICEYIELD
METHOD: LEAST SQUARES
SAMPLE (ADJUSTED): 1829:09 1889:12
INCLUDED OBSERVATIONS: 724 AFTER ADJUSTING END POINTS
NEWEY–WEST HAC STANDARD ERRORS & COVARIANCE (LAG TRUNCATION = 6)

Variable	Coefficient	Std. error	*t*-statistic	Prob.
C	7.825472	0.368081	21.26017	0.0000
TREND	−0.002354	0.001353	−1.739681	0.0823
CABANAGEM2	−0.783256	0.252144	−3.106387	0.0020
FARROP	0.845237	0.270035	3.130107	0.0018
SPMGREV	0.374400	0.149350	2.506856	0.0124
PARAWAR	0.704926	0.115102	6.124355	0.0000
DEBTSTER	−1.35E-08	1.09E-08	−1.230423	0.2189
DIFDBT	3.34E-07	1.20E-07	2.789071	0.0054
GPDUM	0.089482	0.077698	1.151675	0.2498
PORTLOAN	3.426309	0.766906	4.467706	0.0000
BB	−0.713994	0.158202	−4.513179	0.0000
CONVERTIBLE	−0.097625	0.143870	−0.678565	0.4976

R-squared	0.791269	Mean dependent var.	6.793022
Adjusted *R*-squared	0.788044	S.D. dependent var.	1.653736
S.E. of regression	0.761359	Akaike info criterion	2.309011
Sum squared resid.	412.7229	Schwarz criterion	2.385002
Log likelihood	−823.8621	*F*-statistic	245.3712

SOURCE: See pp. 232–235.

the wrong sign. This result no doubt stems from a degree of simultaneity between the level of the debt and the yield (or risk premium). In the absence of sufficient instruments no two-stage, least squares estimate could be pursued.

In London convertibility unsurprisingly reduces the Brazil risk premium by roughly 40 basis points, and is statistically significant. In Rio de Janeiro convertibility has no effect. Finally, in every specification the delegation of monetary authority to the Banco do Brasil reduces sovereign credit risk considerably, in Rio by around 70 basis points, and in London by 180 basis points. Somewhat surprisingly, even this weak and partial delegation had positive effects on the government's credit risk.

All of the OLS specifications in Tables 8.3 through 8.6 exhibited serial correlation. HAC standard errors are employed to guard against generating artificially high *t*-statistics. One other concern with the OLS estimates is the risk of spurious regression, if the data series contain unit roots. Both the Augmented Dickey-Fuller test and Phillips-Perron test fail to reject the null hypothesis of no unit root in levels for nearly every series used here,

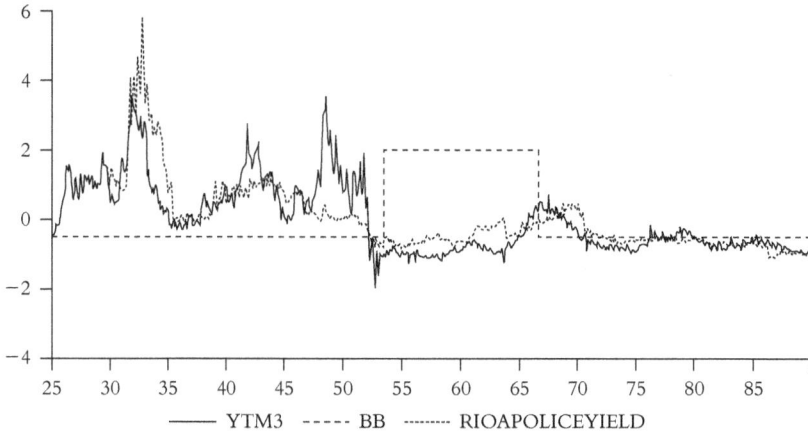

Figure 8.6 Impact of delegation to Banco do Brasil

SOURCE: See pp. 232–235.

NOTE: Normalized representation of London risk premium (YTM3), Rio apólice yield, and Banco do Brasil dummy variable.

including those for dummy variables. In the presence of a high *R*-squared statistic and a low Durbin-Watson statistic, spurious regression is indeed a concern.

To test for a long-term relationship between variables that avoids the risk of spurious regression, we subjected various specifications to Johansen cointegration tests. Many specifications, especially those with multiple dichotomous variables, failed to return results because of near-singular matrices. Nonetheless, a simple specification using the Rio de Janeiro yields, the dummy variable for the period in which Brazil suspended payments on the Portuguese loan, the level of the debt, and the dummy for the Banco do Brasil yielded a significant likelihood ratio and a single cointegrating equation (with standard errors in parentheses):

$$\text{RIOAPOLICEYIELD} = 7.82 + 4.39\text{PORTLOAN} - .0000000422\text{DEBTSTER}$$
$$(0.62) \qquad\qquad (-.000000009)$$

$$- 1.28\text{BB}$$
$$(-0.39)$$

in which the Banco do Brasil dummy variable is significant and takes on the predicted sign.[62] To better illustrate this effect, Figure 8.6 presents a normalized graph of the risk premium in London, yields in Rio de Janeiro, and the Banco do Brasil dummy variable. The Treasury reestablished its monopoly over currency issue early in the war with Paraguay, and the inflation tax became one of the margins on which the war was financed. Government did not give up monetary authority again under the empire. Nonetheless, the period of delegation corresponded to the lowest yields and risk premia of the imperial era.

Conclusions

The continuous access to long-term borrowing at home and abroad that Brazil enjoyed during the empire came at a varying price. Reference to yields on sovereign debt in secondary markets in London and Rio de Janeiro makes it possible to measure changes in Brazil's credit risk. Sovereign credit risk varied enormously over this period. Domestic yields ran as high as 16 percent and as low as 6 percent. The yield to maturity on Brazil's bonds in London varied between 13 percent and 4 percent.

Consistent with both the quantity measures of sovereign credibility and the costs of new borrowing, bond yields reveal that Brazil's credit risk dropped to historically low levels by the early 1850s. Bond markets registered key turning points, as events and policies translated into persistent changes in yields on the government's securities. The political crisis culminating in the end of the first reign, political instability under the regency, the defeat of geopolitical rivals, and Brazil's resumption of debt amortization all registered an impact on perceptions of sovereign credibility. The general tendency, however, was for yields to decline, just as was the case in the primary market for new borrowing.

Notes

1. These propositions are apparent in the literature inspired by the now-classic work by North and Weingast (1989), which both revitalized and historicized the study of politics, public finance, and long-term economic performance.

2. See Tsebelis (2002).

3. See McCubbins, Noll, and Weingast (1989).

4. See, for example, King and Levine (1993); Levine and Zervos (1998); and Rajan and Zingales (1998).

5. Elsewhere (Summerhill 2006) I examine the consequences (or lack thereof) of the revolution in public finance for private financial development.

6. Dawson (1990).

7. Marichal (1989).

8. "Domestic creditor" is a euphemism in many cases, as Spanish American caudillos often levied "loans" in the form of assets, specie, and material under threat of violence.

9. Eichengreen and Hausmann (2005).

10. See Bulow and Rogoff (1989b); and Eaton, Gersovitz, and Stiglitz (1986).

11. See Bulow and Rogoff (1989a); and Cole and Kehoe (1998).

12. Greif, Milgrom, and Weingast (1994); and Weingast (1997).

13. Drazen (1998).

14. See North and Weingast (1989).

15. Hoffman and Norberg (1994); and North and Weingast (1989).

16. Rodrigues (1863, article 179).

17. Ibid., article 15.

18. This is established as an additional possibility result in Stasavage (2003).

19. See Barman (1988); and Macaulay (1986).

20. Brazil, Câmara dos Deputados, *Anais*, June 7, 1831.

21. Drazen (1998) derives results that show how credibility in domestic debt markets mobilizes savings that would not otherwise be made available.

22. Bond prices in the secondary markets provide more reliable information on default risk than do loan costs in the primary market. A government exhibiting an extremely high risk of default may not be able to borrow long at all, such that intervals between bond issues may conceal immeasurably high credit risk. The continuous quotation of Brazilian bonds in the secondary market between 1825 and 1889 avoids this potential pitfall in measuring risk premia.

23. The National Loan of 1822 would seem to provide the opportunity to test directly the impact of the Constitution of 1824. Scrutiny of contemporary newspapers in Rio de Janeiro has not yielded secondary-market quotations for the loan.

24. Sussman and Yafeh (2003); and Stasavage (2002, pp. 164–74).

25. The series from 1829 through 1849 is constructed using the prices of 6 percent apólices.

26. Arquivo Nacional (Rio de Janeiro), Junta de Corretores de Fundos Públicos da Cidade do Rio de Janeiro, "Livros de Registro Oficial de Cotações de Titulos e Valores," 1850–95.

27. Constructing the yield series entailed considerable grunt work but proved necessary since the existing monthly price series for Brazilian bonds is not suitable for the analysis conducted here.

28. Redemption dates for each issue are taken from the amortization provisions detailed in each of the imperial government's loan agreements with the Rothschilds; see Summerhill (2006, chap. 3).

29. Because of debt retirements there was no single Brazilian bond issue that circulated in London for the entire period 1824–89. I have reconstructed monthly prices and yields available for all Brazilian bond issues in London directly from the original sources.

30. *Relatorio do Ministerio da Fazenda*, 1877, p. 32.

31. No similar adjustment for the apólice series is made here, since it was Brazil's counterpart to Britain's consolidated annuity. Such an adjustment might be warranted, if most apólice investors in Brazil had consols as an alternative, and consol investors in Britain had apólices as an alternative. Because of the way in which the government segmented the debt market, consols clearly represented the risk-free alternative to Brazil's bonds in London. It is far from clear that consols were a relevant alternative investment to Brazil's apólices.

32. The best treatment of this episode is found in Macaulay (1986, pp. 240–53).

33. Deveza (1971, pp. 69–72).

34. A related question briefly considered later is that of causality in trans-Atlantic changes in yields and the role of the exchange rate.

35. Willard, Guinnane, and Rosen (1996); and Bai and Perron (1998a, 1998b).

36. Macaulay (1986, pp. 242–53); and Barman (1988, pp. 157–59).

37. However, the regression analysis in the next section does not pick up an effect from the Sabinada on yields. On the revolt, see Kraay (1992).

38. Barman (1988, pp. 200–211).

39. Ibid., pp. 227–28.

40. Deveza (1971, pp. 69–70).

41. See the discussion of this resumption in Summerhill (2006, chap. 3).

42. See Doratioto (2002, pp. 130–88).

43. Ibid., pp. 415–19, 437–55.

44. Barman (1988, pp. 175–78); and Macaulay (1986, pp. 303–5).

45. Barman (1988, p. 177).

46. Javari (1962); and Silva (1895).

47. For a discussion on the 1860 changes in the law regarding incorporation in general, and banks in particular, see Summerhill (2006, chaps. 6, 7).

48. Doratioto (2002, pp. 237–55, 283–84).

49. Ibid., pp. 419–55.

50. Stasavage (2002, pp. 158–64).

51. See North and Weingast (1989, pp. 820–21); and Root (1990).

52. Stasavage (2002, pp. 162–63); and Razaghian (2003).

53. Cavalcanti (1890, 1893); Carreira (1980); and Franco and Pacheco (1979).

54. Policies related to the Banco do Brasil, and the bank's role in currency issue, are discussed further in Summerhill (2006, chap. 7).

55. McCubbins, Noll, and Weingast (1989).

56. There were two variants of the variable for the Cabanagem rebellion: January 1835–May 1836 for the early period in which rebels were successful, and January 1835–June 1840 for the entire conflict.

57. From 1840 through 1889 the party identity of each cabinet is developed by reference to Fleiuss (1925); and Silva (1895). Before the late 1830s party identities were not yet explicit, though the cabinets were generally all Conservative in nature and program. Pre-1840 cabinets are all coded as "Conservative." The *conciliação* cabinet of the 1850s was predominantly Conservative, and coded as such. The *progressista* cabinet members were generally Liberal in their policy positions, and are coded as "Liberal" (Carvalho 1996, pp. 375–77). These categorizations are imperfect, given some instability in party identities and the apparent realignment of both some individual politicians, and party positions, in the 1850s and 1860s.

58. May 1828–September 1834.

59. July 1853–July 1866.

60. The periods during which Brazil's currency was convertible to gold were April 1854–November 1857; August 1858–January 1859; October 1862–September 1864; and June 1889–December 1889.

61. Specifications with a variable for the Sabinada revolt, not reported here, yielded significant coefficients, but of the wrong sign. Specifications including a variable for the Praieira rebellion did not indicate any significance for the event.

62. The estimate uses two lags in the levels of the variables. Other specifications bolster the finding, though they did not yield a unique cointegrating equation. Granger causality tests show bidirectional effects for the risk premium in London and the yield in Rio, and strong unidirectional effects running from the exchange rate to both the London risk premium and the Rio yield. The BB variable might be thought of as operating through the exchange rate. Nonetheless, a specification incorporating both the risk premium and the exchange rate still gave a significant parameter on BB, suggesting that the period in which the bank was responsible for exchange-rate management had an independent effect on yields. From 1828 to 1889 the end-of-month pound–milréis exchange rates are taken from the *JdoC* and the *Diário Oficial do Império do Brazil*. From 1825 through 1828 the rates come from Brazil, *Relatório da Commissão de Inquérito Nomeada por Aviso do Ministério da Fazenda, de 10 de Outubro 1859* (Rio de Janeiro n.d.). There was no spot exchange market in Rio that was quoted in either the commercial press or on the stock exchange. Contracts to be settled within 60 to 90 days serve as the basis of the rates.

References

Bai, Jushan, and Pierre Perron (1998a). "Computation and Analysis of Multiple Structural Change Models." *Journal of Applied Econometrics* 18: 1–22.

——— (1998b). "Estimating and Testing Linear Models with Multiple Structural Changes." *Econometrica* 66: 47–78.

Barman, Roderick J. (1988). *Brazil: The Forging of a Nation, 1798–1852*. Stanford, CA: Stanford University Press.

Brazil (n.d.). *Relatório da Commissão de Inquérito Nomeada por Aviso do Ministério da Fazenda, de 10 de Outubro 1859*. Rio de Janeiro: Imprensa Oficial.

Bulow, Jeremy, and Kenneth Rogoff (1989a). "A Constant Recontracting Model of Sovereign Debt." *The Journal of Political Economy* 97: 155–78.

———— (1989b). "Sovereign Debt: Is to Forgive to Forget?" *The American Economic Review* 79: 43–50.

Carreira, Liberato de Castro (1980). *História Financeira e Orçamentária do Império do Brasil*. Brasília: Senado Federal.

Carvalho, José Murilo de (1996). *A Construção da Ordem— Teatro de Sombras*, 2d ed. Rio de Janeiro: Editora Civilização Brasileira.

Cavalcanti, Amaro (1893). *O Meio Circulante Nacional, Resenha e Compilação Chronologica de Legislação e de Factos*. Rio de Janeiro: Imprensa Nacional.

———— (1890). *Resenha Financeira do Ex-Imperio do Brazil em 1889*. Rio de Janeiro: Imprensa Nacional.

Cole, Harold L., and Patrick J. Kehoe (1998). "Models of Sovereign Debt: Partial Versus General Reputations." *International Economic Review* 39: 55–70.

Dawson, Frank G. (1990). *The First Latin American Debt Crisis: The City of London and the 1822–25 Loan Bubble*. New Haven, CT: Yale University Press.

Deveza, Guilherme (1971). "Política Tributária No Período Imperial." In Sergio Buarque de Holanda and Pedro Moacyr Campos, eds., *História Geral da Civilização Brasileira, vol. 2, Declínio e Queda do Império*. São Paulo: Difel.

Doratioto, Francisco (2002). *Maldita Guerra: Nova História da Guerra do Paraguai*. São Paulo: Companhia das Letras.

Drazen, Allan (1998). "Towards a Political-Economic Theory of Domestic Debt." In Guillermo Calvo and Mervyn King, eds., *The Debt Burden and Its Consequences for Monetary Policy*. New York: Palgrave Macmillan.

Eaton, Jonathan, Mark Gersovitz, and Joseph Stiglitz (1986). "A Pure Theory of Country Risk." *European Economic Review* 30: 481–513.

Eichengreen, Barry, and Ricardo Hausmann (2005). *Other People's Money: Debt Denomination and Financial Instability in Emerging Market Economies*. Chicago: University of Chicago Press.

Fleiuss, Max (1925). *História Administrativa do Brasil*. 2d ed. São Paulo: Melhoramentos.

Franco, Afonso Arinos de Melo, and Claudio Pacheco (1979). *História do Banco do Brasil*. Rio de Janeiro: Banco do Brasil.

Greif, Avner, Paul Milgrom, and Barry R. Weingast (1994). "Coordination, Commitment, and Enforcement: The Case of the Merchant Guild." *Journal of Political Economy* 102: 745–76.

Hoffman, Philip T., and Kathryn Norberg (1994). *Fiscal Crises, Liberty, and*

Representative Government, 1450–1789. Stanford, CA: Stanford University Press.

Javari, Jorge João Dodsworth (1962). *Organizações e Programas Ministeriais: Regime Parlamentar No Império.* 2d ed. Rio de Janeiro: Arquivo Nacional.

King, Robert G., and Ross Levine (1993). "Finance and Growth: Schumpeter Might Be Right." *Quarterly Journal of Economics* 108: 717–37.

Kraay, Hendrik (1992). "'As Terrifying as Unexpected': The Bahian Sabinada, 1837–1838." *Hispanic American Historical Review* 72: 501–27.

Levine, Ross, and Sara Zervos (1998). "Stock Markets, Banks, and Economic Growth." *American Economic Review* 88: 537–58.

Macaulay, Neill (1986). *Dom Pedro: The Struggle for Liberty in Brazil and Portugal, 1798–1834.* Durham, NC: Duke University Press.

Marichal, Carlos (1989). *A Century of Debt Crises in Latin America: From Independence to the Great Depression, 1820–1930.* Princeton, NJ: Princeton University Press.

McCubbins, Matthew D., Roger G. Noll, and Barry R. Weingast (1989). "Structure and Process, Politics and Policy: Administrative Arrangements and the Political Control of Agencies." *Virginia Law Review* 75: 431–82.

North, Douglass C., and Barry R. Weingast (1989). "Constitutions and Commitment: The Evolution of Institutions Governing Public Choice in Seventeenth-Century England." *Journal of Economic History* 49: 803–32.

Rajan, Raghuram G., and Luigi Zingales (1998). "Financial Dependence and Growth." *American Economic Review* 88: 559–86.

Razaghian, Rose (2003). "Establishing Financial Credibility in the United States, 1789–1860: The Impact of Institutions." Ph.D. diss., Columbia University.

Rodrigues, José Carlos (1863). *Constituição Política do Império do Brasil Seguida do Acto Addicional, da Lei da Sua Interpretação e de Outras.* Rio de Janeiro: Imprensa Nacional.

Root, Hilton (1990). "Tying the King's Hands: Credible Commitments and Royal Fiscal Policy During the Old Regime." *Rationality and Society* 1: 240–58.

Silva, João Manuel Pereira da (1895). *Memórias do Meu Tempo.* Rio de Janeiro: Garnier.

Stasavage, David (2003). *Public Debt and the Birth of the Democratic State : France and Great Britain, 1688–1789.* Cambridge, UK: Cambridge University Press.

———— (2002). "Credible Commitment in Early Modern Europe: North and Weingast Revisited." *Journal of Law, Economics, and Organization* 18: 155–86.

Summerhill, William R. (2006). *Inglorious Revolution: Political Institutions, Sovereign Debt and Financial Underdevelopment in Nineteenth-Century Brazil.* Unpublished manuscript.

Sussman, Nathan, and Yishay Yafeh (2003). "Constitutions and Commitment: Evidence on the Relation Between Institutions and the Cost of Capital." CEPR Discussion Paper 4404.

Tsebelis, George (2002). *Veto Players: How Political Institutions Work.* Princeton, NJ: Princeton University Press.

Weingast, Barry R (1997). "The Political Foundations of Limited Government: Parliament and Sovereign Debt in 17th- and 18th-Century England." In John N. Drobak and John V. C. Nye, eds., *The Frontiers of the New Institutional Economics.* New York: Academic Press.

Willard, Kristen L., Timothy W. Guinnane, and Harvey S. Rosen (1996). "Turning Points in the Civil War: Views from the Greenback Market." *American Economic Review* 86: 1001–18.

Chapter 9

Legal Origin vs. the Politics of Creditor Rights
Bond Markets in Brazil, 1850–2002

ALDO MUSACCHIO

Introduction

Do institutions persist over time and determine current economic outcomes? Specifically, does the adoption or inheritance of a legal tradition
in the past determine the subsequent course of institutional and financial
development? This chapter attempts to answer this question by examining
the history of corporate bond markets in Brazil, a civil law country.[1]

Most social scientists agree that institutions are important for economic
development. But there is little agreement about which institutions cause
economic prosperity and which are incidental to growth. To overcome this
endogeneity problem, social scientists have turned to history in their search
for exogenous factors that might explain the variation in the levels of economic development observed around the world today. In particular, they
have wondered whether the conditions at the time the former European
colonies were settled led to the adoption of specific institutions that had
long-term effects on economic growth. Research using current economic
indicators has found a strong correlation between certain early institutions
and contemporary development levels, suggesting that institutions might
exert a persistent effect over time.[2]

This same logic has been used by a growing and influential body of literature, which I refer to as the law and finance literature, to argue that variation in financial development is influenced by differences in legal origin,

specifically, the level of investor protection in any given country. According to this literature, the amount of protection granted to shareholders and creditors determines the degree to which they will be willing to participate in financial markets. Statistical work presented in this literature shows investor protections to significantly explain the variation in financial development in a cross section of 50 countries. Legal origin is thus shown to be a valid exogenous instrument for explaining variation in investor protections across these countries.[3]

The power of the legal origin instrument, according to the law and finance literature, is a consequence of most countries having adopted or inherited their legal traditions before investor protections were chosen by legislators (and even before modern financial markets were created). The explanation goes like this: "Because legal families originated before financial markets had developed, it is unlikely that laws were written primarily in response to market pressures. Rather, the legal families appear to shape the legal rules, which, in turn, influence financial markets" (La Porta, López-de-Silanes, Shleifer, and Vishny [henceforth LLSV] 2000, p. 9). The reason is that, according to LLSV (1998, p. 1126), "countries typically adopted their legal systems involuntarily (through conquest or colonization). The legal family can therefore be treated as exogenous to a country's structure of corporate ownership and finance." The literature's robust statistical findings support the claim that legal origin matters for financial development.

The works of the law and finance literature divide the world into two broad legal traditions, common law and civil law, or four legal families: common law, French civil law, German civil law, and Scandinavian civil law. The law and finance proponents' robust statistical evidence demonstrates that "common law countries have the strongest protection of outside investors—both shareholders and creditors—whereas French civil law countries have the weakest protections" (LLSV 2000, p. 8).

I find research such as is presented in the law and finance literature that links early institutions to current economic outcomes to be explicitly historical in its theoretical setup, but to make historical research irrelevant. Its model is "historical"—events at an earlier time determined the set of institutions (for example, legal traditions) that was established, which sent countries down particular paths of economic development—but historical research is avoided. Historical processes are assumed to be the consequence of institutional variables such as legal tradition just because they are highly correlated with current measures of financial development. The literature is explicit in its historical claims: "History has persistent effects" (LLSV 2000, p. 12).

But implicit in the law and finance literature's statistical results is the idea that a linear relationship exists between legal origin and financial market development that is fairly constant over time (with some standard error allowing for variation over time and across countries of the same legal tradition). If being a civil law country is highly correlated with having small financial markets and poor investor protections today, this relationship between legal origin and financial outcomes should be observable at any time in the country's past. But most of the relevant work has focused on finding relationships between two snapshots of the world, one in the distant past and one today. Research into the historical trajectories of institutions and financial development, which is needed to inform our understanding of how early institutions determined the economic development paths countries followed in subsequent years, is scarce.

If specific legal systems have a path-dependent quality, two things should be true. First, the same cross-sectional variation we see today should be observable in cross sections in the past. Second, if the extent and enforcement of investor protections are determined by the inherited legal tradition, we should not find within cases significant variation in outcomes and investor protections over time.

I construct my argument around the following three tests. First, I test whether the idea that legal origin exerts a persistent effect on financial market size can be defended. The significant variation I find in bond market size and creditor protections over 150 years does not support the notion of persistent effects of legal origin. Second, I test whether a path-dependent effect of legal origin can explain the level of creditor protections in Brazil, finding, following the methodology of LLSV (1998), that creditor rights vary too much over time to be determined by legal origin. I propose that the time variance of investor protections is better explained by the existence of a political economy channel. Finally, I test whether the relationship posited by the law and finance literature between legal origin and creditor rights holds for a (small) cross section of countries in the past. I present evidence that in 1910 legal origin did *not* explain the differences we observe across countries today. In fact, for the few countries I study, French civil law countries had, on average, stronger creditor rights that common law countries.

Preliminary results on variation in financial market size were presented by Rajan and Zingales (2003), who showed that in 1913 the financial markets of many civil law countries were larger (as a percentage of gross domestic product [GDP]) than they are today, as well as larger than those of common law countries at the time. The authors also found the equity markets in a cross section of civil law countries to be significantly larger than those in the majority of large common law countries that year. They documented a significant reversal in equity market size following the Great Depression and accelerated growth at the end of the century for most countries. Their evidence does not support the stable differences among legal families predicted by the law and finance literature.

Rajan and Zingales (2003) propose an interest-group theory to explain the trends they observed in financial market development. They suggested that incumbent businesses opposed financial development because it could breed competition when international cross-border trade and capital flows diminished in the wake of World War I. Using openness to trade and capital as their main exogenous variables (instrumented using a country's distance from its trading partners), the authors found that countries that remained more open to trade experienced a less radical reversal in financial development after the Great Depression. But they did not study what happened to investor protections throughout the twentieth century. We do not know which laws were changed, by which groups, and how.

I find in the case of Brazil significant variation over time in the level of debenture market development.[4] I show that the total stock of private bonds in Brazil was larger at the beginning of the twentieth century than it is today, and find the significant reversal in equity markets observed by Rajan and Zingales (2003) to be more pronounced in bond markets. Even today, Brazil's stock of bonds has not reached the 1913 level.

Creditor rights also exhibit important historical variation. I present evidence that creditor rights were relatively strong in Brazil between 1889 and 1940. In fact, between 1890 and 1908, Brazil had the four protections for creditors deemed by LLSV (1998) to be relevant to the development of a bond market. I maintain, moreover, that variation in creditor rights was accompanied by variation in court enforcement of creditor rights. The law and finance literature assumes creditor rights to be strongly enforced in countries that have good indices of rule of law or institutional development. The lack of indices of rule of law for the past complicates a comparison between past and present. I examined bankruptcy court cases at the National Archive in Brazil to determine the extent to which creditor rights were enforced between 1850 and 1920, the first period of bond market development. The court cases revealed that bondholders had priority in bankruptcy cases. Once a judge declared a company bankrupt, creditors were in control of the firm; they could replace managers immediately and recover their claims by reorganizing or liquidating the company.

Nor was Brazil the only French civil law country that had strong protections for creditors. I present preliminary evidence of creditor rights protection in France, Spain, Belgium, and Argentina circa 1910 that suggests considerable within-country variation over time. Most of these countries had stronger creditor protections in 1910 than in 1995. In fact, they had, on average, stronger protections than some of the common law countries for which I could study the extent of creditor rights protections circa 1910 (that is, the United Kingdom, the United States, Hong Kong, and the Strait Settlements). This is evidence of across- as well as within-country variation over time. If the results obtained from this small sample can be generalized, the implied relationship between common law and strong creditor rights, and French civil law and weak creditor rights, does *not* hold over time.

I argue that the variation over time in creditor rights and their enforcement might be explained by political factors. U.S. bankruptcy law was, according to Berglöf and Rosenthal (2000), the product of an ideological divide in Congress between legislators who supported the use of state bankruptcy laws for debtor relief (after crises) and legislators looking for a federal bankruptcy law with a pro-creditor bias, and Roe (2003) argues that societies with strong worker protections tend to have weak investor protections. In Europe and Japan, protections for workers were consequent to an important shift in social preferences after World War II, a phenomenon Perotti and von Thadden (2003) explain with a model that shows how societies exposed to high inflation in the 1920s moved in the wake of the Great Depression toward greater protection for labor and more concentrated corporate ownership (by banks, the state, or families). A model is also the means by which Pagano and Volpin (2005) explain the political conditions that determine greater or lesser protection for shareholders across countries of the Organization for Economic Cooperation and Development (OECD).[5]

The findings presented here differ from those of Roe (2003) and Perotti and von Thadden (2003) in that the change in investor protections in Brazil cannot be explained by conditions that affected only Europe. Brazil, although not greatly affected by World War II, nevertheless experienced, as did continental Europe, a change in investor protections that favored workers. Inflation might be a more plausible explanation of changes in investor protections in Brazil (a country with a history of high inflation). But high inflation began only in the late 1940s, after creditor rights had been changed to favor labor over creditors. Finally, the ideological divide in Brazil was not between pro-creditors and pro-debtors per se, as in the United States. Debtors benefited from the more lenient bankruptcy procedure the government introduced to protect labor in 1945. But there is no evidence of a pro-debtor lobby in Brazil.[6]

My findings support the general view of Pagano and Volpin (2005) that in Brazil more democratic regimes have tended to be associated with stronger creditor rights. The authoritarian regime of Getulio Vargas traded creditor rights for labor protections to garner support from Brazil's powerful unions.

The exogenous factor that seems to have influenced Brazil to emphasize labor rights over creditor protections was the Great Depression, which, in Brazil, coincided with a revolution that transferred rule from the coalition of republican elites situated in the states of São Paulo and Minas Gerais to the pragmatic military group of the southern state of Rio Grande do Sul. Lacking the support of the coffee exporters and incumbent industrialists, the new ruling group logically viewed labor unions as a source of needed popular support. The unions were responsible for mounting pressure for workers' rights in the 1920s and especially after the Great Depression. The government that came to power in the 1930s traded laws that provided strong protections for workers and weakened creditor rights for massive support.

Brazil is a natural laboratory in which to test the hypothesis that institutional and market outcomes within countries have historically exhibited a great deal of variation. It is (1) a developing civil law country with relatively small equity and bond markets today; (2) by LLSV's (1998) classifications (and as measured in 1995), among the countries least supportive of creditor rights; and (3) ranked poor, by all the current indices of rule of law, in the enforcement of property rights. Brazil is today perceived to be a relatively poor environment in which to do business, rife with corruption and plagued by government repudiation of contracts and poor contract enforcement.

This chapter also articulates new insights into the initial financial revolution in Brazil circa 1882. The accelerated growth of industrial GDP, GDP, and GDP per capita coincides with the emergence of bond and equity markets in Brazil in the 1880s and 1890s. GDP per capita, although it remained flat throughout most of the nineteenth century (Leff 1982), achieved a compound annual growth rate of 1.8% from 1890 to 1945, and GDP grew at approximately 4% per year during the same period.[7] There is little evidence that rapid growth was fueled by bank credit. Because banks were not particularly active in providing long-term financing, most companies financed capital formation during the first half of the twentieth century with equity and bonds (Levy 1977; Triner 2000; Hanley 1995, 1998; Haber 1998; Musacchio 2005).

The sources and methodology used for the present study are discussed in the next section, followed by the main findings and the conclusions.

Sources and Methodology

To test for a time-invariant relationship between legal origin and investor protections, I analyzed the creditor protections contained in Brazil's bankruptcy laws between 1850 and 2005. To ensure as complete a historical perspective as possible, I compiled creditor protections contained in the Commerce Code of 1850; the joint stock company laws of 1882, 1890, and 1891; and the bankruptcy laws of 1902, 1908, 1929, 1945, and 2005. Finally, I analyzed the creditor rights in the bankruptcy law as reformed in June 2005, even though we lack sufficient time to measure their effects.

I use LLSV's (1998) methodology to generate indices of creditor rights that are comparable across time and countries. We would expect to find larger debt markets in countries in which any of the following rights are granted.

1. The most basic right of a secured creditor is the right to repossess collateral in the event of default (with no automatic stay on assets). Legislation that affords excessive protection to managers filing for bankruptcy complicates the repossession of collateral and thereby weakens creditor rights.
2. In many countries workers and the government are accorded priority over secured creditors. But when bondholders are not paid first, investors will exact a premium to compensate for the uncertainty they will face in the event of bankruptcy, which might make funding more difficult to secure.
3. Creditor approval is prerequisite to reorganization and rescheduling debt service. Creditors placed at the mercy of managers granted the right to reorganize or delay payments could find it difficult to recover their investments in the event of financial difficulties.
4. Requiring that existing managers be replaced as part of the reorganization process protects creditors from possible mismanagement and corruption by incumbent managers.

I use a creditor rights index generated by summing the number of rights in each of the bankruptcy laws to compare my results with the results for the 49 countries surveyed by LLSV (1998) in 1995. I also generate creditor rights indices for a cross section of common and French civil law countries circa 1910.

LLSV (1998) hypothesize that bankruptcy laws that do not require that existing managers be replaced as part of the reorganization process reward mismanagement. Such laws reward the managers or stockholders who remain in control of a company that has filed for bankruptcy with time to try to mitigate the consequences of bad decisions or risky activities. Against the interests and at the expense of creditors, these managers or stockholders are likely to try to defer payments to post-reorganization, which would have the effect of diminishing the incentive for investors to buy corporate bonds and banks to lend large amounts of money.[8]

Many economists today use indices of rule of law to measure a country's enforcement of investor rights. These indices in general tend to focus on the commercial relationship between governments and foreign businesses. They measure, for instance, investor perceptions of the "efficiency and integrity of the legal environment as it affects business, particularly foreign firms" (LLSV 1998, p. 1124), a country's law and order tradition (that is, rule of law) as rated by International Country Risk, or the likelihood of a government repudiating a commercial contract. As a matter of fact, none of these indices relates directly to the enforcement of investor rights. Most, in fact, are imperfect measures of the enforcement of property rights in general. As such, they are indices of business conditions, mainly for foreign companies.

I have undertaken to study creditor rights through the surrogate of the enforcement of bankruptcy laws, specifically, to extract from a systematic examination of court cases and their outcomes information about the behavior of managers, shareholders, creditors, and judges during bankruptcy procedures.

I examined all of the bankruptcy court cases of companies that issued bonds, approximately 40 (some companies had more than one case). Most were heard by the Civil and Commercial Tribunal of Rio de Janeiro and are available at the National Archive of Brazil. The sample of cases, albeit relatively small, nevertheless illuminates the workings of bankruptcy procedures at the time. The companies involved, all intensive users of corporate bonds, were from various sectors. Most were chartered in Rio de Janeiro, although some corporations operating in other states brought their cases to court in Rio because it was the legal capital of the country. Rio de Janeiro was Brazil's capital until 1967 and its main financial center until the 1930s.[9] Because space considerations preclude the presentation of all the analyses, I summarize some of the results and present examples of how court cases illustrate the way that enforcement of creditor rights worked.

To establish the representativeness of the sample, it would have been necessary to compare the number of court cases found with the total number of bankruptcies of joint stock companies. But accurate statistics for bankruptcies in Brazil during this period were lacking. Annual summaries of the number of bankruptcies for the period 1906–12 published in the financial newspaper *Restrospecto Comercial do Jornal do Commércio* were the only reliable source available to me.[10] Figure 9.1 compares the number of cases in my sample with the total number of corporate bankruptcies for each year between 1906 and 1912. This period saw between two and three bankruptcy cases per year, save for 1908, in which there were six cases. I found one or two cases per year through 1916.

I used the Rio de Janeiro Stock Exchange annual summaries published in the *Relatorios da Câmara Sindical de Correitores de Fundos Públicos da Bolsa de Valores do Rio de Janeiro* from 1905 to 1931 and 1944 to 1947 to build my estimates of equity and bond market capitalization in Brazil.[11] Additional capitalization data are from the *Anuário da Bolsa de Valores do Rio de Janeiro*, 1932–42. Bond and stock market capitalization data for 1886–1905 were constructed from annual summaries published in the *Jornal do Commércio* and *Retrospecto Comercial do Jornal do Commércio*, the most important financial newspaper published in Rio de Janeiro during this period. Information for São Paulo, when available, is added to the total estimations of stock market capitalization (taking care not to double-count cross-listings). Most of the São Paulo information was taken from Hanley (1998), "Business Finance," and from the *Anuário da Bolsa Oficial de Valores de São Paulo*, 1932–50. Although bond data for São Paulo before 1960 was not added to my estimates because an annual time series was difficult to construct, omission of the São Paulo bond estimates for the first part of the century biases the bond data against my argument that bond markets were larger in the first part of the century than today. Data for stock market capitalization and

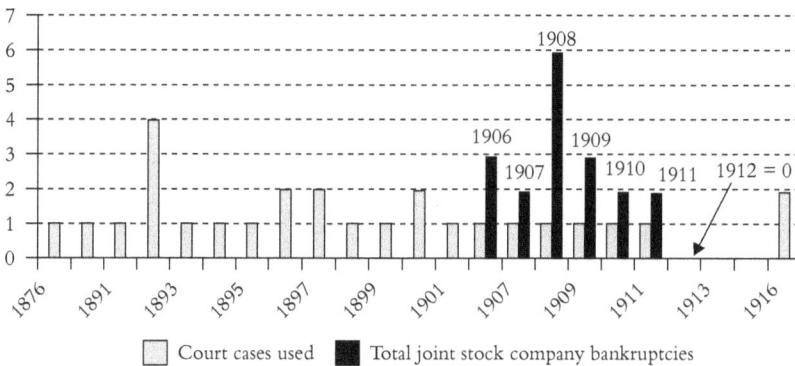

Figure 9.1 Total corporate bankruptcies and cases used

SOURCE: Retrospecto *Comercial do Jornal do Commércio*, 1906–16.

total stock of debentures after 1990 are from *The Brazil Company Handbook*, 1993–2003 and the Brazilian Debenture Service. I normalize stock market and debenture stock data using the GDP estimates compiled by Goldsmith (1986, tables 3.1, 4.2) and current data gathered by the Brazilian Institute of Research in Applied Economics (IPEA).[12]

Findings: Creditor Rights and Bond Markets in Brazil, 1850–2001

BOND MARKETS, 1886–2003

Do bond markets in Brazil follow Rajan and Zingales's (2003) great reversal theory? Figure 9.2 plots the size of equity and debt markets against GDP in Brazil from 1886 to 2002. Two findings revealed by this figure are of particular importance. One, both the equity and bond markets declined relative to the size of the economy after World War I, when flows of international capital to Brazil were reduced drastically and the coffee export sector was experiencing major difficulties. Two, the bond market grew rapidly after 1890, peaked in 1914, and then experienced a more accentuated and permanent decline than equity markets in the decades that followed.

Brazil's bond markets followed the trend documented by Rajan and Zingales (2003) for equity markets around the world, save that the size of Brazil's markets has not returned to 1913 levels relative to GDP. Rajan and Zingales maintain that financial market development recovered during the 1990s when international flows of capital and trade increased to pre–World War I levels. But growth of the stock of bonds in Brazil did not mirror the sharp takeoff in equity markets in the 1990s. The level of bond issues in the first two decades of the twentieth century oscillated between 5% and 12% of GDP, the stock of bonds in the 1990s between 2.5% and 3.5% of GDP.[13]

Two legal changes precipitated the boom in the debenture market after 1890. First, the basic protections for creditors were reformed. Beginning in 1890, debenture holders' status was changed from ordinary to privileged creditors, giving them first priority in the event of bankruptcy. Second, a change in incentives favored the issue of debt over equity. Railroad and port companies were permitted to issue debentures in excess of the value of their declared equity, and other chartered corporations to issue debentures equal in the aggregate to the total book value of their capital. Issuing debentures facilitated the early accumulation of capital to fund operations or the expansion of physical plant.[14] The combined effects of these regulatory changes can be seen in Figure 9.2, which shows the enormous growth

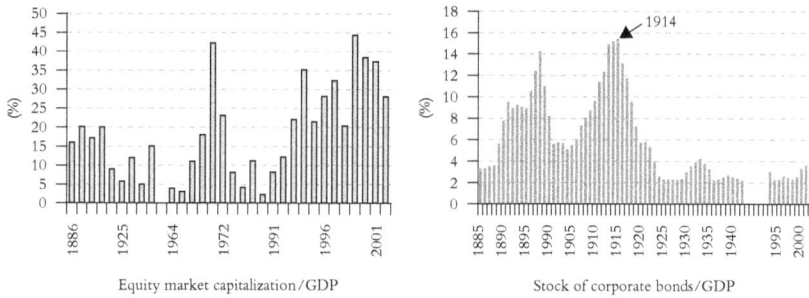

Figure 9.2   Equity and bond market capitalization over GDP in Brazil, 1886–2002

SOURCE: Author's estimates; see text.

NOTES: The uneven horizontal scale is a consequence of many missing data points. São Paulo Stock Exchange equity data are missing for 1920, 1925, and 1935. Data for 1947–64 were excluded because legislation forced all joint stock companies to register at the stock exchange, thus generating data that are not comparable to data for other periods. The stock of bonds before 1940 is an underestimate because it shows only the data for Rio de Janeiro.

of the debenture market over the first two decades of the last century. This growth is more pronounced between 1905 and 1913, when Brazil adopted the gold standard.

Debenture issues denominated in foreign currency were successful outside Brazil because they had low exchange-rate risk and foreign bondholders could appeal to Brazilian courts in the event of default (with a good chance of recovering some of their investment).

The decline in the bond market coincides with bondholders' loss of priority during bankruptcy, the demise of the gold standard during World War I, and the retreat of foreign capital from emerging markets. By the time creditor rights were wiped out of bankruptcy legislation in 1945, the debenture market had become considerably less important.

Investors did not complain about the demise of creditor rights in the 1940s, in part, because preferred shares, introduced in 1932, had substituted debentures as the most popular fixed income securities. Preferred shares were a good substitute for bonds for three reasons. First, they offered investors a minimum fixed dividend as a percentage of net earnings (plus a fluctuating amount determined by company profitability). Second, shareholders holding preferred shares were accorded first priority in recovering their capital in the event of bankruptcy. Third, the real value of preferred shares did not decline as rapidly with high inflation. Once bondholders' priority during bankruptcy was fully eliminated, debentures enjoyed few advantages over preferred shares.

The rise of inflation after the 1940s complicated any future bond market recovery. Sustained inflation had become a problem in the 1940s, and even more so in the 1950s, reaching levels in excess of 80% by the early 1960s. Even with the introduction, in the late 1960s, of indexed debentures the market never regained its 1913 level.

In 2005, Brazil's Congress attempted to rehabilitate credit markets by passing a new bankruptcy law with stronger creditor rights. But the problem now is not so much the reform of creditor rights but how to change the attitudes of the judges who enforce those rights. A majority of judges who responded to a 2003 survey of judges' attitudes toward credit contract enforcement in Brazil insisted that the higher goal of social justice in many instances justifies a violation of credit contracts.[15]

CREDITOR RIGHTS, 1850 – 2001

In this section I explore the hypothesis that investor protections are determined by legal origin. Table 9.1 presents the index of creditor rights protection for Brazil since 1850. The Commercial Code of 1850 established a bankruptcy procedure that was highly protective of creditors. Three of the four provisions LLSV (1998) deem important for the development of debt markets were contained in this legislation. When first priority was added, between 1890 and 1908, all of the creditor protections the LLSV index tracks were present in the bankruptcy law. These four protections were preserved in court rulings during the decade 1910–20.

The priority of bondholders and secured creditors during bankruptcy was changed by the Bankruptcy Law of 1908 only on paper. Although unpaid taxes and some workers' compensations were moved to the top of the priority list, in practice, courts continued to give first priority to creditors. Decree 10,902, issued in 1914, again put again taxes ahead of creditors during bankruptcy, but judges persisted in favoring secured creditors.[16]

To gauge the strength of creditor protections in Brazil before 2005, consider that if in 1995 Brazil had the same creditor protections it had had between 1850 and 1945, when its creditor rights protection index was 3, it would have ranked higher than most countries in the world. We can see in Table 9.2 that with those protections Brazil would have ranked on a par with New Zealand and Thailand (each of which had a creditor rights protection index of 3) in 1995. In fact, Brazilian legislation passed between 1850 and 1929 afforded greater protection for the rights of creditors than contemporary legislation in Australia, Canada, Ireland, and the United

TABLE 9.1

Creditor rights in Brazil since 1850

Law or decree	C. Code of 1850	L. 3150, 12/04/1882	D. 917, 01/17/1890	D. 603, 1891	L. 859, 8/16/1902	Lei 2024, 1908	D. 5746, 9/12/1929	Dec.-Law 7661, 6/21/1945	1995 (LLSV 1998)	Law 11,101, 2005
Repossess collateral (no automatic stay)	1	1	1	1	1	1	1	0	0	1
Secured creditors have first priority[a]	0	0	1	1	1	0	0	0	0	0
Approval of creditors for reorganization (no Chapter 11)	1	1	1	1	1	1	1	0	1	1
Management does not stay (trustees run the company after bankruptcy is declared?)	1	1	1	1	1	1	1	0	0	0
Index	**3**	**3**	**4**	**4**	**4**	**3**	**3**	**0**	**1**	**2**

SOURCES: Brazil, *Coleção das Leis e Decretos*, Law 11,101 of February 9, 2005; see http://www.planalto .gov.br.

[a]Debenture holders in the 1850 Commerce Code had the last priority among all creditors. Between 1890 and 1908 they had absolute and explicit first priority. After 1908 they ceased to have first priority on paper, though judges ignored the legal change.

States (each of which earned a creditor rights protection index of 1). So strong were its creditor protections between 1890 and 1908 that today Brazil would rank next to the top creditor protectors, namely, England, Hong Kong, Malaysia, and Israel (each of which has a creditor rights protection index of 4).

The evidence presented in Tables 9.1 and 9.2 partly contradicts the hypothesis that civil law yields an institutional setup that fails to protect creditors. In fact, the variance in creditor rights over a century and a half should make us wonder about the political economy of bankruptcy legislation. What political factors enabled Brazil to enact such strong creditor protections before 1945? How strongly enforced were those creditor rights? What changed that reversed the institutional settings that had prevailed until 1945?

THE POLITICAL ECONOMY OF BANKRUPTCY LEGISLATION

What accounts for Brazil's strong protection of creditor rights before 1945? Creditor rights included in bankruptcy laws and the commerce code were

TABLE 9.2
Creditor rights in Brazil and around the world in 1995

Country	Repossess collateral	Priority	Approval for reorganization	Management is replaced	Index
England, Hong Kong, Malaysia, Israel, and **Brazil 1890–1908**	1	1	1	1	4
Brazil 1850–90; 1908–45	1	0	1	1	3
New Zealand and Thailand	1	0	1	1	3
Germany and Denmark	1	1	1	0	3
Japan and Uruguay	0	1	0	1	2
Chile, Italy, and the Netherlands	0	1	1	0	2
Taiwan and Belgium	1	1	0	0	2
Brazil after 2005	1	0	1	0	2
Brazil today	0	0	1	0	1
Argentina, Switzerland, and Finland	0	1	0	0	1
Australia, Canada, Ireland, and United States	0	1	0	0	1
France, Mexico, and **Brazil after 1945**	0	0	0	0	0

SOURCES: Table 9.1; and LLSV (1998, table 4).

a product of the interaction of interest groups and lawmakers. In Brazil, bankruptcy laws were usually drafted by Congress in close consultation with business associations. But this was not the case when the 1945 law was drafted and passed by an authoritarian regime without congressional approval. Whereas laws passed by Congress before the authoritarian government of 1937–45 had been more responsive to businessmen or creditors, the 1945 law catered to the interests of labor.

In the wake of its independence (which was granted in 1821), Brazil adopted a constitutional monarchy. The 1824 Constitution established a parliamentarian regime with the emperor responsible for naming the ministers and prime minister. All economic activity in the country was regulated by Congress, which was divided into a senate and lower house, both elected (until 1881) through indirect vote. Voters chose electors who would, by participating in state electoral colleges, choose legislators. Voting was restricted to Brazilian males over 21 years of age who had an income of 100$000 (100 milréis) or more (the income requirement was doubled in 1846).[17]

The newly independent Brazil adopted the Napoleonic Commerce Code of 1807, which was widely used during the last years of the colony. The bankruptcy provisions excluded merchants and were strict with debtors, deeming them criminals and providing jail sentences for some forms of default.

Brazil's first code of commerce was drafted in 1850 in close consultation with businessmen of the time. That same year, Minister of Justice Eusébio de Queiroz established a commission that he made responsible for drafting the code. Queiroz invited congressional specialists in commercial legislation and the viscount of Mauá, the most prolific Brazilian businessman of the nineteenth century. Mauá had built the first railroad from the interior of Rio to the coast, owned several banking houses, and developed infrastructure and utility projects in Rio de Janeiro.

The commerce code protected creditors strongly in its bankruptcy section. As can be seen in Table 9.1, creditors were strongly protected, being allowed, for example, to collect collateral at the time of default and controlling the bankrupt firm during bankruptcy. During this time, debt repudiation by businesses and individuals was considered a crime, frequently punished with jail sentences.

In 1889, a republican movement, in a pacific campaign, overthrew Brazil's monarchy. A federalist republic was quickly established and two years later a new constitution drafted. The 1891 Constitution included direct elections for the president, vice president, and Congress. The president and vice president were elected to four-year terms with no possibility of reelection. Senators served for nine years, lower house representatives for three years. The income requirement was eliminated and a literacy requirement added. The secret ballot that had been employed by the empire was replaced by signed ballots as a way to reduce double voting and other fraudulent practices that had prevailed during the imperial period (Nicolau 2002).

The new political system intensified political competition and encouraged congressmen to court interest groups that could influence large numbers of voters. Commercial associations, because they had a strong political voice and a large base of literate, male voters, were natural targets for politicians. Powerful businessmen and associations could, moreover, finance political campaigns and political parties.

One of the first changes introduced by the republican government in 1890 was to bankruptcy legislation, specifically, to give priority in bankruptcy proceedings to corporate bondholders (debenture holders). Corporate bonds, or debentures, had been legal since 1882, but the issue of this type of security uncommon before 1890, when priority among creditors and other incentives to issue bonds were included in the Company Laws.

During the first republic, Congress consulted business associations about any proposed reforms to bankruptcy law. The 1902 law, and procedural regulations passed in 1903, were circulated among "justice tribunals, the Lawyers Institute, the law schools, the commercial associations of the largest cities, and a great number of legal specialists."[18] In 1928, the congressional commission charged with drafting a new bankruptcy law asked the Commercial Association of São Paulo and Stock Brokers Associations of Rio de Janeiro and São Paulo to propose a new law. The lawyer for the Commercial Association of São Paulo suggested only minor edits to the 1908 law and hinted at complete satisfaction with the current state of the law (Lima 1929).

Getúlio Vargas, who secured the presidency of Brazil in 1930 after a short civil war, immediately installed a provisional government, dismissed Congress, and created a parallel judiciary system to judge political cases. After a short counterrevolutionary movement promoted by the republican political forces of São Paulo in 1932, Vargas's provisional government tried to establish a new social pact by calling a constitutional congress. Vargas was elected president in 1934 under a new constitution and electoral law that restored the secrecy of the ballot and created an Electoral Tribunal. But the improved democratic system was short lived. In 1937, Vargas responded to a revolutionary threat fabricated by his aides by declaring a state of emergency and suspension of powers. The authoritarian regime established in the wake of these actions dismissed the Congress, and Vargas began to build a new social pact much in the spirit of Mussolini's corporatist state.

Vargas had an implicit contract with labor unions, which exchanged political support for labor protections. Vargas drew his main base of support from labor unions, especially those he artificially created in the first years of his presidency. Since the early 1930s his government had promoted labor legislation that introduced such basic protections for workers as a minimum wage, paid vacations, and pension funds.[19] An effort to consolidate labor laws was initiated in 1943 with a piece of legislation called *Consolidação das Leis do Trabalho* (CLT). Most of the changes in labor laws were promoted by the Ministry of Labor under Minister Alexandre Marcondes Filho, whom Vargas had also appointed minister of justice. The new bankruptcy law passed by Filho in 1945 as part of legal reforms intended to make the CLT work, in contrast to earlier revisions to bankruptcy law, radically altered creditor protections. The law was drafted by a committee of lawyers loyal to Vargas and passed as presidential decree-law without congressional approval.[20]

The Bankruptcy Law of 1945 protected incumbent management and labor and eliminated many of the important creditor protections. Its main objective was to promote the survival of the going concern, that is, to encourage the operation even of businesses that under the 1929 bankruptcy legislation would have been under the control of creditors. Under the new law, debtors could avoid liquidation by filing for a reorganization scheme, termed *concordata preventiva*, which prior to 1945 had been applicable only to partnerships. The *concordata preventiva* accommodated rescheduling of payments without creditor approval and permitted management to continue to operate under bankruptcy protection. Finally, under the new legislation, labor social security and labor injury compensations took first priority in the bankruptcy process. After 1945, secured creditors were third in line, after labor and treasury.

BANKRUPTCY COURT CASES AND THE ENFORCEMENT OF CREDITOR RIGHTS IN BRAZIL

The court cases analyzed for the present study reveal Brazilian judges to have been strong enforcers of creditor rights between 1889 and 1930. Bondholders were accorded priority in bankruptcy cases, and a company declared bankrupt was placed under the control of its creditors, who could immediately replace managers and reorganize or liquidate the company to recover their claims.

Two main bankruptcy arrangements prevailed in Brazil between 1850 and 1930. One, forced liquidation, or *liquidação forçada*, after 1908 called simply bankruptcy (*falência*), was similar to the Chapter 7 arrangement in the United States and to the procedure called simply bankruptcy in English legislation.[21] In fact, the Brazilian procedure was quite similar to the English one: creditors first asked the tribunals to declare a company bankrupt, then had to prove that the company was insolvent or had stopped servicing its debts. Judges had 24 hours to check creditor allegations and declare bankruptcy, whereupon the process of handing over management to trustees would begin. The debtor was required to submit a list of creditors to be called by the courts to initiate liquidation.[22]

The second, probably more common, arrangement, called *concordata* (reorganization or agreement), consisted of an agreement to reschedule payments or to pay creditors with equity.[23] In contrast to the Chapter 11 arrangement in the United States, whereby managers are protected from creditors and given time to reorganize the firm, in Brazil *concordata* could occur only after bankruptcy had been declared and trustees had been selected to run the firm. Managers stayed only if creditors approved the continuation of business. The 1945 Bankruptcy Law introduced the *concordata preventiva* (preventive agreement), a reorganization scheme very much in the spirit of Chapter 11 protections in the United States today in providing automatic stay on assets and the continuation of management and extension of payments to debtors.[24]

Concordatas were common for railroad companies. In 1897, the Leopoldina Railway Company was declared bankrupt after Edward Herdman, representing its British debenture holders, showed proof of suspension of payments for two years (the minimum to request forced liquidation was six months). Because he represented a significant portion of the company's debts, Herdman became a trustee for its liquidation and controlled the firm together with Banco da República. With the profits he serviced the company's debt and later entered into an arrangement with the bondholders whereby he swapped debt for equity in order to keep the company working.[25]

The concordata agreement facilitated rapid recuperation of the Leopoldina Railway Company. The *Investor's Monthly Manual* shows the last coupon payment for debentures of the railway company to have been made in July 1895. The bankruptcy process had started in 1897, and by the summer of 1898 the company was trading in London, in lieu of its former gold-denominated bonds, its new ordinary shares. Ordinary shares having no guaranteed dividend in this case, the company did not pay dividends. The company made a new issue of 4% bonds in 1898 and promptly began paying coupons in January 1899. These bonds traded at 83% of par in their first year.[26]

The Leopoldina's bankruptcy case is important to an understanding of Brazil's success in attracting foreign investment before WWI in that it set a precedent for the protection of foreigners in Brazilian courts. Previously, the law had stated that a bankruptcy procedure could be initiated in Brazil only by a merchant registered in the country. After the Leopoldina case, the jurisprudence stated that "the foreign creditor with an address outside of the country can request a bankruptcy procedure for a debtor established here [in Brazil], without having to file a charter in the local registry."[27]

Foreign creditors of the railroad company Sapucaí were among those who benefited from the precedent set by the Leopoldina case. In 1899, after the court had settled a dispute between the company and domestic bondholders, management stopped servicing the company's bonds in pounds sterling. The firm's shareholders and ex-directors proposed to the English bondholders, who had created a bondholders' association and sent a representative to Rio de Janeiro, a swap of debt for equity. This was a sweet deal for bondholders because the Minas Gerais state government guaranteed a dividend of at least 6% on the company's shares. Moreover, the government offered the concession of a new line only if the company was reorganized.[28] Bondholders accepted the deal and ended up owning 80% of total equity.

Smaller companies commonly ended bankruptcy procedures by liquidating their assets to pay creditors. Creditors of the Companhia Vidraria "Carmita," a glass factory, recovered 25% of their debts through the bankruptcy procedure. The case of the Companhia Anonyma Coudelaria Cruzeiro, a horse-breeding company, was similar. Creditors took over and liquidated the company to repay bondholders, whereupon even nonprivileged creditors recovered 25% of their investments. Similarly, the Santa Maria textile mill's assets were auctioned by the trustees in its bankruptcy case to pay its debts.[29]

Bankruptcy procedures also protected creditors from company managers who suspended payments in order to hoard cash accounts. Creditors could appropriate this operating capital through the forced liquidation procedure, as did the trustees of the textile mill Companhia de Tecidos e Fiação Santo Aleixo in 1916; funds were withdrawn from the company's various bank accounts and the debenture holders paid. Similarly, when Cervejaria Bavaria, a beer-brewing company, was declared in forced liquidation in 1898, the trustees took control of the firm and used available cash to pay debenture holders their titles, including past-due coupon payments.[30]

Creditor rights had also been strongly enforced between 1850 and 1889; studies of bankruptcy cases during that period reveal that collateralized creditors had the right to repossess collateral upon default and that creditors were in charge of liquidations and reorganizations (Musacchio 2005).

WITHIN-COUNTRY VS. ACROSS-COUNTRY VARIATION

The evidence presented documents significant variation over time in legal protections for creditors and the size of financial markets within one country. But do these findings hold for other countries? Preliminary evidence of creditor rights in a small cross section of countries reveals more cross-country variation than would seem to be implied in the results reported in the law and finance literature.

Consider the LLSV (1998) index of creditor rights for a cross section of common and French civil law countries presented in Table 9.3. Note first that Brazil is not an outlier; other civil law countries also had stronger protections for creditors circa 1910 than today. Also note that some of the common law countries included in the table had weaker creditor rights protections in 1910 than in 1995. For instance, creditor protections in the colonial bankruptcy codes of Hong Kong and Malaysia circa 1910 earned a creditor rights protection index of only 2 (see Table 9.2), whereas these nations' creditor protections in 1995 were among the strongest, earning a creditor rights protection index of 4 (Table 9.2).

TABLE 9.3
Creditor rights in selected countries, c. 1910

	COMMON LAW				FRENCH CIVIL LAW				
	United Kingdom	United States	Hong Kong	Strait Settlements	France	Belgium	Spain	Argentina	Brazil
1. Secured creditors can repossess collateral (no automatic stay)	1	0	0	0	1	1	1	0	1
2. Secured creditors have first priority	1	1	1	1	1	1	1	1	1
3. Approval of creditors for reorganization	1	1	1	1	1	1	1	1	1
4. Management does not stay for reorganization	1	0	0	0	0	0	0	0	1
Index	**4**	**2**	**2**	**2**	**3**	**3**	**3**	**2**	**4**

SOURCES: United Kingdom: *Companies (Consolidation) Act 1908*; United States: Huberich, *Commercial Laws*; Hong Kong: *Bankruptcy Ordinance* No. 7 1891; Strait Settlements: *An Ordinance to Amend the Law of Bankruptcy* No. 2 1888 (December 3, 1888); France: G. Horn, *Commercial Law*; Belgium: Hennebicq, *Commercial* (based on the Commercial Code of 1872 as amended to 1910); Spain: Benito, *Commercial*; Argentina: Quesada, *Commercial*; Brazil: see Table 9.1 in this chapter.

Finally, the small cross section presented in Table 9.3 shows significant within-country variation in both civil and common law countries in the sample. Circa 1910, the common law countries had weaker creditor rights than the French civil law countries (save for the United Kingdom). Were the results of this sample generalizable, we would conclude that in 1910 common law countries had, on average, weaker creditor protections than French civil law countries. In other words, the implied relationship between legal origin and creditor rights protection found by the law and finance literature would *not* be significant were historical data to be taken into account.

Conclusions

The evidence presented in this chapter points to a weak link between legal origin, investor protections, and financial development. First, it is shown that creditor rights and financial market size are susceptible to continuous change over time. Financial market size seems to be more related to international capital flows than to internal institutions. Creditor rights, on the other hand, vary following the interests of important constituencies. Finally, evidence from 1910 suggests that Brazil is not unique in terms of legal origin not determining creditor rights and financial development. Many

French civil law countries had stronger creditor protections in 1910 than today, and some, such as France and Belgium, enjoyed greater financial market development in the past as well (Rajan and Zingales 2003). Just so, some common law countries that had weak creditor protections in the past became known for much stronger creditor protections in the 1990s.

The chapter has important policy implications inasmuch as the interests of the ruling coalitions determine the legal environment investors face, such as the degree of protection they will be accorded by the law and the extent to which courts and regulatory agencies will enforce those protections. If ruling coalitions determine the legal environment, and the legal environment determines the growth of financial markets, then financial market development is to a large extent dependent on the interests of whoever is in power. This political economy problem relates to what political scientists call the "commitment problem"; any government strong enough to define and protect property rights is also strong enough to abrogate them when necessary.[31] Changes in ruling coalitions can thus complicate the process whereby governments commit to protect investors and ultimately impede financial market growth.

If politics are so important to financial market development, the commitment problem can adversely affect economic welfare as well, there being many causal links between financial market development and economic growth (King and Levine 1993; Levine and Zervos 1998; Rousseau and Sylla 2005).[32]

Perhaps the only way to lock in financial development is to socialize the benefits of financial markets across constituencies. If a strong group stands to gain from reversing financial development, nothing can guarantee a credible commitment from the government to respect investor protections. On the other hand, if everyone in society has something to gain from financial development, it will be hard to reverse investor protections and financial development (save as a consequence of financial crises, sudden stops, and other external determinants of capital flows). For example, workers who win from financial development through private pension funds, mutual funds, and all sorts of saving instruments will have fewer incentives to lobby to alter investor protections.

Notes

Support for this research came from the Social Science History Institute and Center for Democracy, Development of the Rule of Law, both at Stanford University. Additional support came from Ibmec Business School, São Paulo.

Elsa Campos, Silvana Jeha, Veronica A. Santarosa, and Ricardo B. Tancredi offered valuable assistance in different stages of the research. The author would like to thank for their useful comments on earlier versions of the chapter Zephyr Frank, Avner Greif, Peter Gourevitch, Stephen Haber, Phil Hoffman, Phil Keefer, Stephen Krasner, Naomi Lamoreaux, Gary Libecap, David Moss, Jean Laurent Rosenthal, Mary Shirley, Kenneth Sokoloff, William Summerhill, Dick Sylla, Barry Weingast, Gavin Wright, and seminar participants at UCLA, Stanford, the All-UC Graduate Student meeting 2003, Harvard, and NYU-Stern. All errors are the responsibility of the author.

1. Institutions are viewed here as sets of beliefs, norms, and organizational features that regularize and legitimize patterns of behavior (Greif 1994; North 1990).

2. See, for example, Acemoglu, Johnson, and Robinson (2001); and La Porta, López-de-Silanes, Shleifer, and Vishny (LLSV) (1997, 1998).

3. See, for example, LLSV (1997, 1998, 2000); Beck, Demirgüç-Kunt, and Levine (2003a, 2003b); Levine, Loayza, and Beck (2000); Johnson et al. (2000); La Porta and López-de-Silanes (2001); and Glaeser and Shleifer (2002). Berkowitz, Pistor, and Richard (2003) use a similar econometric approach. They argue it is not only about legal origin but about how the legal system is adapted to local conditions.

4. Debentures have been the most common corporate bonds in Brazil since the end of the nineteenth century. These bonds usually have real assets as collateral and have been senior to other private debt during bankruptcy since 1890. The seniority of the government and labor during bankruptcy changed throughout the period of study.

5. See Berglöf and Rosenthal (2000); Roe (2003); Perotti and von Thadden (2003); and Pagano and Volpin (2005).

6. I am not referring to workers as debtors because bankruptcy law deals only with commercial creditors and debtors (e.g., all sorts of corporations and partnerships). Bankruptcy for individuals in most civil law countries is regulated by the civil code rather than the bankruptcy law. The reason is that individuals and businesses have completely different legal "personalities" in the legal system. Individuals are called "physical persons," whereas firms are denominated "moral persons."

7. GDP estimates with data from Goldsmith (1986).

8. There is evidence that in Brazil, banks often favored negotiating terms of payment or forgiving a debtor over repossessing collateral (Triner 2000, pp. 142–43). This makes sense if we consider that the expected discounted return on future payments from a debtor with which a lender maintains a relationship and continues to do business might be greater than the value of repossessed collateral.

9. A review of the books of the first two civil courts in the State of São Paulo, which cover most commercial cases until the first decades of the twen-

tieth century, did not produce a single case of bankruptcy for a corporation. The books can be consulted at the Museu da Justiça in São Paulo.

10. Other annual surveys of the number of bankruptcy cases published in the *Relatório do Ministério da Justiça* did not separate firms by type (joint stock company vs. partnership), and the manner of reporting was changed several times during the period, making comparisons across time difficult.

11. See Câmara Sindical de Corretores de Fundos Públicos da Bolsa de Valores do Rio de Janeiro, *Relatorio da Câmara Sindical de Corretores . . . ,* 1905–30.

12. I did not double-count equity and bond market capitalization for companies that cross-listed shares in São Paulo and Rio. For macrodata and GDP price deflator, see www.ipeadata.gov.br. For current bond stock and turnover rates, see www.debenture.com.br.

13. Because inflation increased rapidly after 1930 and indexed issues were not introduced until the last decades of the century, debentures declined dramatically throughout the twentieth century.

14. Companies established before 1890 could operate with as little as 20% of the value of their shares fully paid, companies established after 1890 with as little as 40% of the value of their shares fully paid. Corporations with only 20% or 40% of their equity fully paid that were able to issue bonds for as much as 100% of their registered value were thus able to raise 1.4 times the book value of capital (100% in debentures and 40% in equity) in a very short time and with little shareholder investment. In 1891, the privilege of issuing bonds in excess of equity was extended to companies with government concessions and those focused on public services.

15. See Pinheiro (2003); and *O Estado de São Paulo*, elections supplement, October 28, 2002.

16. Although this decree stated, in articles 139 and 240, that if a bankrupt debtor was found to owe overdue taxes, the trial would have to become federal with the Ministry of Finance as prosecutor; in practice, the ministry was not involved in bankruptcy cases and usually did not follow the judiciary papers that published bankruptcy notices.

17. Members of the lower house were elected to four-year terms, senators for life. The number of senators was equal to half the number of lower chamber representatives per state. The electoral colleges made lists of the three most-voted candidates for each seat in the senate. The emperor had the right to choose one of the three candidates. Electors and congressmen had to have an income of more than 200 milréis (400 milréis after 1846). See, for example, Nicolau (2002, pp. 10–12).

18. "A novísima lei de fallencias," in *São Paulo Judiciário*, October 2003, p. 157.

19. The Constitution drafted by Vargas in 1937 respected labor rights that had been included in the 1934 Constitution. Specific labor protections were

legislated thereafter. A minimum wage was established in 1938, unions were transformed into state and national unions by profession in 1939, and union contributions made mandatory in 1940. The Justiça do Trabalho (Justice of Labor) was regulated in 1941 by a law that introduced an arbitration panel to resolve all labor disputes. For more information on the Consolidation of Labor Laws legislation that compiled previously legislated labor rights, see CLT in Decree-Law 5,452 of May 1, 1943.

20. Information on Alexandre Marcondes Filho is from Fundação Getúlio Vargas, CPDOC, "A Era Vargas—1° tempo—dos anos 20 a 1945," available at http://www.cpdoc.fgv.br/nav_historia/htm/ev_apresentacao.htm.

21. This was more clearly typified in the compilation of decrees related to Joint Stock Company Laws, Decree 603, October 17, 1891. See articles 233, 234, 235 for forced liquidation. In the Commerce Code of 1850 this type of bankruptcy was called simply *quebra* (bankruptcy).

22. Brazilian procedures were quite similar to English bankruptcy procedures included in 32 & 33 Vict., c. 71 (1869) and 8 Edw. VII, c. 69 (1908). See Bankruptcy Act (1969) and Companies (Consolidation) Act 1908.

23. *Concordata* schemes appeared in the Commerce Code of 1850, articles 842–54.

24. *Concordata preventiva* was a reorganization scheme exclusive to partnerships until 1945 whereby debtor firms could negotiate with the majority of creditors. In permitting debtors to continue to run the business through payments negotiated before bankruptcy was declared, it avoided the intervention of judges and trustees and left management untouched. If creditors approved, judges had to approve the deal as well (*homologação*). See, for example, Faria (1902, p. 146) and other annotated bankruptcy laws.

25. See Corte de Apelação, Estrada de Ferro Leopoldina, 1897.

26. *Investor's Monthly Manual*, foreign railways section, 1894–1908.

27. Extract is from Faria (1902, p. 19) translated by the author. The jurisprudence was originally published in the *Revista de Jurisprudencia*, vol. 2, pp. 84–86, 1897.

28. Corte de Apelação/Viação Férrea Sapucaí (Viação Férrea Sapucahy), 1899.

29. See Corte de Apelação, Companhia Vidraria "Carmita," 1916; Corte de Apelação, Companhia Anonyma Coudelaria Cruzeiro, 1892; and Corte de Apelação, Companhia de Fiação e Tecidos Santa Maria, 1909.

30. Corte de Apelação, Companhia de Tecidos e Fiação Santo Aleixo, 1916; and Corte de Apelação, Cervejaria Bavaria, 1900.

31. See, for example, North and Weingast (1989) for an explanation of how England in the seventeenth century generated credible commitments not to expropriate its creditors when it created the Bank of England.

32. Financial development is measured in general by financial intermediaries' capacity to transfer funds from investors to corporate and individual bor-

rowers. Ways to measure financial development vary from study to study, but the most common estimates use capitalization of equity markets over GDP, number of initial public offerings (IPOs) per year, and number of joint stock companies per million people.

References

Acemoglu, Daron, Simon Johnson, and James Robinson (2001). "The Colonial Origins of Comparative Development: An Empirical Investigation." *American Economic Review* 91: 1369–1401.

Bankruptcy Act (1969). 32 & 33 Vict., c. 71, 1869.

Beck, Thorsten, Asli Demirgüç-Kunt, and Ross Levine (2003a). "Law and Finance: Why Does Legal Origin Matter?" *Journal of Comparative Economics* 31: 653–75.

——— (2003b). "Law, Endowments, and Finance." *Journal of Financial Economics* 70: 137–81.

Berglöf, Erik, and H. Rosenthal (2000). "The Political Economy of American Bankruptcy: Evidence from Roll Call Voting, 1800–1978." Mimeo, Princeton University.

Berkowitz, Daniel, Katharina Pistor, and Jean-Francois Richard (2003). "Economic Development, Legality, and the Transplant Effect." *European Economic Review* 47: 165–95.

Bolsa de Valores do Rio de Janeiro (1932–42). *Anuário da Bolsa de Valores do Rio de Janeiro*. Rio de Janeiro: Typ. Do Jornal do Commércio.

Bolsa Oficial de Valores de São Paulo (1939, 1950). *Anuário da Bolsa Oficial de Valores de São Paulo*. São Paulo: Typ. Do Jornal do Commércio.

Brazil (1993–2003). *Brazil Company Handbook. Data on Major Listed Companies*. São Paulo and Rio de Janeiro: BOVESPA and Rio de Janeiro Stock Exchange.

——— (1906–19). *Retrospecto Comercial do Journal do Commercio*. Rio de Janeiro.

——— (1902–8). *São Paulo Judiciário*. São Paulo.

——— (1897). *Revista de Jurisprudencia*. Vol. 2. Rio de Janeiro.

——— (1890–1930). *Relatório do Ministério da Justiça*. Rio de Janeiro.

——— (1888–1930). *Colecção das Leis e Decretos*. Rio de Janeiro: Imprensa Nacional.

——— (1827–1930). *Jornal do Commercio*. Rio de Janeiro.

——— (1808–88). *Colecção das Leis e Decretos do Império*. Rio de Janeiro: Imprensa Nacional.

Câmara Sindical de Corretores de Fundos Públicos da Bolsa de Valores do Rio de Janeiro (1905–30). *Relatorio da Câmara Sindical de Corretores de Fundos Públicos da Bolsa de Valores do Rio de Janeiro*. Rio de Janeiro: Imprensa Nacional.

Companies (Consolidation) Act 1908 (8 Edw. VII, c. 69, 1908).

Corte de Apelação (1916). Juízo Comercial do Tribunal Civil e Comer-
    cial, No. 188 maço 3051, Réu Companhia de Tecidos e Fiação Santo
    Aleixo/ Autor: Fernandes Moreira & Co., Liquidação Forçada.
———— (1916). No. 1827 maço 3038, 3ª Vara Cível, Réu Companhia Vidraria
    "Carmita," Falência.
———— (1909). No. 3090 maço 3115, Réu Companhia de Fiação e Tecidos
    Santa Maria, Liquidação Forçada.
———— (1900). Juízo Comercial do Tribunal Civil e Comercial, No. 3892
    maço 3133, Réu Cervejaria Bavaria/ Autor: Banco de Depositos e
    Descontos, Liquidação Forçada.
———— (1899). Juízo Comercial do Tribunal Civil e Comercial, No. 581
    maço 262, Réu Companhia Viação Férrea Sapucahy/ Autor: Syndicos da
    Liquidação Forçada da Companhia Viação Férrea Sapucahy, Prestação
    de Contas.
———— (1897). Juízo Câmara Comercial do Tribunal Civil e Criminal, No.
    708 maço 268, Réu Companhia Estrada de Ferro Leopoldina/ Autor:
    Edward Herdman, Liquidação Forçada.
———— (1892). No. 270 maço 3056, Câmara Comercial do Tribunal Civil e
    Criminal, Réu Companhia Anônyma Coudelaria Cruzeiro/ Autor: Emí-
    lio de Barros e Companhia, Liquidação Forçada.
Faria, Antonio Bento de (1902). *Das Fallencias*. Rio de Janeiro: Jacintho Ri-
    beiro dos Santos.
Glaeser, Edward, and Andrei Shleifer (2002). "Legal Origins." *Quarterly Jour-
    nal of Economics* 117: 1193–1230.
Goldsmith, Raymond (1986). *Brasil 1850–1984: Desenvolvimento Financeiro
    sob um Século de Inflação*. Rio de Janeiro: Banco Bamerindus and Editora
    Harper & Row do Brasil.
Greif, Avner (1994). "Cultural Beliefs and the Organization of Society: A
    Historical and Theoretical Reflection on Collectivist and Individualist
    Societies." *Journal of Political Economy* 102: 912–50.
Haber, Stephen (1998). "The Efficiency Consequences of Institutional
    Change: Financial Market Regulation and Industrial Productivity
    Growth in Brazil, 1866–1934." In John Coatsworth and Alan Taylor,
    eds., *Latin America and the World Economy Since 1800*. Cambridge, MA:
    DRCLAS and Harvard University Press.
Hanley, Ann (1998). "Business Finance and the São Paulo Bolsa, 1886–1917."
    In John Coatsworth and Alan Taylor, eds., *Latin America and the World
    Economy Since 1800*. Cambridge, MA: DRCLAS and Harvard University
    Press.
———— (1995). "Capital Markets in the Coffee Economy: Financial Institu-
    tions and Economic Change in São Paulo, Brazil, 1850–1905." Ph.D.
    diss., Stanford University.
Investor's Monthly Manual (1894–1908). London.

Johnson, Simon, Rafael La Porta, Florencio López-de-Silanes, and Andrei Shleifer (2000). "Tunneling." *American Economic Review Papers and Proceedings* 90: 22–27.

King, Robert G., and Ross Levine (1993). "Finance and Growth: Schumpeter Might Be Right." *Quarterly Journal of Economics* 108: 717–37.

La Porta, Rafael, and Florencio López-de-Silanes (2001). "Creditor Protection and Bankruptcy Law Reform." In Stijin Claessens, Simeon Djankov, and Ashoka Mody, eds., *Resolution of Financial Distress: An International Perspective on the Design of Bankruptcy Laws*. Washington, DC: The World Bank.

La Porta, Rafael, Florencio López-de-Silanes, Andrei Shleifer, and Robert Vishny (LLSV) (2000). "Investor Protection and Corporate Governance." *Journal of Financial Economics* 58: 1–25.

——— (1998). "Law and Finance." *Journal of Political Economy* 106: 1113–55.

——— (1997). "Legal Determinants of External Finance." *Journal of Finance* 52: 1131–50.

Leff, Nathaniel (1982). *Economic Structure and Change, 1822–1947*. London: George Allen & Unwin.

Levine, Ross, Norman Loayza, and Thorsten Beck (2000). "Financial Intermediation and Growth: Causality and Causes." *Journal of Monetary Economics* 46: 31–77.

Levine, Ross, and Sara Zervos (1998). "Stock Markets, Banks, and Economic Growth." *American Economic Review* 88: 537–58.

Levy, Maria Barbara (1977). *Historia da Bolsa de Valores do Rio de Janeiro*. Rio de Janeiro: IBMEC.

Lima, Adamastor (1929). *Nova lei das fallencias: decreto n. 5.746 de 9 de dezembro de 1929, comparada com a lei n. 2.024 de 1908*. Rio de Janeiro: Coelho Branco.

Musacchio, Aldo (2006). "Can Civil Law Countries Get Good Institutions? Creditor Rights and Bond Markets in Brazil, 1850–2003." Harvard Business School, Working Paper 06-040.

——— (2005). "Law and Finance in Historical Perspective: Politics, Bankruptcy Law, and Corporate Governance in Brazil, 1850–2002." Ph.D. diss., Stanford University.

Nicolau, Jairo (2002). *História do voto no Brasil*. Rio de Janeiro: Jorge Zahar.

North, Douglass (1990). *Institutions, Institutional Change, and Economic Performance*. Cambridge, UK: Cambridge University Press.

North, Douglass, and Barry Weingast (1989). "Constitutions and Commitment: The Evolution of Institutions Governing Public Choice in Seventeenth Century England." *Journal of Economic History* 49: 803–32.

Pagano, Marco, and Paolo Volpin. 2005. "The Political Economy of Corporate Governance." *American Economic Review* 95: 1005–30.

Perotti, Enrico, and Ernst-Ludwig von Thadden (2003). "The Political Economy of Dominant Investors." CEPR Discussion Paper 3914.

Pinheiro, Armando Catelar (2003). *Reforma do Judiciário. Problemas, Desafios, Perspectivas.* São Paulo: IDESP and Booklink.

Rajan, Raghuram, and Luigi Zingales (2003). "The Great Reversals: The Politics of Financial Development in the 20th Century." *Journal of Financial Economics* 69: 5–50.

Roe, Mark (2003). *The Political Determinants of Corporate Governance: Political Context, Corporate Impact.* Oxford, UK: Oxford University Press.

Rousseau, Peter, and Richard Sylla (2005). "Emerging Financial Markets and Early U.S. Growth." *Explorations in Economic History* 42: 1–26.

Triner, Gail (2000). *Banks and Economic Development: Brazil, 1889–1930.* New York: Palgrave.

Viação Férrea Sapucahy. Proposta de Concordata aos Debenturistas e mais credores da Companhia Viação Férrea Sapucahy, April 14, 1899, in BVRJ, Sociedades Anônimas, Transportes, Notação 6498 a 6527, Caixa 406.

————. Various documents including the agreements between shareholders and debenture holders of the Companhia Viação Férrea Sapucahy 1899–1900, in BVRJ, Sociedades Anônimas, Transportes, Notação 6498 a 6527, Caixa 406.

Chapter 10

Conclusion

Economics, Political Institutions, and Financial Markets

DOUGLASS C. NORTH AND
MARY M. SHIRLEY

What determines the structure of financial markets? This question matters because financial markets matter. Research shows that a country's financial institutions significantly determine the extent of new investment and firm entry, and through them, the rate of long-run economic growth, disparity of income distribution, and incidence of poverty (see Beck et al. 2004; Levine 1997; Levine, Loayza, and Beck 2000 and sources cited therein). If we can explain why some countries evolved financial markets that efficiently allocate resources to more productive uses while others did not, we can begin to explain why some countries are developed and others are not.

Identifying the determinants of financial institutions is not simple. Markets, especially financial markets, are inherently complex structures and tend to become more complex over time (North 2005). History shapes the evolution of financial institutions through intricate interactions between economics, politics, and markets. Politics is especially important because in the real world markets are never free of government influence, and financial markets are arguably more subject to and dependent upon government influence than other markets. Governments influence financial markets through public borrowing and control of the money supply, through the operation of a central bank and other public banks, through direct regulation of private banks and securities markets, and indirectly through regulation and enforcement of property rights and creditor claims. The ability of modern financial markets to mobilize society's resources and disburse them to uses with the highest returns through arm's-length transactions depends upon wealth holders' confidence in government enforcement of a set of formal and informal fiduciary rules. Ross Levine argues that countries can be categorized by whether they rely more on official oversight of banks or more on private monitoring, but the success of private monitoring also depends on government—on government-enforced disclosure rules.

Why have some countries done a better job of building sound financial institutions than others? Some authors attribute the evolution of financial markets to a country's legal origins—common law versus civil or code law. They argue that a country's historical legal family significantly determines the extent to which it protects minority shareholder and creditor rights, shields private property from state predation, and has a legal system that can react flexibly to changing economic circumstances (La Porta et al. 1997, 1998, 1999).[1] These authors show that common law origin is significantly and positively correlated with indices measuring how much a country's current rules protect the rights of minority shareholders and creditors during reorganizations of firms. Beck and Levine (2004) find that such indices are highly correlated with measures of the development of equity markets and the availability and flexibility of financing for firms. They argue that historical differences in legal tradition led to differences in protection of investor, property, and contractual rights and hence to differences in the willingness of savers to invest.

The studies in this volume challenge the legal origins story, pointing out reversals and complications that make it unlikely that greater judicial discretion of judges in nineteenth-century common law countries can adequately explain stronger rules protecting shareholders and creditors today. This book suggests a less linear story, focused on three themes: (1) the primacy of politics; (2) the frequency of reversals; and (3) the role of congruence: the institutional balance between political access and economic access.

The Primacy of Politics

The studies in this volume argue that political institutions are the most important determinants of financial institutions. This is not to suggest that financial markets do not sometimes provoke political change. But it is political institutions as well as their enforcement characteristics that determine which financial institutions are stable in the long run. A society's formal rules and informal constraints determine who the strategic actors are and influence how they make their choices (North 2005). Different political actors hold different beliefs and are accountable to different groups of constituents, and it is the institutional scaffolding that determines which groups' beliefs and incentives matter and how they matter.

One important way in which political institutions shape a country's emerging financial institutions is by determining how powerful and limited is its government. Modern financial markets flourish only under governments that are powerful enough to enforce their monopoly in the use of coercion. Such governments can protect private property rights from theft, create a stable and peaceful environment for investment, and enforce rules to support contracts and encourage third-party transactions and the growth of financial markets to facilitate them.

A powerful government must also be limited for financial markets to flourish. As North and Weingast (1989) have argued, a government that is powerful enough to protect property rights is also powerful enough to expropriate them. Accordingly, "the development of free markets must be accompanied by some credible restrictions on the state's ability to manipulate economic rules to the advantage of itself and its constituents" (North and Weingast 1989, p. 808). Where limits on government are weak or nonexistent, corrupt politicians can subvert regulations created to supervise financial markets in order to extract bribes or create rents for politically important constituencies, as Ross Levine's chapter documents. Under such circumstances financial development, which Levine measured as bank credit to the private sector, is repressed. By setting and honoring limits on its own rent seeking, government makes a credible commitment to investors not to expropriate private property. Such arrangements have to be self-enforcing, since the state is always powerful enough to renege on its own safeguards. Limits are self-enforcing when political actors are motivated to uphold the bargain to protect investors, usually because the agreement also provides a secure stream of government revenues they can use to provide public goods for their constituents.

One way to limit government discretion is through separation of powers, which increases the number of political actors who might veto government's efforts to expropriate property rights. Veto players are those who can overturn policy decisions because of their positions in the polity, and can also reasonably be expected to oppose the dominant elites because of their ideological leanings or their own or their constituents' interests. If veto players represent the interests of creditors, then government will have greater credibility with debt holders (Stasavage 2003). Even autocracies can sometimes craft credible agreements with financiers. In his chapter William Summerhill shows how, by ceding budgetary authority to Parliament from 1824 to 1889, Brazil's autocratic monarchy gained credibility for its sovereign debt. The Parliament aligned the incentives of officeholders with wealth holders, since Brazilian elites were the only groups with the franchise at that time. The delegation of authority to issue currency and manage the exchange rate to an independent central bank further enhanced the credibility of government's promises to repay sovereign debt without manipulating the rules to reduce its value. This enabled the government to borrow increasing amounts in local financial markets while also reducing the cost of its debt.

The more powers are separated—through bicameral legislatures, independent judiciaries, or independent bureaucratic agencies such as central banks—the more opportunities there are for multiple veto players to protect the interests of investors and creditors from expropriation. Independent layers of local governments in federal systems create the same opportunities through a "vertical separation of powers" (Weingast 1995). Federalism can have the added advantage of creating competition between local jurisdictions whenever resources are geographically mobile (Weingast 1995). Politicians in one state will be motivated to uphold limits on their actions if they fear that otherwise resources will move to rival states. Not all federal systems create the conditions for such competition. The heated rivalry between states in the United States throughout its history described in the chapters by Richard Sylla and John Wallis contrasts sharply with the experience of Mexico, as Steve Haber's chapter shows. In the late 1880s Porfirio Díaz undermined the independence of the state governments, distributing rents from private economic activities in ways that cemented the states' subservience to centralized political control well into the late 1990s, as we describe later.

Veto players will be a credible check on government expropriation only if they can be held accountable by those constituents whose interests are threatened, which usually requires competitive elections. Philip Keefer shows that separation of powers and competitive elections increase government's willingness to provide secure property rights and are significant determinants of lending to the private sector. Keefer further argues that voting rights are not enough to secure competitive elections and accountability. Electoral competition also depends on the amount of information voters have by which to judge the credibility of politicians' promises, and the years of experience voters have judging political credibility over continuous competitive elections.

Powerful, limited, and accountable governments have the ability and incentive to protect property rights and provide supportive regulation for financial sector development. But the chapters in this volume do not portray a simple, causal path from empowerment of government, to separation of powers and increasingly competitive elections, to greater protection of property rights, to an expanding and dynamic financial market.[2] The story is a more complicated one of recurring setbacks that sometimes delay and sometimes destroy the movement toward a more efficient financial sector.

Reversals

Several of the countries studied in this book suffered serious setbacks in their efforts to establish modern financial markets. Reversals are not usually aberrations, where a deus ex machina (such as an invasion) causes a U-turn in institutional trends. Rather, reversals are affected by a country's history and, in turn, influence the course of institutional change for a long time to come.

There are two stories of such reversals in Brazil, one involving sovereign debt and the other, private capital markets. As we have seen, the political institutions that the Brazilian monarchy established in 1824 permitted government to tap into domestic savings at levels not found elsewhere in Latin America. The military coup that overturned the empire in 1889 weakened the legislative branch and was followed by serial government defaults on its debt that continued through the twentieth century. Aldo Musacchio portrays reversal in Brazil's bond markets. By the mid-1880s Brazil had put in place legal protections of bondholders, and courts were enforcing creditor rights in bankruptcy cases. Thanks to these protections, Brazil's bond market grew rapidly between 1890 and 1913. Reversal occurred when Brazil's governments became more interested in courting support from labor and institutionalized a system of strong labor protection and weak creditor rights that persisted from 1937 to the present.

The United States also experienced reversals in its financial development. Richard Sylla argues that the United States had none of the key institutional components of a modern financial system in 1788, but had all of them in place by 1795. Its public finance was strong and its money was stable; it had a central bank, a set of state banks, and an expanding private banking system; it also had thriving securities markets and a growing number of private corporations. Thanks to astute political leadership and political institutions that aligned the interests of bankers and political leaders, the new country underwent this financial revolution in the short space of nine years. But the U.S. financial system did not evolve smoothly from this promising beginning into today's efficient, modern financial market. As John Wallis describes, by the early to mid-1880s there was no central bank—the first and second Banks of the United States had been allowed to die. State governments increasingly limited the number of new bank charters and invested state funds in banks as a way to raise revenues without politically unpopular tax increases, and in some cases as a way to reward political friends with lucrative monopolies. The picture that Wallis portrays of banking in the U.S. South, some western states, and New York in the early nineteenth century sounds similar in some ways to Haber's portrayal of banking in Mexico.

The story in Mexico is not one of reversal but one of persistent financial concentration and limited access. In Mexico, the dictator Porfirio Díaz was able to eliminate, undermine, or co-opt the formerly powerful state governors in the late 1880s. He then used his client governors to assure that his preferred candidates were elected to Congress, thereby removing both local government and the legislature as limits on his authority. The repercussions on the financial sector were strong: Díaz removed the power of state governments to issue bank charters and instead gave powerful and loyal groups in each state the right to charter a bank. These state banks had local monopolies, effectively limiting access to bank finance to small groups of politically connected insiders. Because states did not have the rights to charter banks, these barriers to entry could not be challenged by competition among the states. The result was a concentrated banking system that served both the political and financial needs of the ruling elite but repressed Mexico's industrial development. Even after the Díaz dictatorship was overthrown by violent revolution in 1911, subsequent governments found political control of the banking system useful, and Mexico did not begin to create a more open financial system until the late 1990s.

Although some U.S. states evidenced trends toward a politically dominated, concentrated banking system like that of Mexico, these trends did not spread across states or persist. The reversal of financial market development in the United States, unlike those in Brazil, temporarily disrupted its financial revolution but did not permanently derail it. The reasons why the United States returned to its earlier path have to do with federalism and congruence. Steve Haber and John Wallis show how competition among U.S. states led some to innovate and encourage competitive banking, curbing political rent seeking. Another important force for the return to more open financial markets was congruence with political markets.

Congruence

Congruence refers to the balance between institutions providing access to the political system and those providing access to the economic system. A state with relatively open political and economic access is "congruent," as is a state with relatively closed political and economic access. John Wallis argues that when economic and political institutions are not congruent, the situation is inherently unstable and either the political or the economic institutions will change. For example, if a group of individuals possesses sufficient economic power to limit access, such as a monopoly over land-ownership or trade, but does not possess a similar monopoly over political access, the situation is unstable. The economically powerful group will try to use its economic influence to change the political system. Likewise, a group with significant control over political access that does not possess similar economic rights will try to use its political influence to gain control over economic resources. This does not mean that congruent states will never change, since there are other, continual pressures on states to change. Nor does it mean that congruence is bad or good for economic perfor-mance. Rather, it simply predicts that societies with incongruent political and economic institutions will inevitably change.

We can see this in U.S. history. John Wallis and Steve Haber stress the importance of the limited but growing franchise in the early history of the United States in increasing economic as well as political access. In the early nineteenth century, some U.S. states began to limit access to the finan-cial system in order to serve the political interests of the powerful or raise revenues without taxation. In some of these states this created economic institutions that were not congruent with their open-access political insti-tutions. Even when access to the franchise was limited in the early United States, Wallis argues that the ideal of open-access politics dominated po-litical rhetoric and shaped the evolving polity. Haber describes how com-petition among U.S. states for capital and labor led them to expand the franchise, and an expanding franchise undermined the political coalitions that had supported restrictions on the number of bank charters. More and more states introduced de facto or de jure rules that allowed freer entry into banking and into business in general, especially after states defaulted on their debts in 1841–42. Freer entry was a deliberate effort by politi-cal leaders in the states to prevent narrow factions from capturing state government and limiting political access, according to Wallis. Limits on entry created rents that narrow political groups could use to bind the recip-ients and then use their support to obtain control of the state government (Wallis 2004). The exception to the trend to openness was in the Deep South, where limited-access banking was congruent with the southern states' limited political competition.

Peter Gourevitch finds similar congruence between political institutions and corporate governance institutions in developed countries worldwide. He categorizes political institutions in developed countries as either broadly majoritarian, such as the United States, or as broadly consensual, such as much of Europe. Countries with majoritarian political institutions have few veto points, and as a result winners of elections have the power to sharply change policies. These countries tend to develop corporate governance systems that allow flexibility in response to rapidly changing circumstances. Ownership tends to be diffuse and fluid, a situation supported by strong protection of minority shareholder rights; they allow relatively sharp market corrections. Such countries exhibit low coordination among economic groups and less government interference in markets. Countries with consensus political institutions have many veto points, greater coordination among economic groups, more public regulation of markets, and less sharp shifts in policies or markets. Ownership of industry in these consensual countries is concentrated into blockholdings that typically lead to less legal protection of minority shareholders than in countries with more disbursed ownership. In Gourevitch's view each of these systems has advantages and disadvantages, but the main point again is the primacy of politics and the persistence of political and economic institutions that are congruent with one another. This explanation contrasts with the legal origins literature, which portrays stronger minority shareholder protection as a direct product of common law legal traditions rather than a congruent response to majoritarian political characteristics and the diffuse ownership structure they engendered.

Future Research

More research is needed to test whether congruence can explain other instances of reversal and return to track. Although Aldo Musacchio and William Summerhill do not argue this, the reversals they describe in Brazil's financial systems could be explained as a move toward less competitive economic institutions that were congruent with Brazil's less open political system. Brazil's government empowered wealth holders through a parliamentary system and court-enforced property rights, but it never instituted open access to banking or economic activities more broadly.

Congruence is a theory of disequilibrium; it predicts when change is likely to occur, but it does not predict what direction change will take. Most of the U.S. states eventually opened access to their financial markets to fit better with their existing open-access political institutions. Does the reverse occur? Do political institutions adapt to fit better with economic institutions? The movements toward democracy in Chile, Korea, or Taiwan may be instances where open economic access reinforced pressures for political change. The congruence hypothesis predicts that China's combination of competitive markets and repressive style of government is inherently unstable and that one or the other will change. What direction change will take cannot be predicted, however. More research is needed to understand how congruence operates in different institutional settings.

This research also raises other questions. Some important aspects of the financial system are not covered, such as insurance, investment banking, foreign and state-owned banks. How do these structures respond to political institutions? If political institutions determine financial sector institutions in the long run, then what explains the dynamic of political institutions? How do the majoritarian and consensual political systems described by Gourevitch or the different supervisory systems described by Levine emerge? These chapters also suggest that the lessons of history are highly relevant to developing countries, but not simple to interpret. The interaction between state and federal governments in the United States and Mexico, the similarity between the antebellum South and Mexico, and the institutional details behind Brazil's past success and current failures are not the usual subject matter of researchers analyzing financial markets. More comparative microanalysis is needed to better understand how the forces identified in this book operate in other settings.

Notes

1. Common law combines laws passed by the legislature with custom and rules made when judges decide cases that are treated by other judges as precedents for future decisions. Civil or code law requires judges to uphold laws as they were written by the legislature with far less room for judicial interpretation or discretion. Common law originated in England and was installed in its colonies, whereas civil code law is associated originally with Roman law and subsequently with France and the countries conquered by Napoleon and their colonies.

2. The path from politics to market exhibits similar complexity in other countries. In eighteenth-century France, for example, there was enough protection of property rights for private credit markets to flourish despite the absence of elections or separation of powers (Hoffman, Rosenthal, and Postel-Vinay 2000).

References

Beck, Thorsten, Asli Demirgüç-Kunt, Luc Laeven, and Ross Levine (2004). "Finance, Firm Size, and Growth." National Bureau of Economic Research, Working Paper 10983.

Beck, Thorsten, and Ross Levine (2004). "Legal Institutions and Financial Development." In Claude Menard and Mary M. Shirley, eds., *Handbook for New Institutional Economics*. Norwell, MA: Kluwer Academic Press.

Hoffman, Philip T., Jean-Laurent Rosenthal, and Gilles Postel-Vinay (2000). *Priceless Markets: The Political Economy of Credit in Paris, 1660–1870*. Chicago: University of Chicago Press.

La Porta, Rafael, Florencio López-de-Silanes, Andrei Shleifer, and Robert Vishny (1999). "The Quality of Government." *Journal of Law, Economics and Organization* 15: 222–82.

——— (1998). "Law and Finance." *Journal of Political Economy* 106: 1113–55.

——— (1997). "Legal Determinants of External Finance." *Journal of Finance* 52: 1131–50.

Levine, Ross (1997). "Financial Development and Economic Growth: Views and Agenda." *Journal of Economic Literature* 35: 688–726.

Levine, Ross, Norman Loayza, and Thorsten Beck (2000). "Financial Intermediation and Growth: Causality and Causes." *Journal of Monetary Economics* 46: 31–77.

North, Douglass C. (2005). *Understanding the Process of Economic Change*. Princeton, NJ: Princeton University Press.

North, Douglass C., and Barry R. Weingast (1989). "Constitutions and Commitment: The Evolution of Institutions Governing Public Choice in Seventeenth-Century England." *Journal of Economic History* 49: 803–32.

Stasavage, David (2003). *Public Debt and the Birth of the Democratic State: France and Great Britain 1688–1789*. New York: Cambridge University Press.

Wallis, John (2004). "The Concept of Systematic Corruption in American History." Mimeo, Department of Economics, University of Maryland.

Weingast, Barry R. (1995). "The Economic Role of Political Institutions: Market-Preserving Federalism and Economic Development." *Journal of Law, Economics and Organization* 96: 132–63.

INDEX

property rights: commitment problem, 279; contract enforcement and, 14–15; financial development and, 4, 126, 141–44, 152; governments and, 14, 289; in Mexico following independence, 36; politics and, 143–44; as a public good, 129
public credit, Alexander Hamilton's reform of, 68–72
public finance, in Brazil, 227–28
public goods, financial development and, 125–26, 129–30, 151–52
public works projects, 25

Queiroz, Eusébio de, 273

railroad companies, 276
Randolph, Edmund, 72
Real Estate Bank of Arkansas, 107–8
regulatory acts, public goods and, 130
rents, systematic corruption and, 96
Rhode Island, 26, 77, 101, 111
Rio de Janeiro, 266
Rosas, Juan Manuel de, 241, 243
Russia, 214

Sabinada revolt, 240
Santa Anna, Antonio López de, 35, 36
Sapucaí railroad company, 276
Sarbanes-Oxley bill, 203
Scandinavia, 201, 205
Scandinavian law system, 128
scrips, 80
secondary markets, 253n22
Second Bank of the United States, 24
securities markets: government and, 3; United States, 79–83
segmented monopolies, 22, 23–26
selectorate, 210
separation of powers, 289, 290
Sevier family, 108
shareholder concentration. *See* blockholding
shareholder diffusion, 189, 191, 193–95, 216
shareholder protections. *See* minority shareholder protections
silver mining, 36
slave property, 82–83
Smith, Adam, 71, 95

Southern states: bank chartering, 27; banks and paid-in bank capital, *103*; lack of constitutional changes in, 112–14, 115; land banks, 102–9, 113
South Korea, 213–14
sovereign credit risk: Brazil, 232–37, 244–51, 252; government bonds and, 231–32
sovereign debt: Brazil, 227, 230–31, 290; penalties and, 228–29
stakeholder model, 202
State Bank of Arkansas, 107
State Bank of Mississippi, 105
state property taxes, 122n65
states (U.S.): bank chartering, 20–22, 100–103; competition between, 24–26; constitutional changes, 109–14; control of banking policy, 114–16; corporations, 83–84; debt crisis of 1841 and 1842, 109–10; de facto "free banking," 26–27; de jure free banking, 28–31; federal debt assumption, 70; funding of public works projects, 25; land banks, 100, 102–9, 113. *See also* Southern states
stockholders, bankruptcy laws and, 265–66
suffrage. *See* voting rights and restrictions
Sweden, 201
systematic corruption, 96, 111

tariffs, Brazil, 240
taxes: on bank capital, 101; Mexico, 36–37, 41
Taylor, John, 82
Tennessee, 102
textile industry: Brazil, 277; Mexico, 46–47
Thailand, 212
transitional countries, corporate governance patterns and, 209–14
transparency, 210
transplant effect, 214–15
Triple Alliance Treaty, 241, 243

Union Bank of Florida, 107
Union Bank of Louisiana, 108
Union Bank of Massachusetts, 21
Union Bank of Mississippi, 105–7, 118n29

The authorized representative in the EU for product safety and compliance is:
Mare Nostrum Group
B.V Doelen 72
4831 GR Breda
The Netherlands

www.ingramcontent.com/pod-product-compliance
Lightning Source LLC
Chambersburg PA
CBHW021550210326
41599CB00010B/387

* 9 7 8 0 8 0 4 7 5 6 9 3 8 *